Land Grants of the
Middle Neck Hundred
of
Anne Arundel County
Maryland

1650—1704

Robert W. Hall

Heritage Books
2024

HERITAGE BOOKS

AN IMPRINT OF HERITAGE BOOKS, INC.

Books, CDs, and more—Worldwide

For our listing of thousands of titles see our website
at
www.HeritageBooks.com

A Facsimile Reprint
Published 2024 by
HERITAGE BOOKS, INC.
Publishing Division
5810 Ruatan Street
Berwyn Heights, MD 20740

International Standard Book Number
Paperbound: 978-1-58549-675-4

This book is a compilation of patent documents, in synopsis form, and drawings of tracts in the Middle Neck Hundred of Anne Arundel County from 1650-1704. I obtained the information used to prepare each synopsis and drawing from land records held in the Maryland Hall of Records. The original land records and drawings were burned in courthouse fire on October 17, 1704. The patents were re-recorded over a period of years following the fire but the drawings were never replaced.

Surveying in 17th Century Maryland was far from an exact science. In many cases tract size (acreage) does not match the amount certified. Boundaries overlap and often do not "close." There are records of numerous complaints by owners that their acreage was significantly less than the amount certified. It became a common practice for tract owners to request a Special Wart (Warrant) of Resurvey to identify "surplus" land within, or "vacant" land contiguous to, a tract's boundaries and to regrant the tract, including any surplus or vacant land found, to the owner. There are instances of tracts being reduced in acreage because of a conflict with a boundary of a "more ancient" tract. I also found one tract that was certified, surveyed, and granted within the boundaries of an existing tract. Further confusion results from sale of tracts among individuals outside of the patent system. In some instances such tracts were regranted by the Lord Proprietor to the new owner. In other instances the property simply passed from one person to another by indenture or contract. The identification, drawing, and placement of Middle Neck Hundred tracts is like attempting a jig saw puzzle with an unspecified number of pieces and no pattern to follow. There are missing pieces, surplus pieces, pieces that do not fit and all of the pieces come in a box mixed with unpatterned pieces from other puzzles.

Some understanding of the Conditions of Plantation is necessary to appreciate and understand the complexities of land ownership in Maryland during this period and to appreciate the variations found in patent documents. The first conditions were written in 1633, before the settlers arrived. Amendments adjusting the ratio of acreage granted to persons transported were issued in 1636, twice in 1648, and in 1649. Charles, the Third Lord Baltimore, abolished the "land rights" system on April 5, 1684 and, thereafter lands grants were based on purchase. A more complete description of the Conditions of Plantation can be found in *Flowering of the Maryland Palatinate*, by Henry Wright Newman, 1984, Genealogy Publishing Company, Baltimore, Maryland.

Basically, the Conditions of Plantation codified the conditions and terms of the land patent process and served as a contract between the Lord Proprietor and the grantee. Ownership, as we know it today, remained with the Lord Proprietor although the grantee enjoyed all rights of ownership in fee simple including the unrestricted sale, transfer, or bequeathal to others, even before a tract had been patented. In 1648, the Assembly enacted a bill authorizing a 50-acre grant for each indentured servant at the time of service completion. Property granted to persons dying without heirs, failing to pay rents, or abandoning their tracts reverted to the Lord Proprietor through a process called "Escheat." Following Escheat, the property was available to be regranted. Until 1684, land rights were based on either favor with the Lord Proprietor or immigration to and settlement in Maryland. The number, age, social status, and sex of the settlers transported to Maryland by the grantee determined the number of acres granted. Individuals were free to claim land rights based on transporting themselves, family members, servants, and strangers. The conditions also address alienation fees, quick rents and the payment schedule, which was tied to specific religious feast days. In addition to quit rents and alienation fees, grantees were also required to pay recording fees for all official documents including land certifications, surveys, and patents. A fee schedule can be found in the Acts of Assembly, 1650 (L7/33-35 SR7343).

Governor Calvert adopted the "hundred system" in Maryland shortly after the establishment of St.Maries. Hundreds, in Maryland, are usually described as geographical subdivisions that served as voting districts until about 1671. The earliest reference found to a specific hundred (St. Maries) is 1637. According to Newman, "…if there was an official decree or proclamation, it was recorded in one of the early lost libers." The Assembly of February/March 1638/9 established that each hundred be under the management of a commander who was empowered to appoint a high constable and a sergeant to train all men able to bear arms.
Although I found nothing specific concerning the establishment of the Middle Neck Hundred, it is generally accepted that the southern and central areas were located between the South and Severn Rivers. Tax records/rent rolls further include tracts among the Western Branch of the South Runn (South River), westward to the Little Patuxent, northward to Rogue's Harbor Branch (Patuxent River) and eastward to Severn Runn. This excludes a small corridor of South River Hundred tracts extending into the Middle Neck area near present day Staples Corner and running northeasrtward to Route 3. The boundaries (see map on page IV) are based on the location of tracts defined in tax records as being in the Middle Neck Hundred during the period covered.

I have divided the Middle Neck Hundred into the three areas shown on the map on page IV. A brief synopsis of the patent documents, grouped by area and arranged in alphabetical order, precede the drawings, which are presented in the same manner. The drawings show the intended acreage (first number) and the actual acreage. References to land records at the Maryland Hall of Records are included for each tract. I have attempted to retain the special flavor of the patent documents by using the quaint phrasing, misspelled words and grammar as it was found. All names and references of historical or genealogical interest are presented in bold type and are indexed in the "People Index." Preceding the drawings for each area is a "mosaic" of joined tracts developed to aid the reader in finding the relative location of a tract. Not all tracts that were drawn are included in a mosaic. Roughly, 9.5% of the tracts found could not be drawn because of incomplete/inaccurate boundary course data. Approximately 12.5% of the tracts drawn could not be placed (in relation to other tracts or known landmarks) because of vague or missing information in the patent document. Also, tracts that were resurveyed versions of earlier tracts are not included because they occupy the same space. In some instances, tracts bounding tracts that changed "footprints" due to the absorption of surplus or vacant land could not be included because they do not fit. I have also superimposed the boundaries of the Middle Neck Hundred on a current highway map to aid those interested in finding the approximate location of a given patent. Some subtle differences in the shoreline can be seen by comparing the older map with the current version. In a few instances I have included tracts based only on a Certification/Survey when a patent record could not be found. This is limited to historically significant and/or often referenced and occupied tracts that I believe were eventually patented, possibly after the targeted period. In addition, there are a few tracts or owners mentioned in other documents as being in the Middle Neck Hundred for which I could not find records. Tract identification, and subsequently boundary definition, is based on a mix of information from tax records, rent rolls, a few old maps, mentions in a great many books, references in other patent documents, and a frame-by frame-search of 40 reels of microfilmed land records held at the Maryland Hall of Records.

I am indebted to a number of persons for their help and encouragement in preparing this book and would like to give special thanks to Deputy State Archivist Chris Allan and Jennifer Hafner at the Maryland Hall of Records and to my wife Sandy. Without their special help this would not have been possible.

Table of Contents

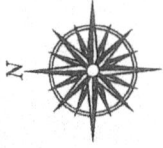

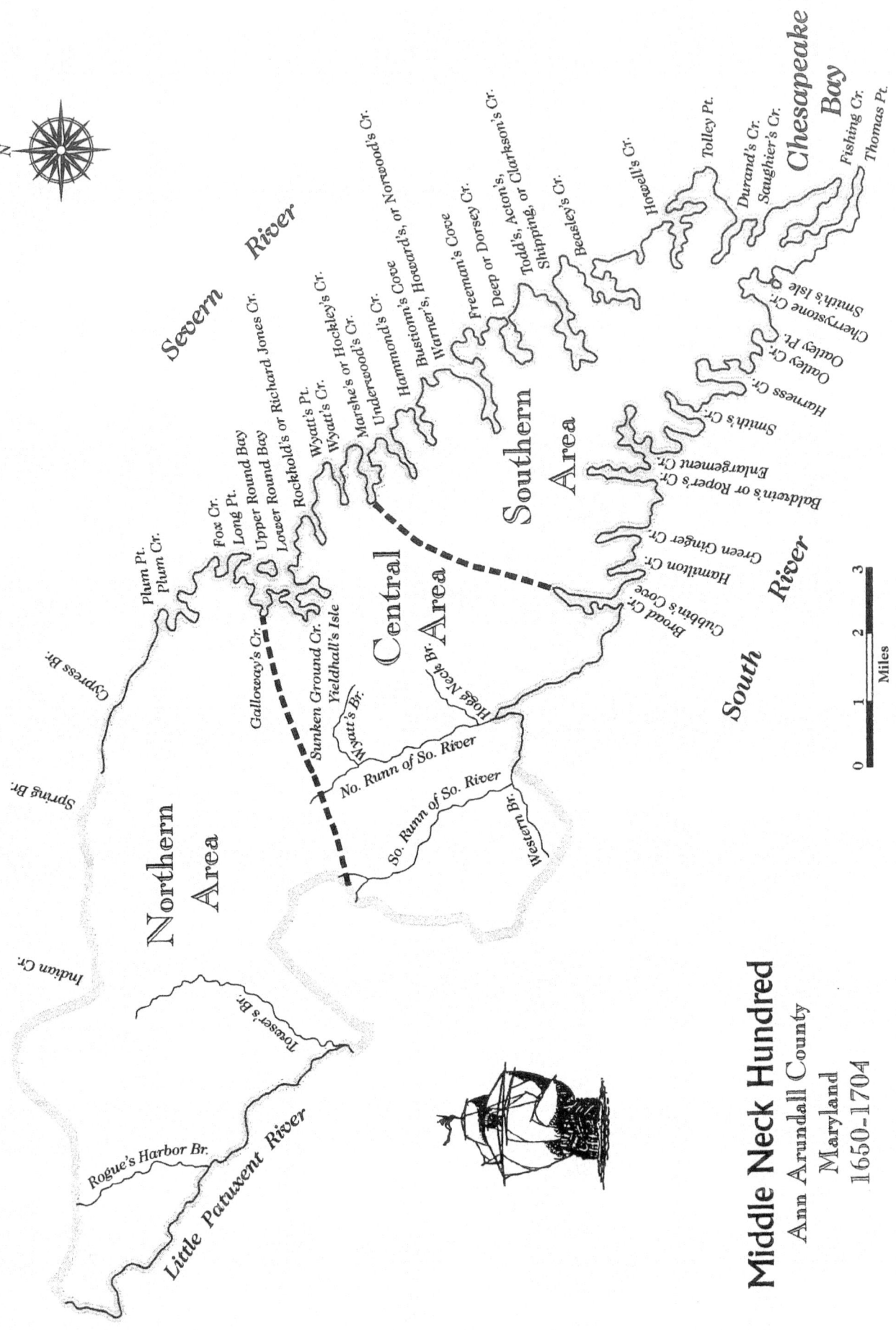

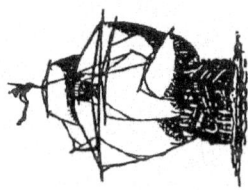

Middle Neck Hundred

Ann Arundell County
Maryland
1650-1704

N

Severn River

Chesapeake Bay

Tolley Pt.

Durand's Cr.
Saughier's Cr.

Howell's Cr.

Fishing Cr.
Thomas Pt.

Beasley's Cr.

Cherrystone Cr.
Smith's Isle

Todd's, Acton's,
Shipping, or Clarkson's Cr.

Deep or Dorsey Cr.

Freeman's Cove

Oakley Cr.
Oakley Pt.

Warner's Cove

Harness Cr.

Bustion's Cove
Howard's, or Norwood's Cr.

Smith's Cr.

Hammond's Cr.

Southern Area

Underwood's Cr.

Enlargement Cr.

Baldwin's or Roper's Cr.

Marshe's or Hockley's Cr.

Wyatt's Cr.

Wyatt's Pt.

Green Ginger Cr.

Rockhold's or Richard Jones Cr.

Hamilton Cr.

South River

Lower Round Bay

Upper Round Bay

Long Pt.

Fox Cr.

Broad Cr.
Cubbin's Cove

Galloway's Cr.

Sunken Ground Cr.
Yieldhall's Isle

Central Area

Hog's Neck Br.

Plum Pt.
Plum Cr.

Wyatt's Br.

No. Runn of So. River

Cypress Br.

So. Runn of So. River

Western Br.

Spring Br.

Northern Area

Indian Cr.

Towser's Br.

Rogue's Harbor Br.

Little Patuxent River

0   1   2   3
Miles

IV

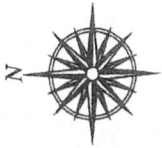

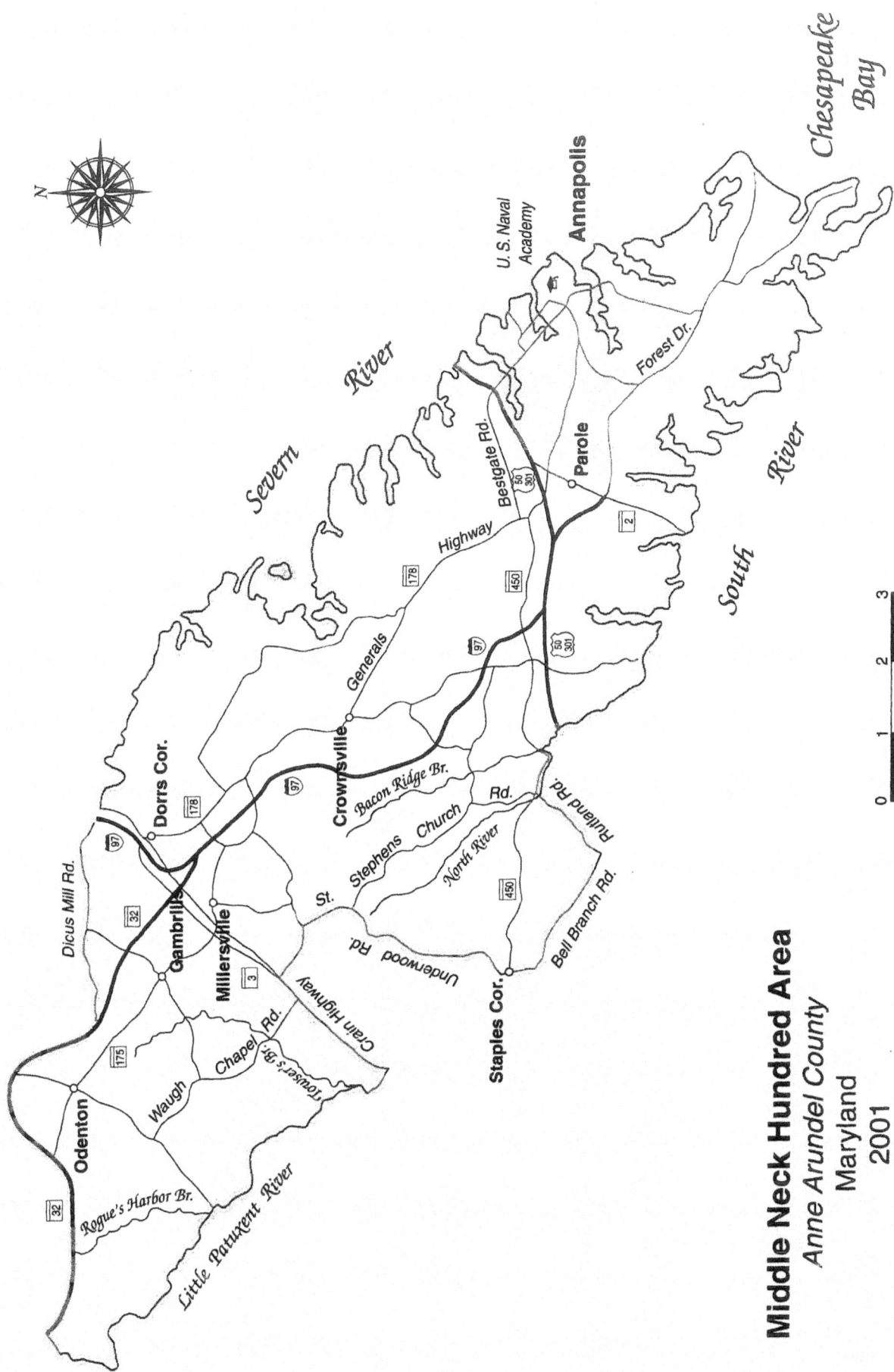

Middle Neck Hundred Area
Anne Arundel County
Maryland
2001

N

Chesapeake Bay

Severn River

U. S. Naval Academy

Annapolis

Bestgate Rd.

Parole

Forest Dr.

50 301

Highway

178

450

2

Generals

97

South River

50 301

Crownsville

Bacon Ridge Br.

Rd.

Dorrs Cor.

178

97

St. Stephens Church

North River

Rutland Rd.

Dicus Mill Rd.

97

178

32

450

Gambrills

Millersville

3

Underwood Rd.

Staples Cor.

Bell Branch Rd.

175

Waugh Chapel Rd.

Touser's Br.

Crain Highway

Odenton

32

Rogue's Harbor Br.

Little Patuxent River

0   1   2   3
Miles

Land Grants in the Middle Neck Hundred
Of Anne Arundel County, Maryland
1650-1704

Northern Area

Abingdon (Robert Proctor & John Gather) 9/20/1664 - 875/876 acres. L7/387 SR 7349. Know Yee that Wee for and in consideration that Robert Proctor and John Gather of this Province, Planters, hath due unto them two hundred and seventy five acres of land by afsignment of **John Mears** and two hundred and fifty acres by afsignment of **Samuel Withers** and three hundred and fifty acres more upon warrant of the s'd Proctor as appears upon record. And, upon such considerations and termes as are exprefsed in our Conditions of Plantation of our Province of Maryland, doe hereby grant unto the s'd Robert Proctor and John Gather a parcell of land lying in Ann Arundel County at the head of the South River about three miles into the woods, adjoining *Freeman's Fancy*. Begins at a marked Oak standing near the main branch of the South Run of the South River. *Adjoins White's Hal (South River Hundred)l, Green Spring, Brandy, Herford, and Freeman's Fancy.*

Abingdon, Part Of (John Gaither) 8/27/1699 – 364/364 acres. LDD5i/44 SR7378. By virtue of a Speciall Warrant granted unto John Gaither and **Jerome Finley** of this County bearing date 5/27/1698, for the resurvey of a certaine tract of land called *Abingdon* lying in the s'd County above the head of the South River granted unto the s'd Gaither and **Robert Proctor** in 1664 for 875 acres. The s'd Gaither and Proctor sold and conveyed six hundred acres to **James Finley** of the County. In order to rectify some errors found in the former course differences and to afford to them the s'd Gaither and Finley the surplus if any appears according to his LOP's late instructions in such cases provided, I have laid out for the s'd Gaither his part of the former grant being what remains after the s'd Finley's six hundred acres were conveyed, beginning at a bounded White Oak standing on a hill on the south side of a small branch falling into the North Branch of the South River. Then issued pattent to the above John for the above land. *Note: Although not mentioned in the patent, it is assumed that this special warrant was issued to John Gaither, Jr. This document clearly states that a patent was, "..then issued to the s'd John for the s'd Land." However, on 5/10/1701, John Gaither again had the same tract resurveyed and regranted (see Abingdon resurveyed). No explanation has been found.*

Abingdon Resurveyed (John Gaither, Jr.) 5/10/1701 – 364/364 acres. LWD/375 SR7372. Know yee that for and in consideration that John Gaither of Ann Arundell County in our Province of Maryland to our Deputy did set forth that he is seized in fee simple of two hundred seventy five acres of land being what remains of a tract called *Abingdon* originally granted **Robert Proctor** and the deceased **John Gaither** in 1664 for eight hundred seventy five acres but supplicating that there might be surplus therein he humbly prayed *(he)* might have our Speciall Warrant for Resurvey thereof and that upon return of Pattent of such, our Letters Pattent might to him be issued. By virtue thereof it is certified unto our Land Office that there is the quantity of eighty nine acres over and above the afsigned quantity. Our instructions to **Coll Henry Darnall** our agent in our s'd Province dated 12/13/1697 *(are that)* 217 pounds of tobacco are to be paid to us being for the Rights of the s'd surplus and also the sum of one pound, sixteen shillings, eight pence, *(and one)* half-penny sterling being for the acres of rent of the s'd surplus from the time of original survey. Wee doe in consideration thereof give, grant, confirm unto him the s'd John Gaither all that remaining part of a tract of land called *Abingdon* beginning at a bounded White Oak standing on a hillside and on the south side of a smaller branch falling in the the North Runn of the South River.

Ben's Discovery (Benjamin Warfield) 1/2/1704 – 380/386 acres. LCD/181 SR7376.
Know yee that for and in consideration that Benjamin Warfield of Ann Arundell County hath due unto him three hundred eighty acres of land within our s'd Province being due unto him by virtue of a warrant of three hundred acres granted to the s'd Warfield 12/15/1701, parte of a warrant also for six hundred eight acres granted to the s'd Warfield the same day and also by virtue of a warrant for fifty five acres granted to the s'd Warfield 12/16/1704 as appears on record. Upon such conditions and terms as are exprefsed in our Conditions of Plantation of this our Province of Maryland, wee doe therefore hereby grant unto the s'd Richard all that tract or parcell of land called *Ben's Discovery* lying on the westernmost side of Towser's Branch beginning at the end of the north by northwest line of a tract called *Granniston.*

Boyde's Chance (John Boyde) 5/4/1685 – 60/80 acres. LNS2i/108 SR7371.
Know yee that for and in consideration that John Boyde, Planter, of Ann Arundell County in our s'd Province of Maryland hath due unto him sixty acres of land within our s'd Province by a warrant for the same quantity granted unto him the s'd Boyde 6/25/1684, as appears on record. Upon such conditions and terms as are exprefsed in our Conditions of Plantation of this our Province, wee doe therefore hereby grant unto the s'd John Boyde all that tract or parcell of land called *Boyde's Chance* lying in the s'd County in the woods beginning at a bounded Red Oake of the land of **Matthew Howard**. *Adjoins Rosse, Howard's 1ˢᵗ Choice, Howard & Porter's Range, and the head of Indian Branch.*

Brandy (Richard Warfield) 8/10/1683 – 300/274 acres. LCB3i/496 SR7367.
Know yee that we for and in consideration that Richard Warfield of Ann Arundell County in our Province of Maryland hath due unto him three hundred acres of land within our s'd Province by afsignment of **Henry Hanslap** the afsignee of **Col. William Burges** part of a warrant for two thousand acres of land granted unto the s'd Burges on 9/28/1680 as appears on record. Upon such conditions and terms as are exprefsed in our Conditions of Plantation of our late father Cecilius of noble memory, wee doe grant unto the s'd Richard Warfield all that tract or parcell of land called *Brandy* lying in Ann Arundell County about three miles from the head of the Ann Arundell River in the woods. Begins at a bound Hickory. *Adjoins Green Springs, Abbingdon, and Haire Hill.*

Brooksby's Point (John Brookesby) 7/7/1681 – 350/369 acres. LCB2i/257 SR7366.
Know yee that we for and in consideration that John Brooksby of Ann Arundell County
in our Province of Maryland hath due unto him three hundred and fifty acres of land
within our s'd Province by afsignment of **George Yate** part of a warrant for four hundred
acres of land granted to the s'd Yate 9/16/1680 as appears on record. Upon such
conditions and terms as are exprefsed in our Conditions of Plantation of our late father
Cecilius of noble memory, wee doe grant unto the s'd John Brooksby all that parcell of
land called *Brooksby's Point* lying in Ann Arundell County on the south side of the Ann
Arundell River beginning at a bound White Oak standing at a branch called the Indian
Branch, the s'd tree being a bound tree of the land of **John Sutton** called *Lancaster*.
*Note 1: The assignment of 350 acres by George Yate follows the patent in the land
records. Note 2: Lancaster, owned by* John Sutton *is described as an adjoining tract.
Lancaster Plaine, owned by* **Richard Warfield** *does adjoin Brooksby's Point. Thus far I
have not found any tracts owned by John Sutton in the land records for the targeted area.
Notes from MSA Tract Index file 73: Sold to* **John Moyatt** *(1686) for 12,000 lbs tobacco.
Moyatt sold 60 acres to* **Thomas Aldrich** *for 3,500 lbs tobacco (1689).*

Brownley (Thomas Browne) 2/15/1659 – 150/147 acres. L4/452 SR7346.
Know yee that we for and in consideration that Thomas Browne of this Province, Planter,
hath due unto him one hundred and fifty acres of land as appears upon record. Upon such
considerations and terms as are exprefsed in our Conditions of Plantation for our s'd
Province of Maryland, doe hereby grant unto this Thomas Brown a parcel of land called
Brownley lying on the west side of the Severne River near unto the head. Begins at a
marked Oak standing on a point by a little marsh. *Adjoins Brown's Encrease, The
Increase (Howard), and Brown's Peace.*

Browne's Chance (Thomas Brown) 10/1/1687 – 98/98 acres. LNSBi/489 SR7370.
Know yee that for and in consideration that Thomas Browne of Ann Arundall County in
this our Province hath due unto him ninety eight acres of land within our s'd Province by
afsignment of **Richard Beard** of the same County part of a warrant for four thousand
acres granted to the s'd Beard 2/27/1685. Upon such conditions and termes as are
exprefsed in our Conditions of Plantation wee doe hereby grant unto the s'd Thomas
Brown all that tract or parcel of land called *Browne's Chance* lying in the s'd County on
the south side of the Ann Arundall River beginning at a bounded White Oake in the north
line of **Richard Warfield's** land *(Warfield's Plain)*. *Notes from MSA Tract Index 73:
Sold to* **Daniel Macomas** *for 4,000 lbs tobacco (1692).*

Brown's Encrease (William Hopkins) 8/8/1670 – 250/200 acres. L13/31 SR7350.
Know Yee that for and in consideration that William Hopkins of the County of Ann
Arundel in our s'd Province of Maryland, Gent, hath due unto him two hundred and fifty
acres of land within our said Province part of a Warrant for 400 acres of land formerly
granted to him the s'd Hopkins as appears upon record. Upon such conditions and terms
as are exprefsed in our Conditions of Plantation, do hereby grant unto the s'd William
Hopkins a parcell of land called Brown's Encrease lying in the s'd County on the south
side of the Ann Arundall River. Begins at a bounded Red Oak on the river side being the
northmost boundary of a parcell of land called *Brown Stone*. *Note 1: The tract cannot be*

drawn with the courses as specified. The courses used are calculations based on other deed courses, location, and boundary angles "borrowed" from adjoining tracts. *Note 2 (from MSA Tract Index 73: Mentioned in deed (**T. Brown** to Sarah Stevens IB#2/117) that a tract called Plum Point (100 acres) is a part of Brown's Encrease. Plum Point is a landmark but no record of a tract patented as Plum Point was found.*

Brown's Folly (Thomas Browne) 7/1/1680 - 270/257 acres. LCB2i/13 SR7366.
Know yee that we for and in consideration that Thomas Browne of Ann Arundell County in our Province of Maryland hath due unto him two hundred and seventy acres of land within our s'd province by afsignment of **George Holland** part of a warrant for one thousand seven hundred and ninety acres granted to the s'd Holland 6/4/1679 as appears on record. Upon such conditions and terms as are exprefsed in our Conditions of Plantation of our late father Cecilius of noble memory, wee do grant unto the s'd Thomas Brown all that parcel of land formerly taken up by **William Hopkins** called *Brown's Folly* lying in Ann Arundell County on the south side of the Ann Arundell River on the north side of Plum Creek. Begins at a bounded Black Oak it being a bound tree of William Hopkins. *Adjoins Shepheard's Range, Weston, and Brown's Encrease.*

Brown's Forrest (Thomas Browne) 3/10/1695 – 387/519 acres. LWD/129 SR7372-2.
Know yee that for and in consideration that Thomas Browne of Ann Arundell County in our Province of Maryland hath due unto him three hundred and eighty seven acres of land within our s'd Province being due unto him by virtue of a warrant for six hundred acres granted to him 2/3/1695 as appears on record in our Land Office. Upon such conditions and terms as are exprefsed in our Conditions of Plantation of this our Province, wee doe therefore hereby grant unto the s'd Thomas Browne all that tract or parcell of land called *Brown's Forrest* lying in Ann Arundell County on the west side of the North Branch of Patuxent River beginning at a bounded Red Oak standing in a branch. *Note: Another Patent of Brown's Forrest is found in LC3i/379 SR7377.*

Brown's Peace (Thomas Browne) 2/20/1677 – 52/51 acres. L20/75 SR7361.
Know yee that we for and in consideration that Thomas Browne of Ann Arundell County of our Province of Maryland hath due unto him fity two acres of land by afsignment of **George Holland** the afsignee of **David Frye** part of a warrant for six hundred acres granted to the s'd Frye on 1/16/1676 as appears on record. And, upon such conditions and terms as are exprefsed in our Conditions of Plantation of our late father Cecilius of noble memory, doe hereby grant unto the s'd Thomas Browne all that parcel of land called *Brown's Peace* lying on the west side of the Ann Arundell River in the woods adjacent to the land of Henry Sewell (*Henry's Increase*). Begins at a bound Oak.

Brownston (Thomas Brown) 2/16/1659 – 100/102 acres. L4/500 SR7346.
Know yee that wee for and in consideration that Thomas Brown of this Province, Planter, hath due unto him one hundred acres of land. Upon such conditions and terms as are exprefsed in our Conditions of Plantation of our Province of Maryland, wee doe hereby grant unto the s'd Thomas Brown a parcell of land called *Brownston* lying on the west side of Chesapeake Bay and on the north side of Severn River next adjoining the land of **Henry Cattline** and **William Hopkins** beginning at Cattline's and Hopkins' easternmost

bound tree. *Note 1: The patent document places Brownston on the north side of the Severn River. However, Baltimore and Ann Arundell County Rent Rolls, 1707-1724 (pg 209) states that Brownston adjoined Brown's Encrease (at that time in the possession of Wm. Hopkins) on the south side of the Severn. Also, the patent for Brown's Encrease states that it adjoins Brownston. Conversely, I have not found any Henry Cattline patents on the south side of the Severn and Brownstone appears to occupy the same space as a tract called Brownly. I have included Brownston because it may have been in the Middle Neck Hundred. Note 2: The boundary courses were incomplete and could not be drawn without borrowing some angles and dimensions from Brown's Encrease and by calculating the shoreline of the river.*

Bruton (John Bruton) June, 1664 – 50/58 acres. L9/114 SR7351.
Laid out for John Bruton of this Province, a parcell of land called *Bruton* lying in Ann Arrundell County in the woods on the south side of Severn River. Begins at a marked Oake near a parcell of land formerly laid out for **John Sisson**. *Adjoins Salmon Hills. Note 1: This tract could not be drawn following the courses as specified in the deed. In order to draw, it was necessary to "borrow" the "direction" from an adjoining course. Note 2: Although a patent was not found, I have included this tract because of the many references to it in other patents and in tax/rent records.*

Bruton Grimes (John Bruton & William Grimes) - 1664 – 150/139 acres. L9/114 SR7351. Laid out for John Bruton and William Grimes of this Province a parcell of Land called Bruton Grimes in the woods on the south side of the Severn River on a ridge above a creek called Plum Creek. Begins at a marked Pokehicory in the line of land laid out for **Henry Sewell**, Planter. *Note: Surveyor's note from Rent Rolls pg 205, "Upon reading the Cert of this land to **Coll Hammond** he informed me that Wm. Grimes possesses this Land but Grimes denyes it nor can I find anyone who claimes it." Note 1: Although a patent was not found, I have included this tract because of the many references to it in other patents and in tax/rent records.*

Chance (Charles Carroll) 3/30/1705 – 203/222 acres. LDD5i/442 SR7378.
By virtue of a warrant for fifteen hundred acres granted unto Charles Carroll bearing date 3/23/1702, these are to certify that I have laid out a parcel of land for the s'd Charles called *Chance* lying in the s'd County above the head of the South River beginning at a bound tree of a parcel of land called Herford now in the pofsefsion of **John Mariott**. Then Pattent issued for the s'd land to the s'd Charles pursuant to the s'd Certificate.

Chilton (Abraham Child) 9/10/1683 – 40/40 acres. LSDA/49 SR7369
The following is from the Survey document. The Patent has faded to the point that it is not legible. The drawing was made from courses specified in the Survey. Certification and Survey: 10/1681 L21/354 SR7362. By Virtue of a warrant granted unto Abraham Child of Ann Arundell County, **I GeorgeYate** hath laid out a parcel of land for the s'd Abraham Child called *Chilton* lying in the County aforesaid on the south side of the Ann Arundell River. Begins at a bound Pine of the land of **Thomas Browne** (*Brown's Encrease)* and bounds Cypress Branch.

Clinke (William Galloway) 1/18/1659 - 100/100 acres. L4/430 SR7346.
Know yee that for and in consideration that William Galloway of Ann Arundell County in our s'd Province of Maryland hath due unto him one hundred acres of land being due unto him by virtue of the s'd Galloway and his wife **Lucy** *(Child)* having completed their time of service in this Province as appears on record. Upon such conditions and terms as are exprefsed in our Conditions of Plantation of this our Province, wee doe therefore hereby grant unto the s'd William Galloway all that parcel of land called *Clinke* lying in Ann Arundell County on the west side of the Chesapeake Bay and on the south side of a river called the Seaverne River on the north side of a creek called Galloway's Creek. Begins at a marked Oak by a marsh. *Note 1: Prior to the granting of this patent (and on the same day) a patent was granted to Wm. Galloway for a tract of 150 acres, also called Clinke (L4/427), located on the western branch of the South Run of the South River. A note in the margin states the following, "This patent is written folio 430 over again because the certificate was in error." Apparently the land office realized that Galloway's rights, as stated in both patents, justified 100 (not 150) acres and corrected the error thereby voiding the first patent. Note 2: The rights to one hundred acres of land were granted to Galloway and his wife Lucy Child, within the Conditions of Plantation, for completion of (indentured) services within this province (July 7, 1659 L4/59). Note 3:* **John Norwood** *received fifty acres for transporting Lucy Child into this province Anno 1658 (July 7, 1659 L4/59).*

Cordwell (John Merriott) 10/15/1680 – 300/296 acres. LCB3i/511 SR7367.
Know yee that wee for and in consideration that John Merriott of Ann Arundell County in our s'd Province of Maryland hath due unto him three hundred acres of land within our Province by afsignment of **Henry Hanslap** part of a warrant for twelve hundred fifty acres granted to the s'd Hanslap on 8/30/1682 as appears on record. Upon such conditions and terms as are exprefsed in our Conditions of Plantation of our late father Cecilius of noble memory, wee doe hereby grant unto the s'd John Merriott all that tract or parcell of land called *Cordwell* lying in the s'd County in the woods about three miles from the head of the Severn River. Begins at a bound tree of a parcell laid out for **Thomas Brown** called *Diamond*, it being in the line of **Matthew Howard** (*Howard's Adventure*). *Also adjoins Green Spring.*

Davistone (Thomas Davis) 10/17/1701 – 240/240 acres. LDD5i/136 SR7378.
By virtue of a warrant for two hundred forty acres of land granted unto Thomas Davis of Ann Arundell County dated 10/20/1701, these are to certify that I have laid out for the s'd Davis a parcell of land called *Davistone* lying in the s'd County between the forke *(of)* the Rogue's Harbor Branch beginning at a bounded White Oak standing at the southwest corner of a tract called *Greenifton*. Then issued Patent to the above pursuant to the above certification.

Dryer's Inheritance (Samuel Dryer) 3/10/1695 – 254/257 acres. LC3i/354 SR7377.
Know yee that for and in consideration that Samuel Dryer of Ann Arundell County in our s'd Province of Maryland hath due to him two hundred and fifty four acres of land within our s'd Province due unto him by assignment of two hundred thirteen acres from **Thomas Brown** of the s'd County out of a warrant for six hundred acres granted to Brown

2/3/1695 and twenty one acres more by afsignment of **John Dodderidge** of the s'd County out of a warrant for three hundred acres granted to the s'd Dodderidge 2/7/1695. The remaining twenty acres by afsignment of **Richard Beard** out of a warrant for three hundred acres granted 10/6/1694, all which warrants appear in our Land Office and were granted upon such conditions and terms as are exprefsed in our Conditions of Plantation of this our Province of Maryland. Wee doe therefore hereby grant unto the s'd Samuel Dryer all that tract or parcell of land called *Dryer's Inheritance* lying on the west side of the North Branch of Patuxent River beginning at a bounded tree of Thomas Brown.

Green Spring (Robert Proctor) 2/20/ 1673 - 200/198 acres. L15/147 SR4327.
In consideration that Robert Proctor, Innholder, of the County of Ann Arundall hath due unto him two hundred acres of land within this Province by virtue of a warrant for the same quantity to him granted on 12/24/1673 as appears on record. And, upon such considerations and terms as are exprefsed in our Conditions of Plantation of our Province of Maryland doe hereby grant unto the s'd Robert Proctor a parcell of land called *Green Spring* lying in Ann Arundall County in the woods beginning at a bound Oak in the line of land formerly laid out for **Jerome White Esq** *(White's Hall)*. *Note: Within weeks of acquiring this tract, Proctor sold a portion to* **Phillip Howard** *via a deed that indicates that all 200 acres were included. However, the "Proctor to Howard" deed courses plot to a different shape and amounted to only 100 acres.*

Greeniston (Nicholas Painter) 5/22/1683 – 700/1,071 acres. LSDA/353 SR7369.
Whereas **James Greeniston** of Ann Arundell County in our s'd Province of Maryland had due unto him seven hundred acres of land within this Province by afsignment of **Henry Hanslap** afsignee of **Coll Wm. Burges** part of a warrant for two thousand acres granted to him 9/23/1681, and had laid out for him the s'd Greeniston a parcell of land for seven hundred acres called *Greeniston* hath now afsigned and sett over unto Nicholas Painter of the same County as appears on record. Upon such conditions and termes as are exprefsed in our Conditions of Plantation of this our Province of Maryland, wee doe hereby grant unto the s'd Nicholas Painter all that tract or parcell of land called *Greeniston* lying in the s'd County about four miles from the Ann Arundell River by a branch side of the SW boundary of the land of **Thomas Brown** called *Diamond*. *Note: Greeniston's survey, dated 9/8/1682, is found in L21/352 SR7362, and again in the same Liber on folio 483. The duplication is noted in the margin without explanation.*

Grime's Addition (William Grimes) 9/10/1672 – 100/81 acres. L17/291 SR7358.
Know Yee that for and in consideration that William Grimes of Ann Arundall County in our s'd Province of Maryland hath due unto him one hundred acres of land within our s'd Province by afsignment from **George Yate**, the afsignee of **Thomas Taylor**, Attorney of **Jerome White Esq.**, as appears upon record. Upon such conditions and terms as are exprefsed in our Conditions of Plantation of our s'd Province, do grant unto him the s'd William Grimes, Gent, all that parcell of land called Grime's Addition lying in Ann Arundall County on the south side of the Ann Arundall River. Begins at a bound White Oake standing in a forke of a creek called Plum Creek. *See note on drawing. Note (from MSA Tract Index 73): Sold to* **John Farthing** *for 4,100 lbs tobacco in 1697 (WH#4/242).*

Grime's Enlargement (William Grimes) 11/10/1695 – 187/186 acres. LWD/105 SR7372-2. Know yee that for and in consideration that William Grimes of Ann Arundell County in our Province of Maryland hath due unto him one hundred thrty acres of land within our Province being due by virtue of a warrant of nineteen hundred acres granted unto **John Norwood** 6/10/1694 the same quantity being by him afsigned unto the s'd Grimes. Thirty eight acres thereof being due him by afsignment of **Charles Stevens**, part of a warrant of three hundred acres granted the twenty fifth day of June of the year aforesaid. Other nineteen acres being due unto him by virtue of a warrant of one thousand acres granted **Daniel Elliott** of Charles County by afsignment of that quantity to the s'd Grimes as appears on record. Upon such conditions and terms as are exprefsed in our Conditions of Plantation of this our Province, wee doe therefore grant unto the s'd William Grimes all that tract or parcell of land called Grime's Enlargement lying on the south side of the Savorn River beginning at a bounded White Oak being a bounded tree of a parcel of land called Salmon's Hill. *Also Adjoins Guy's Will, Grimstin, and Grime's Addition. Note 1: The assignment of land to Grimes is confusing as expressed in the Patent. It appears that one hundred thirty acres was assigned by Norwood, 38 acres by Stevens, and 19 acres by Elliott. Note 2: Another Patent for Grime's Enlargement was found in LC3i/265 SR7377. Note 3 (from MSA Tract Index 73): Sold by William and Ann Grimes to Amos Garratt in 1709 (PK/84).*

Grimeston (William Grimes) 8/25/1665 – 100/98 acres. L8/153 SR7350. Know yee that wee for and in consideration that William Grimes of this Province hath due unto him one hundred acres of land within this Province by afsignment of **Thomas Bradley** as appears upon record. Upon such considerations and terms as are expressed in our Conditions of Plantation of our Province of Maryland, doe hereby grant unto the s'd William Grimes a parcell of land lying in Ann Arundell County on the south side of the Seavern River at the head of the South Branch of Plum Creek. Begins at a marked Oak upon a ridge *(probably Severn Ridge). Note: The tract could not be drawn from the courses as specified. It was necessary to "borrow" some of the course directions from adjoining tracts.*

Guy's Rest (Guy Meeke) 8/8/1670 – 100/98 acres. L13/32 SR7355. Know Yee that we for and in consideration that Guy Meeke of Ann Arundall County in our Province of Maryland hath due unto him one hundred acres of land in our s'd Province by afsignment from **George Yate**, part of a Warrant for fifteen hundred acres upon record. Upon such consideration and termes as are exprefsed in our Conditions of Plantation do hereby grant unto the s'd Guy Meeke a parcell of land called *Guy's Rest* lying in the s'd County on the south side of the Severne River. Begins at a bound White Oak. *Adjoins Rosse and Guy's Will. Note: Several of the courses specified lacked distance or direction. Tract was drawn using calculations based on dimensions of adjoining tracts.*

Guy's Will (Guy Meeke) 5/1/1672 – 100/92 acres. L14/464 SR7356. Know Yee that Guy Meeke of Ann Arundall County in our Province of Maryland hath due unto him one hundred acres of land within our s'd Province by afsignment of **George Yate**, the afsignee of **Richard Ewen** due to the s'd Ewen for transporting **Francis**

Watkins and **Mary Davis** into our s'd Province here to inhabit, as appears on record. And upon such conditions and termes as are exprefsed in the Conditions of Plantation of our s'd Province of Maryland do hereby grant unto the said Guy Meeke all that parcell of land called *Guy's Will* lying in the aforesaid County at the head of the South River. Begins at a bound White Oak of land formerly laid out for the s'd Meeke (*Guy's Rest*). *Adjoins Salmon Hill.*

Hammond's Forrest (Maj. John Hammond) 5/1/1696 – 362/382 acres. LWD/141 SR7372-2. Whereas Maj. John Hammond of Ann Arundell County in our Province of Maryland by his humble petition has sett forth that upon the tenth day of October sixteen hundred and ninety four, surveyed for him by virtue of a warrant duly obtained for three hundred sixty two acres of land but that our grant thereof to him was lapsed. Further that improvements were made by building and clearing and (the tract) consequently was not laid out by common warrant. Our intentions ordering the contrary at that point whereof he was altogether ignorant wherefor he prayed thereon as much that this was prejudiced by his taking up the s'd improved land by a common warrant for same being improved by himself and that this may not be put to charge of a Speciall Warrant and another survey but that would give him our grant for the s'd land upon survey as aforesaid. Know yee that for and in consideration that John Hammond hath due unto him three hundred sixty two acres of land being due unto him by afsignment of **Henry Ridgely Jr.** of that quantity out of a warrant for eight hundred acres granted to the s'd Henry 6/9/1694 as appears on record in our Land Office. Upon such conditions and terms as are exprefsed in our Conditions of Plantation of this our Province, wee doe therefore grant unto the s'd John Hammond all that tract or parcell of land called *Hammond's Forrest* lying at the head of branches of the Ann Arundell River beginning at a bounded Pine tree. *Note 1: On the back of the Cert was written, "On this tract was one twenty foot dwelling house built and a parcel of land cleared but not tended." Note 2: Another Patent for Hammond's Forrest was found in LC3i/331 SR7377.*

Hare Hill (Peter Porter) 9/11/1674 – 100/102 acres. L18/254 SR7359.
Know yee that we for and in consideration that Peter Porter of Ann Arundel County hath due unto him one hundred acres by afsignment of **Richard Wilson**, part of a warrant for one thousand five hundred and twenty acres formerly granted to the s'd Wilson. Upon such conditions and terms as are exprefsed in our Conditions of Plantation of our Province of Maryland, doe hereby grant unto the s'd Peter Porter all that parcell of land called Hare Hilll lying in the woods about three miles from the head of the Ann Arundell River. Begins at a bound White Oak.

Harrisses Beginning (John Harris) 11/10/1695 – 122/139 acres. L23/260 SR7364.
Know yee that wee for and in consideration that John Harris of Ann Arundall County hath due unto him one hundred twenty seven acres of land within our Province by afsignment of **Henry Ridgely** of the s'd County part of a warrant for eighteen hundred acres granted to the s'd Ridgely 6/13/1695 as appears in our land office. Upon such conditions and terms as are exprefsed in our Conditions of Plantation of this our Province of Maryland, wee doe hereby grant unto him the s'd John Harris all that tract or parcell of

land called Harrisses Beginning lying at Hunting Town beginning at a bounded Red Oake by a branch. *Note: a duplicate of this patent is found in L23i/339 SR7365.*

Henry's Addition (Henry Sewell) 4/14/1673 – 30/30 acres L17/504 SR7358.
By virtue of a warrant granted unto **Wheatley** of London, Marriner, for five thousand acres of land in this our s'd Province of Maryland bearing date May 14, 1613, assigned to **Robert Wilson** of the County of Ann Arundall, Gent, by the s'd Wheatley, and 30 acres thereof was assigned by the s'd Wilson to Henry Sewell of the s'd County as appears upon record. These are to certifie in humble manner that I **George Yate** Deputy Surveyor under **Baker Brooke Esq.** have laid out for the s'd Sewell a parcell of land called Henry's Addition lying in the s'd County on a bay called Round Bay. Begins at a bounded Red Oak and runs with the line of **William Galloway**. *Note: The patent erroneously states that the grant of 5,000 acres to Wheatley of London occurred in 1614. However, the document assigning these 30 acres from Robert Wilson to Henry Sewell further identifies Wheatley as **William Wheatley** and shows the year of Wheatley's grant as 1673.*

Henry's Encrease (Henry Sewell) 7/1/1680 – 43/43 acres. LCB2i/41 SR7366.
Know yee that wee for and in consideration that Henry Sewell of Ann Arundell County hath due unto him forty three acres of land in this Province by afsignment of **George Holland** part of a warrant for seven hundred and ninety acres granted to the s'd Holland 6/4/1679 as appears on record. And, upon such conditions and terms as are exprefsed in our Conditions of Plantation of our late father Cecilius of noble memory, wee doe hereby grant unto the s'd Henry Sewell all that parcell of land called *Henry's Increase* lying in Ann Arundell County on the south side of the Ann Arundell River beginning at a bounded Red Oak it being a bounded tree of the land of **Thomas Browne** called *Brown's Increase.*

Herford (Robert Wilson) 5/1/1675 260/228 acres. L16/384 SR7357.
Know yee that for and in consideration that Robert Wilson, Gent, of the County of Ann Arundell in our s'd Province of Maryland hath due unto him two hundred sixty acres of land within our s'd Province by afsignment from **George Yate** part of a warrant for two hundred ninety four acres (*granted*) to the s'd Yate 6/17/1774, as appears on record. Upon such conditions and terms as are exprefsed in our Conditions of Plantation wee doe hereby grant unto the s'd Robert Wilson all that parcell of land called *Herford* lying in Ann Arundell County between the heads of the Ann Arundell and South Rivers beginning at a bound Oak of the land of **John Gater**. *Adjoins Abingdon, North Runn of South River, the land of **Cornelius Howard**, and Howard & Porter's Fancy. Note 1: This tract was patented in 1675. However, MSA Tract Index 73 says that it was sold to **John Hudson** (10/8/1672) and to **Charles Stevens** 1/1/1673 for 6,000 lbs tobacco. No earlier patents have been found.*

Hicory Ridge (Charles Stevens) 11/10/1695 – 262/265 acres. L23/255 SR7364.
Know yee that wee for and in consideration that Charles Stevens of Ann Arundell County in our s'd Province of Maryland hath due unto him two hundred sixty two acres of land in our s'd Province by virtue of a warrant for three hundred acres granted unto him

6/26/1694, as appears in our land office. Upon such conditions and terms as are exprefsed in our Conditions of Plantation of this our Province, wee doe therefore hereby grant unto the s'd Charles Stevens all that tract or parcell of land called *Hicory Ridge* lying in the branches of the Severn River. Begins at a bound tree in the line of land owned by **Capt. John Hammond**. *Note (from MSA Tract Index 73): Charles Stevens willed this tract to his eldest son William Stevens.*

Howard & Porter's Fancy (Cornelius Howard & Peter Porter) 6/13/1668 – 333/316 acres. L12/30 SR7354. Know yee that in consideration that Cornelius Howard of the County of Ann Arundell in our s'd Province hath due unto him 333 acres of land within our s'd Province part of a Warrant for 350 acres to him formerly granted as appears on record. And, upon such conditions and terms as are exprefsed in the Conditions of Plantation of our s'd Province, do hereby grant unto him the aforesaid Cornelius Howard a parcell of land called *Howard and Porter's Fancy.* Begins at a bounded Pine tree of a parcell of land called *Howard and Porter's Range.*

Howard & Porter's Range (Cornelius Howard & Peter Porter) 10/2/1666- 500/1,230 acres. L10/184 SR7352. Know yee that wee for and in consideration that Cornelius Howard and Peter Porter, Planters of this Province, hath due unto them five hundred acres of land within our s'd Province out of a warrant for five hundred acres granted to the s'd Howard and two hundred fifty acres thereof assigned to the s'd Porter by the s'd Howard as appears upon record. And, upon such conditions and terms as are exprefsed in our Conditions of Plantation of our Province of Maryland, doe hereby grant unto the s'd Cornelius Howard and Peter Porter a parcel of land called *Howard and Porter's Range* lying in AA County on the south side of Severn River. Begins at a bounded Hickory by a branch side near the land of **John Hammond**. *Adjoins Howard and Porter's Fancy, Howard's First Choice, Howard's Addition, The Maiden, Boyde's Chance, Howard's Hills, and Warfield's Plaines.*

Howard's Addition (Phillip Howard) 8/10/1685 – 70/72 acres. LNS2i/113 SR7371. Know yee that for and in consideration that Phillip Howard of Ann Arundell County in our s'd Province of Maryland hath due unto him seventy acres of land within our s'd Province being due the s'd Howard by afsignment of **Robert Jones** and **George Yate** parte of a warrant for two thousand acres granted to the s'd Jones and Yate 3/18/1683, as appears on record. Upon such conditions and terms as are exprefsed in our Conditions of Plantation of this our Province, wee doe therefore hereby grant unto the s'd Phillip Howard all that tract or parcel of land called *Howard's Addition* lying in the s'd County in the woods adjacent to the s'd land the s'd Howard now liveth upon. Begins at a bounded Hickory being a bounded tree of *Howard and Porter's Range* by the North Runn of the South River.

Howard's Adventure (Matthew Howard) 8/10/1683–500/502 acres. LCB3i/374 SR7367. Know yee that wee for and in consideration that Matthew Howard of Ann Arundell County in our s'd Province of Maryland hath due unto him five hundred acres of land within our s'd Province by afsignment of **Henry Ridgely** of the s'd County part of a warrant for five hundred thirty seven acres granted to the s'd Ridgely on 8/25/1680 as appears on record. Upon such conditions and terms as are exprefsed in our Condition of Plantation of our late father Cecilius of noble memory, wee doe hereby grant unto the s'd Matthew Howard all that tract or parcell of land called *Howard's Adventure* lying in the s'd County about three miles from the head of the Ann Arrundell River in the woods. Begins at a bound Hickory tree.

Howard's First Choice (Matthew Howard) 5/17/1668 – 160/194 acres. L11/409 SR7353. Matthew Howard, Planter of the County of Anne Arundel in our s'd Province hath due unto him 160 acres of land in our Province part of a Warrant for five hundred acres to him formerly granted. Upon such conditions and termes as exprefsed in our Conditions of Plantation of our Province, do grant unto the s'd Matthew Howard, a parcell of land called *Howard's First Choice* lying in the s'd County on the south side of the Severn River. Begins at a bounded Red Oak in the line of land formerly laid out for **Robert Salmon** called *Salmon's Hill*. *Note: Matthew Howard was granted a warrant for 500 acres on 5/30/1677 (L10/499) for Transporting his wife Sarah Darcy, John Pine, Thomas Gleve, Thomas Stedloe, William Cook, Sarah Driver, Elizabeth Warrenton, Samuel Dryer, and Joan Garnish.*

Howard's Hills (Phillip Howard) 12/10/1679 – 150/42 acres. L21/71/SR7362. Know yee that whereas **John Howard** of Ann Arundell County in our s'd Province of Maryland hath due unto him one hundred fifty acres of land within our s'd Province part of a warrant for five hundred fifty acres granted him 9/7/1665, and had laid out for him a parcel of land called *Howard's Hills* on Seavern Ridge all who's right, title, and interest in and of the s'd parcell the s'd John Howard hath afsigned to Phillip Howard of the s'd County as appears on record. Upon such conditions and terms as are exprefsed in our Conditions of Plantation of our late father Cecilius, of noble memory, wee doe hereby grant unto the s'd Phillip Howard all that parcell of land called *Howard's Hills* lying in the s'd County beginning at a bound Poplar of the land called *Howard and Porter's Fancy*. *Note: The acreage discrepency is unusually high even for surveys of this period. However, the tract fits into the space described for a later adjoining tract (The March) perfectly.*

Lancaster Plaine (John Hudson) 5/1/1676 – 180/151 acres. L19/357 SR7360. Know Yee that Wee for and in consideration that John Hudson of Ann Arundell County hath due unto him one hundred eighty acres of land within this Province by afsignment of **Thomas Hedge** part of a warrant for nine hundred acres granted to the s'd Thomas Hedge on 3/7/1673, as appears on record. And, upon such conditions and terms as are exprefsed in our Conditions of Plantation of our Province of Maryland, doe hereby grant unto the s'd John Hudson all that parcell of land called *Lancaster Plaine* lying in the s'd County in the woods on the south side of the Ann Arundell River. Begins at a bounded Red Oak standing at a branch called the Indian Branch.

Locust Neck (James Horner) s11/22/1651 100/101 acres. LAB&H/254 SR7344. Laid out for James Horner of the County of Ann Arundall, Planter, a parcell of land on the south side of Severn River called *Locust Neck*. Begins at a marked oak standing near a creek called *Locust Creek*. *Note: No record of a patent was found. I included this tract* *because it is mentioned in J.D Warfield's book (The Founders of Anne Arundel and Howard Counties, MD) as being one of the early grants in the Middle Neck Hundred and being located in the Round Bay area.*

Meeke's Rest (Guy Meeke) 5/2/1680 – 350/356 acres. (C) L21/353 SR7362.
By virtue of a warrant granted unto Guy Meeke 11/2/1680 by afsignment of **Henry Hanslap** the afsignee of **William Burges** as appears on record. These therefore in humble manner certifie that I **George Yate**, Deputy Surveyor, hath laid out for the s'd Meeke a parcell of land called *Meeke's Rest* lying in Ann Arundel on the south side of the Ann Arundel River in the woods beginning at a bound White Oak. *Adjoins Salmon Hill and the land of Matthew Howard. Note: Patent was not found for this tract, however, the following was found in Rent Rolls (pg 216) under Meeke's Rest: Resurveyed 10/1/1681, 210 acres, "..the record says this Res. was made by assignmt of 140 a. from Henry Hanslap but mentions not how the rest to make the complement of 210 acres became only concludes the quantity. Poss John Meeke." It is a reasonable assumption that Meeke's Rest was a resurvey of Meeke's that incorporated his adjoining tracts (Rosse, Guy's Will, and Guy's Rest) along with any "surplus" contiguous land.*

Mill Meadow (Capt. Richard Hill) 10/5/1683 – 240/247 acres. LSDA/418 SR7369.
Know yee that for and in consideration that Capt. Richard Hill of Ann Arundell County in our s'd Province of Maryland hath due unto him two hundred forty acres of land by afsignment from **Henry Hanslap** part of a warrant for twelve hundred and fifty acres granted to the s'd Hanslap 8/30/1682 as appears on record. Upon such Conditions and terms as are exprefsed in our Conditions of Plantation of our late father Cecilius, of noble memory, wee doe hereby grant unto the s'd Richard Hill all that tract or parcell of land called *Mill Meadow* lying at the head of the Ann Arundell River beginning at a bound Red Oake standing in the north line of the land of **Henry Sewell** *(Henry's Encrease). Also adjoins Shipley's Choice.*

Owen's Range (Richard Owen) 3/26/1696 – 162/162 acres. LC3i/360 SR7377.
Know yee that for and in consideration that Richard Owen of Ann Arundell County in our s'd Province of Maryland hath due unto him one hundred sixty two acres of land within our s'd Province by afsignment of so much from **Thomas Richardson** of *Baltimore County* out of a warrant for seven hundred ninety eight acres granted the s'd Thomas 10/9/1698 as appears on record in our Land Office. Upon such conditions and terms as are exprefsed in our Conditions of Plantation of this our Province, wee doe therefore hereby grant unto the s'd Richard Owen all that tract or parcell of land called *Owen's Range* beginning at a bounded White Oak in the line of **Jabez Pierpoint.**
Note: The patent document offers nothing in the way of location information except that it adjoins land patented by Jabez Pierpoint. Unfortunately, the only Jabez Pierpoint tract found also does not provide location information. I have included this tract because the Rent Rolls (1701) state that it was located in the Middle Neck Hundred although I can't place it within the area.

<u>Peasley's Neck</u> (Francis Peasley) 1/1/1666 – 250 acres. L9463 SR7351.
Laid out for Francis Peasley of the County of Ann Arundell, Planter, a parcell of land lying on the south side of the Severn River near a creek called Befson's Creek adjoining the land of **Thomas Howell** beginning at Howell's northmost bound tree. *Note 1: A patent document was not found, however, this tract is shown in the Rent Rolls (1701) as being in the Middle Neck Hundred. Note 2: The tract cannot be drawn because four of the five courses specified lack distance, direction, or both.*

Pierpoint's Range (Jabes Pierpoint) 11/10/1695 – 200/200 acres. LWD/136 SR7372-2.Know yee that for and in consideration that Jabes Pierpoint of Ann Arundell County in our Province of Maryland hath due unto him two hundred acres of land within our s'd Province being due unto him by afsignment of **Henry Pierpoint** of the s'd County it being part of a warrant granted the s'd Henry for five hundred acres of land 10/17/1688 as appears on record in our Land Office. Upon such conditions and terms as are exprefsed in our Conditions of Plantation of this our Province of Maryland, wee doe therefore hereby grant unto the s'd Jabes Pierpoint all that tract of parcell of land called *Pierpoint's Range* lying in Ann Arundell County in the woods beginning at a bounded Red Oak of the s'd Pierpoint. *Note 1: Another patent was found for Pierpoint's Range in LC3i/310 SR7377. Note 2: Other than stating that this tract adjoined other property owned by Jabes Pierpoint, the patent document offers no clue as to the location of this tract. Another patent, also without any reference to location (Owen's Range), states that it adjoined the land of Jabez Pierpoint. I included both of these only because they are shown in the Rent Rolls (1701) as being in the Middle Neck Hundred but I am unable to place them within this group.*

Rich Neck (Col. John Hammond) 3/20/1684 – 284/279 acres. L22/183 SR7363.
By Virtue of a warrant granted unto **Richard Beard** of Ann Arundell County for one hundred eighty four acres of land dated 4/24/1684 assigned by the s'd Beard to Col. John Hammond as appears on record. Also, 100 acres being a warrant granted unto **Gabriel Parrott** dated 12/14/1684 was granted by the s'd Parrott unto the s'd Hammond as doth appear. These are therefore to certifie that I have laid out a parcell of land for the s'd Hammond called Rich Neck lying on the east side of the Northernmost Great Branch of the Patuxant River at Huntenton. Begins at a bound Hickory standing by the branch side. Then issued pattent for the above land to the s'd Hammond. *Note: Another patent for this tract was found in LC3i/376 SR7377.*

Ridgely's Beginning (Henry Ridgely Jr.) 11/10/1695 – 282/217 acres. L23/242 SR7365. Know yee that wee for and in consideration that Henry Ridgely Jr. of Ann Arundell County in our Province of Maryland hath due unto him two hundred eighty two acres of land within our s'd Province by virtue of a warrant granted unto him for eighteen hundred acres of land on 6/9/1694. Upon such conditions and terms as are exprefsed in our Conditions of Plantation of our s'd Province of Maryland, we doe therefore hereby grant unto the s'd Henry Ridgely Jr. all that tract or parcell of land called *Ridgely's Beginning,* lying at Huntington *(on the North Branch of the Patuxent River)* beginning at a bound Pine by a branch called Rogue's Harbor Branch (of the Patuxent River).

Ridgely's Chance (William Ridgely) 10/2/1694 – 305/302 acres. LC3/412 SR7377.
Whereas William Ridgely of Ann Arundell County has in his humble petition to us sett forth that he did have surveyed for him three hundred acres of land on 10/1/1694, by virtue of a warrant duly obtained and the Certificate thereof returned but that his grant for the s'd land has been stopped because there was improvements made by building and clearing and by our Instructions could not be taken up by Common Warrant. He humbly prayed that we would issue our letter patent for the s'd land according to the survey. We have thought fitt to condescend unto the rather for that the improvements were made by himself. Know yee that for and in consideration that the s'd Ridgely hath due unto him three hundred and five acres of land within our s'd Province being due him by afsignment of that quantity from **Henry Ridgely Jr.** out of a warrant for eighteen hundred acres granted to the s'd Henry Ridgely 6/9/1694 as appears on record in our Land Office. Upon such conditions and terms as are exprefsed in our Conditions of Plantation of this our Province, wee doe therefore hereby grant unto the s'd William Ridgely all that tract or parcell of land lying in Ann Arundell County on the Forke of a Branch of Patuxent River called Rogue's Harbor Branch beginning at a Bound White Oak standing on the point of the dividing of the Branch.

Ridgely's Forrest (Henry Ridgely) 4/1/1696 – 264/259 acres. LC3i/340 SR7377.
Know yee that Henry Ridgely of Ann Arundell County in our s'd Province of Maryland in his humble petition has sett forth that on June 3, 1686 he had surveyed for him a parcell of land called *Ridgely's Forrest* of two hundred and sixty four acres. But, the patent was not issued because the warrant for the rights to a portion of the land could not be found. However, a warrant was found whereby **John Howard,** of the same County did afsign sufficient acreage to the s'd Ridgely on March 29, 1684 the mistake being that a clerk of our land office did file the s'd afsignment under this date rather than the correct date of March 19, 1684. Upon such conditions and termes as are exprefsed in our Conditions of Plantation of this our Province, wee doe therefore hereby grant unto the s'd Henry Ridgely all that tract of parcell of land called *Ridgely's Forrest* lying on the east side of the North Great Branch of the Patuxant River at Huntington. Begins at a bound Red Oak.

Ridgely's Lott (Henry Ridgely Jr.) 11/10/1695 – 273/177 acres. L23/251 SR7364.
Know yee that wee for and in consideration that Henry Ridgely Jr. of Ann Arundell County in our Province of Maryland hath due unto him two hundred seventy three acres of land in our s'd Province being due unto him by virtue of a warrant of eighteen hundred acres granted unto him on 6/9/1694, as appears in our land office. Upon such conditions and terms as are exprefsed in our Conditions of Plantation of this our Province of Maryland, wee doe therefore hereby grant unto the s'd Ridgely all that tract or parcell of land called Ridgely's Lott lying between Hunting Town and Elk Ridge on the north east side of a branch of the Patuxent River called Ridgely's Great Branch. Begins at a bound White Oak on the east side of the s'd Branch. *Note: Ridgely's Great Branch is believed to be the same as Rogue's Harbor Branch.*

Rosse (Guy Meeke) 5/18/1679 – 136/139 acres. L20/203 SR7361.
Know yee that we for and in consideration that Guy Meeke of Ann Arundell County in our Province of Maryland hath due unto him one hundred and thirty six acres of land by afsignment of **George Yate** part of a warrant for five hundred acres granted to the s'd Yate on 12/21/1678 as appears on record. And, upon such conditions and terms as are exprefsed in our Conditions of Plantation of our late father Cecilius of noble record, doe hereby grant unto the said Guy Meeke all that parcell of land called *Rosse* lying in the s'd county on the south side of the Ann Arundell River in the woods. Begins at a marked Chestnut Tree it being a bound tree of the land of **Matthew Howard** *(Howard's First Choice). Also adjoins Indian Branch, Guy's Rest, Guy's Will, and Salmon's Hill.*

Salmon's Hill (Ralph Salmon) 9/22/1665, 100/100 acres. L8/414 SR7350.
Know yee that wee for and in consideration that Ralph Salmon of this Province, Planter, hath due unto him one hundred acres of land in this Province part of a warrant for two hundred and twenty five acres as appears on record. And under such considerations and terms as are exprefsed in our Conditions of Plantation of our s'd Province of Maryland, doe hereby grant unto the s'd Ralph Salmon a parcell of land called *Salmon's Hill* lying in Ann Arundell County on the south side of the Severn River at the head of Plum Creek. Begins at a marked White Oak.

Sewell's Encrease (Henry Sewell) 5/25/1680 – 500/509 acres. L20/372 SR7361.
By virtue of a warrant granted unto **Henry Ridgely** and **Abraham Childs,** Gents, both of Ann Arundall County for one thousand seventy five acres of land bearing the date 5/13/1680, five hundred thirty seven acres thereof was afsigned by the s'd Ridgely unto Henry Sewell of the s'd County as appears on record. These are to certifie that in humble manner I **George Yate,** Deputy Surveyor, hath laid out for the s'd Sewell a parcel of land called *Sewell's Encrease* lying on the north side of the Ann Arundall River beginning at a bound Pine standing on a point. *Note 1: The rights proved amounted to 37 acres more than the amount granted. No explanation found. Note 2: Although this does not contain the usual grant language, MSA Land Records Index 55 states that this is the patent, and "Patt" does appear in the margin of this document. I'm not convinced that it was patented but I am including it on the chance that it was. Note 3: The tract is described as being on the north side of the Ann Arundall River. However, the patent document for Mill Meadow, which is clearly on the south side of the river, identifies Sewell's Encrease as an adjoining tract. Note 4 (from MSA Tract Index 73): One hundred fifty (of 500) acres devised by will dated 9/29/1699, to son **Henry**. Anticipating that the will might be questioned, elder brother **James** gave up all claims to 150 acres. In 1702, James conveyed 100 acres to brother **Joshua** and 100 acres to brother **Phillip** in accordance with their father's wishes as expressed in his will (WT2/75 &105).*

Shepheard's Choice (Nicholas Shepheard) 6/1/1687 – 240/240 acres. LNS2i/482 SR7371. Know yee that for and in consideration that Nicholas Shepheard of Ann Arundall County in our s'd Province of Maryland hath due unto him two hundred forty acres of land within our s'd Province by afsignment from **John Gray** of the s'd County part of a warrant for five hundred acres granted to the s'd Gray 2/29/1685, as appears on record. Upon such conditons and terms as are exprefsed in our Conditions of Plantation of our s'd Province of Maryland, wee doe therefore hereby grant unto the s'd Nicholas Shepheard all that tract or parcell of land called *Shepheard's Choice* lying in the s'd County on the south side of the Ann Arundall River beginning at a bounded White Oak of land formerly laid out for **John Warfield**.

Shepheards Grove (Nicholas Shepheard) 8/10/1684 – 120/117 acres. LSDA/461 SR7369. Know yee that for and in consideration that Nicholas Shepheard of Ann Arundell County hath due to him one hundred and twenty acres of land within our s'd Province by afsignment from **Henry Hanslap** part of a warrant of twelve hundred fifty acres granted to the s'd Hanslap 4/4/1683 as appears on record. Upon such conditions and terms as are exprefsed in our Conditions of Plantation of our late father Cecilius, of noble memory, wee doe hereby grant unto the s'd Nicholas Shepheard all that tract or parcell of land called *Shepheard's Grove* lying in the s'd County about three miles from the head of the Ann Arundell River. *Note 1: Probably adjoined Shepheard's Chance.*

Shepheard's Range (Nicholas Shepheard) 10/1/1674 – 100/93 acres. L18/260 SR7359. Know yee that wee for and in consideration that Nicholas Shepheard of the County of Ann Arundall hath fifty acres of land due unto him by afsignment of **Robert Wilson** of the s'd County as appears on record. Upon such considerations and terms as are exprefessed in our Conditions of Plantation of our Province of Maryland, doe hereby afsign unto the s'd Nicholas Shepheard a parcell of land called *Shepheard's Range* lying in the s'd County on the south side of the Ann Arundell River. Begins at a bound Red Oak in the line of land formerly laid out for the s'd Shepheard and **William Grimes** (*The Friend's Choice*).

Shepley's Choice (Adam Shipley) 1/20/1681 – 200/205 acres. LCB2i/463 SR7366. Know yee that wee for and in consideration that Adam Shepley of Ann Arundell County in our s'd Province of Maryland hath due unto him two hundred acres of land within our Province by afsignment of **George Yate** the remainder of a warrant for five hundred acres granted to the s'd Yate 3/23/1680 as appears on record. And, upon such conditions and terms as are exprefsed in our Conditions of Plantation of our late father Cecilius of noble memory, wee doe hereby grant unto the s'd Adam Shepley all that parcell of land lying in Ann Arundell County on the south side of the Ann Arundell River called *Shepley's Choice* beginning at a bound Chestnutt tree. *Note 1: Adjoins Brooksby's Point. Note 2 (from MSA Tract Index 73): This tract was apparently devised to Shipley's son **Richard** who gave it to his sisters **Lois Shipley** and **Keturah Barnes** in 1698 (IH#1/82). Note 3: The name in the Patent Document is referred to as both Shipley and Shepley.*

The Addition (William Jones) 10/10/1704 – 50/51 acres. LDSF/517 SR7373-2. Know yee that for and in consideration that William Jones of Ann Arundell County hath due unto him fifty acres of land within our s'd Province by virtue of a warrant for the same quantity granted him 2/7/1770 as appears on record in our Land Office. Upon such conditions and terms as are exprefsed in our Conditions of Plantation of this our Province, wee doe therefore hereby grant unto him the s'd William Jones all that tract or parcell of land called *The Addition* lying in the s'd county on the south side of the

Sevearn River beginning at an old bound Pine on a pond below a small bile.

The Addition (Richard Warfield) 10/8/1680 – 50/50 acres. LCB3i/411 SR7367.
Know yee that wee for and in consideration that Richard Warfield of Ann Arundell
County in our s'd Province of Maryland hath due unto him fifty acres of land within our
s'd Province by afsignment of **Henry Hanslap** part of a warrant for one hundred acres
granted unto him the s'd Hanslap on 7/20/1682 as appears on record. Upon such
conditions and terms as are exprefsed in our Conditions of Plantation of our late father
Cecilius of noble memory, wee doe hereby grant unto the s'd Richard Warfield all that
tract or parcell of land called *The Addition* lying in the s'd County in the woods about
two miles from the head of the Severn River beginning at a bounded White Oak of the
land formerly laid out for **Peter Porter** called *Haire Hill*.

The Desert (Thomas Blackwell) 6/12/1696 – 148/138 acres. LWD/124 SR7372-1.
Know yee that for and in consideration that Thomas Blackwell in our s'd Province of
Maryland hath due unto him one hundred forty eight acres of land within our s'd
Province being due unto him by virtue of a warrant of one hundred sixty acres granted
unto him 12/09/1695 as appears on record in our Land Office. Upon such condition and
terms as are exprefsed in our Conditions of Plantation of this our Province of Maryland,
wee doe therefore hereby grant unto him the s'd Thomas Blackwell all that tract or
parcell of land called *The Desert* lying on the west side of the North Branch of the
Patuxent River beginning at a bounded Red Oak in the woods, it being a bounded tree of
Thomas Brown. *Note: Another patent was found for The Desert in LC3i/387 SR7377.
This version identifies the tract as The Desart, however, the location and boundary
courses are the same in both versions.*

The Diamond (Thomas Brown) 8/10/1684 – 200/207 acres. LSDA/414 SR7369.
Know yee that for and in consideration that Thomas Browne of Ann Arundell County
hath due unto him two hundred acres of land within our s'd Province by afsignment of
Henry Hanslap the afsignee of **Coll William Burges** part of a warrant for two thousand
acres granted unto him the s'd Burges 9/20/1681 as appears on record. Upon such
conditions and terms as are exprefsed in our Conditions of Plantation of our late father
Cecilius, of noble memory, wee doe hereby grant unto the s'd Thomas Brown all that
tract or parcell of land called *The Diamond* lying in the aforesaid county in the woods
about four miles from the head of the Ann Arundell River. Begins at a bounded Red Oak
standing in a marsh.

The Encrease **(Cornelius Howard)** 8/8/1670 – 100 acres. L14/46 SR7356.
Know yee that for and in consideration that Cornelius Howard, Gent, of the County of
Anne Arundall in our Province of Maryland hath due unto him one hundred acres of land
within our said Province by afsignment from **George Yate**, part of a warrant for two
hundred and thirty acres formerly granted to the s'd Yate as appears upon record. And, in
such conditions and terms as exprefsed in our Conditions of Plantation do grant unto him
the s'd Howard a parcell of land called *The Encrease* lying in s'd County on the south
side of the Anne Arundall River. Begins at a bounded White Oak of **William Galloway**.

Note: This tract cannot be drawn because the seventh course lacks distance and direction.

The Friend's Choice (William Grimes & Nicholas Shepheard) 9/10/1672 - 100/92 acres. L17/298 SR7358. Know yee that for and in consideration that William Grimes and Nicholas Shepheard of Ann Arundell County in our s'd Province of Maryland hath due unto them one hundred acres of land within our s'd Province by afsignment from **George Yate** the afsignee of **Thomas Taylor** the attorney of **Jerome White Esq.**, part of a warrant for eleven hundred acres to the s'd White granted the 9th day of April last past as appears on record. And, upon such conditions and terms as are exprefsed in our Conditions of Plantation of the s'd Province wee doe hereby grant unto the s'd Grimes and Shepheard all that parcell of land called *The Friend's Choice* lying in the s'd county on the south side of the Ann Arundell River beginning at a bounded Red Oake standing in a point running up a branch called Spring Branch. *Note 1 (from MSA Tract Index 73): Grimes' interest was devised to Shepheard (9/12/1672). Shepheard conveyed The Friend's Choice and Shepheard's Range to* **Samuel Dryer** *in 1713 (IB#2/84).*

The Friendship (Thomas Browne & William Hopkins) – 5/26/1681 - 100/80 acres. LSDA/94 SR7369. Know yee that for and in consideration that Thomas Browne and William Hopkins of Ann Arundall County in our Province of Maryland hath due unto them one hundred acres of land within our Province it being first due to the s'd Hopkins for transporting **Francis Marlow** and **John Yates** into this Province here to inhabit all whose rights, title, and interest of in and thereunto the s'd William Hopkins afsigned over unto the s'd Thomas Browne who reafsigned the moiety thereof to the s'd Hopkins as appears on record. Upon such conditions and terms as are exprefsed in our Conditions of Plantation of our late father Cecilius, of noble memory, wee doe hereby grant unto the s'd Brown and Hopkins all that tract or parcell of land called *The Friendship* lying in the s'd County about two miles from the head of the Ann Arundell River in the woods. Begins at a bound Hickory. *Adjoins Hare Hill. Note: The patent was found in LSDA/94 SR7369, however, the page has faded to the extent that the patent date cannot be read.*

The Landing (**Robert Proctor**) 9/8/1668 – 70 acres. L5/598 SR 7347 L12/135 SR7354 and L11/482 SR7353. Grant for 70 acres of land ifsued to Robert Proctor of the County of Ann Arundel, Gent, bearing the date 9/8/1668. Consideration by afsignment by **William Bateman** part of a warrant for 100 acres of land formerly granted to the s'd Bateman. Conditions date: 7/2/1649 (with alteration) 9/22/1658. Yearly rent: 1 shilling, five pence the same for a fine upon every alienacon of the same in the usual form. Witnefsed by **Charles Calvert Esq.** *Note 1: Both references (L11/482 and L12/135 show patent without any courses. Note 2 (from MSA Tract Index 73): Sold in 1673 to* **George Puddington.** *Devised in 1674 to* **Edward Burgess.**

The Maiden (Mary Howard) 11/5/1683 – 40/38 acres. LSDA/417 SR7369. Know yee that for and in consideration that Mary Howard of Ann Arundell County in our Province of Maryland hath due unto her forty acres of land within our Province by afsignment of **Henry Hanslap** part of a warrant for one thousand acres granted to the s'd Hanslap 9/15/1682 as appears on record. Upon such conditions and terms as are exprefsed in our Conditions of Plantation of our late father Cecilius, of noble memory, wee doe hereby grant unto the s'd Mary Howard all that tract or parcell of land called *The Maiden* lying in the s'd County on the south side of the Severn River beginning at a bound Poplar of *Howard and Porter's Range. Note 1 (from MSA Tract Index 73): Devised to brother Cornelius Howard Jr. and sold by him to Phillip Howard in 1687. Note 2 (from MSA Tract Index 73): Sold to Richard Owen in 1685. Sold by him to Jabez Pierpoint in 1696. According to Index 73 the tract adjoining Warfield's Marsh laid out for Ed Gardner. A Patent for Warfield's Marsh was not found.*

The March (Edward Gardner) 6/1/1687 - 110/113 acres. LNS2i/280 SR7371.
Whereas Edward Gardner of Ann Arundell County in our s'd Province of Maryland had surveyed and laid out for him the seventh day of June, 1673, a certaine tract or parcell of land containing one hundred and ten acres called *The March* lying in the s'd County by afsignment of **George Yate**, Gent, of the same County, the afsignee of **Coll William Burges** part of a warrant for 1,250 acres granted the s'd Burges 4/11/1672 as appears on record. But, by reason of a surveyor's *(delayed)* return of the Certificate hereof into our Office for Land, it was resurveyed. Whereupon he supplicated our Council for Land to allowe an examination thereof and soe to be recorded in our office in order that our letters of Pattent might be issued for him. Which was granted provided Rights had been made good for same. Know yee that for and in consideration of the promises being fully satisfied and the s'd Gardner's performance of our Conditions of Plantation in formerly making good rights, wee, not willing to take any advantage for the lapse of time aforesaid, give and grant unto the s'd Edward Gardner all that aforementioned parcell of land called *The March* lying in the s'd County about two miles from the head of the Ann Arundell River beginning at a bounded Oak of the land called *Howard and Porter's Range. (Also adjoins Howard and Porter's Fancy, Warfield's Plain, and Howard's Hills.)*

The Range (Thomas Lytfoote) 8/10/1684 – 384/430 acres. LSDA/484 SR7369.
Know yee that for and in consideration that Thomas Lytfoote of Ann Arundell County hath due unto him three hundred eighty four acres of land within our Province by afsignment of **Capt. Richard Hill** being part of a warrant for twelve hundred acres granted to the s'd Hill 6/7/1684 as appears on record. Upon such conditions and terms as are exprefsed in our Conditions of Plantation of this our Province, wee doe hereby grant unto the s'd Lytfoote all that tract or parcell of land called *The Range* lying in the s'd County about a mile from the head of the Ann Arundell River beginning at a bound Red Oak in the line of land laid out for **Richard Warfield**.

Timber Neck (Charles Stevens) 11/101695 – 303/298 acres. LDW/143 SR7372-2.
Know yee that for and in consideration that Charles Stevens of Ann Arundell County in our Province of Maryland hath due unto him three hundred and three acres of land within our s'd Province by afsignment of **Thomas Richardson** of Baltimore County out of a warrant for seven hundred and ninety eight acres of land granted unto him the s'd Richardson 10/9/1685 as appears on record in our Land Office. Upon such conditions and terms as are exprefsed in our Conditions of Plantation of this our Province, wee doe therefore hereby grant unto the s'd Charles Stevens all that tract or parcell of land called *Timber Neck* lying in Ann Arundell County in the woods beginning at a bounded Pine

standing in the line of **Jabes Pierpoint**. *Note: Another patent was found for Timber Neck in LC3i/313 SR7377.*

Turkey Island (Neale Clarke) 3/26/1696 – 333/335 acres. LC3i/351 SR7377.
Know yee that for and in consideration that Neale Clarke of Ann Arundell County in our s'd Province of Maryland hath due unto him three hundred thirty three acres of land within our s'd Province by virtue of an afsignment of so much from **Richard Beard** of the same County out of a warrant for one thousand acres granted unto the s'd Richard 6/8/1694 and remains upon record in our Land Office. Upon such conditions and terms as are exprefsed in our Conditions of Plantation of this our Province, wee doe therefore hereby grant unto the s'd Neale Clark all that tract or parcell of land called *Turkey Island* lying on the NE side of Patuxent River on the south side of Rogue's Harbor Branch beginning at a bounded Gumm standing in the s'd branch.

Warfield's Forrest (Richard Warfield) 4/11/1678 – 182/141 acres. L20/59 SR7361.
Know yee that we for and in consideration that Richard Warfield of Ann Arundell County hath due unto him one hundred and eighty two acres of land by afsignment of **George Yate** the afsignee of **William Burges** on 4/17/1765 as appears on record. Upon such conditions and terms as are exprefsed in our Conditions of Plantation of our late father Cecilius of noble record, doe hereby grant unto the s'd Richard Warfield all that parcell of land called *Warfield's Forrest* lying in the s'd County in the woods. Begins at a bound White Oak.

Warfield's Plaines (Richard Warfield) 1/6/1680 – 300/315 acres. LCB2i/412 SR7366.
Know yee that wee for and in consideration that Richard Warfield of Ann Arundell County in our Province of Maryland hath due unto him three hundred acres of land by afsignment of **George Yate** part of a warrant for five hundred acres granted to the s'd Yate on 2/23/1680 as appears on record. Upon such conditions and terms as are exprefsed in our Conditions of Plantation of our Province of Maryland, wee doe grant unto the s'd Richard Warfield all that parcell of land lying in Ann Arundell County on the south side of the Ann Arundell River beginning at a bounded Red Oak at the head of Indian Cabin Branch and running with the line of a tract called *Lancaster (Lancaster Plaine)*. *Note: Although unmentioned in this grant, Richard Warfield proved rights to 50 acres for Service 2/15/1664- L18/165.*

Weston (Guy Meeke) 8/4/1683 – 130/129 acres. LSDA/101 SR7369.
Know yee that for and in consideration that Guy Meeke of Ann Arundell County in our Province of Maryland hath due unto him one hundred thirty acres of land within our s'd Province by afsignment of **Henry Hanslap** the afsignee of **Coll William Burges** part of a warrant for two thousand acres granted to the s'd Burges on the three and twentieth day of September 1681 as appears on record. Upon such conditions and terms as are exprefsed in our Conditions of Plantation of our late father Cecilius of noble memory, wee doe hereby grant unto the s'd Guy Meeke all that parcell of land called *Weston* lying in the s'd County on the south side of the Ann Arundell River up the branches of Plum Creek. Begins at a bound White Oak on the NW by N line of a tract called *Meeke's Rest*.

What Is Left (Amos Pierpoint) 6/4/1702 – 105/110 acres. LSDF/403 SR7373-2.
Know yee that for and in consideration that Amos Pierpoint of Ann Arundall County in
our s'd Province of Maryland hath due unto him one hundred and five acres of land
within our s'd Province by virtue of a warrant for the same quantity granted unto him the
s'd Amos Pierpoint 10/19/1700 as appears on record in our Land Office. Upon such
conditions and terms as are exprefsed in our Conditions of Plantation of this our
Province, wee doe therefore hereby grant unto him the s'd Amos Pierpoint all that tract or
parcell of land called *What Is Left* lying in the same County on a branch of Patuxent
River called Taylor's Branch beginning at a bounded Red Oak standing on the end of the
NW line of the land called *Cordwell. Adjoins Greeniston, The Diamond, and What You
Please.*

What You Please (Charles Stevens) 11/10/1695 – 72/48 acres. LC3i/303 SR7377.
Know yee that for and in consideration that Charles Stevens of Ann Arundell County in
our s'd Province of Maryland hath due unto him seaventy two acres of land within our
s'd Province due him by virtue of a warrant for seven hundred ninety eight acres granted
to **Thomas Richardson** on 10/9/1688 and inasmuch as the s'd quantity of seaventy two
acres was afsigned by the s'd Richardson out of a warrant unto **Michael Taylor** of the s'd
County, deceased, who's administrator the s'd Stevens is with s'd warrant as appears on
record. Upon such conditions and terms as are exprefsed in our Conditions of Plantation
of this our Province of Maryland, wee doe therefore hereby grant unto the s'd Stevens all
that tract or parcell of land called *What you Please* lying in Ann Arundell County in the
woods beginning at a bound tree of **Matthew Howard.** *Adjoins Brandy.*

What You Will (John Duvall) 6/1/1700 – 373/379 acres. LIB&IBLC/344 SR7368-1.
Know yee that wee for and in consideration that John Duvall of Ann Arundell County in
our s'd Province of Maryland hath due unto him three hundred and seventy three acres of
land within our Province by virtue of a warrant for foure hundred acres granted to him
10/15/1699 as appears on record. Upon such conditions and terms as are exprefsed in our
Conditions of Plantation of this our Province of Maryland, wee doe therefore hereby
grant unto the s'd John Duvall all that tract or parcell of land called *What You Will* lying
in Ann Arundell County above the South River beginning at a bounded White Oak it
being the first bound tree of *White's Hall* standing on the south side of the South Runn of
the afores'd River. *Note: The Certification (LCC4/153 SR7375) states that this tract
adjoined Abingdon. Adjoins Wilson's Grove and Abingdon.*

Wilson's Grove (Robert Wilson) 7/5/1672 - 200/188 acres. L16/385 SR7357.
Know yee that for and in consideration that Robert Wilson, Gent, of Ann Arundell
County in our s'd Province of Maryland hath due unto him two hundred acres of land
within our s'd Province part of a warrant for six hundred fifty acres to him granted
6/17/1671, as appears on record. Upon such conditions and terms as are exprefsed in our
Conditions of Plantation of this our Province of Maryland we doe hereby grant unto the
s'd Robert Wilson all that parcell of land called *Wilson's Grove* lying in the s'd County
between the heads of the Severn and South Rivers beginning at a bounded Red Oak of a
parcel of land formerly laid out for **Robert Proctor** and **John Gaither** of the s'd County.
Adjoins Abingdon and What You Will.

Middle Neck Hundred
Central Area

Bear Ridge (Nicholas Wyatt) 8/11/1664 - 175/209 acres. L7/355 SR7349.
Know yee that wee for and in consideration that Nicholas Wyatt of this Province, Planter, hath due unto him one hundred seventy and five acres of land within this Province being part of a warrant for three hundred acres as appears on record. Upon such considerations and termes as are exprefsed in our Conditions of Plantation of our Province of Maryland doe hereby grant unto the s'd Nicholas Wyatt a parcell of land called *Bear Ridge* lying in Ann Arundell County on the South side of the Severn River adjoining *Wyatt's Ridge*. Begins at a marked Oak near the head of a swamp.

Beetenson's Adventure **(Edward Beetenson)** 9/23/1680 - 82 acres. LCB2i/47 SR7366.
Know yee that we for and in consideration that Edward Beetenson of Ann Arundell County in our Province of Maryland hath due unto him eighty two acres of land within our s'd Province by afsignment of **George Yate** of the same County part of a warrant for two thousand eight hundred and ninety acres granted unto the s'd Yate the seventeenth day of March last paft, as appears on record. Upon such conditions and terms as are exprefsed in our Conditions of Plantation of our late father Cecilius of noble memory, wee doe grant unto the s'd Edward Beetenson all that parcell of land called *Beetenson's Adventure* lying in Ann Arundell County on the North side of the South River beginning at a bounded White Oak it being a bounded tree of land formerly granted to Thomas Bell. *Note 1(from MSA Tract Index 73): Sold by Beetenson to **Anthony Ruly** in 1707 (WH#2/628) who gave it to his daughter in 1710. Note 2: The tract cannot be drawn because the third course lacks both distance and direction. This course follows a creek called Harriss'es Creek and ends at the boundary of the plantation Beetenson "...now liveth upon." I found no mention of Harriss'es Creek or of Beetenson's home plantaion. I have been unable to position this tract in relation to other tracts. The certification (L20/357 SR7361) does not provide any information helpful in placing this tract. It is included only because it is shown in the Rent Rolls of 1701 as being in the Middle Neck Hundred. Based on the fact that it adjoined Bell's Haven (also unplaced), my best guess is that it was located in the Central Area near what is today Bell Station Road.*

Bell's Haven (Thomas Bell) 8/25/1665 – 100/122 acres. L9/146 SR7351.
Know ye that we for and in consideration that Thomas Bell of this Province, Planter, hath due unto him one hundred acres of land within this Province for Transporting himself and his wife **Elizabeth** in Anno 1659 into this Province here to inhabit as appears on record. And, upon such considerations and terms as are exprefsed in our Conditions of Plantation of our Province of Maryland, do grant unto the s'd Thomas Bell a parcell of land called *Bell's Haven* lying in Ann Arrundel County upon a creek called Befson's Creek. Begins at a bound Popler upon Befson's Creek. *Note: I have been unable to place this tract in relation to other tracts. Befson's (Besson's) Creek is not mentioned in any other tracts*

found in other patent documents and it is not shown on any of the old maps I have used to find the location of branches and creeks. My best guess, based on the location of present day Bell Station Road, is that it was located in the Central Area. It is included only because it is shown in the Rent Rolls of 1701 as being in the Middle Neck Hundred.

Bell's Haven Resurveyed (Richard and Elizabeth Bell) 6/30/1684 - 50/58 acres.
L22/94 SR7363. By Virtue of a Speciall Warrant granted to Richard Bell and his wife **Elizabeth** dated 11/28/1682 to resurvey a parcel of land called *Bell's Haven* lying in Ann Arundell County on the north side of the South River these presence are to certify that I in a humble manner have laid out and resurveyed the aforesaid parcell as follows, beginning at a bounded White Oak standing in a swamp. *Surveyor's Note: "Formerly laid out for 100 acres but now for fifty five acres by reason that the lines of the first survey run into the land of a more ancient survey." Note: I have been unable to place this tract. The patent for Bell's Haven makes reference to Befson's Creek, which I have been unable to locate (see footnote for previous tract). It is included only because it is shown in the Rent Rolls of 1701 as being in the Middle Neck Hundred.*

Broome (Richard Beard) 2/15/1659 - 220/202 acres. L4/441 SR 7346.
Know yee that wee for and in consideration that Richard Beard of this Province, Planter, hath due unto him two hundred and twenty acres of land in this Province. And upon such considerations and terms as are exprefsed in our Conditions of Plantation of our s'd Province of Maryland doe hereby grant unto the s'd Richard Beard a parcell of land lying on the west side of Chesapeake Bay on the north side of a river in this Bay called South River and on the west side of a creek in the said South River called the *Broad Creek.* Begins at a marked Oak by a swamp side near the head of this creek. *Note: On 9/8/1670, Richard Beard requested a special warrant to resurvey Broome and three months later sold the tract to Henry Ridgely.*

Broome Resurveyed (Henry Ridgely) 11/12/1670 - 220/153 acres. L16/23 SR7357.
Whereas **Richard Beard** hath caused the s'd parcell to be resurveyed and demands that the former (survey) be vacated on record and it appears that the s'd Beard hath afsigned, sold, and made over to Henry Ridgely, Gent, of the County of Ann Arundell, all his rights, titles, and interest in and to the same parcell of land, We do hereby grant and confirm unto the s'd Henry Ridgely all that parcell of land now resurveyed called *Broome* lying on the west side of Chesapeake Bay on the north side of the South River and on the west side of a creek called Broad Creek. Begins at bound Oak standing on a point called Deep Cove Point. *Note: The resurvey was requested by Richard Beard on 9/8/1670. Note 2: As shown in the tract drawings, Broome and Broome Resurveyed bear no resemblence to each other. In terms of actual acreage, the latter version is 52 acres smaller. The original Broome began on the west side at the head of Broad Creek and both began at a place called "Deep Cove Point," which is described in the patent as being at the head of Broad Creek. Actually, it was closer to the mouth of the creek. The resurveyed version also begins at Deep Cove Point, however, no reference is made to the head of Broad Creek.*

Bruton's Hope (John Bruton) 4/10/1671 – 40/55 acres. L14/207 SR7356.
Know ye that John Bruton of the County of Ann Arrundall in our Province of Maryland
hath due unto him forty acres of land by afsignment of **Matthew Howard** out of a
warrant for five hundred acres granted to the s'd Matthew Howard bearing the date of
10/16/1667, as appears upon record. And upon such conditions and termes as are
exprefsed in our Conditions of Plantation doe hereby grant unto the s'd John Bruton all
that parcell of land called *Bruton's Hope* lying in the aforesaid County on the south side
of the Seavern River. Begins at a bounded White Oak of the land formerly laid out for
Ralph Salmon (*Salmon Hill*). *Note 1: Note found in MSA Tract Index 73: Bruton's
Hope (40 acres) with part of Huckleberry Forrest (114 acres) willed to* **Thomas Rolls,**
Cooper, and sold in 1704 to **Edward Hall.** *Note 2: Several courses lack distance and
direction. The tract was drawn using the angles and distances of adjoining tracts.
Note 3: MSA Tract Index 73 shows the name as John Burton.*

Burntwood (Robert Gudgeon) 5/1/1676 – 100/176 acres. L19/350 SR7360.
Know yee that wee for and in consideration that Robert Gudgeon of Ann Arundell
County hath due unto him one hundred acres of land within our Province by afsignment
of **Thomas Hedge** part of a warrant for nine hundred and fifty acres of land granted unto
the said Thomas Hedge on 3/1/1673, as appears on record. And, upon such conditions
and terms as are exprefsed in our Conditions of Plantation of our Province of Maryland,
doe hereby grant unto the s'd Robert Gudgeon all that parcell of land called *Burntwood*
lying in the s'd County between the branches of the South and Ann Arundell Rivers.
Begins at a bound White Oak standing in the line of the land of **Larrance Richardson.**
Notes found in MSA Tract Index 73: 1692- sold to **Thomas Blackwell** *who bequeathed it
to son-in-law* **John Dorsey.** *1708 – Sold by John &* **Comfort Dorsey** *to* **Amos Garrett** *as
part of a package including Dorsey's Addition, Upper Toynton, Howard's Interest and
Mill Land.*

Burntwood Common (Robert & Lawrence Gudgeon) 6/1/1685 – 50/55 acres.
LIB&ILC/224 SR7368-2. Know yee that wee for and in consideration that Robert and
Lawrence Gudgeon of Ann Arundall County in our s'd Province of Maryland hath due
unto them fifty acres of land within our s'd Province by afsignment of **George Yate** part
of a warrant for three hundred and forty six acres granted to the s'd Yate bearing date
6/25/1684, and remaining on record in our Province of Maryland. Upon such conditions
and terms as are expressed in our Conditions of Plantation of our late father Cecilius of
noble memory, wee doe hereby grant unto the s'd Robert and Lawrence Gudgeon all that
tract or parcel of land called *Burntwood Common* lying in the s'd County on a branch of
the Ann Arundall River called Rockhold's Creek beginning at a bounded Oak by the s'd
Creek. *Note: Found in MSA Tract Index 73: Conveyed to* **John Rockhold** *5/17/1687,
and willed to his son* **Jacob,** *2/17/1698. Subsequently sold by Jacob Rockhold to* **Amos
Garrett.**

Charles' Hills (Charles Stevens) 7/23/1679 – 271/271 acres. L20/255 SR7361.
Know yee that we for and in consideration that Charles Stevens of Ann Arundell County
hath due unto him two hundred and seventy acres of land within our Province by

afsignment of **George Yate** part of a warrant for two thousand eight hundred and ninety six acres of land assigned to the s'd Yate on 3/7/1678, as appears on record. And, upon such conditions and terms as are exprefsed in our Conditions of Plantation of our late father Cecilius of noble memory, doe hereby grant unto the s'd Charles Stevens all that parcell of land called *Charles' Hills* lying in the s'd county on the west side of the Ann Arundell River beginning at a bound Oak standing on a point. *Note: MSA index 74 indicates that in 1766, this tract was resurveyed and 200 acres "laid out" (but not patented) for Orphan's Inheritance (Elizabeth Sisson) and also that 50 acres were conveyed to **William Yieldhall**. Also, 50 acres were sold but never conveyed to **Edward Hall**. Orphan's Inheritance was eventually patented by **Amos Garrett** as Providence).*

Clarke's Enlargement (Neale Clarke) 9/1/1687 - 265/286 acres. LNS2i/438 SR 7371.
Know yee that for and in consideration that Neale Clarke, Planter, of Ann Arundell County in our s'd Province of Maryland hath due unto him two hundred sixty five acres of land within our s'd Province by afsignment of severall parcells of land one of two hundred thirty acres from **Andrew Norwood** of the s'd County, part of a warrant for fourteen hundred acres granted to the s'd Norwood in February 1685, and the other of six and thirty acres from **Robert Proctor** of the aforesaid County, part of a warrant for two hundred acres granted to the s'd Proctor 2/21/1685, as appears on record. Upon such conditions and terms as are exprefsed in our Conditions of Plantation of this our Province of Maryland, wee doe therefore hereby grant unto the s'd Neale Clark all that tract or parcell of land called *Clarke's Enlargement* lying on the north side of the South River beginning at a bounded Pine of **Henry Ridgely's** land (*Wardridge*). *Note: Adjoins Hog Neck, land of **John Hammond**, and the Main Branch of Broad Creek.*

Clarke's Luck (Neale Clarke) 6/5/1685 - 60/60 acres. LNSBi/415 SR 7370.
Know yee that for and in consideration that Neale Clarke of Ann Arundall County in our s'd Province of Maryland hath due unto him sixty acres of land within our s'd Province by afsignment of **Richard Beard** part of a warrant for one thousand acres granted to the s'd Beard 4/9/1684 as appears on record. Upon such conditions and terms as are exprefsed in our Conditions of Plantation of this our Province, wee doe hereby grant unto the s'd Neale Clark all that tract or parcell of land called *Clarke's Luck* lying on the north side of the South River in this County beginning at the southmost bounded tree of a parcel of land formerly laid out for **Edward Hope** and **Thobey Butler** called *Hodge Neck (Hog Neck)* and running from the said tree on the said land northeast by east to a bounded White Oak standing in the northmost line of a parcel of land formerly laid out for **James Wardner** and **Henry Ridgely** of this County and running with the said land south southwest to a bounded Red Oak it being the easternmost of a parcel of land formerly laid out for Neale Clarke of this County called the *Landing Place*. *Note from MSA Tract Index 73: Sold by Clarke to **William Griffith** for 3,000 lbs of tobacco (IH&IL/72-5).*

Covell's Cove (Ann Covell Mott Lambert) 1661 - 430/425 acres. L5/292 SR 7347.
Know yee that for and in consideration that Ann Covell, widow and relict of **John Covell,** deceased, hath due unto her four hundred thirty acres of land within this Province

as appears on record. Upon such conditions and terms as are exprefsed in our Conditions of Plantation of our Province of Maryland, wee doe hereby grant unto the s'd Ann Covell a parcell of land called *Covell's Cove* lying on the north side of the South River next adjoining the land of **Neale Clark** (*Nealson*), Planter. Begins at the s'd Clarke's easternmost bound tree at the river, a Pine tree. *Note: This property was patented as Covell's Cove by Ann Covell Mott Lambert on the date shown. An 80 acre portion of this tract was sold to **Samuel White** in 1682, and a 50 acre portion to **John Robinson** in 1683. On both occasions the property was deeded as Covell's Troubles, which is, apparently, the name Lambert used to identify this property during her lifetime. This tract cannot be drawn following the deed courses specified because the final course, which follows the line of the South River, omitted distance. However, I have calculated a final course to approximate the actual course and produced a drawing that is within five acres of the granted amount.*

Crouchfield (William Crouch) 7/9/1659 – 150/120 acres. L4/87 SR7346.
Know yee that wee for and in consideration that William Crouch of the County of Ann Arundell hath transported **Josias and Rachell** his children into this Province here to inhabit in Anno 1650, and upon such conditions and terms as are exprefsed in our Conditions of Plantation in our Province of Maryland doe hereby grant unto the s'd William Crouch a parcell of land called *Crouchfield* (150 acres) lying in Ann Arrundell County on the south side of the Ann Arundell (Severn) River near Marsh's Creek. Begins at a marked White Oak in a valley called *Crouche's Valley*. *Note 1: In a later patent a second parcel called North Crouchfield (300 acres) was granted for transporting his daughters **Mary** and **Elizabeth**. North Crouchfield is located on the north side of the Ann Arundell (Severn) River. Note 2: This tract could not be drawn from the courses as stated in the patent. It was necessary to calculate distance for the third course based on acreage.*

Dorsey's Addition (Joshua Dorsey) 5/10/168? – 50/50 acres. LNSBi/433 SR7370.
Know yee that for and in consideration that Joshua Dorsey of Ann Arundell County in our s'd Province of Maryland hath due unto him fifty acres of land within our s'd Province being due to the s'd Dorsey by warrant for the same quantity granted him 10/9/1683 as appears on record. Upon such conditions and terms as are exprefsed in our Conditions of Plantation of this our Province, wee do hereby grant to the s'd Joshua Dorsey all that tract or parcell of land called *Dorsey's Addition* lying in the woods beginning at a bound Hickory. Adjoins *Orphan's Addition, Howard's Interest* and the Main Branch of Broad Creek. *Note: The exact patent year cannot be determined. The date shown on the patent document (5/10/1680) predates the Survey by nearly three years and must have been a clerk's error. The patent preceding Dorsey's Addition in Liber NSBi is dated 1686, and the patent following Dorsey's addition is dated 1685.*

Freeman's Fancy (John Freeman) 5/27/1663 – 300/250 acres. L5/289 SR7347.
Know yee that wee for and in consideration that John Freeman of this Province hath due unto him three hundred acres of land in this Province for the Transportation of severall

persons into this Province as appears on record. Upon such conditions and terms as are exprefsed in our Conditions of Plantation of our Province of Maryland, wee doe grant unto the s'd John Freeman a parcell of land called *Freeman's Fancy* lying a mile and a half from the head of the South River in the County of Ann Arundall at the end of land formerly conveyed to him beginning at his southmost bounded Oak in the woods. *Note from MSA Tract Index 73: Clarke devised this tract to his widow* **Elizabeth** *who married* **Robert Proctor**. *In 1673, Robert and Elizabeth Proctor sold to George Puddington who in 1764 devised the tract to* **Edward Burges.**

Free Manston (John Freeman) 2/15/1659 –150/131 acres. L4/429 SR7346.
Know yee that wee for and in consideration that John Freeman of this Province, Planter, hath due unto him one hundred fifty acres of land within this Province. Upon such conditions and terms as are exprefsed in our Conditions of Plantation of this our Province of Maryland, wee do hereby grant unto the s'd John Freeman a parcell of land called *Freeman's Neck* or *Free Manston (Note: shown both ways in card files of MHR)* lying on the west side of Chesapeake Bay in a river of the s'd Bay called the South River near to the head of the said river between the two main branches of the river. Begins at a marked Oak on the east side of the West Branch. *Note: A note in the margin of this grant refers to the tract as Freeman's Neck. The Index of Tracts at the Maryland Hall of Records shows both names. However, the text of the grant is clear that the tract being granted was called Free Manston. Note from MSA Tract Index 73: Clarke devised this tract to his widow* **Elizabeth** *who married* **Robert Proctor**. *In 1673, Robert and Elizabeth Proctor sold to* **George Puddington** *who, in 1764 devised the tract to* **Edward Burges.**

Gardner's Warfield (Richard Warfield & Edward Gardner) 10/10/1669 – 60/ 62 acres. L12/328 SR7354. By virtue of a warrant granted unto **George Yate** of Ann Arundell County, Gent, for 230 acres of land dated 5/18/?, *(we)* doe grant unto Richard Warfield and Edward Gardner of the County aforesaid, Planters, by afsignement of George Yate, a parcell of land called *Gardner's Warfield* lying in the s'd County on the north side of the South River. Begins at the NW bounded Tree of land formerly laid out for **Nicholas Wyatt** now in the occupacion of Gardner and Warfield. *Note: The assignment of all rights, title, and interest in this tract follows the patent in the land records.*

Gater's Range (John Gater) 9/10/1675 - 200/*147* acres. L17/293 SR 7358.
Know yee that we for and in consideration that John Gater of Ann Arundell County in our s'd Province of Maryland, Planter, hath due unto him two hundred acres of land within our s'd Province by afsignment from **George Yate** the afsignee of **Thomas Taylor**, attorney for **Jerome White, Esq.**, part of a warrant for eleven hundred fifty acres to the s'd White granted 4/9/1672, as appears on record. Upon such conditions and terms as are exprefsed in our Conditions of Plantation of this our Province of Maryland we doe hereby grant unto the s'd Gater a parcell of land called *Gater's Ridge* lying in the said County on the head of the South River. Begins at a bounded Red Oak standing on the west side of the North Runn of the South River. *Note: Adjoins Freemans Fancy and the North Runn of the South River.*

Hog Neck formerly Broome (Edw. Hope) 6/24/1663 - 250/233 acres. L5/353 SR7347.
Know yee that we for and in consideration that Edward Hope of this Province hath due
unto him two hundred and fifty acres of land in this Province as appears upon record.
And, upon such considerations and terms as are exprefsed in our Conditions of Plantation
of our Province of Maryland, do hereby grant unto the s'd Edward Hope a parcel of land
formerly surveyed to **Tobias Butler** called *Hog Neck*, formerly surveyed for Tobias
Butler and called *Coombe*, lying on the north side of the South River in the County of
Ann Arundell. Begins at a marked Oak by cove side. *Note: This tract bears no
resemblence to Coombe which was laid out for 150 acres. At some point before
assigning the tract to Hope, Butler must have added 100 acres to Coombe. No record
has been found of this, however.*

Honest Man's Lott (John Duvall) 7/23/1704 –110/119 acres. LCDi/220 SR7376.
Know yee that for and in consideration that John Duvall of Ann Arundell County in our
Province of Maryland hath due unto him 110.5 acres of land within our s'd Province
being due unto him by virtue of a warrant for two hundred ten acres granted him
6/24/1704 as appears on record. Upon such conditions and terms as are exprefsed in our
Conditions of Plantation of our Province of Maryland, wee doe therefore hereby grant
unto the s'd Duvall all that tract or parcell of land called *Honest Man's Lott* lying in the
s'd County on the North Branch of the head of the South River beginning at a bound
Poplar standing by a gate post which stands by a roadside which leads from the house of
Richard Warfield to **Mrs. Ruth Howard's** door. *Note: Adjoins The Good Mother's
Endeavor and Howard and Porter's Range.*

Hope (Henry Sewell) 8/8/1664 - 100/107 acres. L7/343 SR7349.
Know yee that wee for and in consideration that Henry Sewell of this Province, Planter,
hath due unto him one hundred acres of land within this Province for transporting himself
and **William Rinthell** into this Province here to inhabit. Do hereby grant unto him, the
s'd Sewell, a parcell of land called *Hope*. Lying in Anne Arundel County in the woods on
the south side of the Severn River about a mile from the head of Plum Creek. Begins at a
marked Oak by an Indian path on a ridge. *Note: The Indian path referred to is present
day MD Route 178 (General's Highway). Adjoins Wayfield. Note from MSA Tract
Index73: Sold to **John Minter** 12/16/1675 and following his death, devised to Elizabeth
Williston (Winchester).*

Howard's Discovery (John Howard) 5/1/1697 – 50/50 acres. LCD/18 SR7376
Know yee that for and in consideration that John Howard of Ann Arundell County by his
humble petition presented to our Deputy did set forth that there was a small parcell of
vacant cultivated land containing about fifty acres adjoining to a tract of land of his that
which he could not take up by a common warrant. Wherefore he humbly prayed that he
might have a Speciall Warrant to take up the same which was granted him as appears in
our Land Office. And upon such conditions and terms as are exprefsed in our Conditions
of Plantation of our Province of Maryland, wee doe therefore hereby grant unto him the
s'd John Howard all that tract or parcell of land called *Howard's Discovery* beginning at
a bound Red Oak standing by Hockley Creek and running down the s'd creek. *Note:
Also adjoins Severn River and the mouth of Wyatt's Creek.*

Howard's Interest (John Howard) 8/4/1664 - 150/209 acres. L7/252 SR7349.
Know yee that we for and in consideration that John Howard of this Province, Planter, hath due unto him one hundred and fifty acres of land within this Province being part of a warrant for nine hundred acres granted unto him and his three brothers **Samuel**, **Cornelius**, and **Matthew Howard** as appears on record. And, upon such considerations and terms as are exprefsed in our Conditions of Plantation of our Province of Maryland do grant unto the s'd John Howard a parcell of land called *Howard's Interest* lying in Anne Arundel County on the south side of the Severn River. Begins at a marked White Oak on the north side of Hockley Creek.

Howard's Mount (John Howard) 4/12/1678 – 80/76 acres. L20/69 SR7361.
Know yee that we for and in consideration that John Howard of Ann Arundell County hath due unto him eighty acres of land within our s'd Province part of a warrant for five hundred acres granted unto him 12/7/1665, as appears on record. Upon such conditions and terms as are exprefsed in our Conditions of Plantation of our late father Cecilius of noble memory, doe hereby grant unto the s'd John Howard all that parcell of land called *Howard's Mount* lying in the s'd county on the south side of the Ann Arundell River near the Round Bay. Begins at a bound White Oak. *Note: Adjoins Howard's Search, Bear Neck and Stony Hill.*

Howard's Search (John Howard) 12/10/1690 – 121/119 acres. LCC4/13 SR7375.
Know yee that for and in consideration that John Howard of Ann Arundell County in our s'd Province of Maryland hath due one hundred twenty one acres of land being due unto him by virtue of warrants for twenty nine acres (and) the other for ninety two acres both granted him 6/29/1696 as appears on record in our Land Office. Upon such conditions and terms as are exprefsed in our Conditions of Plantation of our Province of Maryland, wee doe therefore hereby grant unto the s'd John Howard all that tract or parcell of land called *Howard's Search* lying on the south side of the Severn River near the Round Bay beginning at the northeast boundary of a parcell of land called *Howard's Mount* and running with the s'd Land.

Howard's Thickett (**John Howard**) 10/2/1666 – 50 acres. L10/186 SR7352.
Know ye that we for and in consideration that John Howard of this Province, Gent, hath due unto him fifty acres of land within this Province part of a warrant for five hundred fifty acres formerly granted to the s'd Howard as appears on record. And, upon such conditions and terms as are exprefsed in our Conditions of Plantation of our Province of Maryland, doe hereby grant unto the s'd John Howard a parcell of land called *Howard's Thickett* lying in Anne Arundel County on the south side of the Seaverne River. Begins at a bound White Oak on the Land of **Charles Stevens**. *Note: This tract (and a portion of the Woodyard) was eventually resurveyed into the The Good Mother's Endeavour. The tract cannot be drawn because the second course gives conflicting direction and the fourth (final) course lacks direction.*

Jane's Inheritance (Jane Sisson) 6/20/1668 – 50/51 acres. L12/28 SR7354.
Know yee that we for and in consideration that **John Sifson** late of the County of Ann
Arrundell deceased, had due unto him fifty acres of land for Transportion of **John
Hermon** into our s'd Province to inhabit as appears upon record. And, upon such
conditions and terms as are exprefsed in our Conditions of Plantation in our s'd Province
of Maryland, doe grant unto Jane Sisfon a parcell of land called *Jane's Inheritance* lying
on the south side of the Seavern River and on a creek called Sunken Green Creek.
*Note: The courses specified lack distance and direction. Courses used in the drawing are
calculated based on location, adjoining property, and acreage.*

Long Venture (John Stimson) 7/20/1673 - 250/278 acres. L17/170 SR 7358.
Know yee that wee for and in consideration that John Stimson of Ann Arundell County in
our s'd Province of Maryland hath due unto him two hundred fifty acres of land within
our s'd Province by afsignment of **Robert Wilson** being part of a warrant for two
thousand acres granted to the s'd Wilson 4/9/1672 as appears on record. Upon such
conditions and terms as are exprefsed in our Conditions of Plantation, wee doe hereby
grant unto the s'd John Stimson all that parcell of land called *Long Venture* lying in Anne
Arundel County between the head of the South River and Anne Arrundel (Severn) River.
Begins at a bounded Red Oak on the land of **Henry Pierpoint**. *Note 1: Adjoins
Pierpoint's Lott, Vennall's Inheritance, and Wyatt's Ridge.* (Survey: 1/22/1651 **AB&H**
264 SR7344.) *Note 2: Cannot be drawn following the course order specified in the
patent. It was drawn by beginning with patent course 7 and ending with course 6.*

Medcalfe's Chance (John Medcalfe) 8/10/1683 – 80/71 acres. LSDA/104 SR7369.
Know yee that for and in consideration that John Medcalfe of Ann Arundell County in
our Province of Maryland hath due unto him eighty acres of land within our s'd Province
by afsignemnt of **Henry Hanslap** the afsignee of **Coll William Burges** part of a warrant
for two thousand acres granted to the s'd Burges on 9/23/1681 as appears on record.
Upon such conditions and terms as are exprefsed in our Conditions of Plantation of our
late father Cecilius of noble memory, wee doe hereby grant unto the s'd John Medcalfe
all that tract or parcell of land called *Medcalfe's Chance* lying in the s'd County between
the branches of the South River. Begins at a bound Hickory of a tract called *Howard and
Porter's Range*. *Note: Also adjoins Medcalfe's Mount.*

Medcalfe's Mount (John Medcalf) 5/10/1685 – 70/70 acres. LNSBi/174 SR7370.
Know yee that for and in consideration that John Medcalfe of Ann Arundell County in
our s'd Province of Maryland hath due unto him seventy acres of land within our s'd
Province being due to him the s'd Medcalfe by afsignment of **Robert Jones** and **George
Yate** part of a warrant for two thousand acres granted to the s'd Jones and Yate
3/25/1683 as appears on record. Upon such conditions and terms as are exprefsed in our
Conditions of Plantation of this our Province of Maryland, wee doe hereby grant unto the
s'd John Medcalfe all that tract or parcell of land called *Medcalfe's Mount* lying in the s'd
County in the woods between the North Runn Branches of the South River beginning at a
bound Red Oak. *Note: Adjoins Howard and Porter's Range and Medcalfe's Chance.*

Mill Land (Robert Proctor) 5/10/1683 - 100/101 acres. LNS2i/111 SR7371.
Know yee that for and in consideration that Robert Proctor of Ann Arundell County in
our s'd Province of Maryland hath due unto him 100 acres of land within our s'd
Province by a warrant granted to him for six hundred acres of land bearing the date
2/17/1683 as appears on record. Upon such conditions and terms as are exprefsed in our
Conditions of Plantation of this our Province, wee doe hereby grant unto the s'd Robert
Proctor all that tract or parcell of land called *Mill Land* lying in the s'd County on the
north side of the South River and on the Main Branch of Broad Creek. Begins at a
Bounded Oak standing by the s'd Creek. *Note: Adjoins Hockley in the Hole.*

Narrow Neck (William Yieldhall) 10/5/1683 – 41/39 acres. LSDA/420 SR7369.
Know yee that for and in consideration that William Yieldhall of Ann Arrundell County
in our s'd Province of Maryland hath due unto him forty one acres of land within our s'd
Province by afsignment of **Henry Hanslap** part of a warrant for twelve hundred fifty
acres granted the s'd Hanslap 8/30/1682 as appears on record. Upon such conditions and
terms as are exprefsed in our Conditions of Plantation of our late father Cecilius, of noble
memory, wee doe hereby grant unto the s'd William Yieldhall all that tract or parcell of
land called Narrow Neck lying in the s'd County on the south side of the Ann Arrundell
River by a bay called *Round Bay* at the head of Sunken Ground Creek.

Nealson (Neale Clark) 2/15/1659 - 100/100 acres. L4/383 SR7346.
Know yee that we for and in consideration that Neale Clarke of this Province, Planter,
hath due unto him one hundred acres of land. And upon such considerations and terms as
are exprefsed in our Conditions of Plantation of our s'd Province of Maryland, do hereby
grant unto the s'd Neale Clark a parcell of land called *Nealson* lying on the west side of
Chesapeake Bay and on the east side of a river in the said Bay called the South River.
Beginning at a marked Pine tree standing by the riverside under a hill near to a bile called
Neale's Bile running north up the river. *Note: Nealson also bounded Broad Creek on the
east (AA County Abstracts of Land Records, Vol. III, page 88).*

Norwood's Fancy (John Norwood) 2/16/1659 420/381 acres. L4/426 SR7346.
Know ye that for and in consideration that John Norwood, Boatwright, hath transported
himself and his wife and sons **Andrew** and **John** and servants **John Hage, Elizabeth
Hills** in Anno 1658, **Thomas Hall** and **George Barrett** in Anno 1657 (LQ/29) and that
there is twenty of acres of land yet due to the said Norwood for transporting **Lucy Child**
and hath further acres due to him fifty acres more (LQ/29). Do hereby grant unto him the
said Norwood a parcell of land called *Norwood's Fancy* lying on the east side of
Chesapeake Bay and on the south side of a river called Severine River on the west side of
a creek called Round Bay. Begins at a marked Ash tree standing by a fresh branch.
Note: John Norwood is referred to as Capt. Norwood in Abstracts, Vol. 4, page 61.
*Notes from MSA Tract Index 73: Norwood willed "moiety' to children Andrew, Hannah,
and Ann Norwood, and Elizabeth Beall. Andrew sold to William Yieldhall who died
intestate. Yieldhall's brother Charles sold the tract to William Griffith.*

Pierpoint's Lott (Henry Pierpoint) 9/15/1666 - 150/*207* acres. L10/106 SR7352.
Know yee that wee for and in consideration that Henry Pierpoint of this Province hath
due unto him one hundred and fifty acres of land within our said Province out of a
warrant for three hundred fifty acres formerly granted to the s'd Pierpoint as appears on
record. And, upon such conditions and terms as are exprefsed in our Conditions of
Plantation of our Province of Maryland, wee doe hereby grant unto him the s'd Henry
Pierpoint all that parcell of land called *Pierpoint's Lott* lying in the said County in the
woods about two miles from Ann Arundell River. Begins at a bounded Hickory.
*Note 1: Adjoins Long Venture, Rawling's Purchase, Vennall's Inheritance, and Wyatt's
Ridge. Note 2: Henry Pierpoint was issued a warrant for 350 acres on 1/11/1666 for
transporting himself, Elizabeth his wife, Arnis his oldest son, Jabes Pierpoint and
Elizabeth and Hanna Mopes (L9/34). Note 3: The survey indicates that Pierpoint's Lott
was laid out for 200 acres. A marginal note on the patent states that, "This patent let fall
and a warrant of resurvey granted to the said Pierpoint." (LibMM /149) Apparently the
resurvey erroneously resulted in a reduction of the acreage to the 150 acres shown in the
patent and when this property was eventually sold in 1695 by Jabez Pierpoint (son of
Henry), the deed of sale (C#3/311 SR7377) indicates that at that time the tract contained
200 acres of land. My drawing, which follows the courses shown in the patent and resale
deeds, resulted in a tract of 207 acres of land. Note 4 (from MSA Land Tract Index 73):
In 1683, Pierpoint sold 50-acre portions to sons Jabez and Amos with each paying 2,000
lbs of tobacco (WH4/57 and 162). Jabez sold his portion to Amos in 1694 for
12 lbs. sterling.*

Pierpoint's Rocks (Henry Pierpoint) 4/1/1672 – 80/*57* acres. L14/489 SR7356.
Know yee that for and in consideration that Henry Pierpoint of Ann Arundel County in
our Province of Maryland, Planter, hath due unto him eighty acres of land, part of a
warrant for 350 acres granted to him bearing the date of the first day of November 1665,
as appears on record. And, upon such conditions and terms as are exprefsed in our
Conditions of Plantation do hereby grant unto the s'd Henry Pierpoint all that parcell of
land called *Pierpoint's Rocks* lying in s'd County on the north side of the South River and
on the north west side of Broad Creek. Begins at a bound Oak of a tract laid out for **John
Covill.**

Plumpton (**George Walker**) 6/22/1663 – 280 acres. L5/357 SR7347.
Know yee that wee for and in consideration that George Walker of this Province, Planter,
hath due unto him one hundred eighty acres of land afsigned to him by **Robert Clarkson**
and one hundred acres more from **George Puddington** both of this Province, Planters, as
appears on record. Upon such conditions and terms as are exprefsed in our Conditions of
Plantation of our Province of Maryland, wee doe hereby grant unto the s'd George
Walker a parcell of land called *Plumpton* lying in the west side of the South River near
the land of **Marin Duvall** in the County of Ann Arundell beginning at a marked Oak on a
hill by a great swamp. *Note: The grant conveys two adjoining tracts with a combined
acreage of 280 acres. Neither can be drawn because the courses are incomplete.*

Providence (Amos Garrett) 8/20/1710 – 200/200 acres. LDD5i/633 SR7378.
The bounds of a tract of land containing two hundred acres formerly called the *Orphan's Inheritance* laid out and resurveyed for **Elizabeth Sifson** the orphan of **John Sifson**, dec'd, by afsignment of **William Crouch** of the s'd County of Ann Arundell one hundred acres being a warrant granted unto the s'd Crouch for one hundred acres and by afsignment from **John Howard** of the s'd County for one hundred acres it being parte of a warrant for five hundred fifty acres. A parcell of land lying in the s'd county called *Orphan's Inheritance* beginning at a bounded Red Oake upon a point by a bay side in the Seavern River called The Round Bay the Oake being the northmost bound tree of *Norwood's Fancy*. *Note: This tract was surveyed for Elizabeth Sisson on 5/21/1666 (L9/465 SR7351). Apparently it was not patented by her. The following preceded the above (Providence) patent: " Know all men by these prefents that we Thomas Brown and Elizabeth his wife, formally Elizabeth Sifson, for a valuable consideration have as by these prefents wee doe afsign, sell, and make over to Amos Pierpoint and his heirs forever all right, title, and interest in and of a certaine Certificate dated 5/21/1666, for two hundred acres of land called The Orphan's Inheritance and then laid out for the above named Elizabeth Sifson the orphan of John Sifson. The tract was then renamed Providence and patented by Amos Pierpoint (same liber and folio).*

Rawling's Purchase (Richard Rawlings) 8/30/1682 – 50/48 acres. LCB3i/146 SR7367.
Whereas, **John Vennell,** late, of Ann Arundell County was granted a parcell called *Vennel's Inheritance* of one hundred acres in the s'd County, fifty acres of the s'd one hundred acres John Vennell in his lifetime alienated and let fall and the remaining fifty acres escheated to us for lack of an heir to the s'd John Vennell by the judgement of the Provincial Court held at St. Maries City on 10/8/1679. Whereas Richard Rawlings of the s'd County having lately purchased of us the s'd fifty acres now our rights and has humbly supplicated a Special Warrant to resurvey and lay out the same to the metes and bounds thereof and a Patent of Confirmation to him be granted. Wee doe therefore hereby give, grant, and confirm unto him the s'd Richard Rawlings all that parcel now resurveyed called *Rawling's Purchase* and part of a parcel of the aforementioned one hundred acres also called *Vennel's Inheritance* being situated in Ann Arundell County on the north side of a runn called *Hog Neck Runn* beginning at a bounded tree standing on a hill by the side of a branch of land formerly laid out for **Nicholas Wyatt** (*Wyatt's Ridge*). *Note 1: Also adjoins Pierpoint's Lott and Long Venture. Note 2: Like the courses specified in the grant for Vennel's Inheritance, the 5th and 6th boundary courses lacked a combination of distance and direction. The tract was drawn by measuring the angles of Hog Neck Branch and the distance from the southwestern most point of Long Ridge, following the North Runn of the South River to Hog Neck Branch.*

Richardson's Joy (Lawrence Richardson) 6/23/1663 - 200/195 acres. L5/344 SR7347.
Know yee that we for and in consideration that Lawrence Richardson of this Province hath transported himself, his wife **Sarah**, and his children **Thomas** and **Sarah**, all in Anno 1649. And, upon such considerations and terms as are exprefsed in our Conditions of Plantation of our Province of Maryland, do hereby grant unto the said Lawrence Richardson a parcel of land called *Richardson's Joy* lying in the County of Ann Arundall on the south side of the Severn River on south end of Round Bay. Begins at a marked

Oak tree in a valley by the riverside. *Note: On August 9, 1666, Larrance Richardson was granted 50 acres for transporting* **Gilbert Thurston** *in Anno 1662.*

Ridgely's Beginning (Wm. Ridgely) 5/18/1679 - 40/60 acres. L20/205 SR7361.
Know yee that we for and in consideration that William Ridgely of Ann Arundell County in our Province of Maryland hath due unto him forty acres of land by afsignment of **George Yate** *(1/15/1678 - L15/767)* part of a warrant for five hundred acres granted to the s'd Yate on 10/21/1678 as appears on record. And, upon such conditions and terms as are exprefsed in our Conditions of Plantation of our late father Cecilius of noble memory, doe hereby grant unto the s'd William Ridgely all that parcel of land called *Ridgely's Beginning* in the s'd County lying on the north side of the South River and in a neck of land called Hog Neck. Begins at a marked stump. *Note: Adjoins Hog Neck, Clarke's Enlargement, and Vennall's Inheritance.*

Rocky Point (Ann Lambert) 7/18/1680 - 50/12 acres. LCB2i/13 SR7366.
Know yee that we for and in consideration that Ann Lambert of Ann Arundell County hath due unto her fifty acres of land by afsignment of **George Holland** part of a warrant for seven hundred sixty acres granted unto the s'd Holland 10/4/1679 as appears on record. Upon such conditions and terms as are exprefsed in our Conditions of Plantation of our late father Cecilus of noble memory, we do therefore grant unto the s'd Ann Lambert all that parcell of land called *Rocky Point* lying in Ann Arundell County on the north side of the South River and on the south side of a branch called Forked Branch. *Note: The discrepency in acreage is unusually great, even for this period. The boundary courses specified in the deed have been correctly drawn and it has been determined that these courses are the same as those specified for Rocky Point in the initial survey as well as in two subsequent deeds of sale (Lomas to Dorsey and Dulany to Jordan).*

Roundabout Hill (John Gaither) 9/1/1687 - 120/121 acres. LNS2i/396 SR7371.
Know yee that for and in consideration that John Gaither of Ann Arundell County in our s'd Province of Maryland hath due unto him one hundred twenty acres of land by afsignment of **Robert Proctor** of the s'd County part of a warrant for two hundred acres granted the s'd Proctor 2/25/1685 as appears on record. Upon such conditions and terms as are exprefsed in our Conditions of Plantation of this our Province wee doe therefore grant unto the s'd John Gaither all that tract or parcell of land called called *Round About Hill* lying in the s'd County beginning in the north west by north line of a parcell of land called *Free Manston.* Lying in Ann Arundel County on the west side of the South Runn of the South River, begining at the nw by north line of *Free Manston.*

Stony Hills (Richard Everet) 1/10/1695 - 36/26 acres. LWD/126 SR7372-2.
Know yee that for and in consideration that Richard Everet of Ann Arundall County in our s'd Province of Maryland hath due unto him thirty six acres of land within our Province being due unto him by afsignment of **Charles Hopkins** of the s'd County out of a warrant for two hundred seventy acres granted to Hopkins 7/25/1695 as appears on record in our Land Office. Upon such conditions and terms as are exprefsed in our Conditions of Plantation of this our Province, wee doe therefore hereby grant unto the s'd Richard Everet all that tract or parcel of land called *Stony Hills* lying in Ann Arundall

County beginning at a bounded Red Oak of **John Howard**. *Note: Another patent was found for Stony Hills in LC3i/328 SR7377.*

The Adventure (William Frizzell) 9/13/1663 - 50/43 acres. L5/574 SR7347.
Know yee that we for and in consideration that William Frizzell of this Province, Planter, hath due unto him fifty acres of land for compleating his time of service in this Province and upon such considerations and terms as are exprefsed in our Conditions of Plantation of our Province of Maryland do grant unto the s'd William Frizzell a parcell of land called *The Adventure* lying in Ann Arundall County on the north side of the South River, and on the west side of Broad Creek adjoining the land of **Nicholas Wyatt** (*Wyatt's Ridge*). *Note: Purchased from Frizzell 6/26/1670 by **John Hammond** (BC&GS 45 Folio 205 SR 7752). Purchased again (6/1677) by **Henry Ridgely.***

The Coombe (Tobias Butler) 1/22/1659 - 150/*149* acres. *L6/432* SR 7346.
Know yee that we for and in consideration that **Edward Lloyd, Esq.**, hath afsigned the rights to three hundred acres of land to him formerly entered unto **Richard Deaver** who thereupon had warrant for so much upon the eastern shore of this our said Province that the s'd Deaver now afsigned unto **Marin Duvall** who hath also afsigned the s'd warrant unto Tobias Butler who hath upon the western shore served. Upon such considerations and terms as are exprefsed in our Conditions of Plantation of our Province of Maryland, do hereby grant unto the s'd Tobias Butler a parcell of land called *The Coombe* lying on the west side of Chesapeake Bay and on the side of a river in this Bay called the South River near the head respecting the land of **John Freeman** to the south. Begins at a marked Oak by the riverside.

The Encrease (John Minter) 5/15/1668 – 50/33 acres. L11/407 SR7353.
Know ye that John Minter, Planter, of Ann Arundell County in our s'd Province hath due unto him for his time of service performed within our Province as appears upon record. And, upon such Conditions of Plantations doe grant unto him the s'd John Minter a parcel of land called *The Encrease* lying on the south side of the Seaverne River. Begins at a bound Oake of the land laid out for **Henry Sewell**.

The Good Mother's Endeavor (Eleanor Howard) 6/1/1698 - 285/285 acres. LBBB3i /537 SR7374. Know yee that whereas Elinor Howard has humbly put to our Deputy for Management of Land Affairs did set forth that her husband **John Howard**, deceased, by his last will and testament in writing did bequeath unto her and her heirs a certain tract of land in the s'd county called *Howard's Thickett* originally laid out for fifty acres or more. Adjoining to the same being the remainder of a tract of land of one hundred acres called *The Woodyard* the other hundred acres being by the s'd Howard in his lifetime conveyed to his daughter **Ann Gremmell**. But, concerning that there may be some surplus land within the bounds of the aforesaid *Howard's Thickett* and the same fifty acres part of the aforesaid tract called *The Woodyard*. She humbly prayed that she might have our special warrant and as well to ascertaine their bounds and to bring them into one tract. Whereupon such special warrant was ordered to you by virtue of our instructions. Whereof it is certified into our Land Office that there is surplus land within the bounds of the s'd *Howard's Thickett* and the remaining part of *The Woodyard* over and above the quantity for which it was first laid out. The quantity of one hundred and eighty five acres for which the s'd Elinor has pursuant to a clause of our instructions to **Coll Henry Darnall**, our agent in our Province being dated 12/6/1697. Secured to the aforesaid unto us the quantity of four hundred and forty five pounds of tobacco regarding rights to the surplus and also the sum of 5lbs, 8 shillings and 10 pence sterling being for the errors of rent from the time of the original survey. Wee doe therefore hereby give, grant, and confirme unto the s'd Elinor Howard all that tract or parcell of land called *The Good Mother's Endeavor* beginning at a Pine tree. *Note: Located on the north side of the South River on the North Runn, adjoining the land of Edward Dorsey.*

The Landing Place (Neale Clarke) 9/25/1663 - 50/*31* acres. L5/597 SR7347.
Know yee that we for and in consideration that Neale Clarke, Planter, of this Province hath due unto him fifty acres of land in this Province the remainder of a warrant granted for five hundred acres of land to **William Jones**, assignee of the said Clarke and another fifty acres of land granted unto the s'd Clarke by **Nathaniel Dolphin** and also another fifty acres granted unto the s'd Clarke for Transporting **John Stimson** (Note: *who later married Clarke's widow Rachel Beard Clarke)*, Anno 1650, into this Province here to inhabit. And, upon such considerations and terms as are exprefsed in our Conditions of Plantation of our Province of Maryland do grant unto the s'd Neale Clark a parcell of land called *The Landing Place* lying in Ann Arrundall County and on the north side of South River, adjoining to his plantation he now liveth upon *(Nealson).* Begins at a marked Pine being the northernmost bound tree of the said plantation and running for breadth up the river. *Note 1: This grant conveys The Landing Place (50 acres) and Turkey Quarter (150 acres) for a total of 200 acres. However, the "rights" as stated in the patent document add up to only 150 acres. No explanation found. Note 2 (from MSA Tract Index 73): Sold to Thomas Reynolds for 140 lbs sterling in 1704.*

The Woodyard (John Hayward) *(Howard)* 6/10/1671 – 150/159 acres. L14/242 SR7356. Know yee that we for and in consideration that John Howard of the County of Anne Arundel in our Province of Maryland hath due unto him one hundred and fifty acres of land by afsignment from **Matthew Howard** part of a warrant for two hundred and thirty acres formerly granted to the s'd Matthew Howard and **Cornelius Howard** and the remaining fifty acres due to him bring part of his own share of the s'd warrant for two hundred thirty acres above mentioned as appears upon record. And upon such considerations and terms as are exprefsed in our Conditions of Plantation do hereby grant unto the s'd John Howard all that parcell of land lying on the south side of the Severn River near the Round Bay, called *The Woodyard.* Adjoins *Wayfield* and the sw boundary meets *Wyatt's Ridge* and *Howard's Interest.* Begins at a marked White Oak. *Note: The certification (L6/109 SR7346) issued for this land was to John Hammond and Charles Stevens. The intended acreage certified (150 acres) and basic landmarks are the same as those in the patent. However, the courses vary slightly resulting in a twenty acre increase in size in the later description.*

Turkey Quarter (Neale Clarke) 9/25/1663 – 150/*176* acres. L5/598 SR7347.
Know yee that we for and in consideration that Neale Clarke, Planter, of this Province hath due unto him fifty acres of land in this Province the remainder of a warrant granted

for five hundred acres of land to **William Jones**, assignee of the said Clarke and another fifty acres of land granted unto the s'd Clarke by **Nathaniel Dolphin** and also another fifty acres granted unto the s'd Clarke for Transporting **John Stimson** (*who later married Clarke's widow Rachel Beard Clarke*), Anno 1650, into this Province here to inhabit. And, upon such considerations and terms as are exprefsed in our Conditions of Plantation of our Province of Maryland do grant unto the s'd Neale Clark a parcell of land called *The Landing Place* lying in Ann Arrundall County and on the north side of South River, adjoining to his plantation he now liveth upon (*Nealson*). Begins at a marked Oak on a hill. *Note 1: This grant conveys two tracts: The Landing Place (50 acres) and Turkey Quarter (150 acres) for a total of 200 acres. However, the "rights" as stated in the patent document add up to only 150 acres. No explanation found. Note 2 (from MSA Tract Index 73): Sold to Amos Garrett, 1707 (WT#2/622).*

Upper Toynton (Larrance Richardson) 8/15/1666 – 280/280 acres. L10/20 SR7352. Know yee that wee for and in consideration that Larrance Richardson of this our Province of Maryland, Planter, for Transporting himself, **Sarah** his wife, and his daughter in Anno 1649, here to inhabit hath due unto him two hundred acres of land within this Province. Upon such conditions and terms as are exprefsed in our Conditions of Plantation of our Province of Maryland, doe hereby grant unto the s'd Larrance Richardson, Planter, a parcell of land called *Upper Toynton* lying in Ann Arundall County on the south side of the Severn River adjoining the east line of the land he now liveth upon. *Note 1: The deed is incorrect. Upper Toynton adjoins the land that he then lived on (Richardson's Joy) on its southwestern boundary. Note 2: The patent indicates that Richardson "hath due" 200 acres of land. However, the grant was for 280 acres. No explanation was found. Note 3 (from MSA Tract Index 73): Willed by Larrance Richardson to sons John & Larrance who became sole owner following John's death. One hundred sixty six acres sold to Joshua Dorsey (1680) who willed to his son John. John and wife Comfort sold the tract (still 166 acres) to Amos Garratt in 1708 (PK/7) along with Dorsey's Addition, Burntwood, Howard's Interest and Mill Land.*

Venall's Inheritance (**John Venall**) 10/10/1671 - 100 acres. L14/ 363 SR 7356. Know yee that for and in consideration that John Vennall of Ann Arundall County hath due unto him one hundred acres of land within our s'd Province by afsignment of **Robert Wilson** part of a warrant for four hundred thirty acres of land granted him 6/19/1672 as appears on record. Upon such conditions and terms as are exprefsed in our Conditions of Plantation of this our Province of Maryland, wee doe hereby grant unto the s'd John Vennall all that parcell of land called *Vennall's Inheritance* lying in the County of Ann Arundall on the east side of the North Run of the South River beginning at a bounded Pine Tree of a parcell of land formerly laid out for **Tobias Butler**. *Note 1: Adjoins Pierpoint's Lott, Long Venture, and Hog Neck. Note 2: The tract cannot be drawn because the course data is insufficient.* Note 3 (from MSA Tract Index 73): Fifty acres sold by John Venall to **John Barber** who sold it to **William Ridgely**. William and wife **Elizabeth** sold it to **Amos Garratt** in 1710.

Wardridge (James Wardner & Henry Ridgely) 6/26/1663 - 600/524 acres. L5/355 SR 7347. Know yee that we for and in consideration that James Wardner and Henry

Ridgely of this Province, Planters, hath due unto them six hundred acres of land in this Province as appears upon record. And, upon such considerations and terms as are exprefsed in our Conditions of Plantation in our s'd Province of Maryland, doe hereby grant unto the s'd James Wardner and Henry Ridgely a parcell of land called *Wardridge* lying on the north side of the South River in the County of Ann Arundell adjoining the land called *Broome*, formerly laid out for **Richard Beard** of this province, Planter. Beginning at a marked Oak in the northernmost line of the said land and running west. *Note: Henry Ridgely transferred 200 acres of Wardridge to his son Henry Ridgely Jr. on 5/25/1700. Abstracts of AA Deeds Vol. 2 pg. 11. Adjoins the land of Richard Beard.*

Warfield's Right (Richard Warfield) 7/14/1675 – 50/37 acres. L19/45 SR7360.
Know yee that wee for and in consideration that Richard Warfield of the County of Ann Arundell hath due unto him fifty acres of land within our s'd Province for his time of service performed in our S'd Province as appears on record. Upon such conditions and terms as are exprefsed in our Conditions of Plantation of our Province of Maryland, doe hereby grant unto the said Richard Warfield all that parcell of land called *Warfield's Right* lying in the s'd county on the South side of Severn River by a bay called The Round Bay. Begins at bound Red Oak standing on a hill, it being a bound tree of the land of **John Rockhold.**

Wayfield (Nicholas Wyatt) 8/11/1664 – 100/80 acres. L7/353 SR7349.
Know ye that we for and in consideration that Nicholas Wyatt of this Province, Planter, hath due unto him one hundred acres of land part of a warrant for three hundred acres as appears on record. Upon such considerations and terms as are exprefsed in our Conditions of Plantation of our Province of Maryland do hereby grant unto the s'd Nicholas Wyatt a parcell of land called *Wayfield* lying in Ann Arundall County on the south side of the Severn River at the head of a creek in the woods. Begins at marked Oak by an Indian path (Note: *present day MD Route 178, General's Highway*) being a bound tree of the land of **Henry Sewell** *(Hope)*. *Note (from MSA Tract Index 73): Wyatt sold the tract to **Richard Warfield** & **Ed Gardner** for 3,000 lbs of tobacco in 1668 (JH2/181).*

Wyatt's Harbour **(Nicholas Wyatt)** 5/2/1668 – 100 acres. L11/361 SR7357.
Know Yee that Nicholas Wyatt of the County of Ann Arundell in our s'd Province of Maryland, Gent, hath due unto him one hundred acres of land within our s'd Province by afsignment of **George Yate** (L10/509), the afsignee of **Daniell Jennifer**, part of a warrant for four hundred acres formerly granted to the s'd Jennifer as appears upon record. And upon such conditions and terms as are exprefsed in our Conditions of Plantation of our s'd Province doe hereby grant unto the s'd Nicholas Wyatt a parcell of land called *Wyatt's Harbour* lying in Ann Arundell County, aforesaid. Begins at a bounded Cedar upon a point called Wyatt's Point. *Note: This tract cannot be drawn because the 2nd and 3rd courses lack direction.*

Wyatt's Hills (Nicholas Wyatt) 8/8/1681 - 60/54 acres. L7/345 SR7349.
Know Yee that Wee for and in consideration that Nicholas Wyatt of this Province, Planter, hath due unto him sixty acres of land being part of a warrant for three hundred acres as appears on record. And, upon such considerations and terms as are exprefsed in

our Conditions of Plantation of our Province of Maryland do hereby grant unto the s'd
Nicholas Wyatt a parcell of land called *Wyatt's Hills* lying in Ann Arundall County on
the south side of the Severn River next adjoining the land he now liveth upon. Begins at
a marked Chestnut at the head of the Neck

Wyatt's Ridge (Nicholas Wyatt) 8/4/1664 - 450/504 acres. L7/237 SR7349.
Know yee that we for and in consideration that Nicholas Wyatt of this Province, Planter,
hath due unto him two hundred acres of land by afsignment of **Thomas Turner**, afsignee
of **Richard Preston**, as appears on record. And, upon such considerations and terms as
are exprefsed in our Conditions of Plantation of our Province of Maryland, do hereby
grant unto the s'd Nicholas Wyatt a parcell of land called *Wyatt's Ridge* lying in Ann
Arundall County between the branches of the South River and the main branch of Broad
Creek. Begins at a marked Pokehikary tree. *Note: **Thomas Griffith** of Virginia claimed
350 acres of land in February 1664 for Transporting Nicholas Wyatt and others to this
Province to inhabit (L7/507 SR7349).*

Middle Neck Hundred
Southern Area

Acton (Richard Acton) 8/11/1658 – 100/107 acres. LQ/117 SR7345.
Know yee that we for and in consideration that **Thomas Todd** transported one able
bodied servant into this Province here to inhabit and upon such conditions and terms as
are exprefsed in our Conditions of Plantation of this our Province of Maryland, wee doe
hereby grant unto Richard Acton, Carpenter, the afsignee (as appears on record) of
Thomas Todd all that parcel of land lying on the west side of Chesapeake Bay near the
River Seavern beginning at the mouth of a branch of Todd's Creek. *Note: The tract is not
named in this patent and is identified only as, "Land of Richrd Acton." Another tract
named Acton (300 acres) was laid out for Richard Acton in Talbott County on 4/29/1665
(L9/106 SR7351). The two final deed courses lack distance and direction. These were
approximated using the dimensions of adjoining tracts.*

All Cussack's Land. **(Michael Birmingham)** 5/28/1692 - LBBB/451 SR747374.
Whereas it had been manifestly made clear to me that **Michael Cussack** of the Province
of Maryland, deceased, was in his lifetime legally entitled to and pofsefsed of about two
hundred acres of land in the County of Ann Arrundall between the South and Severn
Rivers in two or more parcells as by pattents for same as set forth. And whereas the s'd
Michael Cussack made no disposition of the land or any part thereof and dyed without
heirs of his body begotten, all the s'd lands should and ought to of right revert to and
devolve again to the **Honorable Charles**, Land Barron of the s'd province. Know yee
that for and in consideration of the singular love and affection I have for Michael
Birmingham of London, Gent, he being *(an)* uncle and, likewise to prevent further
charges *(could be changes)* concerning the s'd lands in the Office of Escheat or
otherwise, I do for *(myself)* and my heirs and succefsors release and forever quit claim
unto the s'd Michael Birmingham his heirs and afsignees forever my rights, property,
claims, and interest whatsoever in or to the s'd lands and furthermore that Michael
Birmingham shall by virtue of these presents have, hold, pofsefs and enjoy all the s'd
lands belonging to the s'd Michael Cussack as is above exprefsed. *Note 1: Signed by*
C. Baltimore. *Note 2: On the back of the preceding Michael Birmingham acknowledges
that he has sold and sett over to* **Richard Hill** *of Ann Arundall County all right, title,
claim, and interest in and to the land and premises (7/16/1692). Note 3: Boundary
courses and acreage are not shown in the patent document.*

Baldwin's Addition (John Baldwin) 8/11/1664 120/102 acres. L7/356 SR7349.
Know yee that Wee for and in consideration that John Baldwin, Planter, of this Province
hath due unto him one hundred and twenty acres of land in this Province the remainder of
a warrant for six hundred acres as appears on record. Upon such considerations and
terms as are exprefsed in our Conditions of Plantation of our Province of Maryland, do

hereby grant unto the s'd John Baldwin a parcell of land lying in Ann Arundall County on the north side of the South River in the woods at the head of the plantation he now liveth upon called *Baldwin's Neck*. Begins at a marked Oak tree. *Note: John Baldwin (and his wife **Ruth**) patented another tract also named Baldwin's Addition (70 acres) which was located well south of the Middle Neck in the Herring Creek area of Anne Arundel County.*

Baldwin's Chance (John Baldwin) 11/10/1695 – 415/493 acres. L23/265 SR7364. Know yee that we for and in consideration that John Baldwin of Ann Arundell County of this our Province of Maryland hath due unto him four hundred fifteen acres of land within this Province by virtue of an afsignment of three hundred forty acres from **Richard Beard** part of a warrant for one thousand acres granted unto Beard and seventy two acres by afsignment of **Daniel Ellet** of Charles County, out of a warrant for one thousand acres as appears on record in this land office. Upon such conditions and terms as are exprefsed in our Conditions of Plantation of this our Province of Maryland, wee doe therefore hereby grant unto the s'd John Baldwin all that tract or parcell of land called *Baldwin's Chance* lying in Ann Arundell County on the north side of the South River beginning at *Baldwin's Point*. *Note 1: Adjoins Brushy Neck, Baldwin's Addition, Freeborne's Enlargement, and Baldwin's Creek. Note 2: A duplicate of this patent is found in L23i/336 SR7365. Note 3 (from MSA Tract Index 73): Following the death of John Baldwin (1729) this tract was divided among his children **James, Thomas, and Catherine** (wife of **Charles Griffin** (TI/133). Note 4: An adjoining tract called Baldwin's Neck (260 acres) was laid out for John Baldwin 1/7/1761. However, records at the Maryland Hall of Records indicate that this tract was not patented until 1741 (EI#6/131).*

Beard's Dock (Richard Beard) 9/28/1663 – 250/254 acres. L5/585 SR7347. Know yee that we for and in consideration that Richard Beard of this Province, Planter, hath due unto him two hundred and fifty acres of land for the Transportation of **Richard** and **Rachell** his children and **Thomas Gearfe** into this Province here to inhabit Anno 1650. And, upon such considerations and terms as are exprefsed in our Conditions of Plantation of our Province of Maryland, do hereby grant unto the s'd Richard Beard a parcell of land called *Beard's Dock* lying on the west side of Chesapeake Bay on the north side of South River. Begins at a marked Oak at the head of Beard's Branch. *Note 1: Adjoins The Favor. Note 2: On the same day, Richard Beard made the following assignment of his rights to Beard's Dock, "The patent of Richard Beard for 250 acres he hath afssigned over to **John Taylor**, his heirs, executors forever." Note 3: The third and fourth courses lack direction and distance. These were approximated using dimensions from adjoining tracts.*

Beasley's Neck Resurveyed (Richard Hill) 2/3/1673 – 150/162 acres. L15/347 SR4327. By virtue of a special warrant granted unto Richard Hill of Ann Arundell County, Gent. These are in humble manner to certifie that I **George Yate** Deputy Surveyor under **Baker Brook,** Surveyor Generall, have laid out unto and resurveyed for the s'd Hill all that parcell of land called *Beasly's Neck* lying in the s'd county at the mouth of the Ann Arundell River and in a creek called Beasley's Creek. Begins at a Persimmen tree standing on a point of marsh at the mouth of s'd creek and bounds on the s'd river. *Note: To the Right Honorable the Lord Proprietory: The humble petition of Richard Hill sheweth that on 3/18/1672, the Petitioner purchased of* **John Beasley**, *son and heir of* **Francis Beasley**, *a parcel of land called Beasley's Neck of 200 acres. Upon a resurvey by virtue of a special warrant the tract was found to be but on 159 acres and no more. Your petitioner asks that he be granted rights to the balance of 90 acres. Petition Granted. A warrant of 490 acres granted to Richard Hill one hundred acres thereof by the renewal of a warrant in that quantity and 90 acres more resulting from his Lordship's grant of the remainder of rights to 250 acres due to Francis Beasley (5/31/1676 - L15/480, SR4327. Also see L19/2276 SR7360).*

Brampton (Richard Beard) 2/28/1659 – 100/91 acres. L4/442 SR 7346.
Know Yee that We for and in consideration that Richard Beard of this Province, Planter, hath due unto him one hundred acres of land in this Province. And, upon such conditions and terms as are exprefsed in our Conditions of Plantation of our s'd Province of Maryland do hereby grant unto the s'd Richard Beard a parcell of land called *Brampton* lying in Ann Arundel County on the north side of the South River, east side of Broad Creek, and on the east side of Bear Cove. Begins at a marked Pine standing on the creek side. *Note 1: Beard sold the parcel to* **John McCubbin** *on 11/13/1666. Note 2: In order to draw this tract it was necessary to calculate course three based on the angle of the adjoining creek and river.*

<u>Brick Tenement & Two Lotts</u> **(Charles Carroll)** 10/10/1701 - LWD/371 SR7372-2.
Whereas Charles Carroll of Ann Arundell County in our Province of Maryland by his humble petition to us has sett forth that one **John Perry** late of the s'd County and Province was in his lifetime seized in fee simple of and in a certaine brick house or tenement and two lotts of ground containing about one acre and three quarters of an acre of land or thereabout lying and being in the s'd county in a place now commonly known as or called by the name of The Port of Annapolis. And that the s'd John died intestate and without heirs whereby the s'd tenement with the lotts of ground aforesaid escheated unto us. And further, the s'd Charles has sett forth that he has purchased from **Sarah Perry**, now **Evans**, the widow and relict of the s'd John all the rights and interest, claim, and dominance the s'd Sarah by title of Dower or any custom or wage of our s'd Province whatsoever hath and ought to have in the s'd premises. Wherefore he prayed that wee would grant our right and interest therein unto him upon such conditions and termes as to us should seem reasonable. Know yee that for and in consideration of the goode deeds and services to us done by the s'd Charles and to better enable him to continue in the performance of like goode services for the future sons and heirs, wee do for us and our heirs give, grant, release, and confirm unto the s'd Charles all that aforesaid house or tenement with the two lotts of ground and all other appurtanances thereon belonging to and all other rights, title and interest, claims and domain therein and thereunto. *Note: The location, acreage, and boundary courses for the two lots is not included in the patent document.*

Brushy Neck (John Baldwin) 8/24/1665 – 150/151 acres. L8/148 SR7350.
Know yee that wee for and in consideration that John Baldwin, Carpenter, of this Province hath due unto him one hundred and fifty acres of land within this Province, the

remainder of a warrant for three hundred and forty acres as appears upon record. Upon such conditions and terms as are exprefsed in our Conditions of Plantation of our Province of Maryland, doe hereby grant unto the s'd John Baldwin a parcell of land called *Brushy Neck* lying in Ann Arundell County on the north side of the South River. Begins at a marked Walnutt tree near the plantation he now liveth upon B*ounds Acton's Creek. Note 1: Adjoins Harris His Mount. Note 2 (from MSA Tract Index 73): Between 1665 and 1704 this tract was owned by the following Mr. Johnson, Mr. Summerland, Ed. Bates, back to Summerland, then Samuel Young, and finally Amos Garrett.*

Brushy Neck Resurveyed (Thomas Francis) 10/7/1683 – 390/390 acres. L22/106 SR7363. By Virtue of a Special Warrant of Resurvey granted unto Capt. Thomas Francis bearing the date 10/14/1682 as appears on record. These are therefore to certify in humble manner that I **George Yate**, Deputy Surveyor under **Vincent Long**, Esq, Surveyor Generall, hath laid out and resurveyed for the s'd Francis all that parcell of land called *Brushy Neck* formerly laid out for two hundred acres. Begins at a bound tree by the creek called Todd's Creek and by some of Clarkson's Creek. *Adjoins Pond's Hill.*

Chance (William Frizzell) 8/8/1664 100/100 acres. L7/342 SR7349.
Know ye that in consideration that William Frizzell of this Province, Planter, hath due unto him one hundred acres of land within this Province for the transportacion of **Ann Potter** his wife, into this Province here to inhabit as appears upon record. And upon such conditions and terms as are expressed in our Conditions of Plantation of our Province do hereby grant unto him, the s'd Frizzell, a parcell of land called *Chance* lying on the north side of the South River and on the east side of a creek called Green Ginger Creek. Beginning at a marked Oak by a branch. (May have been surveyed "into" **C. Howard's** *Inheritance* at some point.)

Chelsy (Lawrence Draper) 3/26/1695 – 117/108 acres. LWD/132 SR7372-2.
Know yee that for and in consideration that Lawrence Draper of Ann Arundell County in our Province of Maryland hath due unto him one hundred and seaventeen acres of land within our s'd Province by virtue of a warrant granted unto him for three hundred acres 11/14/1695 as appears on record in our Land Office. Upon such conditions and terms as are exprefsed in our Conditions of Plantation of this our Province, wee doe therefore hereby grant unto the s'd Lawrence Draper all that tract or parcell of land called *Chelsy* lying in Ann Arundell County beginning at a creek called Saughier's Creek. *Note: Another patent for this tract was found in LC3i/369 SR7377.*

Clarkston (Matthew Clark) 2/28/1659 – 100/130 acres. L4/490 SR7346.
Know yee that we for and in consideration that Matthew Clark of Ann Arundell County in our s'd Province of Maryland hath due unto him one hundred acres of land within our s'd Province. Upon such conditions and terms as are exprefsed in our Conditions of Plantation of our s'd Province, wee doe hereby grant unto the s'd Matthew Clark all that tract or parcell of land called Clarkston lying on the west side of Chesapeake Bay near to a creek called Dorrell's Creek beginning at a marked Oake upon a point called Clark's Point.

Come by Chance (George Yate) 8/10/1684 – 214/179 acres. LSDA/434 SR7369.
Know ye that Whereas **Henry Hanslap** of Ann Arundell County in our s'd Province of
Maryland hath due unto him two hundred and fourteen acres of land part of a warrant for
one thousand acres granted 9/15/1682 and laid out for him a tract of land called Come by
Chance. And the s'd Hanslap hath afsigned and sett over all title, right, and interest in to
George Yate of the same County as appears on record. Upon such conditions and terms
as are exprefsed in our Conditions of Plantation of our late father Cecilius, of noble
memory, wee do hereby grant unto the s'd George Yate all that tract or parcel of land
called *Come by Chance* lying in the s'd County on the north side of the *South River* in the
woods beginning at a bound Red Oake by a branch. *Adjoins the land of Walter Smith,
the land of Zephaniah Smith, and Wither's Outlet. See Garrets Town.*

Cossill (John Collier) 1/21/1659 - 200/196 acres. L4/501 SR7346.
Know yee that we for and in consideration that John Collier of this Province, Planter,
hath due unto him two hundred acres of land in this Province. Upon such considerations
and terms as are exprefsed in our Conditions of Plantation of our s'd Province of
Maryland doe hereby grant unto the s'd John Collier a parcell of land called *Cossill* lying
on the west side of Chesapeake Bay and on the south side of a river in the said Bay called
the Severne River and on the south side of a creek in the said river called Todd's Creek.
Begins at a marked Pine at the mouth of a branch called Collier's Branch. *Note: In 1663,
this tract was assigned to **Patrick Dunkin** and by him (and his wife **Margaret**) to **Robert
Clarkson**. Upon Clarkson's death the tract was willed to his daughter **Mary** the wife of
Samuel Young.*

Devise (Thomas Davies) 2/22/1659 – 150/150 acres. L4/527 SR7346.
Know yee that we for and in consideration that Thomas Davies of this Province, Planter,
hath due unto him one hundred and fifty acres of land in this Province. And, upon such
conditions and terms as are exprefsed in our Conditions of Plantation of our s'd Province
of Maryland, do hereby grant unto the s'd Thomas Davies a parcel of land lying on the
west side of Chesapeake Bay next adjoining the land of **Sampson Warren**
(*Warringston*). Begins at Warren's southmost bound tree.

Dorsey (Edward Dorsey) 9/16/1668 – 60/93 acres. L12/136 SR7354.
Grant for 60 acres of land ifsued to Edward Dorsey of the County of Ann Arundal,
Planter, bearing the date 9/16/1668. Consideration by afsignment from **George Yate** the
afsignee of **Capt. James Conaway** part of a Wart for 510 acres of land formerly granted
to the s'd Conaway. Applicable Conditions of Plantation dated 7/2/1649 as amended
9/22/1658. Cert GG Folio 43 name Dorsey. Manor of Ann Arundell. Yearly rent one
shilling two pence, halfpenny. The same fine upon every alienacon of the land in the
usual form. Witnessed: **Charles Calvert Esq**. The patent reference cited in the MSA
index *did not include a land description or boundary courses. The second reference
found included incomplete course information. The tract was drawn using the one
complete course, calculating the creek, river and cove angles and distance, and
borrowing the angle of the south line of the northward adjoining tract (Norwood).*

Dunken's Luck (Patrick Dunken) 9/1/1687 – 52/52 acres. LNS2i/399 SR7371.
Know yee that for and in consideration that Patrick Dunken of Ann Arundell County in our s'd Province of Maryland hath due unto him fifty two acres of land by afsignment of **John Dorsey** of the s'd County part of a warrant for two hundred acres granted to the s'd Dorsey 4/10/1684 as appears on record. Upon such conditions and terms as are exprefsed in our Conditions of Plantation of this our Province of Maryland, wee doe therefore hereby grant unto the s'd Patrick Dunken all that tract or parcell of land called Dunken's Luck lying in the s'd County on the north side of the South River and on the east side of a creek called Hambilton Creek. Begins at a bounded Pine standing by the s'd creek it being a bounded tree of land formerly laid out for **Edward Skidmore** *(Hamilton)*.
*Note (from MSA Tract Index 73): Sold to **Samuel Young** in 1695 (IH#1/199).*

Edge's Addition (Daniel Edge) 9/10/1684 – 50/42 acres. LSDA/456 SR7369.
Know yee that for and in consideration that Daniel Edge of Ann Arundell County hath due unto him fifty acres of land within our s'd Province by Afsignment of **Robert Jones** and **George Yate** part of a warrant for two thousand acres granted to the s'd Jones and Yate 3/28/1683 as appears on record. Upon such conditions and terms as are exprefsed in our Conditions of Plantation of this our Province of Maryland, wee doe hereby grant unto the s'd Daniel Edge all that tract or parcell of land called *Edge's Addition* lying in the aforesaid County between the South and Ann Arundell Rivers. Begins at a bound Oak by a branch.

Edward's Neck (John Edwards) 5/4/1688 – 100/92 acres. L11/354 SR7353.
Know yee that for and in consideration that John Edwards of the County of Ann Arundal hath one hundred acres of land due to him by afsignment of **Irasaus Yateman** for the s'd Yateman transporting himself into our Province to inhabit. Upon such conditions and terms as are exprefsed in our Conditions of Plantation of this our Province of Maryland, wee doe hereby grant unto the s'd John Edwards a parcell of land called *Edward's Neck* lying on the north side of the South River in Ann Arundal County. Begins at a marked Pohickary standing on a point at the mouth of a creek called Fishing Creek. *Note: Apparently this was not the initial patent of this land. A record of sale in 1684 (**Gassaway** to **Anthony Ruley** was found (TA#2/165).*

Freeborne's Enlargement (Thomas Freeborn) 10/7/1694 – 80/81 acres. L23/260 SR7364. Know yee that we for and in consideration that Thomas Freeborne of Ann Arundell County in our s'd Province of Maryland hath due unto him eighty acres of land within our s'd Province being due to him by virtue of an afsignment by **Daniel Ellet** of Charles County out of a warrant for one thousand acres granted to the s'd Ellet on 9/4/1694 as appears in our Land Office. Upon such conditions and terms as are exprefsed in our Conditions of Plantation of this our Province of Maryland, wee doe therefore hereby grant unto the s'd Thomas Freeborne all that tract of parcell called *Freeborne's Enlargement* lying in Ann Arundell County on the north side of the South River beginning at a bounded Oak of the land of **John Baldwin** *(Baldwin's Addition)*. Also adjoins *Norwood's Angles*. *Note: A duplicate of this patent is found in L23i/328 SR7365.*

Fuller's Point (Phillip Thomas) 4/12/1664 – Two Ajoining Tracts. Tract 1 – 70/73 acres. Tract 2 - 50/39 acres L9/292 SR7351. Laid out for Phillip Thomas, Planter, of this Province, a parcell of land called *Fuller's Point.* Lying in Ann Arrundell County on the west side of Chesapeake Bay. Tract 1 begins at a marked White Oak standing on the beach and runs down the Chesapeake Bay. Tract *2 begins at the same marked White Oak. Bounded by Chesapeake Bay, on the Fishing Creek,* and the South River. *Note 1: Land Rights were based on Phillip Thomas having transported himself, his wife Sarah, and his children Caleb, Phillip, Sarah, and Elizabeth and Arnold Jackson (LQ/425 SR 7345). Note 2: Two adjoining tracts were laid out on the same day for a combined total of 120 acres. The deed courses for Tract 1 were incomplete. Drawing is based on calculations of distance and direction for the third and fourth courses. The calculations were based on proximity to the Bay, South River, and Fishing Creek and the acreage. Note 3: Patent not found. Note 4: This is currently known as Thomas Point.*

Garrett's Town (Michael Cussack) 8/12/1685 – 59/59 acres. LNSBi/414 SR7370. Know yee that whereas **Thomas Winddell** of Ann Arundell County in our s'd Province of Maryland by afsignment of **George Yate** the afsignee of **Thomas Richardson,** part of a warrant for one thousand acres granted to the s'd Richardson 4/8/1684 and had surveyed and laid out for him a tract of land for fifty nine acres called Garrett's Town lying in the s'd County on the north side of the South River and on the east side of the creek called The Broad Creek all whole right, title, and interest of and in to the s'd land the s'd Thomas Windell hath afsigned and made over unto Michael Cussack of the same County. Upon such conditions and terms as are exprefsed in our Conditions of Plantation of this our Province, wee doe hereby grant unto the s'd Michael Cussack all that tract or parcel of land called Garrett's Town lying in the s'd County on the north side of the South River and on the east side of Broad Creek beginning at a bounded Red Oake standing at the head of a cove. *Note: A surveyor's note found in* Rent Rolls *(PG 75) states the following, "Cussack dead and can find no heirs." The following was extracted from a grant to* **Michael Birmingham** *(LBBB/451 SR7373 – 5/29/1692): Whereupon it has been manifestly made clear to me that Michael Cussack of the Province of Maryland, deceased, was in his lifetime legally possessed of about two hundred acres of land in the County of Ann Arundell between the South and Severn Rivers and two or more parcells as by patents for same as is sett forth. And Whereas the s'd Michael Cussack made no disposition of the land or any part thereof and dyed without heirs to his body begotten, all the s'd lands ought of right to revert to and devolve again to the* **Honorable Charles,** *Land Barron of Baltimore his heirs and afsignees as Chief Land and Proprietor of the s'd Province. Know yee that for and in consideration of the singular love and affection I have for Michael Birmingham of London, Gent, and alone being uncle to ye s'd deed and likewise to prevent further charges (changes?) concerning the s'd lands in the Office of Escheat or otherwise, I do for and my heirs as succeed release and quit claime unto the s'd Michael Birmingham his heirs and afsigns forever my rights, property, claimes and interest whatsoever in or to the s'd and furthermore that Michael Birmingham shall by virtue of these prefents have, hold, pofsefs and enjoy all the s'd lands belonging to the s'd Michael Cussack as is above exprefsed. Signed, C. Baltimore. According to* Rent Rolls, *Michael Cussack owned the following four tracts in Ann Arundel County: Garret's Town (59 Acres), Welfare (184 acres), Cussack's Forrest (596 acres), and Come By Chance*

*(200 acres). However, there is some doubt as to whether the tract Come By Chance was included in the tracts granted above to Michael Birmingham. A patent found for Come by Chance (LSDA/434 SR7369, 8/10/1684) shows that it was granted to George Yate. A note on the back of the grant to Michael Birmingham shows that on 7/16/1692, about two months after receiving all of the lands formerly granted to Michael Cussack, Birmingham sold these rights to **Richard Hill** of Ann Arundell County. Rent Rolls 1700-1707 shows all of the Cussack tracts, except Come by Chance, in the possession of the heirs of Richard Hill.*

Gatenby (Thomas Gates, Ensign) 2/7/1650 - 100/121 acres. LQ/392 SR7345.
Know yee that we for and in consideration that Thomas Gates hath transported himself in the year 1648 into this Province here to inhabit. Upon such conditions and terms as are exprefsed in our Conditions of Plantation of our s'd Province of Maryland wee doe hereby grant unto the s'd Thomas Gates all that tract called *Gatenby* lying on the west side of Chesapeak Bay on the south side of the Severn River and on the north side of Dorsey's Creek. Begins at a marked Pine tree, a bound tree of a 10 acre tract formerly laid out for the s'd Gatenby. *Note: The tract was granted to Gates, within the Conditions of Plantation, for transporting himself to this Province on 7/7/1749, here to inhabit. Gates died before August 1659. His will, dated 5/2/2659, left Gatenby jointly to **Michael Bellot** and **John Holloway** with his personal goods and debts to Bellot*

Georgeston (George Saughier) 2/16/1659 – 190/132 acres. L4/503 SR7346.
Know yee that we for and in consideration that George Saughier of this Province, Planter, hath due unto him one hundred ninety acres of land in this Province. And, upon such considerations and terms as are exprefsed in our Conditions of Plantation of our s'd Province of Maryland, do hereby grant unto the s'd George Saughier parcell of land called *Georgeston* lying on the west side of Chesapeake Bay near to a creek in the s'd Bay called Durand's Creek. Begins at the mouth of said creek and runs west by the Bayside. *Note: The tract cannot be drawn from the courses as specified. Drawing was possible using a calculated distance for the sixth course and closing on the "bayside" course.*

Griffith's Lott (William Griffith) 11/10/1695 – 197/190 acres. L23/256 SR7364.
Know yee that wee for and in consideration that William Griffith of Ann Arundell County in our Province of Maryland hath due unto him one hundred ninety seven acres of land within this Province being due unto him by afsignment of **Henry Ridgely** of the s'd County out of a warrant for eighteen hundred acres of land granted to him the s'd Ridgely on 6/9/1694 as appears in our land office. Upon such conditions and terms as are exprefsed in our Conditions of Plantation of this our Province of Maryland, we doe therefore hereby grant unto the s'd William Griffith all that tract or parcell of land called *Griffith's Lott* lying in Ann Arundell County beginning at a bound Water Oake of **William Ridgely**. *Note 1: A duplicate of this patent is found in L23i/320 SR7365. Note 2: Maryland Rent Rolls Baltimore and Anne Arundel Counties (Pg. 224) locates this tract between the South and Severn Rivers in the Middle Neck Hundred.*

Gross's Increase (Thomas Gross) 6/1/1685 – 180/182 acres. LNS2i/116 SR7371.
Know yee that whereas Thomas Gross of Ann Arundell County had granted unto him by
earlier pattent a tract of land called *Gross's Increase* lying in the s'd County on the north
side of the South River in the woods and whereas the s'd Gross hath informed the
Councill of a surveyor's mistake returned in the Certificate viz a south line to his fifth
bounded tree whereas he ought to have an east line ninety eight perches to a White Oake
of the east side of a branch then south two hundred eighteen perches to a bounded stake.
And that if the error was not corrected he had not half the land granted to him. And,
forasmuch as the land Gross hath humbly brought to our last Councill to return another
Certificate for the s'd land according to the first survey and that pattent should issue
hereupon to him and his heirs. Whereupon it was by our s'd Councill decided that
official warrant should issue to resurvey this land according to the true intended metes
and bounds thereof. And whereas the land hath been resurveyed the first day of July
1684, according to the actual intended metes and bounds and a Certificate returned into
our Land Office as appears on record, Wee doe hereby grant unto the s'd Thomas Gross
all that tract or parcell of land called *Gross's Increase* beginning at a bounded Hickory
tree. *Adjoins Wardrop Ridge.*

Hamilton (Edward Skidmore) 8/4/1665 - 350/350 acres. L7/238 SR7349.
Know Yee that wee for and in consideration that Edward Skidmore of this Province,
Planter, hath due unto him one hundred fifty acres of land for transporting **Ellenor (&)**
Abraham Ursulead and **Elias Goddfrey** into this province here to inhabit, and two
hundred acres more by assignment of **Oliver Sprye** as appears on record. And, upon
such considerations and terms as are exprefsed in our Conditions of Plantation of our
Province of Maryland, do hereby grant unto the s'd Edward Skidmore a parcel of land
called *Hamilton* lying in Anne Arundel County on the north side of the South River.
Begins at a marked Pine at the mouth of McCubbins Cove. *Adjoins property of*
McCubbin and extends to Hamilton Creek on the southeast. Note 1: This tract was
surveyed as Hambleton on 11/28/1662 (L5/621). Note 2: The following "confirmation"
of Skidmore's patent was found in Liber 12/249, dated 4/30/1669. Note 2 (from MSA
Tract Index 73): Skidmore sold the tract to Joseph Struther who later was convicted of
murder and, through the escheat process, the tract was returned to Skidmore on
4/30/1669. Later that year Skidmore then sold the tract to Patrick Dunken for 6,000 lbs
tobacco. Portions of the text are missing because of a hole in the page and the meaning
is not clear but it appears that at some point the tract was Vested in one Joseph Finder
(could be Fincher) who later forfeited the land.

Hammond's Pasture (John Hammond) 2/11/1688 - 118/116 acres. LNSBI/623
SR7370. Know yee that we for and in consideration that John Hammond of Ann Arundell
County in our s'd Province of Maryland hath due unto him one hundred eighteen acres of
land within our s'd Province by afsignment of **Thomas Richardson** of Baltimore County
part of a warrant for two thousand eight hundred eighty two acres granted to the s'd
Richardson 2/27/1687 as appears on record. Upon such conditions and terms as are
exprefsed in our Conditions of Plantation of this our Province, wee doe hereby grant unto
the s'd John Hammond all that tract or parcel of land called *Hammond's Pasture* lying on
the north side of the South River beginning at a point of marsh near the mouth of a creek

called Green Gingerville Creek, being the westernmost boundary of a parcell formerly laid out for **Thomas Roper**. *Adjoins the land of Thomas Jeff (Jeffe's Encrease) and the head of Green Gingerville Creek.*

Harness (**William Harness**) 10/27/1652 - 400 acres. LQ/236 SR7345.
Know ye that we for and in consideration that William Harness transported himself, **Susan** his wife, and **William** and **Isaac**, his children, into this province here to inhabit, wee doe hereby grant to the s'd William Harness all that tract of land called *Harness* lying on the west side of the Chesapeake Bay and on the north side of the South River beginning at a marked Pohikary at the head of a branch called *Harness Branch. Note: Harness was sold to Joseph Hill on March 8, 1701, by Jacob Harness (son of Wm.) and his wife Ellinor. Excluded from this sale was the, "...six or eight feet square wherein William Harness, dec., lies interred." (Abstracts of Ann Arundell County Land Records, Vol 2, pg 29). Note: the tract cannot be drawn because the fourth (final) course lacks distance.*

Harnesses Gift (**Jacob Harness**) 5/27/1684 – 51 acres. L22/33 SR7363.
By virtue of a warrant granted unto **Robert Jones** for one thousand four hundred and fifty acres of land whereof fifty one acres was afsigned over unto Jacob Harness of Ann Arundell County on 5/16/1684 as appears on record. There are in humble manner to certifie that I **George Yate**, Deputy Surveyor, hath surveyed for the s'd Harness a parcell of land called *Harnesses Gift* lying on the west side of Chesapeake Bay and on the north side of the South River beginning at an old stump of a bounded tree of Harness'. *The tract cannot be drawn because of insufficient course detail. The above reference is shown in MHS Tract Index 55, as the patent document.*

Harris His Mount (**Wm. Harris**) 1677 – 100 acres. L11/211 SR7353.
Know ye that wee for and in Consideration that William Harris hath due unto him one hundred acres of land in this Province by afsignment of **John Wheeler** for transporting himself, the s'd Wheeler and **Mary Bark** to this Province to inhabit as appears upon record. And upon such Conditions and Termes as are exprefsed in our Conditions of Plantation of our s'd province of Maryland doe hereby grant unto him the s'd Harris a parcell of land lying in Anne Arrundall County on the north side of the South River. Beginning at a bounded Oak in the line of land laid out for **John Baldwin** called *Brushy Neck. Note 1: This tract cannot be drawn because the third course follows a creek and does not indicate either distance or direction. Note 2 (from MSA Tract Index 73): Upon the death of Harris, his widow Elizabeth Harris sold the tract to John Summerland for 4,000 lbs tobacco. Summerland sold the tract to Samuel Young in 1699.*

Hockley in the Hole (**Edward, Joshua & John Dorsey**) 8/225/1664 - 400 acres. L7/378 SR7349. Know Yee that Wee for and in consideration that Edward, Joshua, and John Dorsey of this Province, Planters, hath due unto them four hundred acres of land within this Province being the plantation they now liveth upon called *Hockley In The Hole* lying in Ann Arundall County on the south side of the Severn River in the woods. Upon such considerations and terms as are exprefsed in our Conditions of Plantation of our Province of Maryland, do hereby grant unto the s'd Edward, Joshua, and John Dorsey a parcell of land called *Hockley in the Hole* lying on the South side of the Severn River in the woods beginning at a marked Red Oak, it being a bound tree of **Cornelius** and **Samuel Howard.** *Note 1: The present day Annapolis Water Works is located within the bounds of this parcel. Note 2: Edward Warfield (<u>The Founders of Anne Arundel and Howard Counties,</u> reprinted by Heritage Publishers, 1995, pg. 30) notes that, "In 1664, the three sons of Edward Dorsey took up and patented their father's survey of Hockley In The Hole." However, this patent makes no mention of an early survey. Note 3: The tract cannot be drawn because the fourth boiundary course lacks distance*

Hockley In The Hole Resurveyed (John Dorsey) 7/15/1686 - 842/770 acres. LIB&IL2/225 SR7368-1. Whereas, John Dorsey of Ann Arundell County in our s'd Province of Maryland had granted unto himself and his brothers **Edward** and **Joshua Dorsey,** the 25th day of August, 1664, a parcell of land called *Hockley In The Hole* and whereas the s'd John Dorsey did humbly sett forth to our Councill for Land that he has purchased the interest of his two brothers and that the fee simple and inheritance of the land did lye in him. He therefore humbly prayed that a Speciall Warrant of Resurvey for the aforesaid tract and what surplus land should appear within the lines of the tract that the liberty be granted to him to take it up proving good rights for the land which was accordingly granted. Whereupon, **George Yate,** Deputy Surveyor for Ann Arundell County found the land contained eight hundred and forty two acres being four hundred forty two acres more than was exprefsed in the former survey. Whereupon it was found by our Councill that you the petitioner are to pay tenn thousand pounds of tobacco. Know yee that for and in consideration of the payment of tenn thousand pounds of tobacco by the s'd John Dorsey, we do grant and confirm to him all that aforementioned tract called *Hockley in the Hole* beginning at a bounded Red Oak of the line of **Cornelius** and **Samuel Howard.**

Horne Neck (Robert Clarkson) 9/20/1665 – 300/304 acres. L8/404 SR7350. Know yee that wee for and in consideration that Robert Clarkson of this Province of Maryland hath due unto him three hundred acres of land within this Province by afsignment of **Daniel Jennifer** out of a greater quantity afsigned him from severall persons as appears upon record. And, upon such considerations and terms as are exprefsed in our Conditions of Plantation of our Province of Maryland, doe hereby grant to him the s'd Robert Clarkson a parcell of land called *Horne Neck* formerly surveyed and laid out for him the S'd Clarkson of which no return thereof made unto our Secretary's Office. Lying in Ann Arundall County on the south side of Seavern River bounding on the said river and Todd's Creek on the north and bounds the head of Beafsley's Creek.

Howard's Heirship (Cornelius Howard) 8/4/1664 - 420/390 acres. L7/249 SR7349. Know yee that we for and in consideration that Cornelius Howard of this Province, Planter, hath due unto him four hundred and twenty acres of land within this Province being part of a warrant for nine hundred acres granted to him and his three brothers **Matthew, Samuel,** and **John Howard** as appears on record. And upon such considerations and terms as are exprefsed in our Conditions of Plantation of our Province of Maryland, doe hereby grant unto the s'd'Cornelius Howard a parcell of land called

Howard's Heirship lying in Anne Arundel County on the south side of the Severn River at the head of Hockley Creek. Begins at a marked Red Oak by Crouch's Creek.

Howard's Hill (Cornelius Howard) 9/10/1672 – 200/200 acres. L17/297 SR7358. Know Yee that for and in consideration that Cornelius Howard of the Ann Arundell County in our s'd Province of Maryland hath due unto him two hundred acres of land within our s'd Province by afsignment of **Charles Stevens** being due to the s'd Stevens by afsignment of **William Luffman** due unto the s'd Luffman for Transporting himself into this Province to inhabit. Fifty acres more due unto the s'd Stevens by afsignment from **John Norwood** due to the s'd Norwood for Transporting **John Arrington** into s'd Province to inhabit. The remaining fifty acres being due to the s'd Howard by afsignment from **George Yate**, the afsignee of **Thomas Taylor**, attorney of **Jerome White Esq.**, part of a warrant for nine hundred acres granted to the s'd White on the nineth day of April last past, as appears upon record. Upon such conditions and termes as are exprefsed in the Conditions of Plantation of our s'd Province of Maryland, do grant unto the s'd Cornelius Howard a parcell of land lying in Ann Arundell County on the south side of the Ann Arundell River at Underwood's Creek. Begins at a marked Oak standing on the north side of Underwood's Creek.

Howard's Hope (Samuel Howard) 8/4/1664 - 100/77 acres. L7/251 SR 7349. Know yee that for and in consideration that Samuel Howard of this Province, Planter, hath due unto him one hundred acres of land within this Province being a part of a Wart for nine hundred acres of land granted unto him and his three brothers **Cornelius, Matthew** and **John Howard** as appears on record. And, upon such considerations and terms as are exprefsed in our Conditions of Plantation of our Province of Maryland, do hereby grant unto the s'd Samuel Howard a parcell of land called Howard's Hope lying on the south side of the Severn River in Anne Arundel County. Begins at a marked Oak tree.

Howard's Inheritance (Samuel Howard) 5/1/1700 – 449/446 acres. LCD/45 SR7376. Know yee that Samuel Howard of Ann Arundell County in our s'd Province of Maryland has by his humble petition to our Deputy sett forth that he is seized in fee simple of one hundred acres of land being parte of a tract of two hundred acres called *The Chance* granted to one **Cornelius Howard** 8/20/1664 as also two other parcells containing about one hundred acres each formerly belonging to **James Warner**, decd. All of which severall parcells of land are adjoining and contiguous the one to the other but concerning that there may be some surplus within the ancient metes and bounds of the s'd severall parcells more than the original quantity for which they were laid out. He humbly prayed that he might have a speciall warrant to resurvey and that upon realization of a fact of such resurvey he might have a letter of patents for the same which was granted. Whereupon, it was certified in our land office that there is of surplus within the bounds of the severall three aforesaid parcells the quantity of one hundred forty nine acres for which the s'd Samuel Howard has, pursuant to a clause of our instructions bearing the date 12/2/1697 to **Coll Henry Darnall** our agent in our s'd Province secured to be paid out the quantity of three hundred sixty pounds of tobacco for rights to the same and also the sum of 5 lbs and 10 shillings sterling being for the arrears in rent of the s'd surplus from the time of the original survey. Wee doe therefore hereby grant unto the s'd Samuel Howard all those severall parcells with the surplus in them now contained called *Howard's Inheritance* beginning at a White Oak marked with four notches. *Adjoins Hockley in the Hole and Warner's Neck. Replaces The Chance and two tracts owned by* **John Warner**.

James' Hill (John James) 8/4/1664 - 100/69 acres. L7/225 SR7349.
Know yee that wee for and in consideration that John James of this Province, Planter, hath due unto him one hundred acres of land in this Province for Transporting **Robert Bab** and **Edmond Thomas** into this Province here to inhabit as appears on record. And, upon such considerations and terms as are exprefsed in our Conditions of Plantation of our Province of Maryland, do hereby grant unto the said John James a parcel of land lying in Anne Arundel County on the south side of the Severn River adjoining the land of **Samuel Withers**. Begins at a marked Sassafrass tree, a bound tree of the s'd Withers. *Note: The patent states that the property is in Talbot County. However, the references to the Severn River and the adjoining of property owned by Samuel Withers (Wither's Durand) are convincing evidence that the tract was actually located in Anne Arundel County.*

Jeffe's Encrease (Thomas Jeffe) 10/5/1683 – 180/100 acres. LSDA/176 SR7369.
Know yee that for and in consideration that Thomas Jeffe of Ann Arundell County in our s'd Province of Maryland hath due unto him one hundred and eighty acres of land within our Province by afsignment of **Henry Hanslap** part of a warrant for seven hundred ninety three acres granted to the s'd Hanslap on 7/24/1682 as appears on record. Upon such conditions and terms as are exprefsed in our Conditions of Plantation of our late father Cecilius of noble memory, wee doe hereby grant unto the s'd Thomas Jeffe all that tract or parcel of land called *Jeffe's Encrease* lying in the s'd County on the north side of the South River in the woods beginning at a bounded Hickory. *Adjoins Wardrop Ridge and Hammond's Pasture. Note: Tract was resurveyed at the request of the owner and found to be 180 acres (L22/95 SR7365, 7/13/1684).*

Jeff's Search (William Jeff) 2/18/1688 – 39/39 acres. LNSBi/676 SR7370.
Know yee that for and in consideration that William Jeff of Ann Arundell County in our s'd Province of Maryland hath due unto him thirty nine acres of land within our s'd Province by afsignment of **Thomas Richardson** of Baltimore County, part of a warrant for two thousand eight hundred eighty two acres granted the s'd Richardson 2/27/1687 as appears on record. Upon such conditions and terms as are exprefsed in our Conditions of Plantation of this our Province, wee doe hereby grant unto the s'd William Jeff all that tract or parcell of land called *Jeff's Search* lying on the north side of the South River beginning at a bounded White Oak in the line of **Robert Parnaby**. *Also adjoins land of* **John Dorsey, Samuel Howard and William Fergueson**.

Lydia's Rest Resurveyed (John Baldwin) 7/8/1681 - 210/134 acres. LCBi/148 SR7366. Whereas a Provincial Court held at our City of St. Marie's on 6/14/1679, a parcel of land called *Oatley's Choice* formerly granted to **Christopher Oatley** for 400 acres of land lying in Ann Arundell County on the north side of the South River was by the Justices of our s'd Court adjudged escheated unto us for lack of an heir of **Elizabeth**

Caplyn daughter of **Henry Caplyn** deceased who married with **Thomas Watkins**, deceased, who was the former husband of **Lydia** the now wife of **Edmund Beetenson** of the County aforesaid. And, whereas the s'd Lydia during the time of her widowhood purchased of us our rights, title and interest of the s'd tract and obtained our Special Warrant for a patent to be drawn for the s'd land in whose name whosoever the s'd Lydia should appoint. And, whereas the s'd Beetenson and Lydia his wife hath informed us that upon inquiry made into the metes and bounds of the s'd tract they concluded that severall mistakes had been made in the former survey and humbly supplicated us for a Special Warrant to Resurvey the s'd tract according to the ancient metes and bounds thereof without prejudice to us or any person whatsoever. And upon Resurvey our letters and confirmation might convey unto them the s'd Beetenson and his wife Lydia and their heirs forever which was conveyed to them with all right, title, and interest. The s'd Edmund Beetenson and Lydia his wife hath granted afsigned and set over unto John Baldwin of Ann Arundell County as appears on record. And, upon such conditions and terms as are exprefsed in our Conditions of Plantation of our late father Cecilius of noble memory we doe hereby grant unto the s'd John Baldwin all that parcell of land called *Oatley's Choice* now *Lydia's Rest Resurveyed* being in Ann Arundell County on the north side of the South River at a point of land called Oatley's Point at the mouth of Oatley's Creek

Major's Fancy (Major Edward Dorsey) 11/10/1695 – 186/187 acres. L23/257 SR7364. Know yee that wee for and in consideration that Major Edward Dorsey of Ann Arundell County in our s'd Province of Maryland hath due unto him one hundred eighty six acres of land within this Province due unto him by virtue of a warrant for eight hundred fifty acres granted to him by the s'd Dorsey on 3/1/1694, as appears in this land office. Upon such conditions and terms as are exprefsed in our Conditions of Plantation of this our Province of Maryland, we doe therefore hereby grant unto the s'd Major Edward Dorsey all that tract of parcell of land called *Major's Fancy* lying in the s'd County between the South and Severn Rivers beginning at a bound tree on the land of **Captain Richard Hill** called *Littleworth*. *Note 1: The location of this tract is not certain. The grant document states that the tract is located between the South and Severn Rivers adjoining a tract called Littleworth. Maryland Rent Rolls pg. 224 also states that it is so located and includes it among Middle Neck Hundred tracts but does not indicate an adjoining tract. Page 258 (Rent Rolls) further indicates that Littleworth is located on the north side of the Severn River as does the patent document (IB&IL Ci/181 SR7368-1). I have included this tract because it may be in the targeted area. Note 2: A duplicate of this patent is found in L23i/313 AR7365. Note 3: (from MSA Tract Index 73): By agreement between Edward and **Samuel Dorsey**, Samuel to give up claim of title to Round Bay to brother **Joshua Dorsey** in return for rights for Major's Fancy from Edward (PK1708/417).*

Mayden Croft (Lawrence Draper) 2/11/1688 –128/139 acres. LNSBi/618 SR7370. Know yee that for and in consideration that Lawrence Draper of Ann Arundell County in our s'd Province of Maryland hath due unto him one hundred and twenty eight acres of land within our s'd Province by afsignment of **Thomas Richardson** of Baltimore County part of a warrant for twenty eight hundred acres of land granted to the s'd Richardson 2/27/1687/8, as appears on record. Upon such conditions and terms as are exprefsed in our Conditions of Plantation of this our Province wee doe hereby grant unto the s'd Lawrence Draper all that tract or parcell of land called *Maiden Croft* lying on the bayside between the South and Ann Arundell Rivers. Begins at a bounded Hickory. *Adjoins Saughier's Creek and the Chesapeake Bay.*

Mountain Neck (Thomas Hammond) 8/24/1665 – 190/266 acres. *(Two Tracts. Tract 1 – 145/211 acres. Tract 2 – 45/55 Acres.)* L8/118 SR7350. Know Yee that for and in consideration that Thomas Hammond hath due unto him one hundred fifty acres of land within our Province and forty acres more being his *Right and Terms of Town Land* due unto him. And, upon such conditions and terms as are exprefsed in our Conditions of Plantation of our s'd Province of Maryland, doe grant unto him the s'd Thomas Hammond a parcell of land called *Mountain Neck* lying in Ann Arundall County on the south side of the Ann Arundall River. Tract 1 begins at a marked Oak standing by Hammond's Creek at his landing. Tract 2 begins at a marked Oak on the north side of a pond by the riverside. *Note: These tracts do not adjoin.*

Norwood (John Norwood) 2/8/1650 – 230/333 acres. LQ/396 SR7345.
Know yee that we for and in consideration that John Norwood hath transported his sons **John** and **Arthur Norwood** into this Province in the year 1650 and his servant **Elizabeth Fletcher** in the year 1657 here to inhabit and upon such conditions and terms as are exprefsed in our Conditions of Plantation of our s'd Province of Maryland, wee doe therefore grant unto the s'd John Norwood all that tract or parcel of land called *Norwood* lying in Anne Arundel County on the west side of Chesapeake Bay and on the south side of a river called the Seavern River adjoining land formerly laid out for **Nicholas Wyatt** (*Wayfield*). Begins at a marked Oak by a cove called Norwood's Cove. *Note: This tract could not be drawn from the deed course stated in the patent. It was necessary to "borrow" a boundary angle from an adjoining tract and to calculate the closing distance. Note 2: "John Norwood demands land for transporting **John Harrington** into this Province here to inhabit." Fifty acres granted (1658 – L5/485 SR7347).*

Norwood's Angles (Andrew Norwood) 8/10/1684 – 103/109 acres. LSDA/446 SR7369. Know yee that for and in consideration that Andrew Norwood of Ann Arundell County in our s'd Province of Maryland hath due unto him one hundred three acres of land within our s'd province by afsignment of **Robert Jones** and **George Yate** part of a warrant for two thousand acres granted to the s'd Jones and Yate 3/28/1683 as appears on record. Upon such conditions and terms as are exprefsed in our Conditions of Plantation of our late father Cecilius, of noble memory, wee doe hereby grant unto the s'd Andrew Norwood all that tract or parcell of land called *Norwood's Angles* lying in the s'd County on the branches of a creek called Todd's Creek beginning at a bound White Oak of **Daniel Edge's** land and the land laid out for **Richard Petticoate**. *Note 1 (from MSA Tract Index 73): Sold to **Thomas Freeborne** 8/18/1687 for 4,000 lbs tobacco (IH#3/35).*

Norwood's Recovery (Andrew Norwood) 6/10/1686 – 104/103 acres. LIB&ILCi/229 SR7368-1. Know yee that wee for and in consideration that Andrew Norwood of Ann Arundell County in our s'd Province of Maryland hath due unto him 104 acres of land within our s'd Province part of a warrant for five hundred acres granted to him 2/25/1685 as appears on record. Upon such conditions and terms as are exprefsed in our Conditions of Plantation of this our Province, wee doe hereby grant unto the s'd Andrew Norwood all that tract or parcell of land called *Norwood's Recovery* lying on the south side of the Ann Arundall River beginning at a bounded Black Walnut it being a bound tree of land formerly laid out for **John Norwood** on the north side of Norwood's Cove. *Adjoins Norwood, Norwood's Creek and Freeman's Cove.*

Oatley (Christopher Oatley) 9/14/1659 – 400 acres. L4/101 SR 7346.
Know yee that wee for and in consideration that Christopher Oatley and **Sampson Warring** have transported themselves and two servants into this Province here to inhabit and upon such conditions and Terms as are exprefsed in our Conditions of Plantation of our s'd Province of Maryland do hereby grant unto Christopher Oatley of Ann Arundell County, Planter, all that parcell of land called *Oatley* lying on the west side of Chesapeake Bay and on the north side of a river called the South River beginning at a marked Oak standing on a point called Oatley's Point. *Note 1: The grant is based on Oatley and Warring transporting four persons (including themselves) but the grant is to Oakley. There is no mention of a transfer of rights from Warring to Oakley in the deed. Note 2: The tract cannot be drawn because the third course lacks direction and the fourth course lacks distance. Note 3: Petition to the Honorable Governor from* **Thomas Watkins**, *of AA County found in L19/60 written on 9/22/1677: Thomas Watkins, Petitioner, sheweth that Christopher Oatley, now deceased, was granted a 400 acre tract called Oatley on 9/14/1659 which he subsequently sold to* **Henry Cateline**. *Upon Cateline's death the tract was passed to his daughter* **Josie Elizabeth**, *also deceased and without issue, the former wife of the petitioner. Thereafter, the land was Escheat to his Lordship, who was pleased to grant the same land to the petitioner as by the affidavit of* **Col. Taylor** *and* **Col. Burges**. *Since his Lordship granted this land to the petitioner an "accident happened whereby his house was burnt," along with the original patent and the later Confirmation of Patent granted by your Lordship. The petitioner humbly prays your honor order the Secretary for a Patent of Confirmation for the s'd land. Then, Col's. Taylor and Burgess made oath before the Secretary that that land was granted by his Lordship to the petitioner. Note 2: The tract cannot be drawn because the third and fourth courses lack distance and/or direction,*

Orphans Addition (Robert & Lawrence Guggeon) – 5/10/1685 - 85/90 **acres.**
LNSBi/150 SR7370. Know yee that wee for and in consideration that Robert & Lawrence Guggeon of Ann Arundell County in our s'd Province of Maryland hath due unto them eighty five acres of land in our s'd Province by afsignment of **George Yate** part of a warrant for three hundred forty six acres granted to the s'd Yate 6/25/1684 as appears on record. Upon such conditions and terms as are exprefsed in our Conditions of Plantation of this our Province, wee doe hereby grant unto the s'd Robert Guggeon and Lawrence Guggeon all that tract or parcell of land called *Orphans Addition* lying in Ann Arundell County in the woods between the South and Arundel Rivers. Begins at a bounded Oak by a Great Branch. *Note 1: Adjoins Dorsey's Addition, Howard's Interest, and the main branch of Broad Creek. Note 2 (from MSA Tract Index 73): Sold to* **John Dorsey** *in 1697. Dorsey conveyed Orphan's Addition with part of Hockley in the Hole and Howard's Heirship to son* **Caleb Dorsey** *by deed of gift (WT#1/288).*

Petticoate's Rest (Wm. Petticoat) 9/9/1679 – 100/52 acres. L21/99 SR7362.
Know yee that wee for and in consideration that William Petticoate of Ann Arundell
County in our Province of Maryland hath due unto him one hundred acres of land within
our s'd Province as appears on record. Upon such conditions and terms as are exprefsed
in our Conditions of Plantation of our late father Cecilius of noble memory, doe hereby
grant unto the s'd William Petticoate all that parcel of land called Petticoate's Rest lying
in the s'd County in the woods. Begins at a bound Hickory of **Daniel Edge** *(Edge's
Addition). Also adjoins Norwood's Angles and The Advance. Note 1: The courses
specified in the Patent and in the Survey are complete but erroneous. The tract was
drawn using some courses from this Patent and some from an adjoining tract (Norwood's
Angles). Note 2 (from MSA Tract Index 73): Sold to* **Thomas Freeborne** *in 1684
(IH#3/16).*

Piney Point (**Thomas Phelps**) 1/30/1668 – 50 acres. L12/423 SR7354.
In consideration that Thomas Phelps hath due fifty acres of land due unto him for
completion of his time of service in this Province and upon such consideration and termes
as are exprefsed in our Conditions of Plantation of our s'd Province of Maryland, do
hereby grant unto the s'd Thomas Phelps a parcell of land called *Piney Point.* Lying in
Ann Arundall County on the south side of a creek called Clarkson's Creek and adjoining
the land laid for the s'd **Robert Clarkson** *(Horne Neck).* Begins at a bounded Oak of the
s'd Clarkson. *Note: this tract cannot be drawn because the final course lacks distance.
Also adjoins The Addition (**Richard Hill**).*

Porter's Hill (Peter Porter, Jr.) 9/19/1659 – 200/130 acres. L4/129 SR7346, Survey.
Know yee that for and in consideration that Peter Porter of Ann Arundell County in our
s'd Province of Maryland hath due unto him two hundred acres of land for transporting
himself and his wife **Frances** into this Province here to inhabit and upon such conditions
and terms as are exprefsed in our Conditions of Plantation of our s'd Province of
Maryland wee doe hereby grant unto **Peter Porter** (the younger), son and heir of the s'd
Peter Porter, all that tract or parcel of land called *Porter's Hill* lying on the west side of
Chesapeake bay on the south side of the s'd (Severn) River beginning at a point, a cove of
Bustions Point and running up the river. *Note: The "rights' for this tract were initially
certified to Peter Porter (the elder) and his wife **Frances**, under the Conditions of
Plantation, for transporting themsleves to this province here to inhabit. The year of their
arrival is not mentioned in the patent.*

Proctor's Chance (Robt. Proctor) 6/28/1680 – 30/14 acres. LCB2i/13 SR7366.
Know yee that we for and in consideration that Robert Proctor of Ann Arundell County
in our Province of Maryland hath due unto him thirty acres of land by afsignment of
George Holland part of a warrant for one thousand six hundred and seventy nine acres
granted unto the s'd Holland 6/14/1679 as appears on record. Upon such conditions and
terms as are exprefsed in our Conditions of Plantation of our late father Cecilius of noble
memory, we do hereby grant unto the s'd Robert Proctor all that parcell of land called
Proctor's Chance lying in Ann Arundell County on the south side of the Severn River
beginning at a marked Hickory it being a bound tree of a parcell of land called *Intack.*

Adjoins Intacke, Todd's Range, and The Advance. Note 1: Direction for the northern boundary was not included in the deed courses and the heading for the southern boundary of the adjoining tract was used to make this drawing. Note 2 (from MSA Tract Index 73): Proctor's Chance along with Intack and Mill Land conveyed by gift deed to **Richard Hill** *in 1694.*

Proctor's Forrest (Robt. Proctor) 7/20/1673 – 100/100 acres. L15/87 SR4327. Know yee that wee for and in consideration that Robert Proctor, Innholder, of Ann Arundall County in our s'd Province of Maryland hath due unto him one hundred acres of land within this Province by afsignment of **Robert Wilson** as appears on record. And, upon such conditions and terms as are exprefsed in our Conditions of Plantation of our Province of Maryland, wee doe hereby grant unto the s'd Robert Proctor all that parcell of land called *Proctor's Forrest* lying in Ann Arundell County on the north side of the South River beginning at a bounded Hickory Tree and running by the line of **Robert Clarkson**. *Adjoins land of **John Baldwin** and **John Taylor**.*

Range (John Medcalfe) 4/2/1706 – 75/45 acres. LWD/5512 SR7372-3. Know yee that whereas John Medcalfe of Ann Arundell County by his humble petition heretofore presented did sett forth that he is seized in fee simple of and in a certaine tract of land in the County called *Baldwin's Addition* originally surveyed for **John Baldwin** within the bounds whereof he conceived some surplus and vacant land contiguous. Wherefore he prayed our Speciall Warrant for the resurvey thereof to include the surplus and add thereto what vacant land he should find contiguous which the s'd John pattented by virtue of a warrant for sixty acres granted to him 3/4/1704, and also by virtue of a warrant for five acres granted 4/25/1706 as appears on record in our Land Office. Upon such conditions and terms as are exprefsed in our Conditions of Plantation of our Province of Maryland, wee doe therefore hereby grant unto the s'd John all that tract or parcell of land called *Range* beginning at a bounded Gumm being a bound tree of the s'd tract.

Read's Lott (William Read) 9/15/1665 – 40/20 acres. L8/290 SR7350. Know ye that wee for and in consideration that William Read of this Province, Planter, hath due unto him forty acres, part of a warrant for seventy acres as appears upon record. Upon such conditions and terms as are exprefsed in our Conditions of Plantation of our Province of Maryland, doe hereby grant unto the s'd William Read a parcell of land called Read's Lott lying in Ann Arundell County on the south side of the Severn River at the Head of a creek called Beasley's Creek. Begins at a bound Red Oak. Adjoins land of **Robert Clarkson**. *Note: in order to draw this tract it was necessary to follow a course order of 3-1-2, because deed course 2 specifies the reverse heading (direction) of course one.*

Roper's Neck Resurveyed (Thomas Roper) 3/1/1673 – 300/348 acres. L15/153 SR4327. Whereas we did by your deed of grant bearing date of 9/18/1664 for the considerations therein named grant over to Thomas Roper of Ann Arundell County a parcell of land called *Roper's Neck* lying in the s'd County on the east side of Chesapeake Bay and on the north side of the South River containing and then laid out for two hundred acres of land. And Whereas we did also by our other deed of grant (9/10/1665) make grant unto the s'd Thomas Roper a parcell of land called *Chance* adjoining to the above-mentioned parcell containing fifteen acres that the s'd Thomas Roper hath surrendered up the s'd two patents to the Secretary's Office and there caused the same to be vacated upon record and had a warrant to recover the same as appears on record. And, upon which resurvey it was found to be three hundred acres now. For that the s'd Thomas Roper hath due unto him ninety acres of land within our province forty acres there being the remainder of the warrant for two hundred acres formerly granted and fifty acres by afsignment of **Daniel Edge** for his time of Service in this Province. And upon such conditions and terms as are exprefsed in our Conditions of Plantation of our Province of Maryland, doe grant unto the s'd Thomas Roper all that parcell of land resurveyed called *Roper's Neck* lying in the s'd county on the north side of the South River and on the west side of the mouth of a creek called *Roper's Creek* and bounding on the river. *Adjoins The Little Cove, a marsh on the east side of Green Gingerville Creek, the land of John Baldwin and land already owned by Thomas Roper (Chance). Note: The following preceded the above patent document (same reference and date): "To his Excellency the Captane Generall, The humble petition of Thomas Roper of Ann Arundell County showith unto your Excellency that whereas your Excellency was pleased to grant unto your petitioner a warrant of resurvey for 255(sic) acres of land bearing date 8/29/1688. Upon which your Petitioner did surrender up unto the Secretarye's office as appears. And now, may it please your excellency, your petitioner cannot get pattent for the same without your excellency's order for the making of the s'd pattent as he is in duty bound shall we ever pray. Granted, Charles Calvert.*

Ruly's Search (Anthony Ruly) 8/6/1696 – 74/109 acres. LBBB3i/486 SR7374.
Know yee that for and in consideration that Anthony Ruly of Ann Arundell County in our s'd Province hath due unto him seventy four acres of land within our Province by virtue of a special warrant granted him 6/20/1696 for the taking and resurveying for him the s'd Ruly cleared land before taken up which lay contiguous to a tract of land of the s'd Ruly called *Edward His Neck* lying in the s'd county and taking up one hundred acres. And forasmuch as upon the survey of the s'd land above it was found that there was seventy four acres thereof and that the s'd Ruly has given mention in our Land Office for the same according to our Conditions of Plantation. Wee doe therefore hereby grant unto him the the s'd Anthony Ruly all that tract or parcell of land called *Ruly's Search* lying on the north side of the South River beginning at a bounded Red Oak of a parcel of land called *Edward His Neck*. *Also adjoins Smith's Rest.*

Smith's Neck (**Richard Owen**) 2/12/1650 – 685 acres. LQ/408 SR7345.
In consideration that **Zephaniah Smith** hath transported himself, **Robert Thompson**, **Robert Knight**, **Rich. Vaughn**, **James Copes**, **Grace Wells**, and **Phillip Baggley** to this province in 1651, here to inhabit, Do hereby grant unto Richard Owens, Merchant, assignee of s'd Smith all that parcel of land formerly surveyed for the s'd Zephaniah and now called *Smith's Neck* lying on the west side of Chesapeake Bay and near a river called South River, bounding on a branch of s'd River called Smith's Branch. *Note 1: Two adjoining tracts (585 and 100 acres) were laid out. The deed courses for both lacked the combination of distance and direction and cannot be drawn. Note 2: The deed does not*

identify this tract by name. Note 3: Based on the acreage, owner's name, and location, this tract was identified using information found in Maryland Rent Rolls 1700-1707, 1705-1724, Baltimore and Anne Arundel Counties, Genealogical Publishing Company, Baltimore Maryland, 1972, page 192. Note 4: On April 4, 1684, Col Thomas Taylor obtained a Special Warrant, on behalf on Ann Owens, widow and relict of Richard Owens, merchant, then deceased, to resurvey Smith's Neck and an unnamed adjoining tract. It is assumed that this is the same unnamed adjoining tract included in the 1658 survey for 685 acres (LQ/408). The land was resurveyed by George Yate, Deputy Surveyor under George Talbot, Surveyor Generall, on May 5, 1684. The resurvey document indicates that it is likely that the resurvey was conducted solely within the confines of the Surveyor's Office making use of the "ancient" plots to recalculate acreage. The resulting 412 acres found (both tracts) differs significantly from 685 acres found in the 1658 survey of what can only be assumed to be the same two tracts. There is no evidence to the contrary. Also, the "resurveyed" courses shown for both tracts are in summary form, e.g., "then by severall courfes and diftances to a bound tree near the head of Smith's Creek," and cannot be drawn.

Smith's Rest (Walter Smith) 8/26/1651 150/188 acres. L7/288 SR7349.
Know Yee that Wee for and in consideration that Walter Smith of this Province, Planter, hath due unto him one hundred and fifty acres, being land formerly laid out for the s'd Smith that he now liveth upon lying in Anne Arundel County on the north side of the South River beginning at a marked Cedar upon a point of land a bile of the s'd River. *Note 1: Because the third course (of nine) lacked distance, the tract cannot be drawn following the course order specified in the patent. The drawing was made by beginning at course four and ending (closing) on the third course. Note 2 (from MSA Tract Index 73): Devised to son Manuell Smith who sold the tract to Lawrence Draper.*

The Addition (John Hammond) 1/5/1687 – 22/20 acres. LIB&ILC/315 SR7368-1.
Know yee that wee for and in consideration that John Hammond of Ann Arundel County in our s'd Province of Maryland hath due him two and twenty acres of land within our s'd Province part of a warrant for five hundred acres granted until him 5/30/1685 as appears on record. Upon such conditions and terms as are exprefsed in our Conditions of Plantation of our Province of Maryland, wee doe hereby grant unto the s'd John Hammond all that tract or parcel of land called The Addition lying in the aforesaid County on the south side of the Ann Arundell River at a bounded White Oak it being a bound tree of **Thomas Hammond** *(Mountain Neck)*.

The Addition (Capt. Richard Hill) 6/1/1687 – 60/60 acres. LNS2i/321 SR7371.
Know yee that for and in consideration that Capt. Richard Hill of Ann Arundell County in our s'd Province of Maryland hath due unto him sixty acres of land within our s'd Province being due unto him by a warrant for the same quantity granted to him 6/23/1674 as appears on record. Upon such conditions and terms as are exprefsed in our Conditions of Plantation of this our s'd Province of Maryland, wee doe therefore grant unto the s'd Capt. Richard Hill all that tract or parcell of land called *The Addition* lying in the s'd County on the south side of a creek called Todd's Creek beginning at a bounded White

Oak marked with four notches it being a bound tree of **Robert Clarkson** *(Horne Neck).*
Also adjoins Read's Lott, Brushy Neck and Piney Point.

The Addition (Samuel Young) 10/20/1704 – 80/80 acres. LSDF/540 SR7373-2.
Know yee that for and in consideration that Samuel Young of Ann Arundell County in
our s'd Province hath due unto him eighty acres of land within our s'd Province being
due unto him by virtue of a warrant for the same quantity granted unto him 10/13/1701 as
appears on record. Upon such conditions and terms as are exprefsed in our Conditions of
Plantation of our s'd Province, wee doe therefore hereby grant unto him the s'd Samuel
Young all that tract or parcell of land known as *The Addition* lying in the s'd County on
the north side of the South River beginning at a bounded White Oak in the line of **Robert
Clarkson** now in the occupation of the s'd Young.

The Advance (Daniel Edge) 5/10/1676 – 42/41 acres. L19/245 SR 7360.
Know Yee that Wee for and in consideration that Daniel Edge of Ann Arundell county
hath due unto him forty two acres of land within this Province as appears on record.
Upon such considerations and terms as are exprefsed in our Conditions of Plantation of
our late father Cecilius of noble memory, doe hereby grant unto the s'd Daniel Edge all
that parcell of land called *The Advance* lying in the s'd county between the South and
Ann Arundall Rivers and on a creek called Norwood's Creek. Begins at a bound Pine
standing by the s'd creekside it being a bound tree of the land of **John Norwood.**

The Advantage (Richard Moss) 8/24/1665 – 40/23 acres. L8/110 SR7350.
Know Yee that Wee for and in consideration that Richard Moss of Ann Arundell County
hath due forty acres of land out of a warrant for three hundred acres granted to him the
s'd Richard. Upon such conditions and terms as are exprefsed in the Conditions of
Plantation of this our Province, wee doe hereby grant unto the s'd Richard Moss all that
parcell of land called *The Advantage* lying in Anne Arundel County on the south side of
the Severn River in the woods. Begins at a marked White Oak on the side of a hill by the
line of land formerly laid out for **Thomas Turner**. *Adjoins land owned by **Richard
Young**.*

The Angle (Capt. Richard Hill) 6/1/1687 – 7/7 acres. LNS2i/321 SR7371.
Know yee that wee for and in consideration that Capt. Richard Hill of Ann Arundell
County in our Province of Maryland hath due unto him seven acres of land being part of
a warrant for seventy acres granted unto him 6/23/1684 as appears on record. Upon such
conditions and terms as are exprefsed in our Conditions of Plantation of our Province of
Maryland, wee doe hereby grant unto him the s'd Capt. Richard Hill all that tract or
Parcell of land called *The Angle* lying in the s'd County on the south side of the Ann
Arundell River and on a creek called Dorsey's Creek. Begins at a bounded Pine by the
s'd creek. *Adjoins Smith and Enlargement Creek. Note: This tract is within the bounds
of the Town of Annapolis, Rent Rolls pg. 220.*

The Batchellor's Hope **(Walter Phelps & Nicholas Green)** 10/20/1665 - 240 acres.
L10/253 SR7352. Know yee that we for and in consideration that Walter Phelps and
Nicholas Greene of the County of Ann Arundell, Planters, by afsignment of **Robert**

Franklin, Merchant, for forty acres. Rights of the assignee of **John Shale** of the s'd County being part of a warrant for four hundred acres and by afsignment from **James Chilcott** of the s'd County, Merchant, being a warrant granted to the s'd Chilcott for 200 acres. And, upon such conditions and terms as are exprefsed in our Conditions of Plantation of our Province of Maryland, do hereby grant unto the s'd Walter Phelps and Nicholas Greene a parcell lying on the north side of the South River and on the eastern side of Broad Creek. Begins at a bounded Red Oake. *Note: This tract cannot be drawn because the 7ᵗʰ and 8ᵗʰ courses lack direction*

The Chance (Cornelius Howard) 8/25/1664 - 200/173 acres. L7/379 SR7349.
Know Yee that Wee for and in consideration that Cornelius Howard of this Province, Planter, hath due unto him two hundred acres of land in this Province for Transporting himself, **Henry Kettlewell** and **John Sherin** into this Province here to inhabit. And, upon such conditions and terms as are exprefsed in our Conditions of Plantation of our Province of Maryland, do hereby grant unto the s'd Cornelius Howard a parcel of land called *The Chance* lying in Anne Arundel County on the south side of the Severn River in the woods adjoining the land of **Wm. Frizzell** and **James Warner**. Begins at a bound tree of s'd Warner.

The Chance (Thomas Roper) 9/10/1665 – 15/10 acres. L8/408 SR7350.
Know yee that wee for and in consideration that Thomas Roper of this s'd Province, Planter, hath due unto him fifteen acres within this Province part of a warrant for two hundred acres as appears upon record. And, upon such considerations and terms as are exprefsed in our Conditions of Plantation of our Province of Maryland doe hereby grant unto the said Thomas Roper a parcell of land called *The Chance* lying in Ann Arundell County on the south side of the Severn River in the woods adjoining the land of **William Frizzell.** *Note: The marginal note by the Certification (same Liber and Folio) indicates that the grant was for 150 acres. However the marginal notes and the text are clear that the grant was for 15 acres.*

The Favour (Benjamin Bond) 4/2/1696 – 123/121 acres. LC3i/420 SR7377.
Know yee that Benjamin Bond of Ann Arundell County in our s'd Province of Maryland had obtained on 3/7/1681 a Speciall Warrant to resurvey a certaine tract of land on the north side of the South River formerly pofsefsed by **George Paddington** (*Puddington*) for two hundred ninety acres and by the s'd Paddington afsigned to **William Pennington** and by the s'd Pennington afsigned to **Ester Gossum** and by the s'd Gossum unto **Adam Desapp** and by the s'd Desapp to Benjamin Bond. All of which afsignments do appear upon the records of our s'd County. Upon which s'd Speciall Warrant was Certified by **George Yate,** then Deputy Surveyor of Ann Arundell County, that the tract contained but one hundred twenty three acres of land. Whereas the s'd Benjamin Bond by his humble petition has sett forth that the s'd Cert was never yet recorded in our Land Office and consequently our grant to him was never issued. Wherefore he prayed that the s'd Cert may be recorded and our Letters of Pattents issued hereupon which we have thought fitt to condescend unto *(him)* under the conditions and limitations hereinafter expfessed. We doe therefore hereby grant unto the s'd Benjamin Bond all that tract or parcell of land as after resurvey called *The Favour* lying in the s'd County on the north side of the South

River beginning at a bounded Red Oak standing at the mouth of Oatley Creek. *Adjoins Beard's Branch and Beard's Dock.*

The Friendship (**William Frizzell**) 8/20/1683 – 30acres. LCBi//484 SR7367.
Know ye that wee for and in consideration that William Frizzell of Ann Arundell County in our Province of Maryland hath due unto him thirty acres of land by afsignment of **George Yate** part of a warrant for fifty acres of land on 3/1/1680 as appears on record. Upon such conditions and terms as are exprefsed in our Conditions of Plantation of our late father Cecilius of noble memory, wee,doe hereby grant unto the s'd William Frizzell all that tract or parcell of land called *The Friendship* lying in Ann Arundell County on the north side of the South River bounding on the east side of a creek called the Broad Creek. *Note: The tract cannot be drawn because the first (of three) courses specified lacks direction and third lacks distance and direction.*

The Intacke (John Norwood) 1/18/1659 – 100/155 acres. L4/225 SR7346.
Know yee that we for and in consideration that John Norwood hath transported **John Field** and **Joanne Barrington** into this Province here to inhabit and upon such conditions and terms as are exprefsed in our Conditions of Plantation of our Province of Maryland, wee doe hereby grant unto the s'd John Norwood a parcell of land lying on the west side of Chesapeake Bay in Anne Arundel County on the south side of the Severn River on the west side of Dorsey's Creek. Begins at a marked Oak of the land where he now liveth. *Adjoins Proctor's Chance, Dorsey's Creek, the land of **Richard Yate**, and the land of **Wyatt** (now in the possession of **John Freeman**). Note: **Phillip Calvert Esq**, patented a 57 acre tract called Intacke near St. Mary's City (10/5/1677- L19/510 SR7360.*

The Levell (John Cross) 10/5/1683 – 260/272 acres. LCB3i/510 SR7367.
Know yee that wee for and in consideration that John Cross of Ann Arundell County in this our Province of Maryland hath due unto him two hundred and sixty acres of land within our s'd Province by afsignment of **Henry Hanslap** part of a warrant granted unto the s'd Hanslap for twelve hundred fifty acres on 8/30/1680. Upon such conditions and terms as are exprefsed in our Conditions of Plantation of our late father Cecilius, wee doe grant unto the s'd John Cross all that parcell of land called *The Levell* lying in the s'd County in the woods adjoining the land formerly laid out for **Zephaniah Smith**. Begins at a bounded White Oak of another tract of the s'd Smith standing by Enlargement Creek.

The Neglect (Patrick Dunkin) 5/4/1683 - 30/9 acres. LCB3i/280 SR7367.
Know yee that for and in consideration that Patrick Dunkin of Ann Arundell County in our s'd Province of Maryland hath due unto him thirty acres of land within our Province the remainder of fifty acres afsigned him by **Thomas Bland** out of a warrant for two hundred fifty acres granted to the s'd Bland 8/2/1681 as appears on record. Upon such conditions and terms as are exprefsed in our Conditions of Plantation of our late father Cecilius, of noble memory, wee doe hereby grant unto the s'd Patrick Dunkin all that tract or parcell of land called *The Neglect* lying in Ann Arundell County on the north side of the South River beginning at a bound White Oak by a cove side of Broad Creek. *Note 1 (from MSA Tract Index 73): In 1684 this tract was conveyed as a gift to son-in-law **John Frissell**.*

<u>The Roper's Yard</u> (**Thomas Roper**) 9/13/1664 - 200 acres. L7/431 SR7349.
Know Yee that Wee for and in consideration that **John Edwards** of this Province, Planter, hath due unto him one hundred acres of land by afsignment of **Quentin Camell** the afsignee of **Erasmus Yeatman** for his Transportacon (*Transportation*) in Anno 1651 and one hundred acres more for the s'd Edwards (*for*) his own transportacon into this Province here to inhabit who for right, title, and interest thereto the s'd two hundred acres hath afsigned and made over to Thomas Roper as appears on record. And, upon such considerations and terms as are exprefsed in our Conditions of Plantation of our Province of Maryland do hereby grant unto the s'd Thomas Roper a parcell of land called *The Roper's Yard* lying in Anne Arundel County on the north side of the South River beginning at a marked Oak by the riverside. *Note: this tract cannot be drawn because the first course lacks distance and the sixth and the seventh (final) courses lack direction.*

Timber Neck (**John Macubbin**) 9/15/1665 – **40/24 acres**. L8/294 SR7350
Know yee that wee for and in consideration that John Macubbin of this Province, Planter, hath due unto him forty acres of land in this Province. Upon such conditions and terms as are exprefsed in our Conditions of Plantation of our s'd Province of Maryland, doe hereby grant unto the s'd John Maccubbin a parcell of land called *Timber Neck* lying on a creek called the Broad Creek. Begins at a bounded pine of the s'd John Macubbin near the mouth of s'd creek. *Adjoins Smith's Neck and land already laid out for Macubbin.*

Todd (**Thomas Todd**) 6/8/1651 - **100/117 acres**. LAB&H/288 SR7344.
Laid out for Thomas Todd for the County of Ann Arrundell, Shipwright, a parcell of land lying on the west side of Chesapeake Bay upon the River Severn and on the south side of the s'd river beginning at a marked White Oak standing upon an oyster shell point. *Adjoins the Severn River and the land of **Thomas Hall** (Hall's patent not found). Note 1: This tract was probably not patented, however, it is included in the Rent Rolls (1705-1724). Note 2: The boundary courses specified are incomplete. The tract was drawn using a combination of those courses that were complete, boundaries of adjoining tracts, and a calculation of the angles and distances of the river and adjoining creeks. Note 3 (from MSA Tract Index 73): Todd's Harbor, Todd's Pasture, Todd's Range, and an unnamed tract of 100 acres surveyed 7/8/1751. The unnamed tract was most likely Todd, which was sold by **Lancellot Todd** for 16,000 lbs tobacco in 1713 to **Thomas Larkin** and **Thomas Bordley**, Gentlemen (IB#2/171).*

Todd's Harbour (**Thomas Todd**) 4/10/1671 – **120/113 acres**. L14/191 SR7356.
Know yee that we for and in consideration that Thomas Todd of the county of Anne Arundel in our Province of Maryland hath due unto him one hundred and twenty acres of land within our Province by afsignment from **Robert Wilson** bearing the date 12/16/1670, as appears on record. And upon such conditions and termes as are exprefsed in our Conditions of Plantation do hereby grant unto him the said Thomas Todd all that parcell of land called *Todd's Harbour* lying in Anne Arundel County on the west side of the Anne Arundel River. Begins at a bound White Oak. *Bounds Dorsey's Creek, the land of **Richard Acton**, and the land of **Thomas Hall**. Note: Included land formerly*

certified to Thomas Todd called Todd Surveyed 7/8/1651, that adjoined Acton's land in Annapolis Town.

Todd's Pasture (Thomas Todd) 6/29/1675 – 29/24 acres. L19/122 SR7360.
Know Yee that Wee for and in consideration that Thomas Todd of the County of Ann Arundell hath due unto him twenty nine acres of land in this Province by afsignment of **George Yate** part of a warrant granted unto the s'd Yate for one hundred thirty acres as appears on record. Upon such considerations and terms as are exprefsed in our Conditions of Plantation of our Province of Maryland, doe hereby grant unto the s'd Thomas Todd all that parcel of land called Todd's Pasture lying in the s'd County and in a neck of land called *Todd's Neck.* Begins at a marked Locust stump.

Todd's Range (Thomas Todd) 5/4/1664 120/136 acres. L7/244 SR7349.
Know Yee that Wee for and in consideration that Thomas Todd of this Province hath due to him one hundred and twenty acres of land being part of the rights of land for Transporting **Joyce Bayne, John Barker**, and **Matthew Burin** into this Province here to inhabit as appears on records. And, upon such considerations and terms as are exprefsed in our Conditions of Plantation of our Province of Maryland, do hereby grant unto the s'd Thomas Todd a parcell of land called *Todd's Range* lying on the south side of the Severn River in Anne Arundel County adjoining the plantation he now liveth upon. Begins at a marked Pine tree. *Extends to the head of Dorsey's Creek. Note 1: The following appears in Rent Rolls, "...located in the town of Annapolis as is confirmed." Note 2: A **Captain Thomas Todd** of Baltimore County patented a 400-acre tract called Todd's Range on the north side of the Patapsco River (8/8/1670 Pat JJ376 L12/307).*

Tolley's Point Resurveyed (Capt. Richard Hill) 4/16/1684 – 140/141 acres. LSDA/319 SR7369. Whereas **Thomas Tolley**, late, of Ann Arundell County in our s'd Province of Maryland deceased 9/14/1664 bought and purchased of **William Durand** a tract or parcell of land about one hundred and forty acres as by a certaine writing or bargain of sale they doth appear. Whereas the s'd Tolley not mistrusting the title of the s'd Durand to the s'd land did build and improve quietly using the same during his life and **Thomas Tolley Junior**, sonne and heir of the s'd Thomas Tolley dec'd hath since the death of his father hath enjoyed the same and paid over rents for the same and no person hath molested or troubled him in the quiet enjoyment thereof. But, the s'd Durand's title not appearing on record the s'd Thomas Tolley Junior was in great fear not only of losing his s'd land but also his labor, cost, and trouble in improving and building upon the same unless wee should relieve him in and thereupon he humbly supplicated and obtained our Special Warrant to resurvey the same. Whereupon Capt. Richard Hill of Ann Arundell County hath informed us that the s'd Tolley pursuant to our Special Warrant caused the land to be resurveyed and laid out according to the terms of the Special Warrant. But, before he could return the certificate to us he dyed having first made sale of the s'd land to the s'd Hill as the s'd Hill made appear unto us. Whereupon the s'd Hill supplecated us to grant him a Pattent of Confirmation for the same to him and his heirs and having made return of the Certificate of Resurvey aforesaid to same, Wee doe therefore hereby give, grant and confirm unto him the s'd Capt. Richard Hill all that tract or parcell of land now resurveyed called *Tolley's Point* lying in the s'd County on the west side of Chesapeake

Bay *beginning at a marked stake by the Bayside. Apparently the resurvey referred to was conducted prior to the granting of the Certificate of Resurvey as described in the following: Tolley's Point (Thomas Tolley) c9/9/1683 –140 acres. L22/60 SR7363 "...By virtue of a warrant granted unto Thomas Tolley of Ann Arundell County dated 10/18/1683 as appears on record. These are in humble manner to certifie that I **George Yate**, Deputy Surveyor under **George Talbot** Esq, Surveyor Generall, hath laid out and surveyed according to the directions of the neighborhood that are here with best known and good acquainted, all that parcel of land called and known by the name Tolley's Point lying in the s'd County on the west side of Chesapeake Bay." Patent not found.*

Warner's Neck **(James Warner)** 1/5/1658s – 320 acres. LQ/237 SR7345.
Grant based on John Warner Transporting himself, **Joan** his wife, one child (unnamed) and **John Mathews** (servant) in 1650. Located near the Severn River beginning at a marked Oak near a creek called *Warner's Creek*. Adjoins *Porter's Hills, Mountain Neck, and The Chance. Note 1: On May 30, 1667, James Warner delivered his patent, bearing date of 1/5/1658, for Warner's Neck near the Severn River, to the Land Office requesting that it be reissued showing the correct acreage and returned to him. Warrant then issued to the s'd James Warner that a resurvey of the s'd land be made with all convenience (L10/499). Note 2: Tract could not be drawn because the 4th (final) course lacks distance and direction. The missing course runs along Warner's Creek near Bustion's Cove.*

Wardner's Neck Resurveyed (James Wardner) 6/20/1668 – 320/293 acres. L12/24
SR7354. Whereas our deed of grant bearing the date of the fifth day of January 1659, unto James Wardner of the County of Ann Arundell under the considerations therein mentioned, we did grant unto the s'd James Wardner all that tract of land called Wardner's Neck near the Severne River containing and laid out for three hundred and twenty acres of land. The s'd James Wardner *(Warner)* hath since resurveyed and delivered the Patent to this Office with request that a new grant of the s'd land according to the Metes and Bounds of Certificate of Resurvey might be to him granted. And upon such considerations and terms as are exprefsed in our Conditions of Plantation of our Province of Maryland, do hereby grant unto the s'd James Wardner all that parcel of land resurveyed called *Wardner's Neck Resurveyed* beginning at a marked Oak by Wardner's Creek. *Note (from MSA Tract Index 73): During his lifetime James Warner conveyed 100 Acres to **Phillip Howard** and 100 acres to **Samuel Howard**. After his death 120 acres were devised to widow **Elizabeth Warner** who willed the tract to their daughter **Johana Sewell** the wife of **John Sewell**.*

Wardrop (James Wardner) 6/26/1663 - 200/150 acres. L5/354 SR7347.
Know yee that wee for and in consideration that James Wardner of this Province, Planter, hath due unto him two hundred acres of land as appears upon record. And, upon such considerations and terms as are exprefsed in our Conditions of Plantation of our Province of Maryland, do grant unto him the s'd James Wardner a parcell of land called Wardrop lying on the north side of South River and on the east side of a creek called the Broad Creek in the County of Ann Arundall. Begins at a marked Oak in a bile by a swamp. *Note 1: This tract cannot be drawn per the deed courses. The drawing, which should be considered an approximation only, eliminates a partial fourth course which appears to*

be an error on the part of the individual transcribing the surveyor's notes. The direction specified for the first and fifth courses is the same (although drawn from opposing directions) and, due to the generally rectangular shape of nearby tracts, the same "distance" was used for both of these courses. Also, the deed does not specify distance or direction for the boundary following Broad Creek. This has been drawn by connecting the ends of the first and fifth courses with a straight line, which appears to be an often-used technique by surveyors of the time to simplify laying out irregular shoreline courses. Note 2 (from MSA Tract Index 73): Sold to **Patrick Dunkin** *in 1671 (WH#4/142). Dunkin sold to* **Mary Gibbs** *for 4,500 lbs tobacco in 1671 (WH#4 145). Mary Gibbs sold to* **John Maccubbin** *in 1675 (WH#4/146). John Maccubbin sold to* **Charles Carroll** *in 1706 (WT#2/354).*

Wardrop Ridge (Patrick Dunkin) 5/12/1663 - 100/75 acres. LCB3i/283 SR7367. Know yee that wee for and in consideration that Patrick Dunkin of our s'd Province of Maryland had surveyed and laid out for him on 12/10/1683, a parcel of land for one hundred acres called *Wardrop Ridge* lying on the north side of the South River in Ann Arundell County. By virtue of a Special Warrant to him granted on 4/6/1676 to resurvey and whereas the s'd Patrick Dunkin hath due unto him one hundred acres of land within our s'd Province fifty acres thereof for transporting **Thomas Bland** into this province to inhabit on 8/26/1681 as appears on record. And, upon such conditions and terms as are exprefsed in our Conditions of Plantation of our late father Cecilius of noble memory, wee doe hereby grant unto the s'd Patrick Dunkin all that tract or parcell of land called *Wardrop Ridge* lying in Ann Arundell County on the north side of the South River respecting the land of the s'd Dunkin to the west called *Wardrop*. Begins at a bounded White Oak. *Note 1: A note written in the margin of the first Certification (L6/108 SR 7348) reads as follows: " This cert again entered Lib LL Folio 492 and warrant resurveyed granted Lib WC Folio 194. ____ granted by order of the Councill Lib CB Folio 228 upon condition of making good one right which is due Lib WCN 4 Folio 219 having already made one good. Note 2: This tract could not be drawn using the courses in the first Certification. However, the tract was resurveyed on 4/6/1678 at the request of Patrick Dunkin. The resurveyd courses were changed slightly and the tract has been drawn using these later courses (L19/344 SR7360).*

Waringston (Sampson Waring) 9/2/1663 - 200/200 acres. L7/75 SR7349. Know yee that for and in consideration that **John Covell, Gent,** of this Province has due unto him two hundred acres of land for transporting two servants into this Province here to inhabit, do hereby grant to Sampson Waring, asignee of s'd Covell, all that parcell of land lying on the west side of Chesapeake Bay next adjoining the land of **William Durand**. Beginning at a marked Gum tree, being Durand's southmost bound tree and running down the Bay. *Adjoins Devise on the south.*

West Quarter (Jacob Brimingham) 6/20/1663 – 100/100 acres. L5/352 SR7347. Know yee that we for and in consideration that Jacob Birmingham of this Province, Carpenter, hath one hundred acres of land due unto him for the transportation of himself and one servant named **Mary Combs** into this Province here to inhabit in the year 1659, as appears upon record. And, upon such considerations and terms as are exprefsed in our

Conditions of Plantation of our s'd Province of Maryland doe hereby grant unto the said Jacob Birmingham a parcell of land called *West Quarter* lying on the south side of the Severn River and the south side of Howell's Creek on the north side of the West Branch (of South River) in the County of Ann Arundall. Begins at a marked Oak by the side of a branch. *Note 1 (from MSA Tract Index 73): West Quarter is within the bounds of Read's Lott and The Widow's Addition.*

Widow's Addition (Elizabeth Read) 5/181679 – 130/134 acres. L20/199 SR7361.
Know yee that we for and in consideration that Elizabeth Reade of Ann Arundell County, widow, hath due unto her by afsignment of **George Yate** *(1/10/1678) - L15/766)* part of a warrant for five hundred acres granted to the s'd Yate 10/21/1678 as appears on record. And, upon such conditions and terms as are exprefsed in our Conditions of Plantation of our late father Cecilius of noble record do hereby grant unto the s'd Elizabeth Reade all that parcell of land called *Widow's Addition* lying on the south side of the Ann Arundell River in the woods *(adjoining Howard).* Begins at a bound Oak it being a bound tree of land formerly laid out for **William Reade** called *Reade's Lott. Note 1: George Yate assigned 130 acres to Elizabeth Read for a valuable consideration. Note 2: The patent document spells the name Read in both of the ways shown here.*

Wither's Durand **(Samuel Withers)** - 5/20/1663 250 acres. Liber 5/266. SR7347.
Know yee that we for and in consideration that Samuel Withers of this Province hath due unto him two hundred fifty acres of land in this Province and upon such consideratioins and terms as are exprefsed in our Conditions of Plantation of our Province of Maryland do grant unto the s'd Samuel Withers a parcel of land lying on the south side of the Severn River in Ann Arundel County. Beginning at a Sasafrax tree standing by a creek called Howell's Creek adjoining land now in the possession of **Thomas Tolley**. *Note: Cannot be drawn because the fourth and fifth (final) courses lack distance.*

Wither's Outlet (Samuel Withers) 8/5/1664 - 100/91 acres. L7/283 SR 7349.
Know Yee that Wee for and in consideration that Samuel Withers, Gent, of this County hath due unto him one hundred acres of land within this Province being part of a warrant for three hundred and fifty acres as appears on record. Do hereby grant him the said Samuel Withers a parcell of land called *Wither's Outlet* lying in Ann Arundel County on the south side Seavern River at the head of a creek called Saughier's Creek.
Note 1: Adjoins Come by Chance. Note 2 (from MSA Tract Index 73): Devised to son **Samuel Withers Jr.**, *and sold by him to* **Richard Hill** *in 1685.*

Drawn and Placed Northern Area Tracts

B - Bruton
BC - Boyde's Chance
BE - Brown's Encrease
BCH - Brown's Chance
BG - Bruton Grimes
BH - Bruton's Hope

BP - Brown's Peace
BST - Brownston
C - Chilton
CL Clinke
D - Diamond
DS - Davistone

FC - Friend's Choice
GA - Grime's Addition
GE - Grime's Enlargement
GR - Guy's Rest
GRS - Grimeston
GS - Green Spring

GW - Guy's Will
H - Howard's Hills
HA - Howard's Addition
HE - Henry's Encrease

Sewell's Encrease
Mill Meadow
Sewell's Cove
Indian Cr.
Cypress Cr.
Plum Cr.
Shipley's Choice
Brooksby's Pt.
TJ
C
Pierpoint's Range
FC
Brown's Folly
BE
Owen's Range
BCH
SR
Weston
LP
Warfield's Plaine
D
Ben's Discovery
D
TF
WF
TAW
GR
GW
GE
GA
Brownley
TD
WL
W
TM
Rosse
SH
GRS
C
BST
Brandy
HH
H
BC
B
BH
BP
L
HA
Greeniston
Cordwell
GS
H&P's Fancy
HFC
BG
Fox Cr.
Ridgely's Chance
Abbingdon
H&P's Range
Galloway's Cr.
Herford
md
ha
Dividing point of Rogue's Harbor Br and No. Br. of Patuxent
What You Will
WG
No. Br. of South River

7400.00 feet

1:88800

HFC - Howard's First Choice
HH - Hare Hill
LP - Lancaster Plaine
MD - The Maiden
MM - Mill Meadow
SC - Shipley's Choice

SG - Shepheard's Grove
SH - Salmon Hills
SR - Shepheard's Range
TAW - The Addn. (Warfield)
TD - The Desert
TF - The Friendship (B&H)

TJ - The Addn. (Jones)
TM - The March
W - What You Please
WF Warfield's Forrest
WG - Wilson's Grove
WL - What is Left

69

Marked Oak by side
of North Run of
South River

Marked Oak standing
on a Sevell

Abingdon 875/876 Acres
Robert Proctor & John Gather 9/20/1664
(L7/387 SR7349)

Intersects line of
Freeman's Fancy

Marked Oak standing
near main branch of
South River

2600.00 feet
1:31200

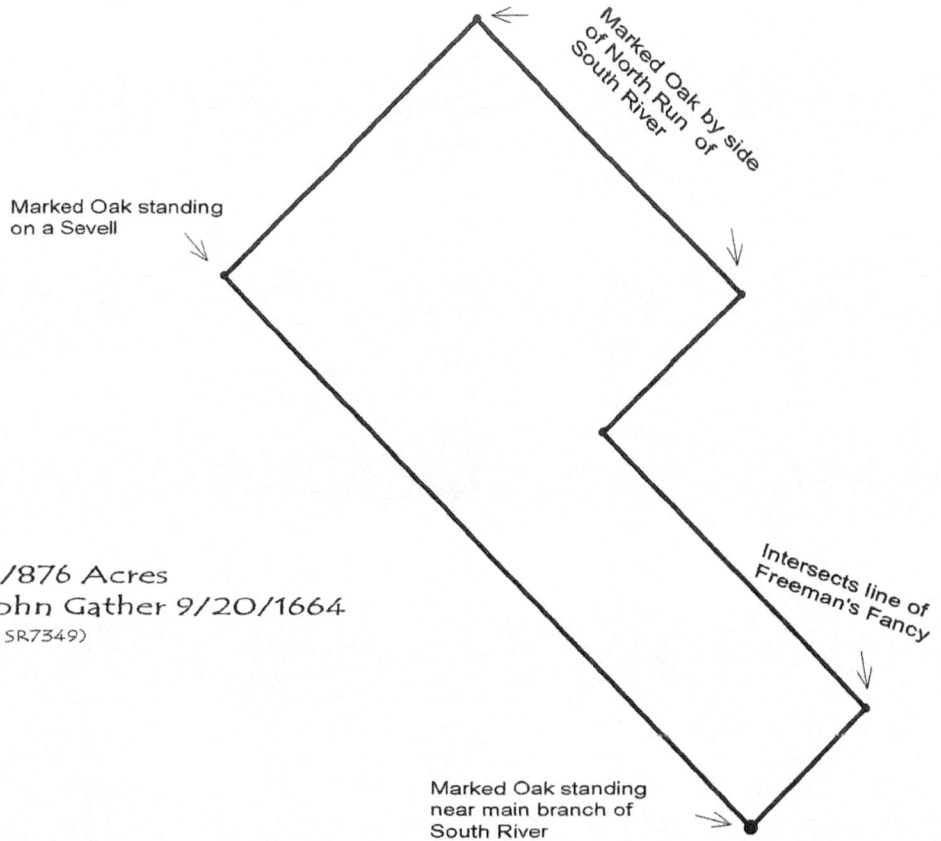

70

Bound White
Oak

Abingdon Part Of 364/364 Acres
John Gaither 8/27/1699
(LDD5i/44 SR7378)

N

1200.00 feet

1:14400

Bound Spanish
Oak

Bound White Oak
on a hill by a smale
branch falling into
No. Be, of South
River

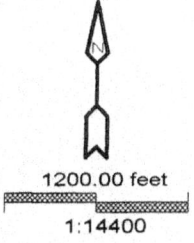

Abingdon Resurveyed 364/364 Acres
John Gaither Jr. 5/10/1701
(LWD/375 SR7372)

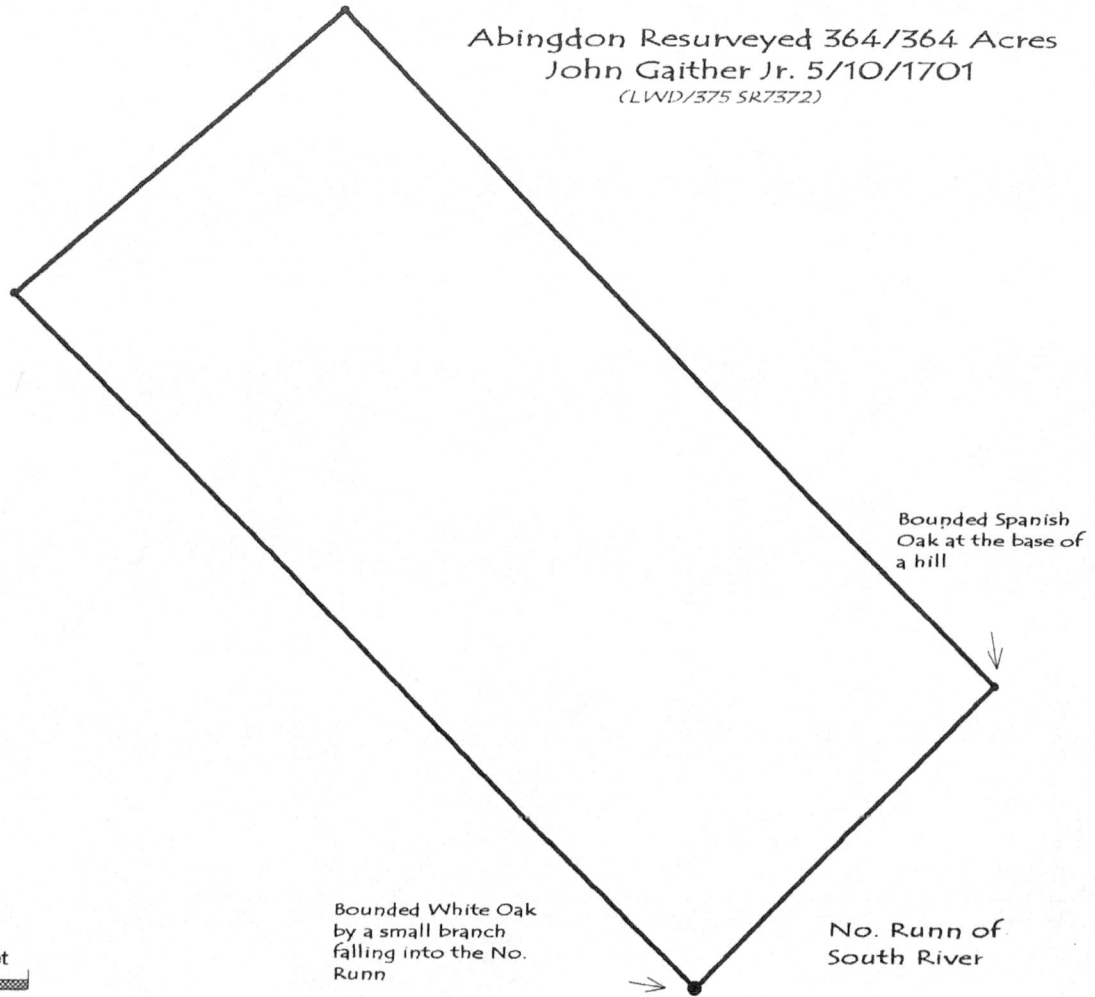

Bounded Spanish
Oak at the base of
a hill

Bounded White Oak
by a small branch
falling into the No.
Runn

No. Runn of
South River

1200.00 feet

1:14400

Ben's Discovery 380/386 Acres
Benjamin Warfield 1/2/1704
(LCD/181 SR7376)

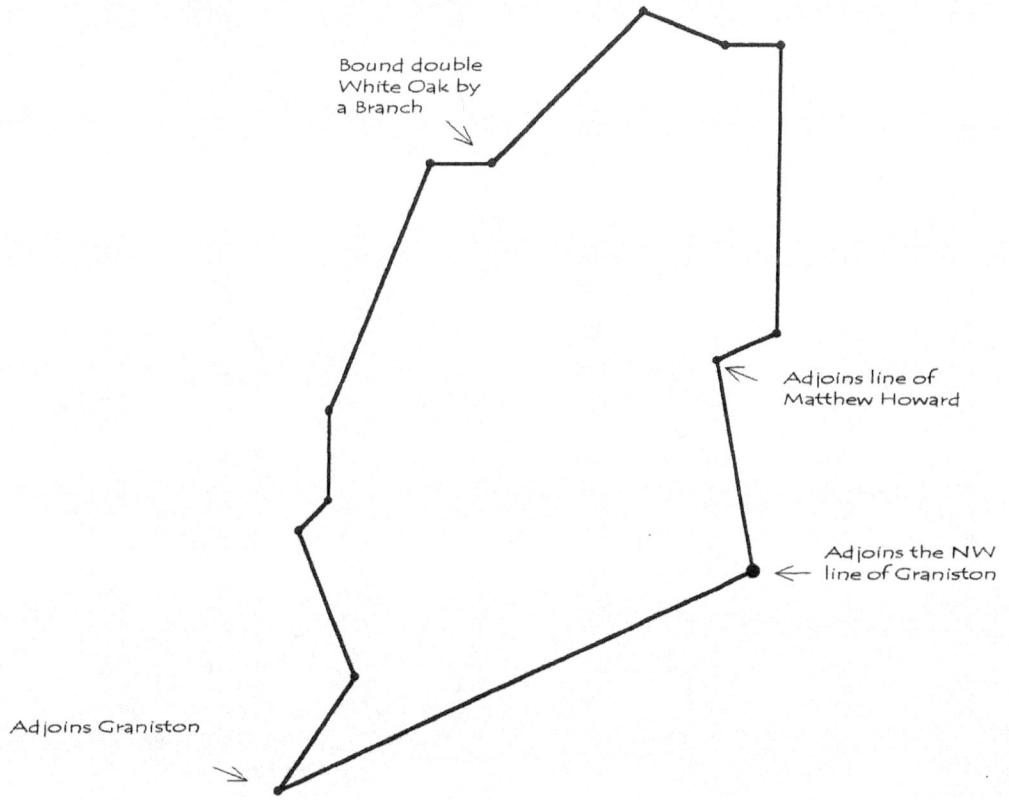

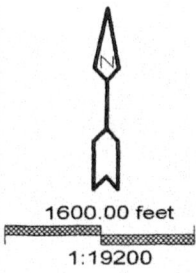

Bound double
White Oak by
a Branch

Adjoins line of
Matthew Howard

Adjoins the NW
line of Graniston

Adjoins Graniston

N

1600.00 feet

1:19200

Boyde's Chance 60/80 Acres
John Boyde 5/4/1685
(LNS2i/108 SR7371)

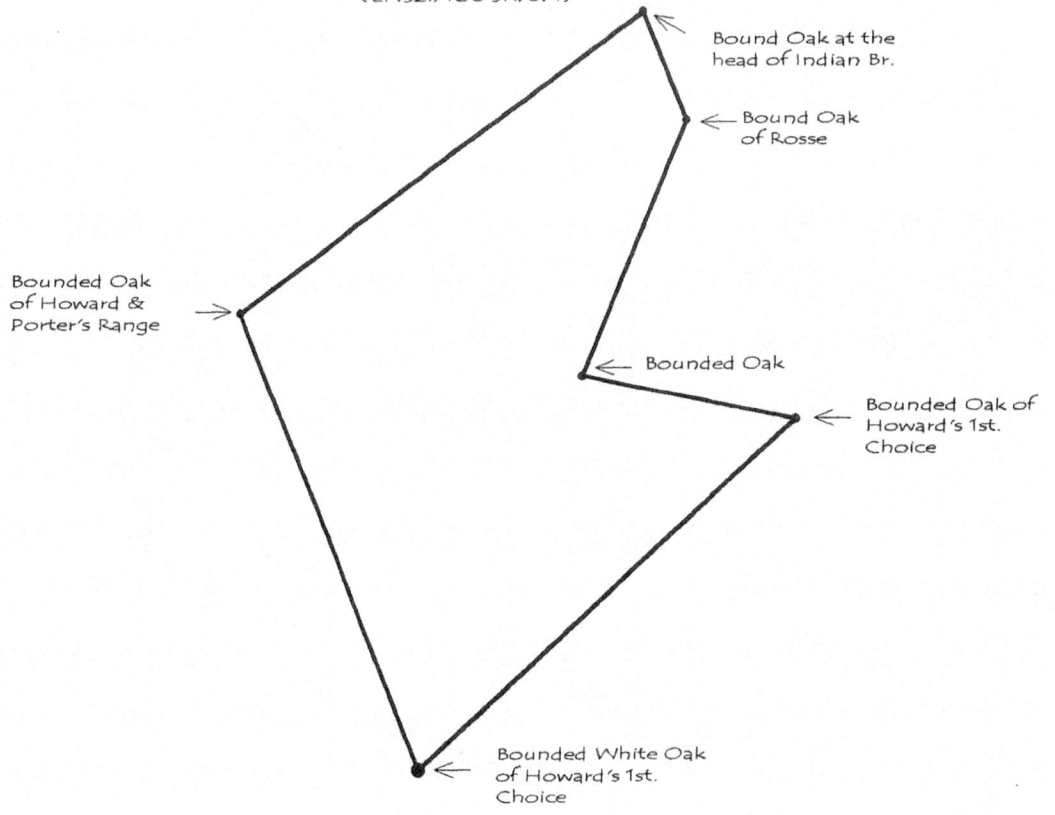

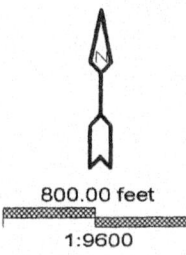

Bound Oak at the
head of Indian Br.

Bound Oak
of Rosse

Bounded Oak
of Howard &
Porter's Range

Bounded Oak

Bounded Oak of
Howard's 1st.
Choice

Bounded White Oak
of Howard's 1st.
Choice

800.00 feet

1:9600

Brandy 300/274 Acres
Richard Warfield 8/10/1683
(LCB3i/496 SR7367)

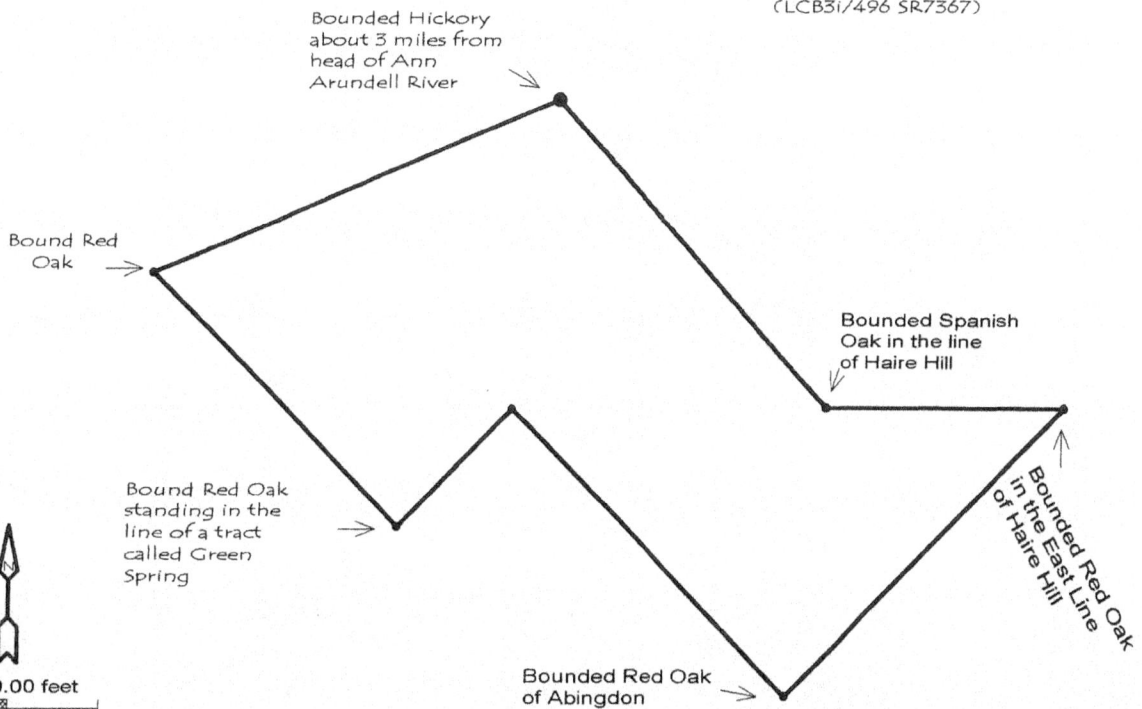

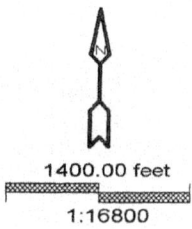

Bounded Hickory
about 3 miles from
head of Ann
Arundell River

Bound Red
Oak

Bounded Spanish
Oak in the line
of Haire Hill

Bound Red Oak
standing in the
line of a tract
called Green
Spring

Bounded Red Oak
in the East Line
of Haire Hill

Bounded Red Oak
of Abingdon

N

1400.00 feet
1:16800

Brooksby's Point 350/369 Acres
John Brooksby 7/7/1684
(LCB2i/257 SR7366)

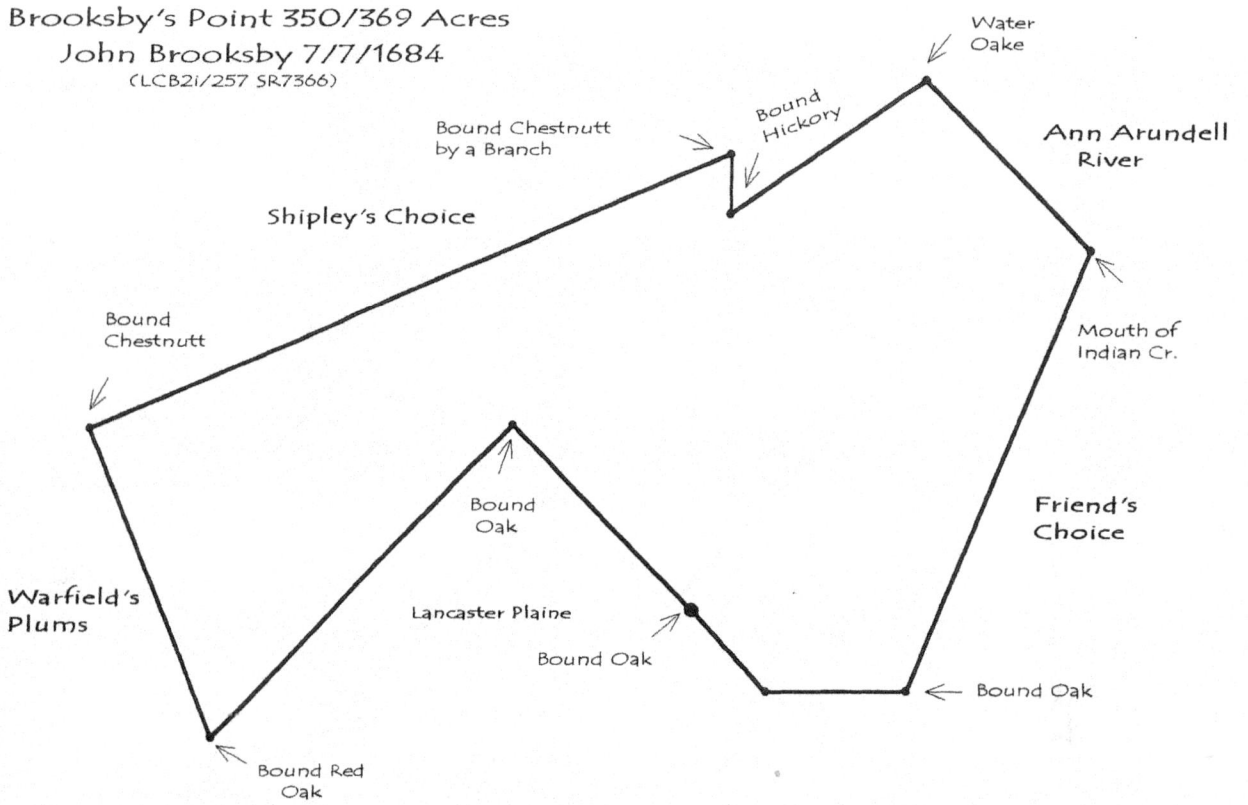

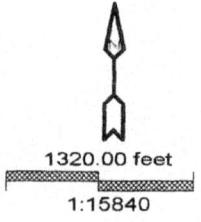

Water Oake

Bound Chestnutt
by a Branch

Bound Hickory

Ann Arundell River

Shipley's Choice

Bound Chestnutt

Mouth of Indian Cr.

Bound Oak

Friend's Choice

Warfield's Plums

Lancaster Plaine

Bound Oak

Bound Oak

Bound Red Oak

N

1320.00 feet
1:15840

Brownley 150/147 Acres
Thomas Brown 2/15/1659
(L4/452 SR7346)

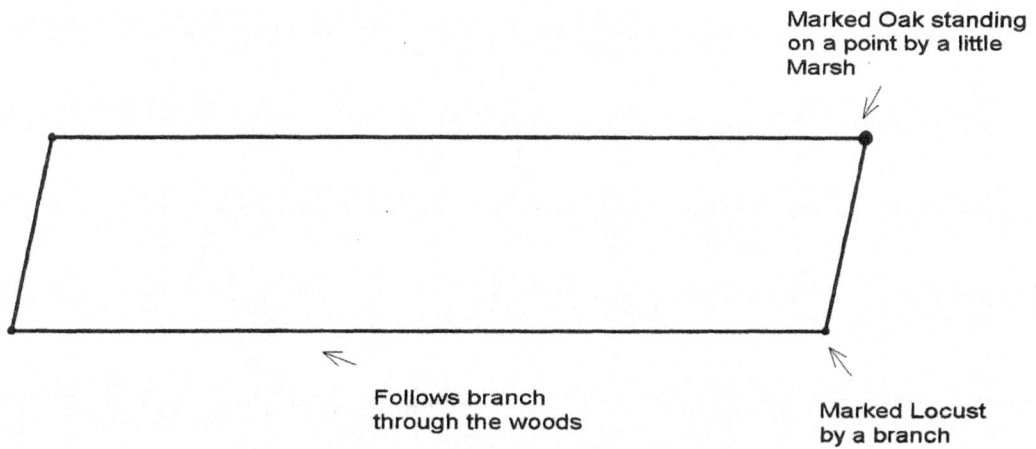

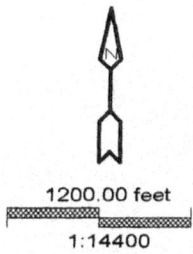

Marked Oak standing
on a point by a little
Marsh

Follows branch
through the woods

Marked Locust
by a branch

1200.00 feet

1:14400

Browne's Chance 98/98 Acres
Thomas Browne 10/1/1687
(LNSBi/489 SR7370)

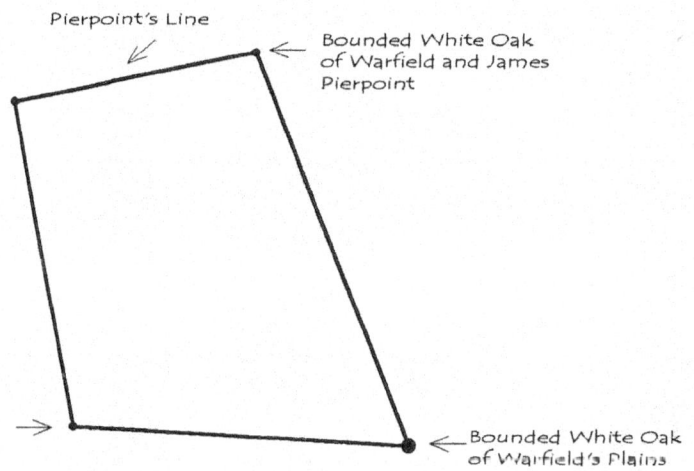

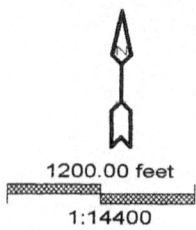

Pierpoint's Line

Bounded White Oak
of Warfield and James
Pierpoint

Bounded White Oak
of the March

Bounded White Oak
of Warfield's Plains

1200.00 feet
1:14400

Brown's Encrease 250/200 Acres
William Hopkins 8/8/1670
(Liber 13/31 SR7350)

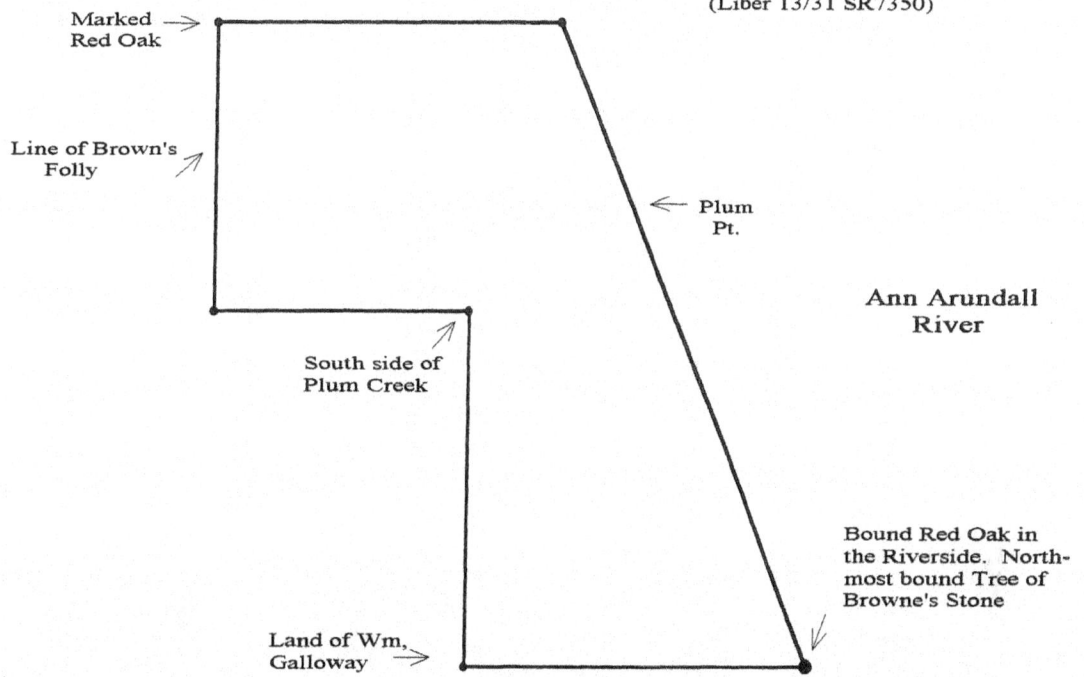

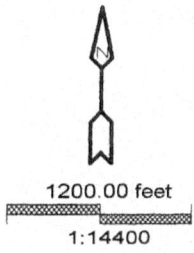

Marked
Red Oak →

Line of Brown's
Folly →

← Plum
Pt.

Ann Arundall
River

South side of
Plum Creek

1200.00 feet
1:14400

Bound Red Oak in
the Riverside. North-
most bound Tree of
Browne's Stone

Land of Wm,
Galloway →

Browne's Folly 270/257 Acres
Thomas Browne 7/1/1680
(LCB2i/13 SR7366)

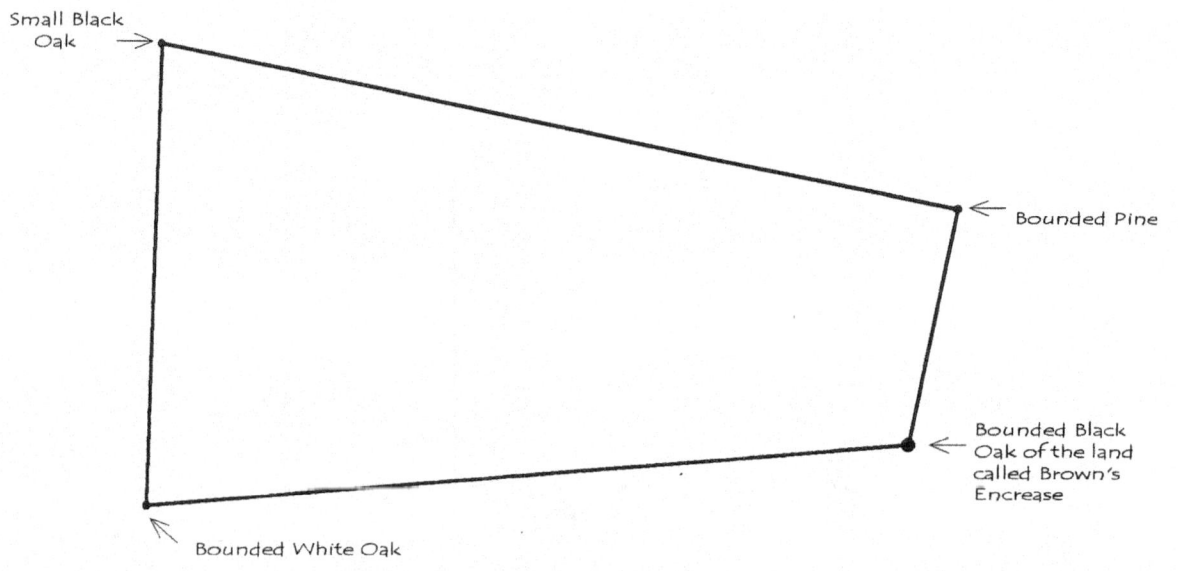

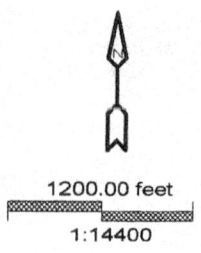

Small Black Oak

Bounded Pine

Bounded Black Oak of the land called Brown's Encrease

Bounded White Oak

1200.00 feet
1:14400

Brown's Forrest 387/519 Acres
Thomas Browne 3/10/1695
(LWD/129 SR7372-2)

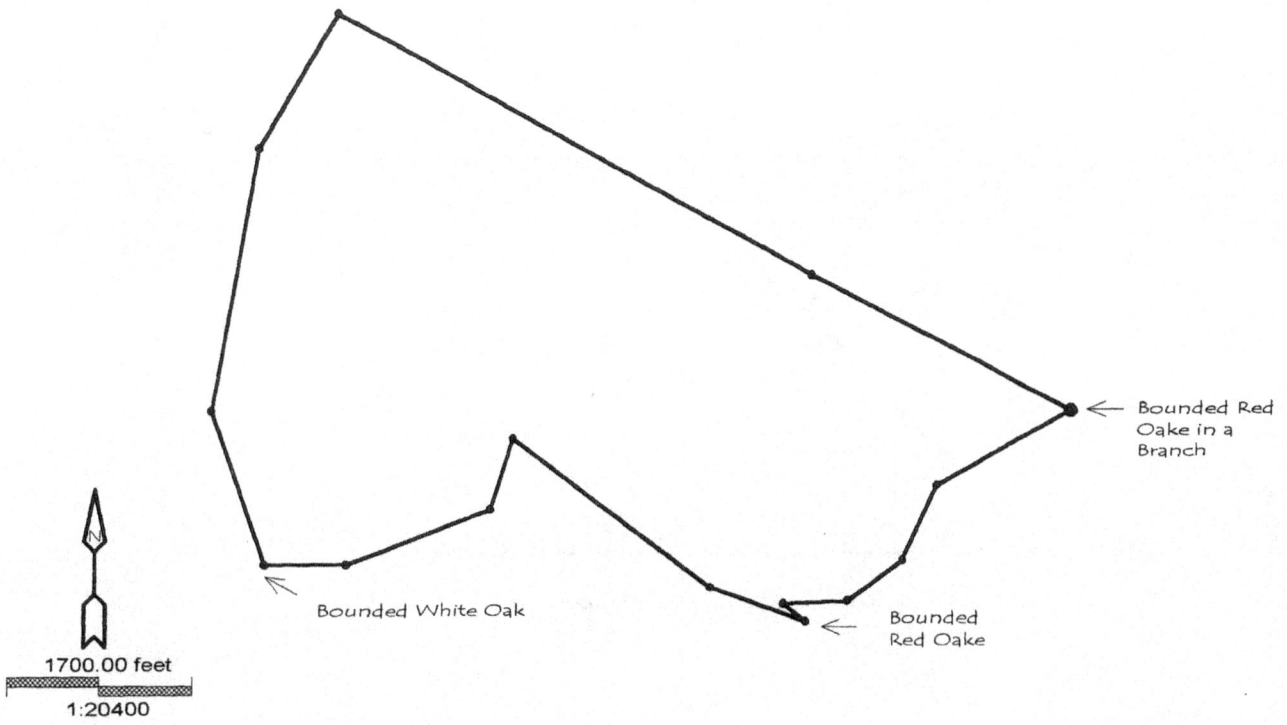

Bounded Red
Oake in a
Branch

Bounded White Oak

Bounded
Red Oake

1700.00 feet
1:20400

Brown's Peace 52/51 Acres
Thomas Browne 2/20/1677
(Liber 20/75 SR7361)

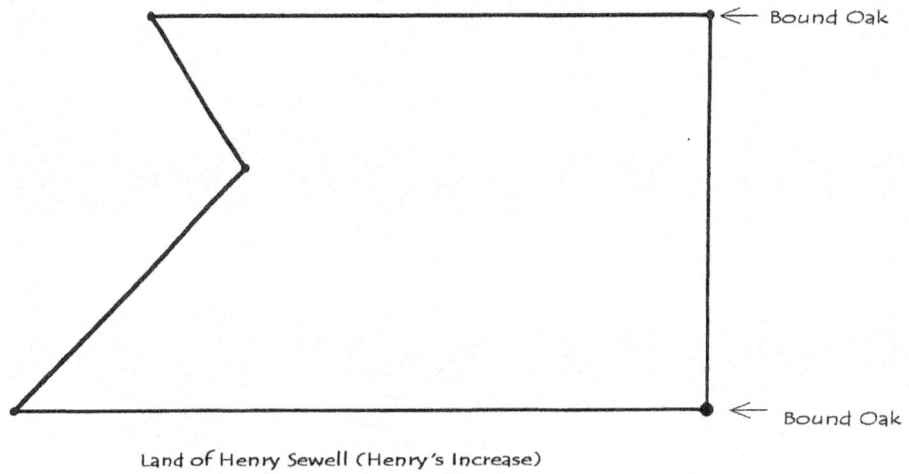

← Bound Oak

← Bound Oak

Land of Henry Sewell (Henry's Increase)

600.00 feet

1:7200

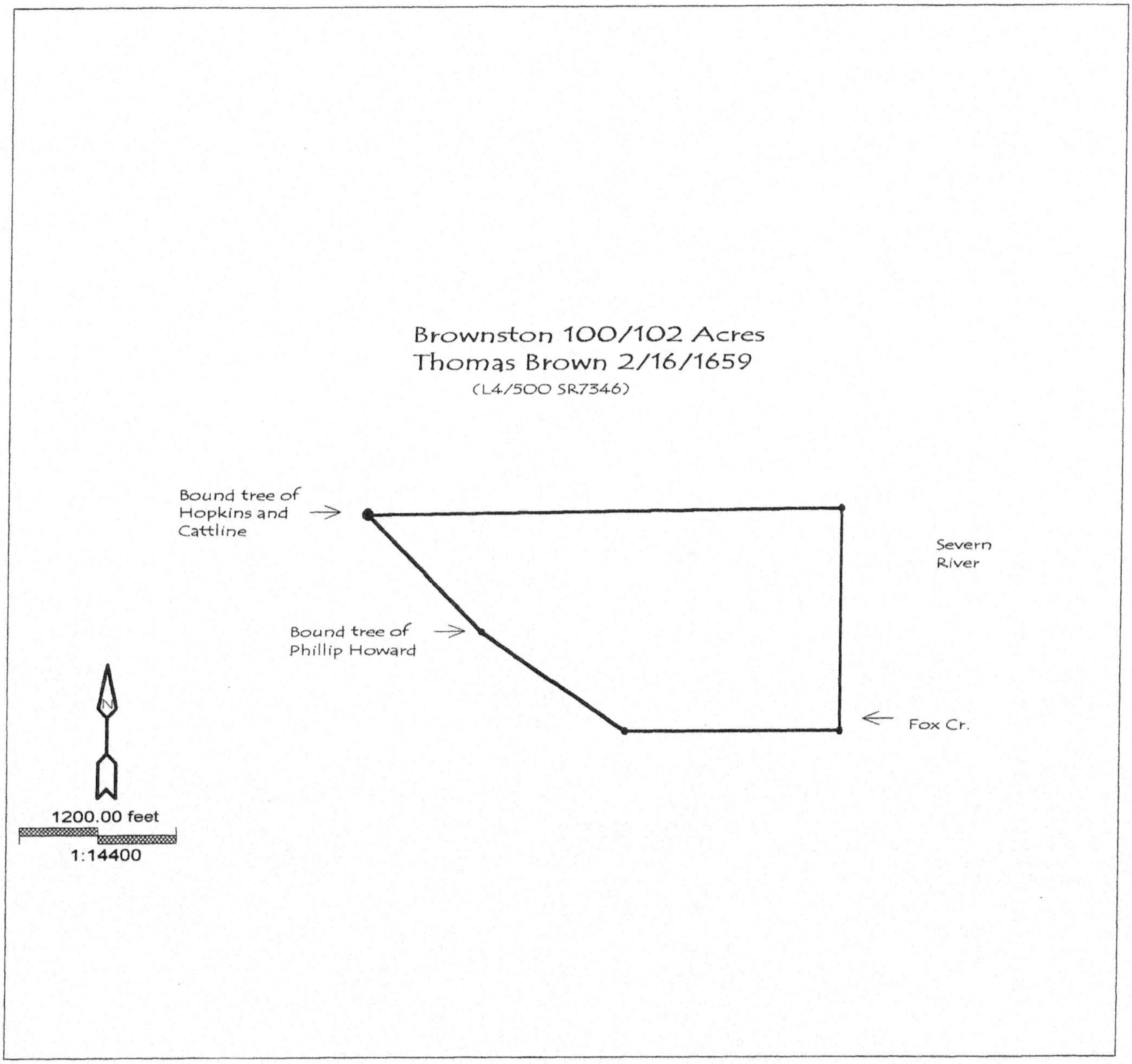

Brownston 100/102 Acres
Thomas Brown 2/16/1659
(L4/500 SR7346)

Bound tree of
Hopkins and
Cattline

Severn
River

Bound tree of
Phillip Howard

Fox Cr.

1200.00 feet
1:14400

Bruton 50/58 Acres
John Bruton 6/1664 (Cert)
(L9/114 SR7351)

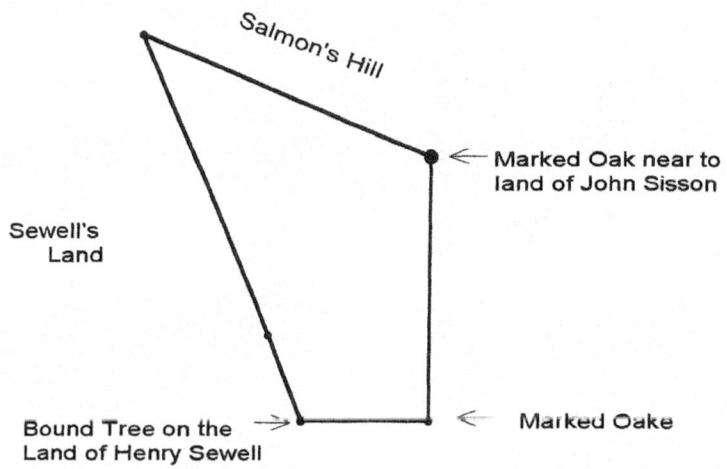

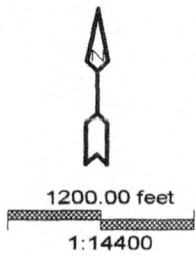

Salmon's Hill

← Marked Oak near to
land of John Sisson

Sewell's
Land

Bound Tree on the →
Land of Henry Sewell

← Marked Oake

1200.00 feet

1:14400

Bruton Grimes 150/139 Acres
John Burton and William Grimes 1664
(Liber 9/114 SR7351)

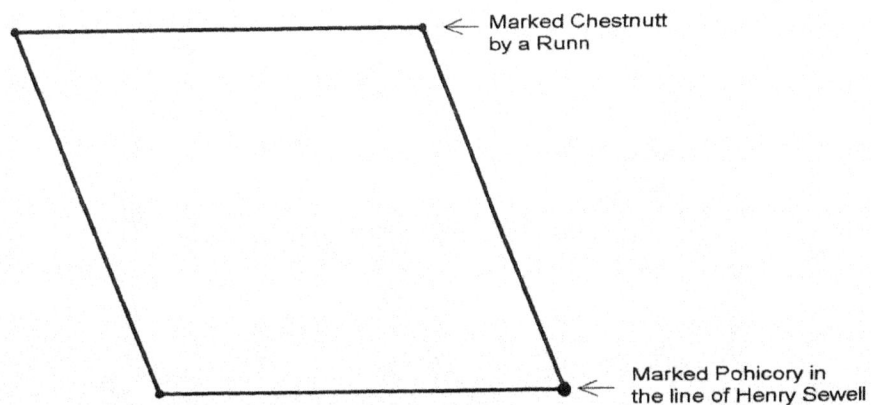

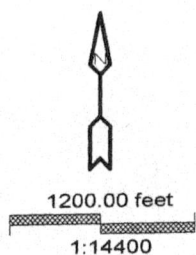

← Marked Chestnutt
by a Runn

← Marked Pohicory in
the line of Henry Sewell

1200.00 feet
1:14400

Chance 203/222 Acres
Chas. Carroll 3/30/1705
(LDD5i/442 SR7378)

Bound White Oak of
Abingdon by a Branch
falling in the So. Runn

Line of Herford

Bound Tree of
Herford

North Br.

Adjoins Freeman's
Fancy

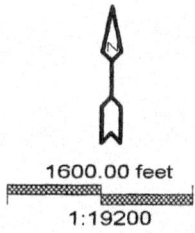

1600.00 feet
1:19200

Chilton 40/40 Acres
Abraham Child 9/10/1683
(LSDA/49 SR7369)

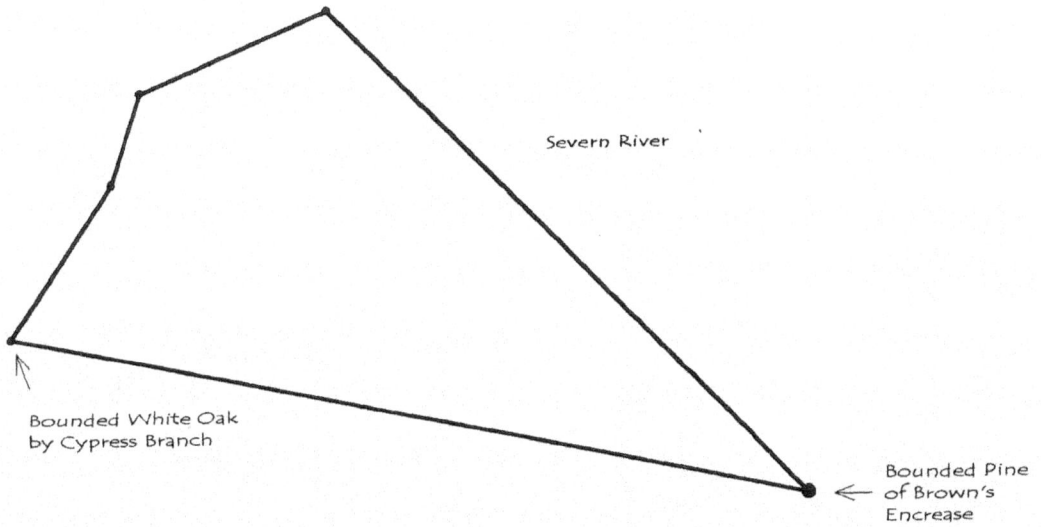

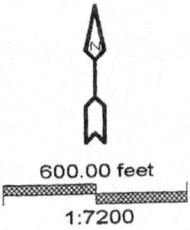

Severn River

Bounded White Oak
by Cypress Branch

Bounded Pine
of Brown's
Encrease

N

600.00 feet

1:7200

Clinke 100/100 Acres
William Galloway 1/8/1659
(L4/430 SR7376)

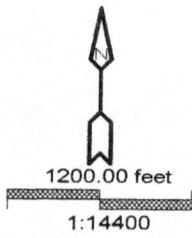

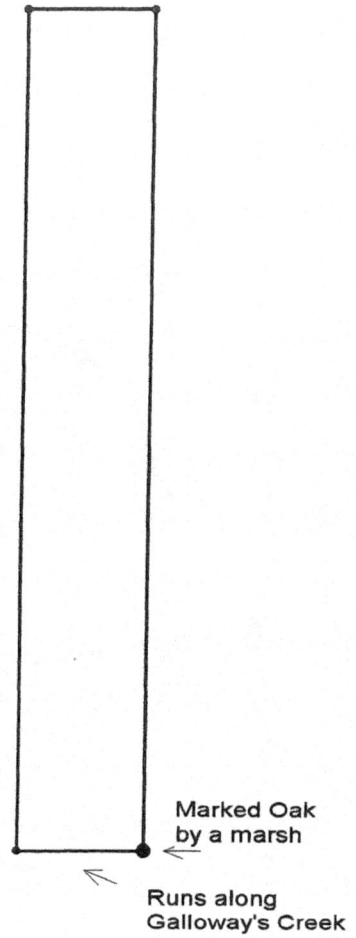

1200.00 feet
1:14400

Marked Oak
by a marsh

Runs along
Galloway's Creek

Cordwell 300/296 Acres
John Merriott 10/5/1680
(LCB3i/511 SR7367)

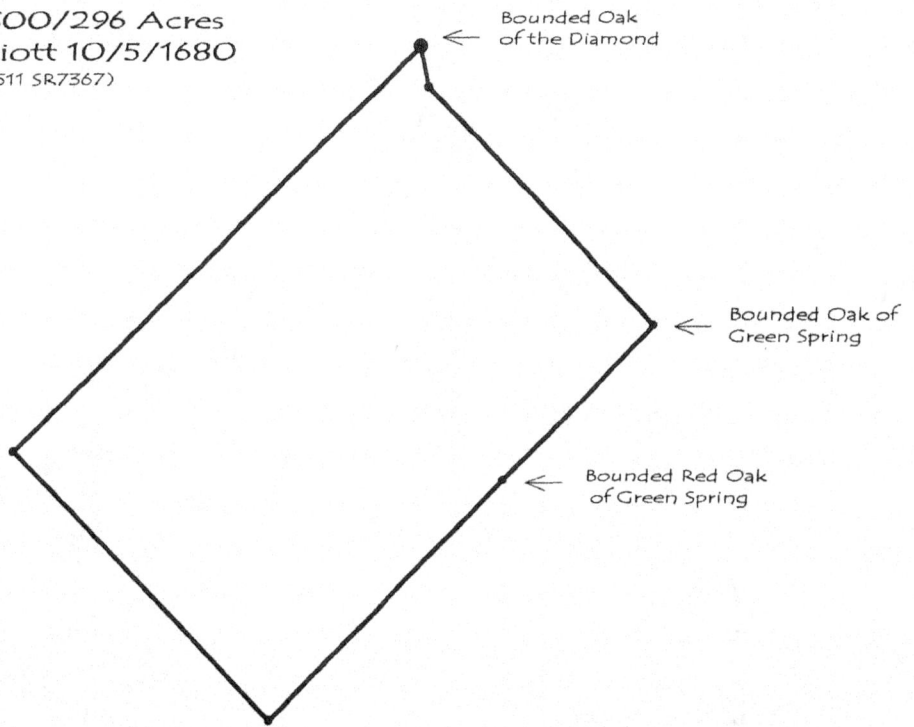

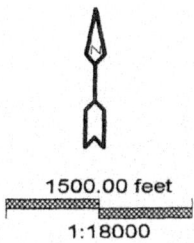

Bounded Oak
of the Diamond

Bounded Oak of
Green Spring

Bounded Red Oak
of Green Spring

1500.00 feet

1:18000

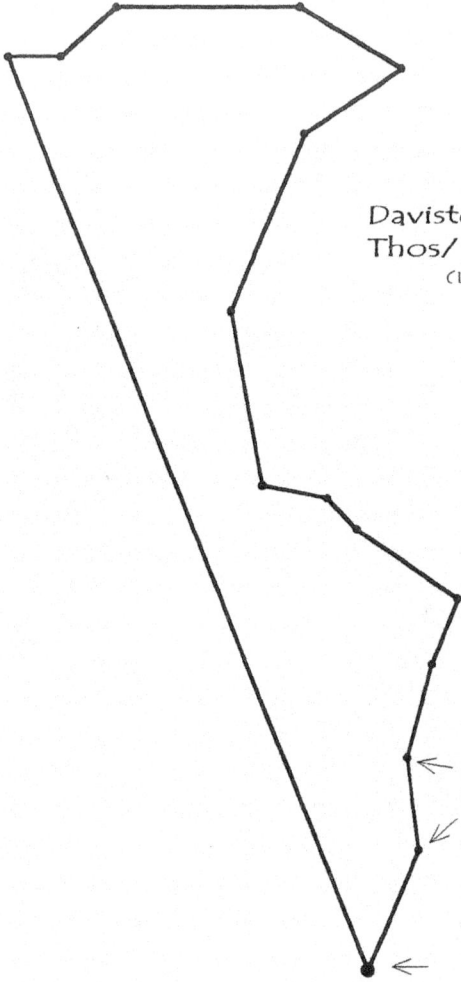

Davistone 240/240 Acres
Thos/ Davis 10/17/1701
(LDD5i/136 SR7378)

Bounded White Oak
by a branch

Bound White Oak at
the South SW boundary
of Greeniston

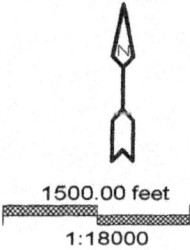

1500.00 feet

1:18000

Dryer's Inheritance 254/257 Acres
Samuel Dryer 3/10/1695
LC3i/334 SR7377)

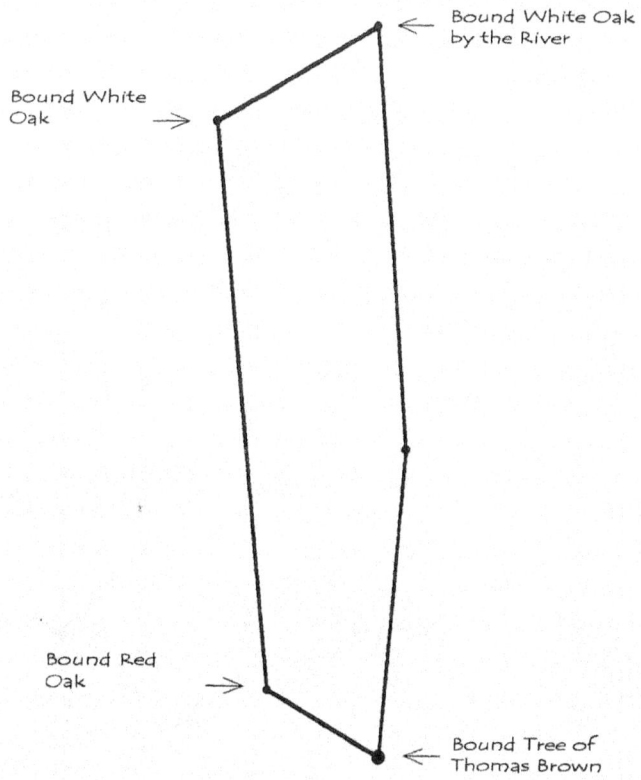

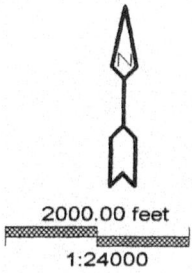

Bound White Oak
by the River

Bound White
Oak

Bound Red
Oak

Bound Tree of
Thomas Brown

2000.00 feet

1:24000

Green Spring 200/198 Acres
Robert Proctor 2/20/1673
(L15/147 SR4327)

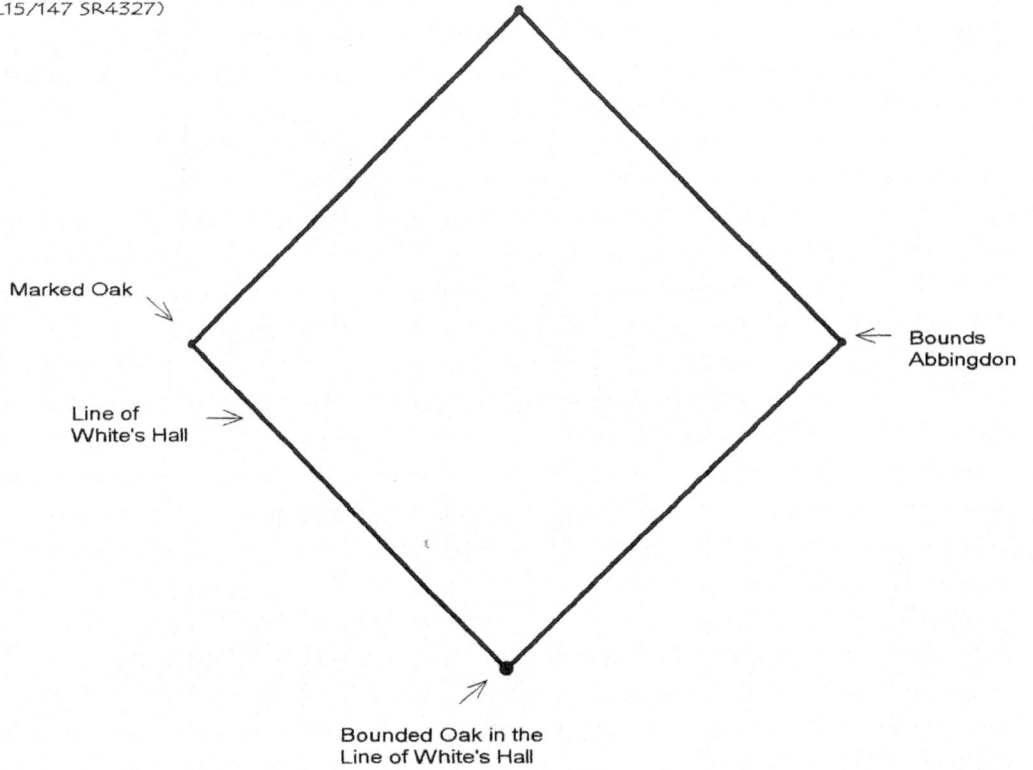

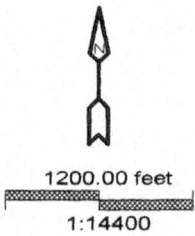

Marked Oak

Bounds
Abbingdon

Line of
White's Hall

1200.00 feet
1:14400

Bounded Oak in the
Line of White's Hall

Greeniston 700/1,071 Acres
Nicholas Painter 5/22/1683
(LSDA/353 SR7369)

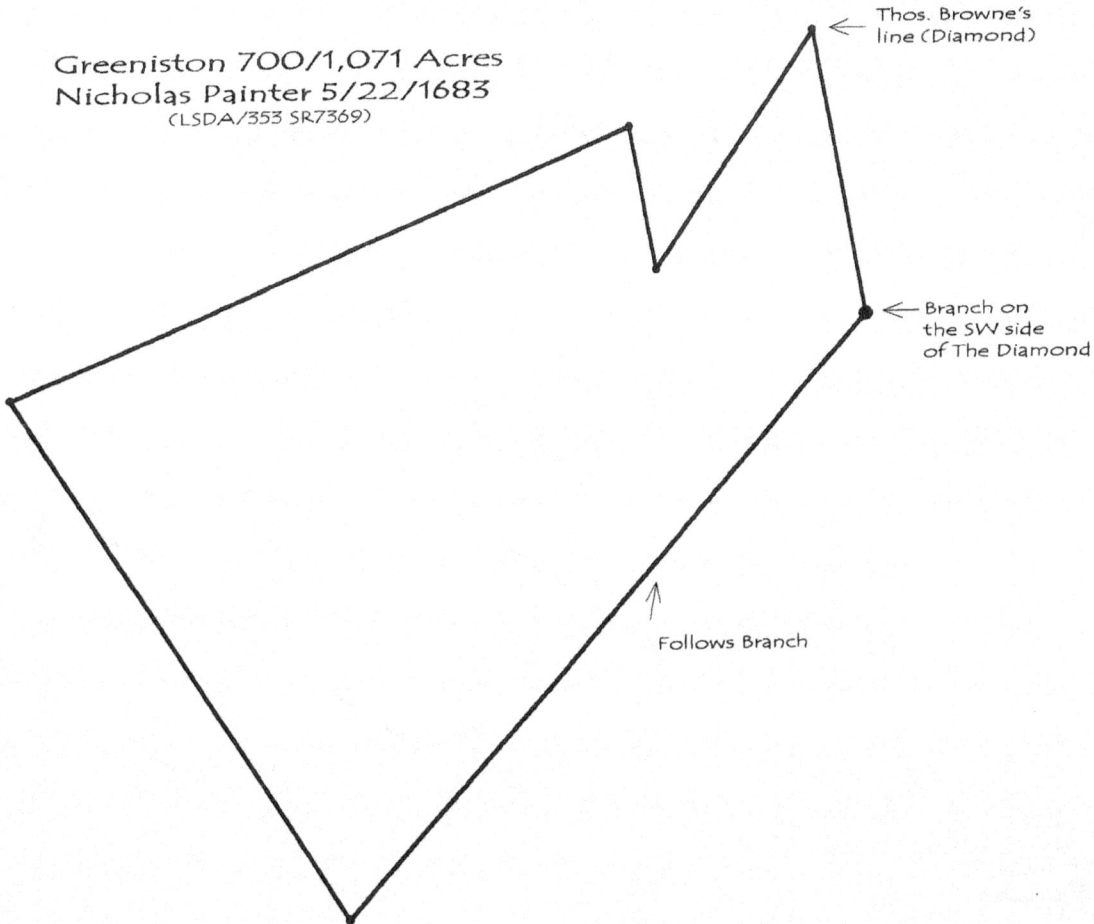

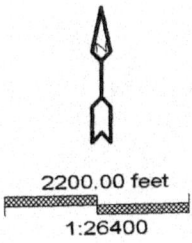

Thos. Browne's
line (Diamond)

Branch on
the SW side
of The Diamond

Follows Branch

2200.00 feet
1:26400

Grime's Addition 100/81 Acres
William Grimes 9/10/1672
(L17/291 SR7358)

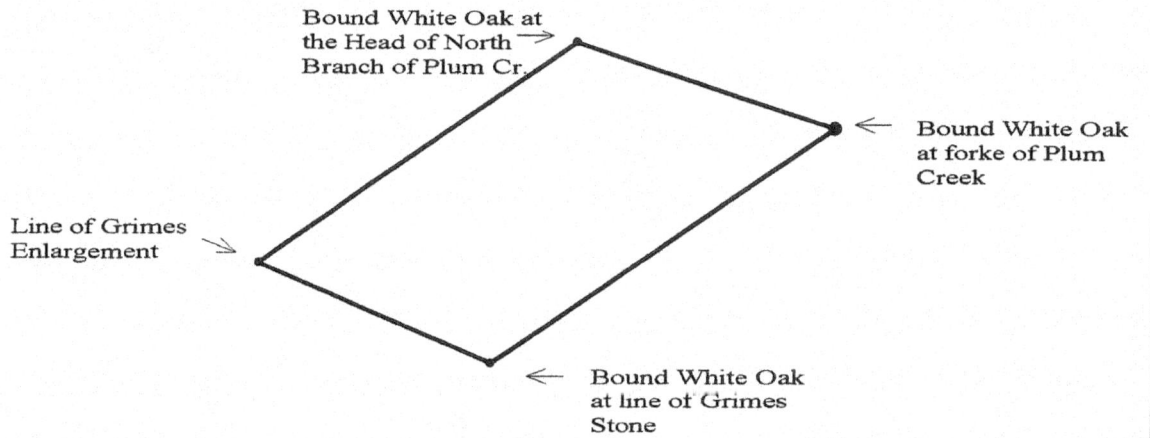

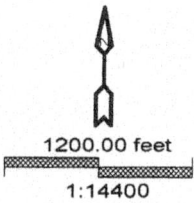

Bound White Oak at
the Head of North →
Branch of Plum Cr.

← Bound White Oak
at forke of Plum
Creek

Line of Grimes
Enlargement →

← Bound White Oak
at line of Grimes
Stone

1200.00 feet
1:14400

Grimes Enlargement 187/186 Acres
William Grimes 11/10/1695
(LWD/105 SR7372-2)

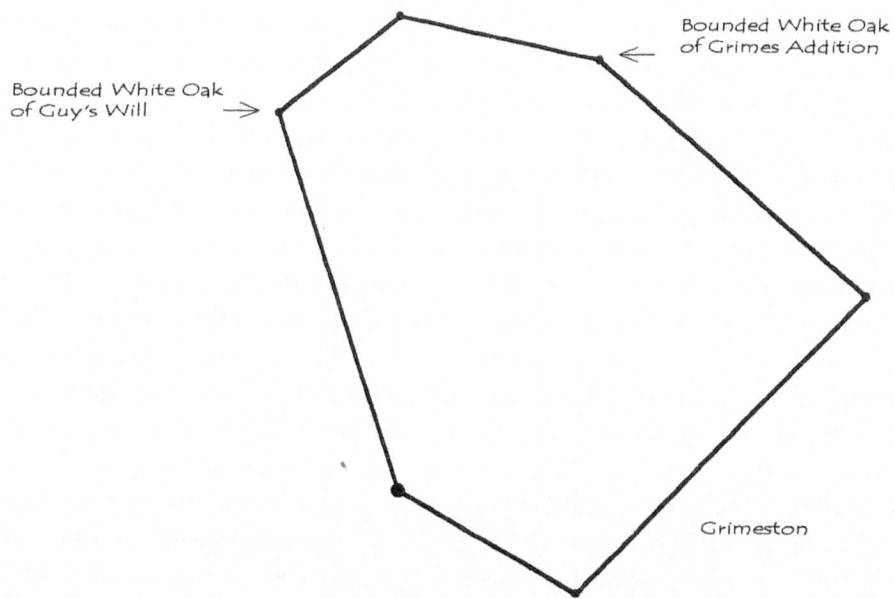

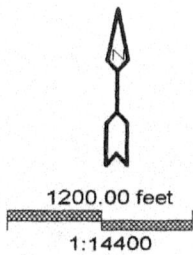

Bounded White Oak
of Grimes Addition

Bounded White Oak
of Guy's Will

Grimeston

1200.00 feet

1:14400

Grimeston 100/98 Acres
William Grimes 8/25/1665
(L8/153 SR7350)

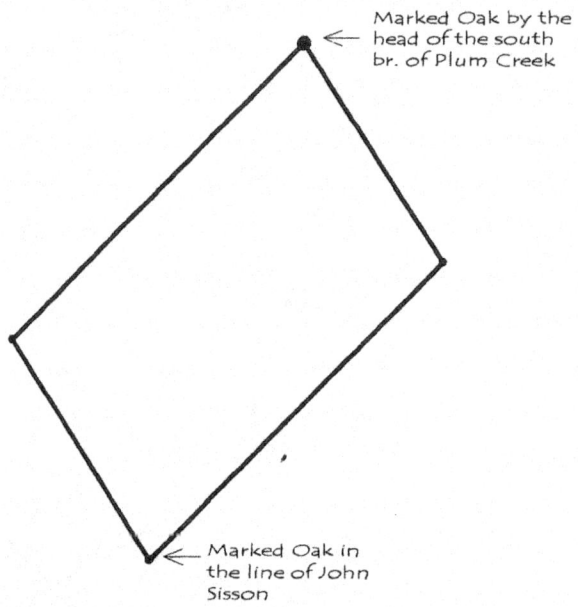

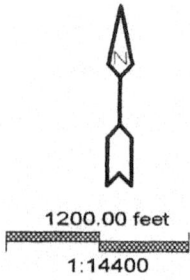

Marked Oak by the
← head of the south
br. of Plum Creek

N

Marked Oak in
← the line of John
Sisson

1200.00 feet
1:14400

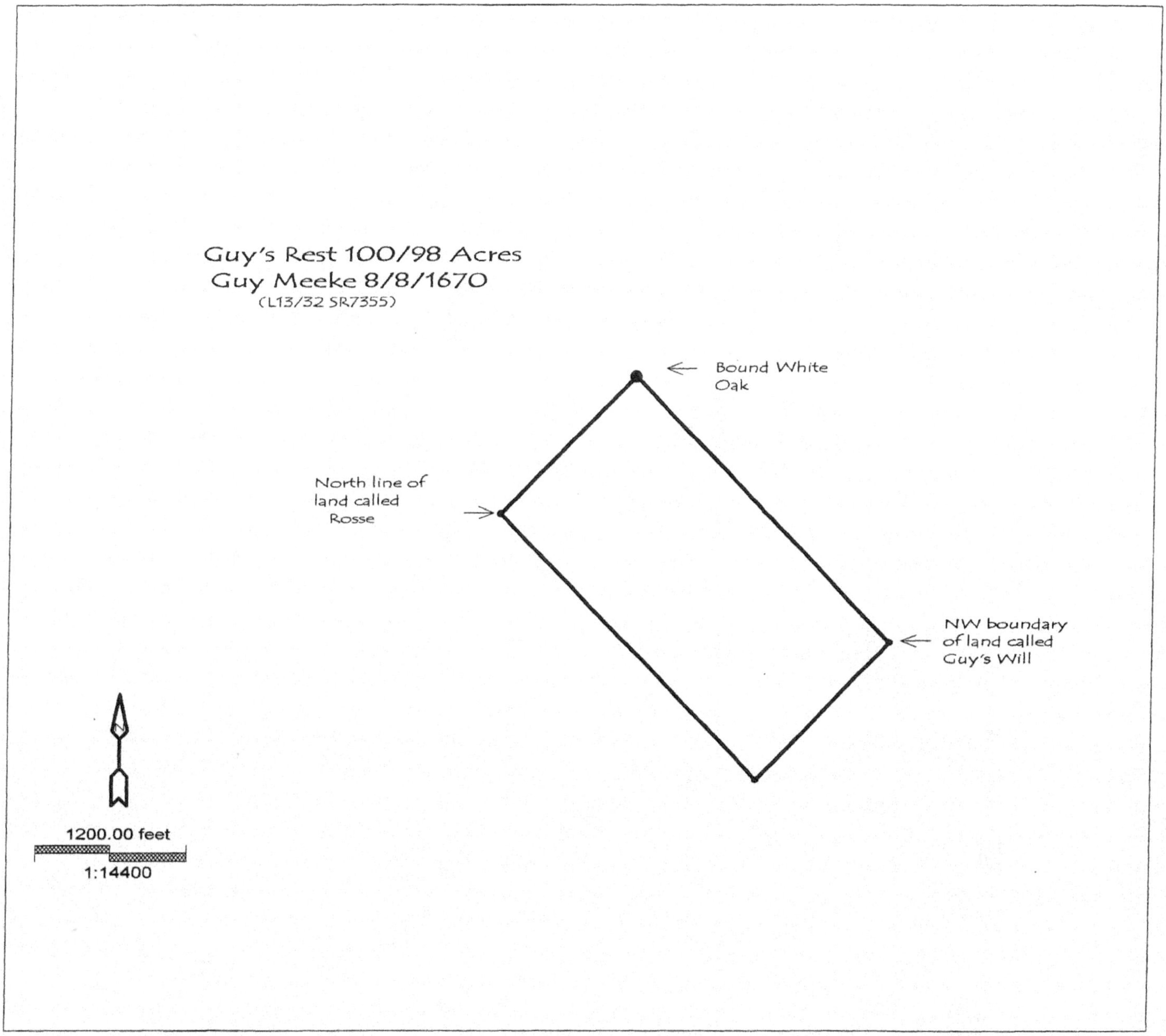

Guy's Rest 100/98 Acres
Guy Meeke 8/8/1670
(L13/32 SR7355)

← Bound White
Oak

North line of
land called
Rosse →

← NW boundary
of land called
Guy's Will

1200.00 feet
1:14400

Guy's Will 100/92 Acres
Guy Meeke 5/1/1672
(L14/464 SR7356)

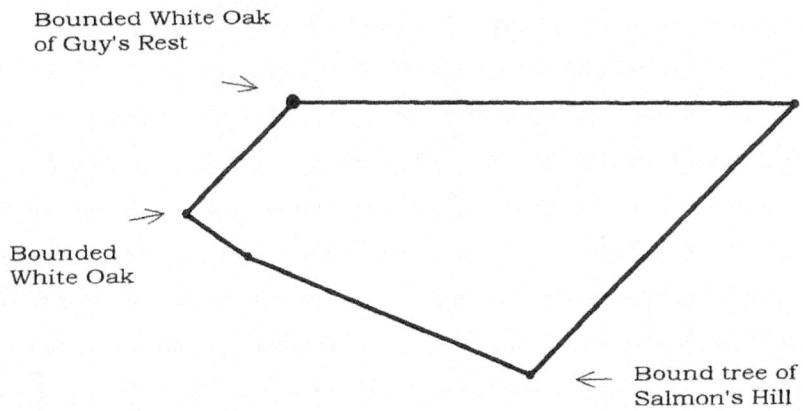

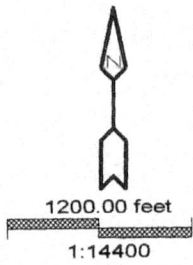

Bounded White Oak
of Guy's Rest

Bounded
White Oak

Bound tree of
Salmon's Hill

1200.00 feet

1:14400

Hammond's Forrest 362/382 Acres
Maj. John Hammond 5/1/1696
(LWD/141 SR7372-2)

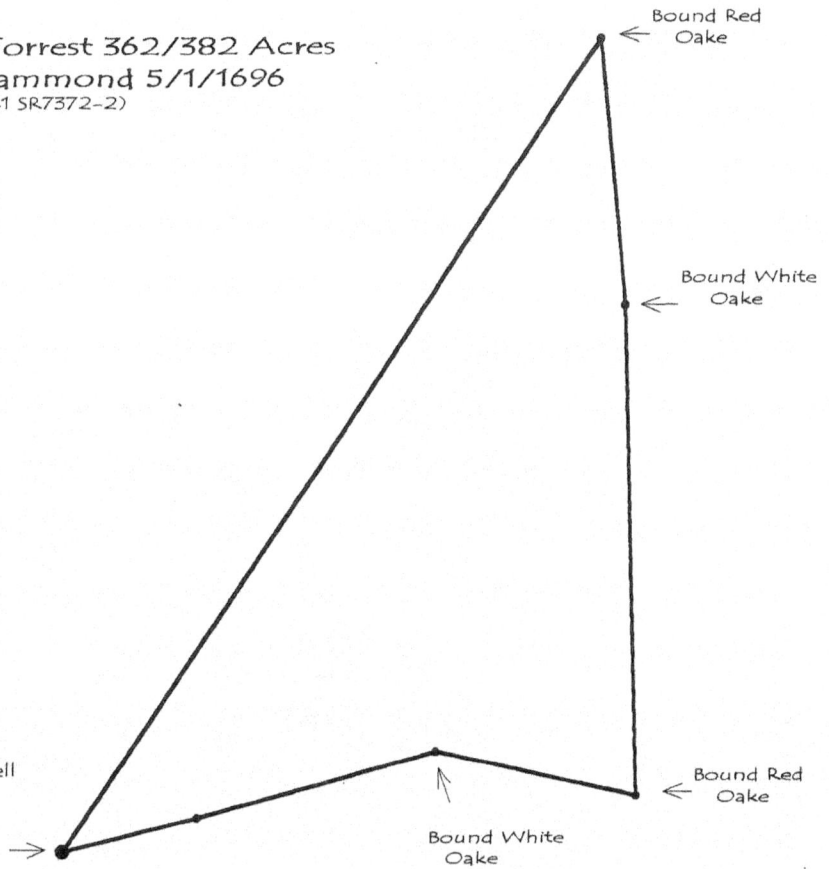

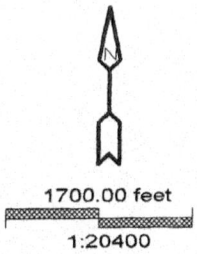

Bound Red
Oake ←

Bound White
Oake ←

Bound Red
Oake ←

Bound White
Oake ↑

N

1700.00 feet

1:20400

Bound Pine at the
head of Branches
of the Ann Arundell
River →

Hare Hill 100/102 Acres
Peter Porter 9/11/1674
(Liber 18/254 SR7359)

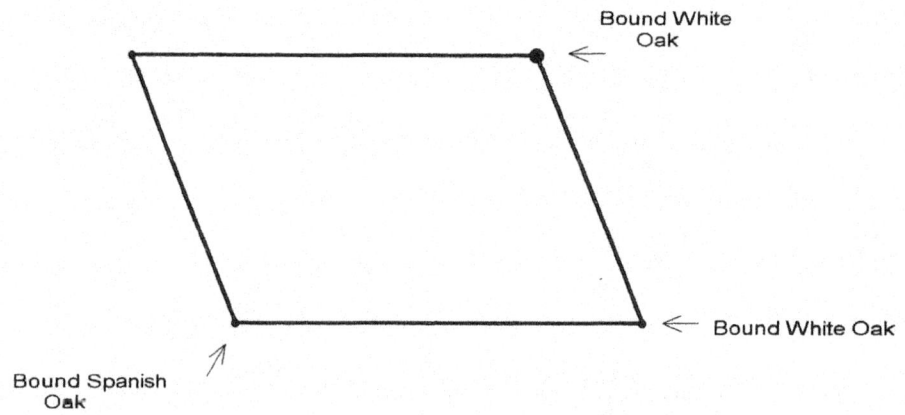

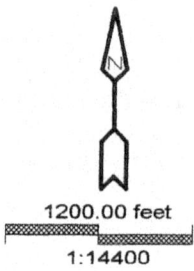

Bound White
Oak

← Bound White Oak

Bound Spanish
Oak

1200.00 feet

1:14400

Harrisses Beginning 122/139 Acres
John Harris 11/10/1695
(L23/260 SR7364)

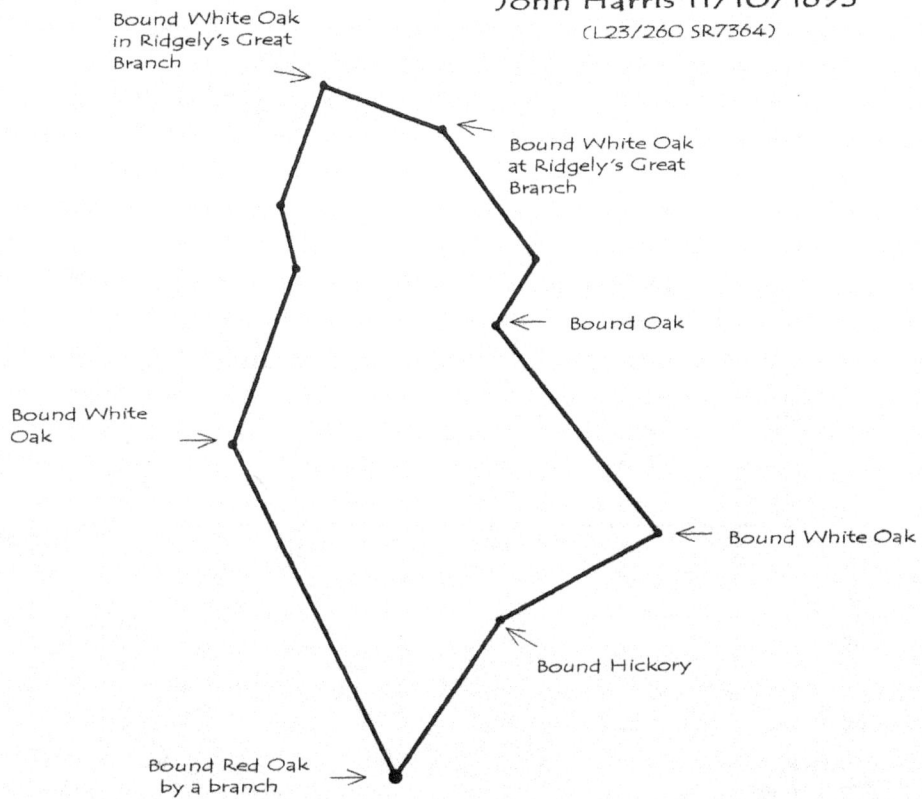

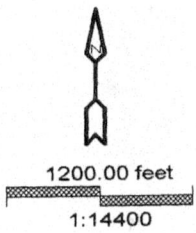

Bound White Oak
in Ridgely's Great
Branch

Bound White Oak
at Ridgely's Great
Branch

Bound Oak

Bound White
Oak

Bound White Oak

Bound Hickory

Bound Red Oak
by a branch

N

1200.00 feet
1:14400

Henry's Addition 30/30 Acres
Henry Sewell 4/14/1673
(L17/504 SR7358)

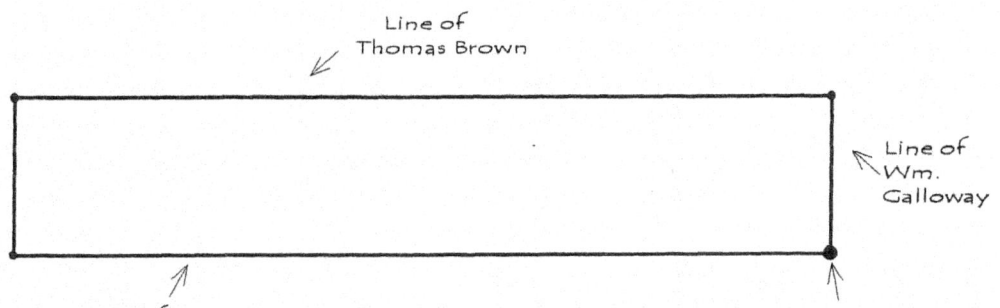

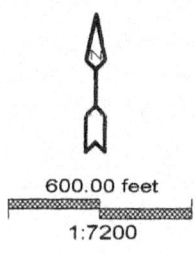

Line of
Thomas Brown

Line of
Wm.
Galloway

Line of
Elizabeth
Sisson

Bound Red Oak
bounding Round
Bay

600.00 feet
1:7200

Henry's Encrease 43/43 Acres
Henry Sewell 7/1/1680
(LCB2i/41 SR7366)

Thomas Brown's Line

Bounded Red Oak
of Thomas Brown

Bounded
Red Oak

Bound White
Oak on a hill

Bound Chestnutt
of Charles' Stevens
land

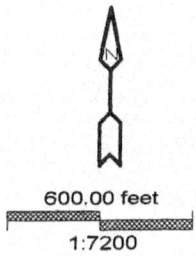

600.00 feet
1:7200

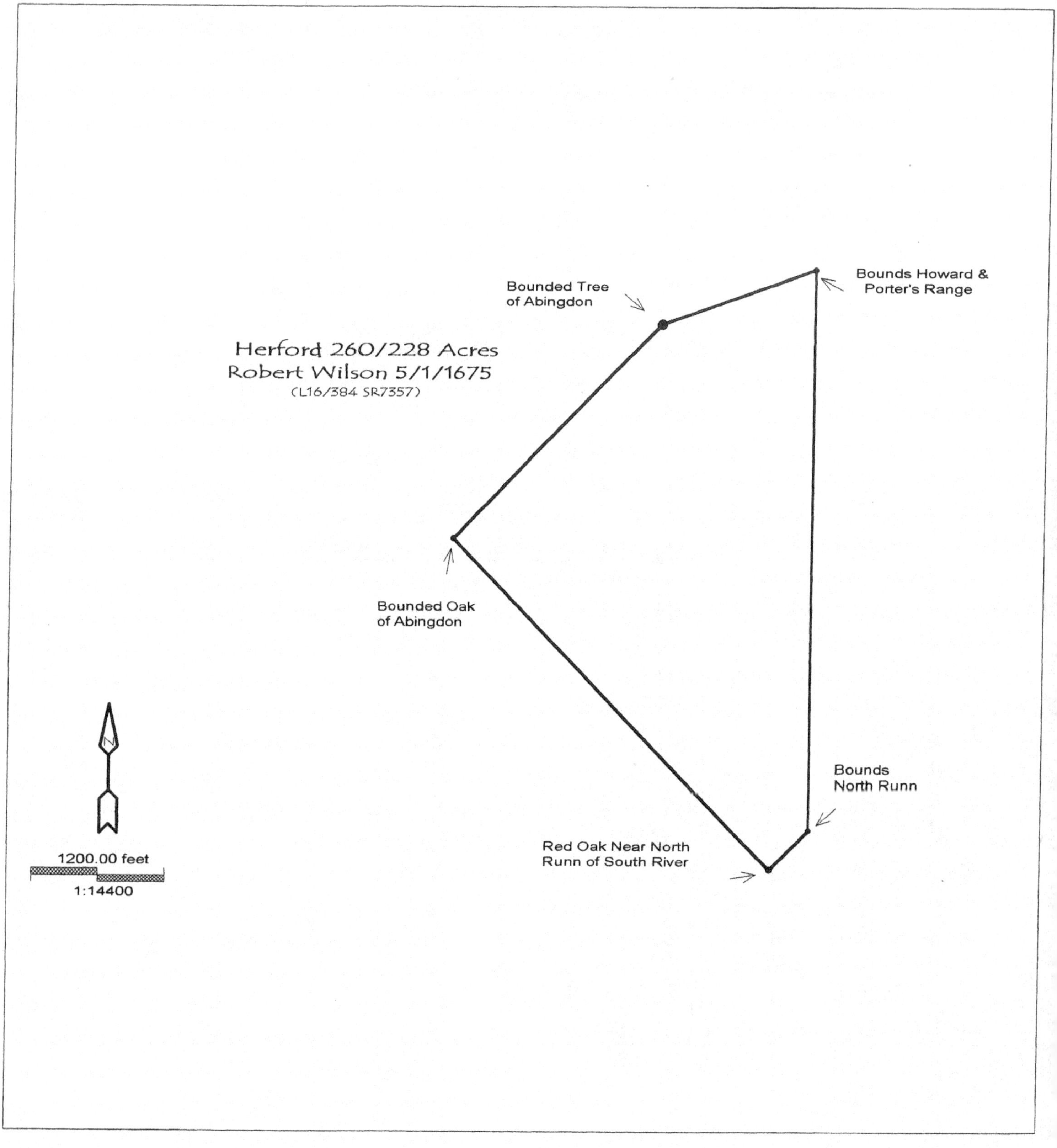

Herford 260/228 Acres
Robert Wilson 5/1/1675
(L16/384 SR7357)

Bounded Tree
of Abingdon

Bounds Howard &
Porter's Range

Bounded Oak
of Abingdon

Bounds
North Runn

Red Oak Near North
Runn of South River

1200.00 feet

1:14400

Hicory Ridge 262/265 Acres
Charles Stevens 11/10/1695
(L23/255 SR7364)

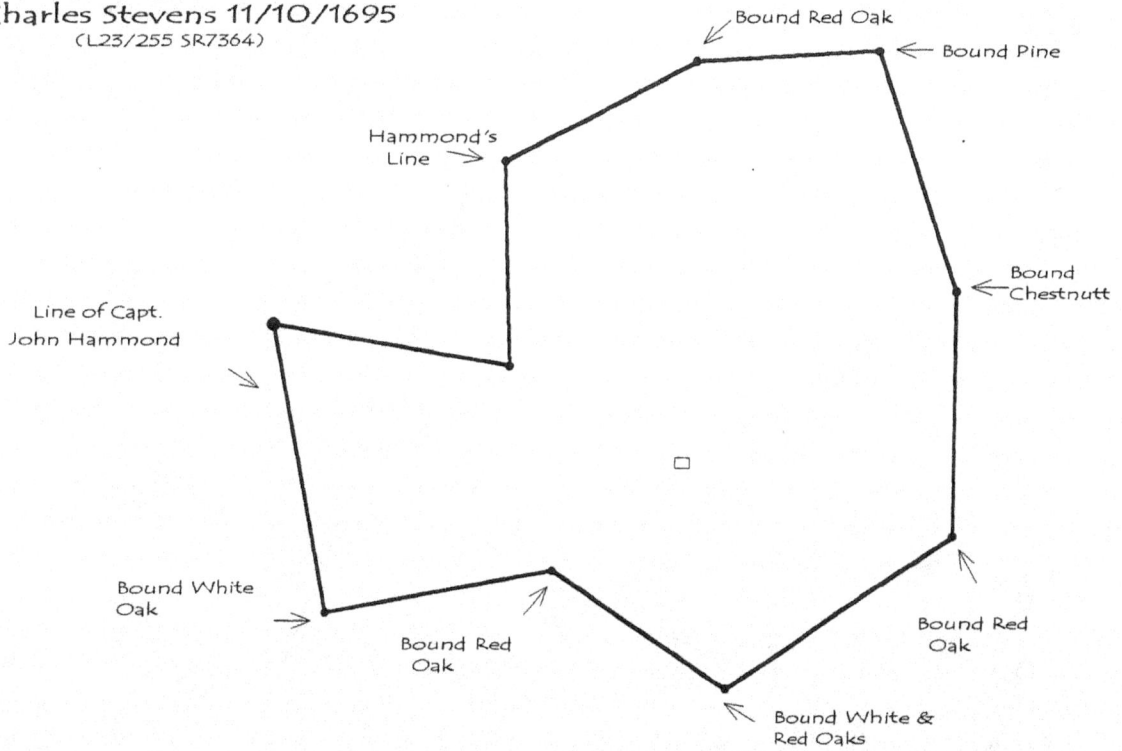

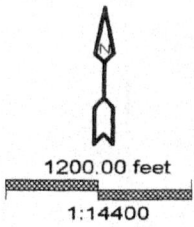

Bound Red Oak
Bound Pine

Hammond's Line

Bound Chestnutt

Line of Capt. John Hammond

Bound White Oak

Bound Red Oak

Bound Red Oak

Bound White & Red Oaks

N

1200.00 feet
1:14400

Howard & Porter's Fancy 333/316 Acres
Cornelius Howard 6/13/1668

(Liber 12/30 SR7354)

Bounded Popler
of Howard &
Porter's Range

Bound Red
Oak

Follows
Branch

Great Branch
Side

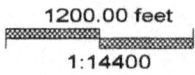

1200.00 feet
1:14400

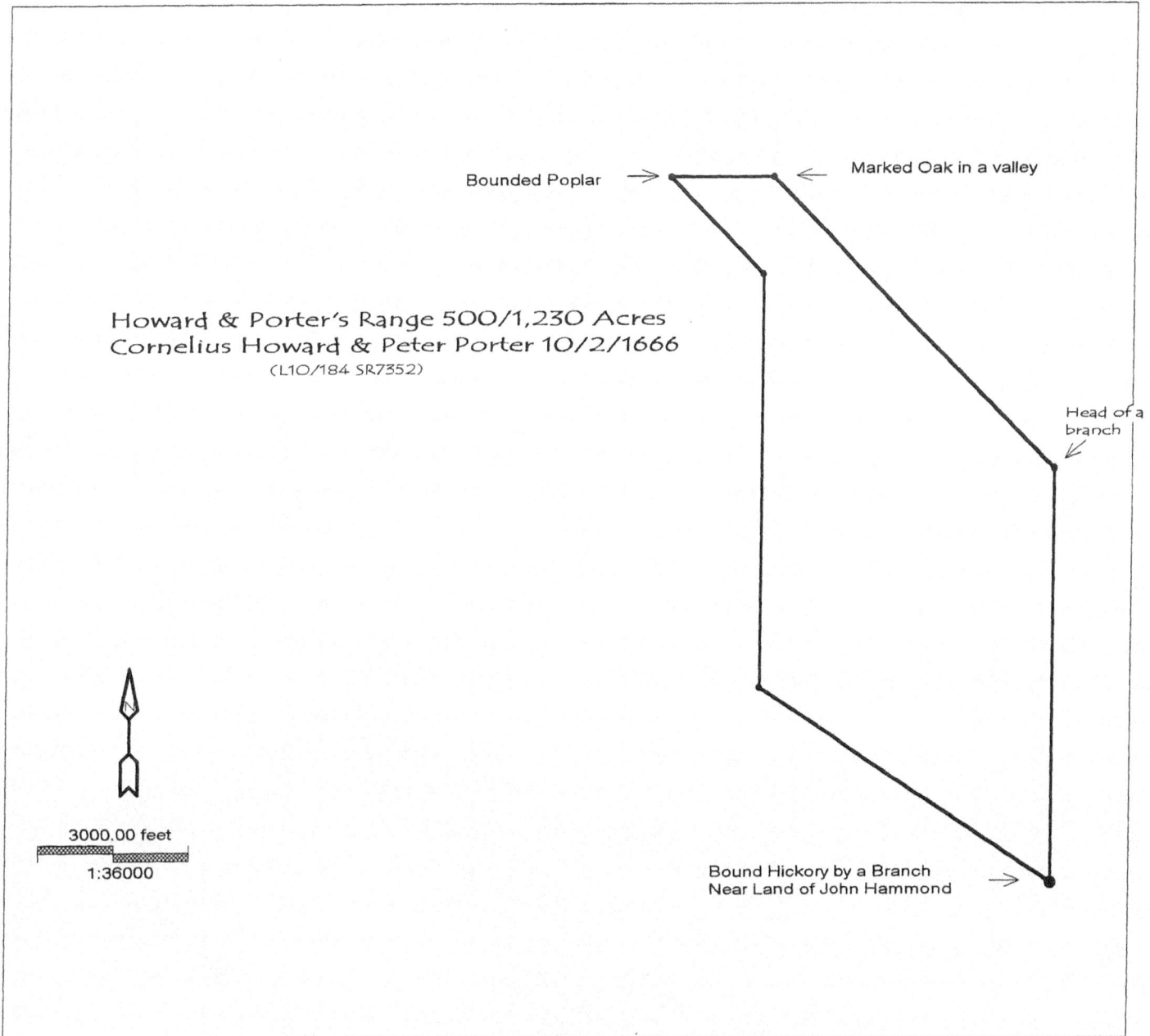

Bounded Poplar →

← Marked Oak in a valley

Howard & Porter's Range 500/1,230 Acres
Cornelius Howard & Peter Porter 10/2/1666
(L10/184 SR7352)

Head of a
branch
↙

3000.00 feet

1:36000

Bound Hickory by a Branch
Near Land of John Hammond →

Bounded Tree of
Howard's Addition
& The Mayden

Bounded Gum by
No. Runn of
South River

Howard's Addition 70/72 Acres
Phillip Howard 8/10/1685
(LNS2i/113 SR7371)

N

1200.00 feet

1:14400

Bound Hickory of
Howard & Porter's
Range standing by
the North Runn of
South River

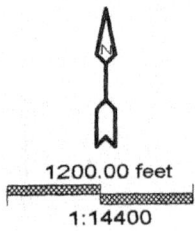

Howard's Adventure 500/502 Acres
Matthew Howard 8/10/1683
(LCB3i/374 SR7367)

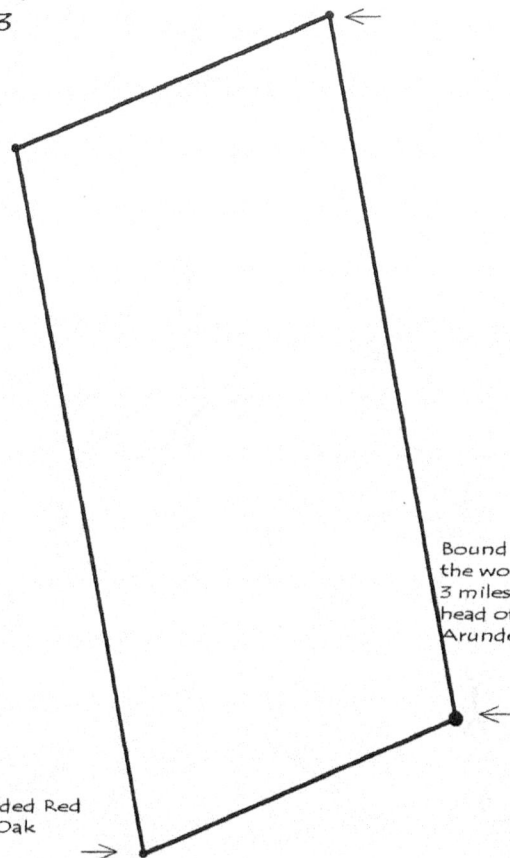

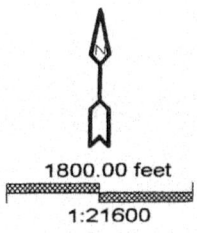

Bound Hickory in
the woods about
3 miles from the
head of the Ann
Arundell River

1800.00 feet

1:21600

Bounded Red
Oak

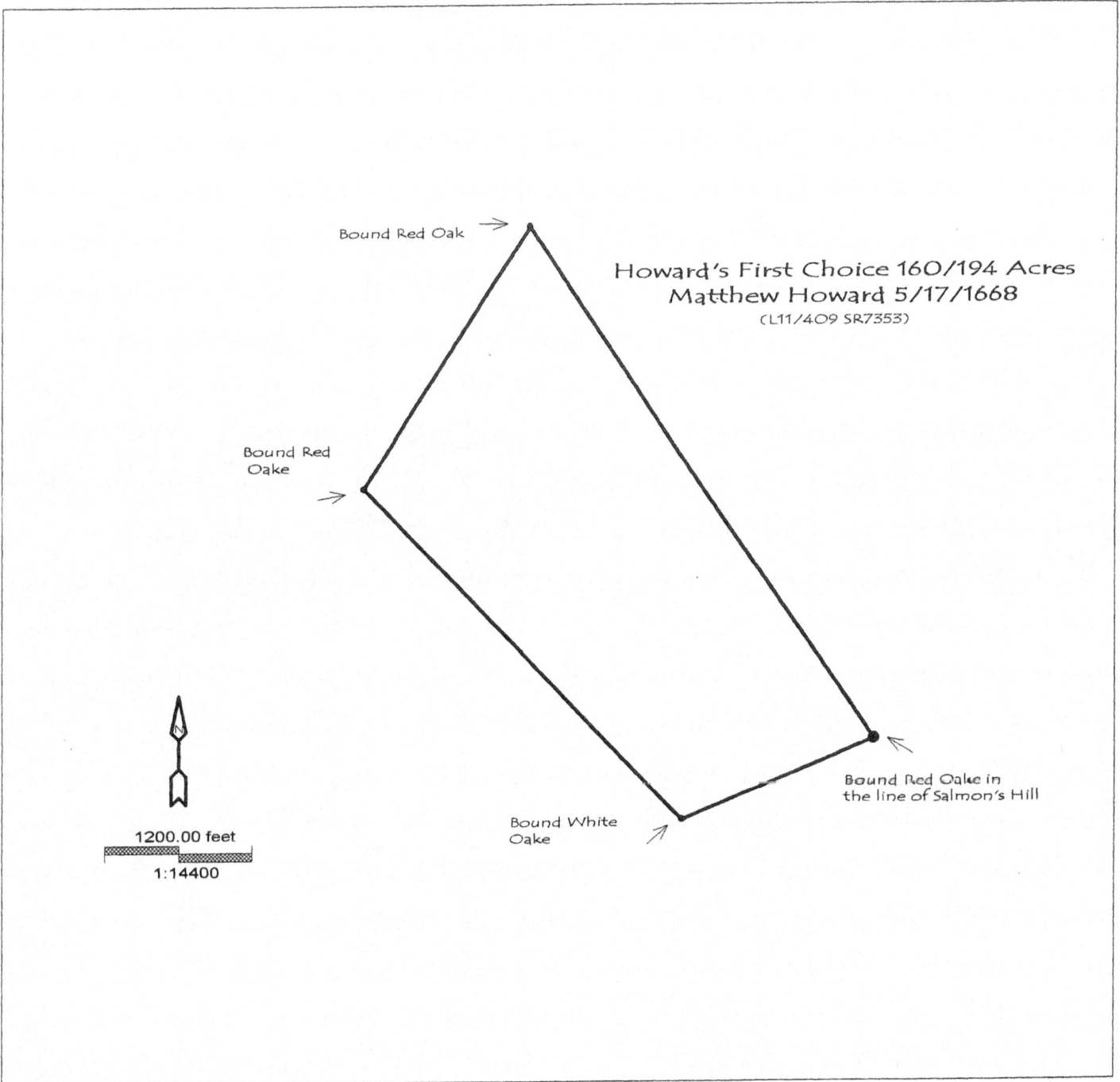

Bound Red Oak

Howard's First Choice 160/194 Acres
Matthew Howard 5/17/1668
(L11/409 SR7353)

Bound Red
Oake

Bound Red Oake in
the line of Salmon's Hill

Bound White
Oake

N

1200.00 feet
1:14400

Howard's Hills 150/42 Acres
Phillip Howard 12/10/1679
(L21/71 SR7362)

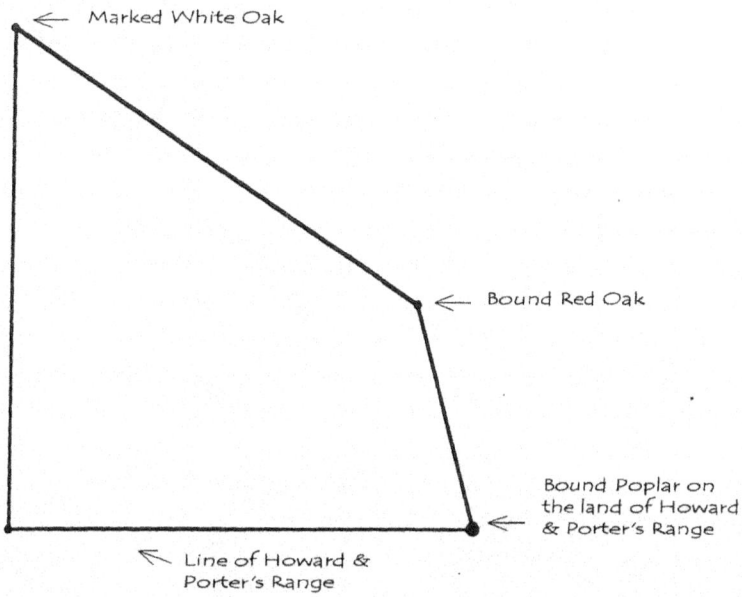

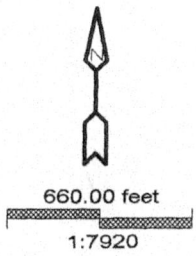

← Marked White Oak

← Bound Red Oak

Bound Poplar on
the land of Howard
& Porter's Range

← Line of Howard &
Porter's Range

660.00 feet
1:7920

Lancanster Plaine 180/151 Acres
John Hudson 5/1/1676
(L19/357 SR7360)

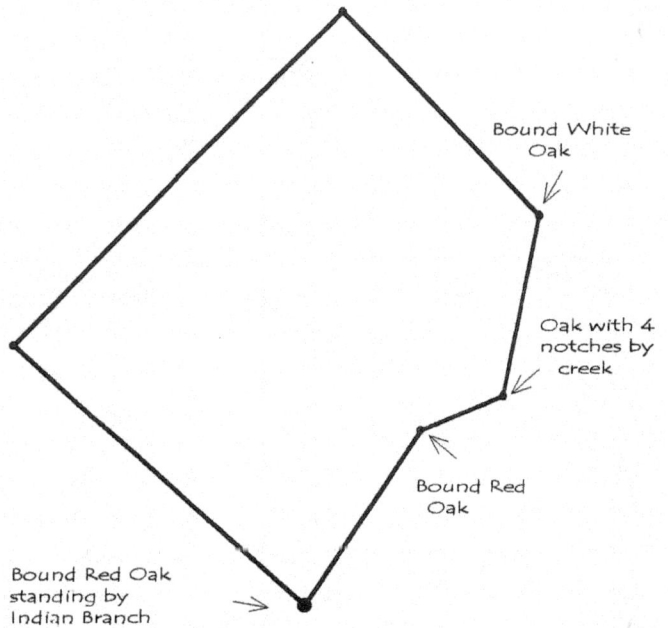

Bound White
Oak

Oak with 4
notches by
creek

Bound Red
Oak

Bound Red Oak
standing by
Indian Branch

1200.00 feet
1:14400

Locust Neck 100/101 Acres
James Horner s11/22/1651
(LAB&H/254 SR7344)

Marked Oak in
another deep
Valley →

← Deep valley

Severn River

Marked Oak near
Locust Creek ←

Locust Cr.

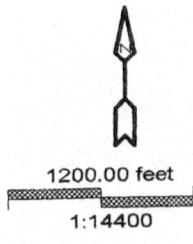

1200.00 feet

1:14400

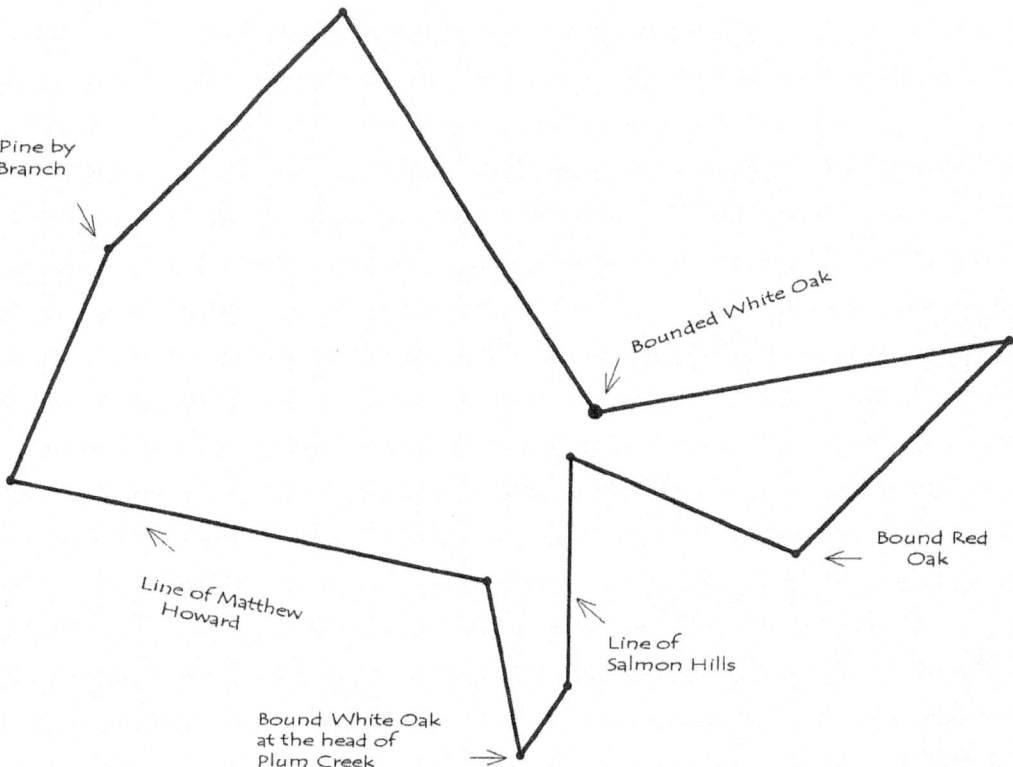

Meeke's Rest Resurveyed 350/356 Acres
Guy Meeke 5/2/1680
(L21/353 SR7362)

Bound Pine by
Indian Branch

Bounded White Oak

Bound Red
Oak

Line of Matthew
Howard

Line of
Salmon Hills

Bound White Oak
at the head of
Plum Creek

1500.00 feet
1:18000

114

Mill Meadow 240/247 Acres
Capt. Richard Hill 10/5/1683
(LSDA/418 SR7369)

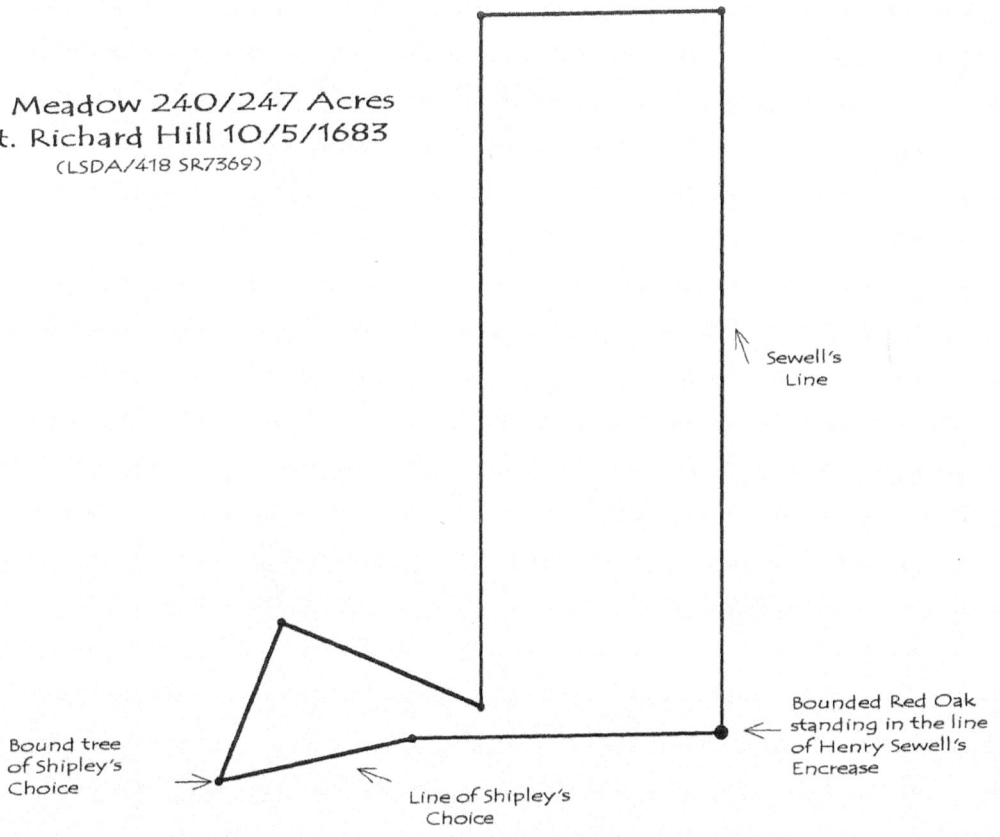

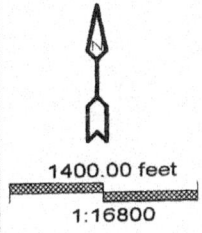

Sewell's
Line

Bounded Red Oak
standing in the line
of Henry Sewell's
Encrease

Bound tree
of Shipley's
Choice

Line of Shipley's
Choice

1400.00 feet

1:16800

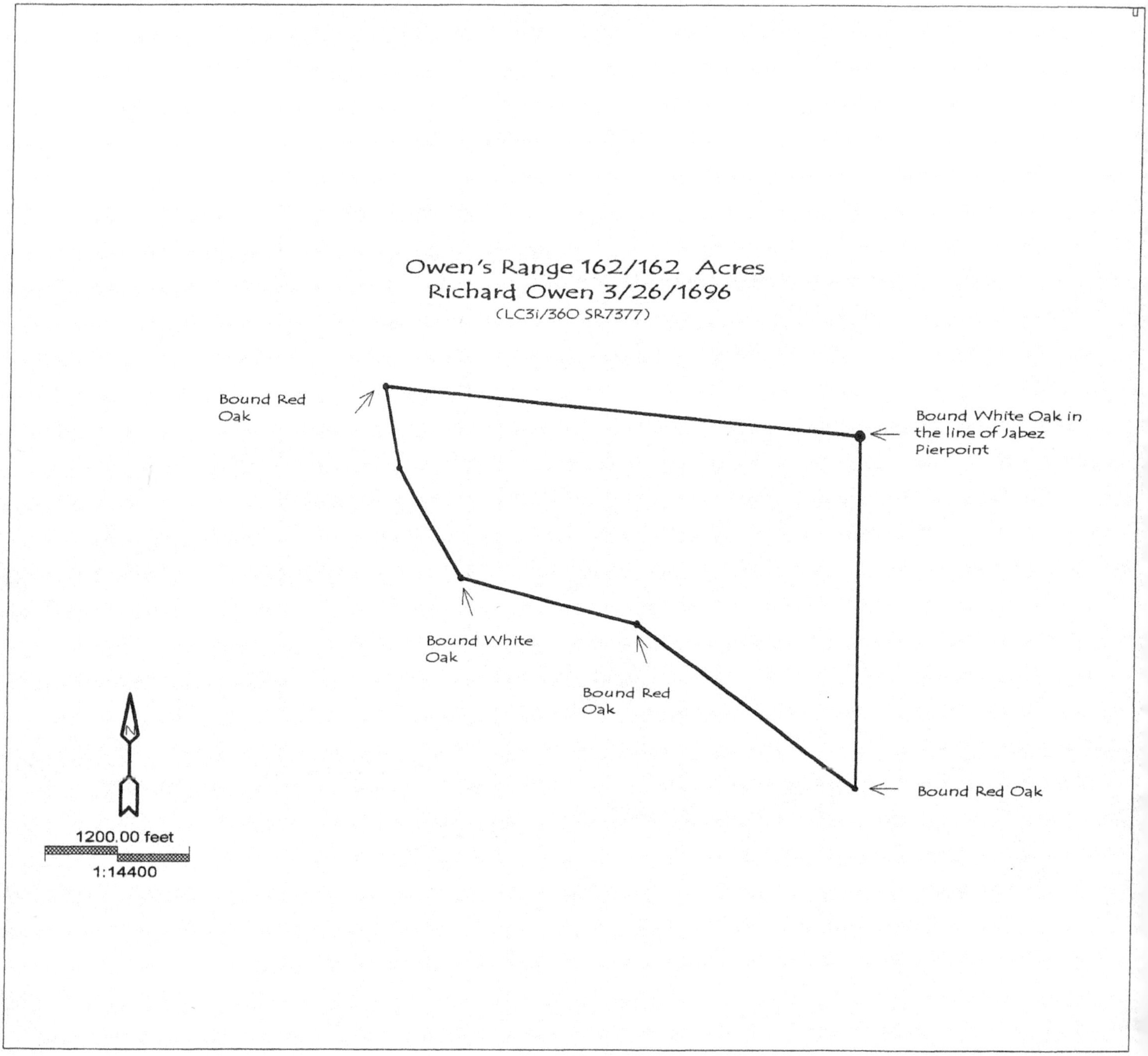

Owen's Range 162/162 Acres
Richard Owen 3/26/1696
(LC3i/360 SR7377)

Bound Red
Oak

Bound White Oak in
the line of Jabez
Pierpoint

Bound White
Oak

Bound Red
Oak

Bound Red Oak

1200.00 feet
1:14400

Pierpoint's Range 200/200 Acres
Jabes Pierpoint 11/10/1695
(LWD/136 SR7372-2)

Bound
Gumm

Bounded Red
Oake

Bound White Oak
of Pierpoints adj.
land

Bounded White
Oake

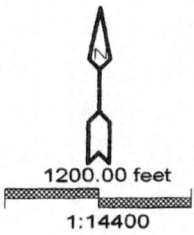

N

1200.00 feet

1:14400

117

Bound Hicory by
by Northmost Great
Branch of Patuxent
River at Huntenton

Rich Neck 284/279 Acres
Col. John Hammond 3/20/1784
(L22/183 SR7363)

1320.00 feet
1:15840

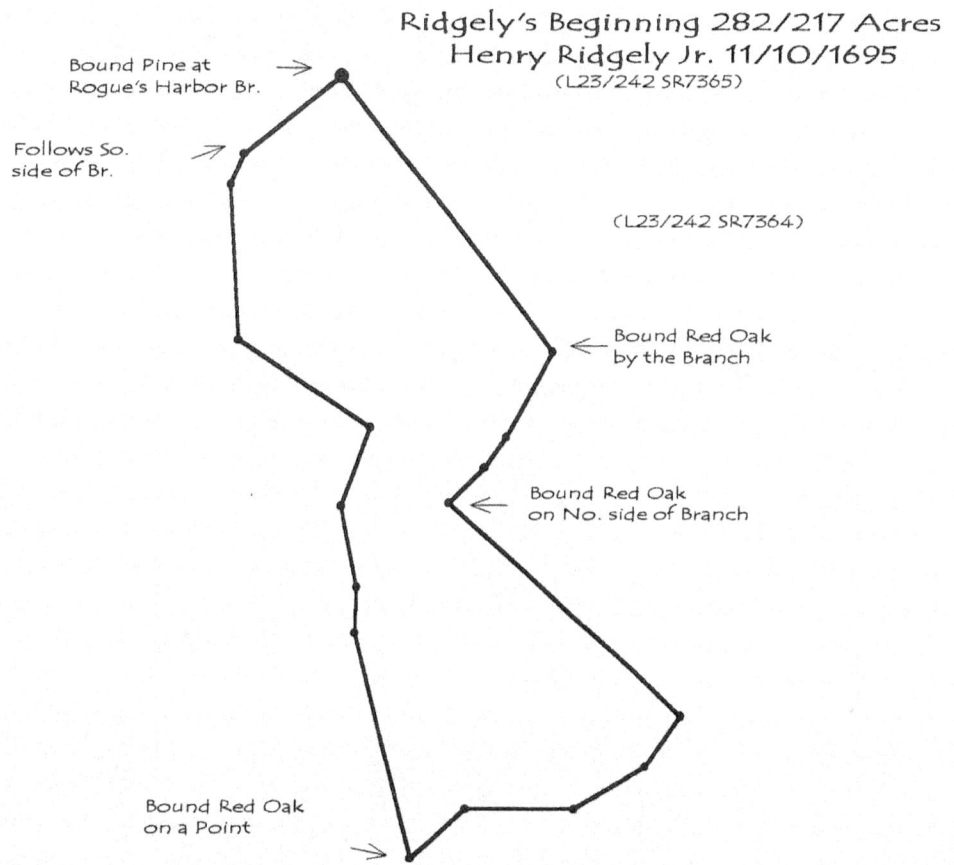

Ridgely's Beginning 282/217 Acres
Henry Ridgely Jr. 11/10/1695
(L23/242 SR7365)

(L23/242 SR7364)

Bound Pine at
Rogue's Harbor Br.

Follows So.
side of Br.

Bound Red Oak
by the Branch

Bound Red Oak
on No. side of Branch

Bound Red Oak
on a Point

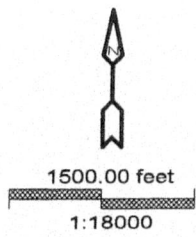

N

1500.00 feet

1:18000

Ridgely's Chance 305/302 Acres
William Ridgely 10/2/1694
(LC3/412 SR7377)

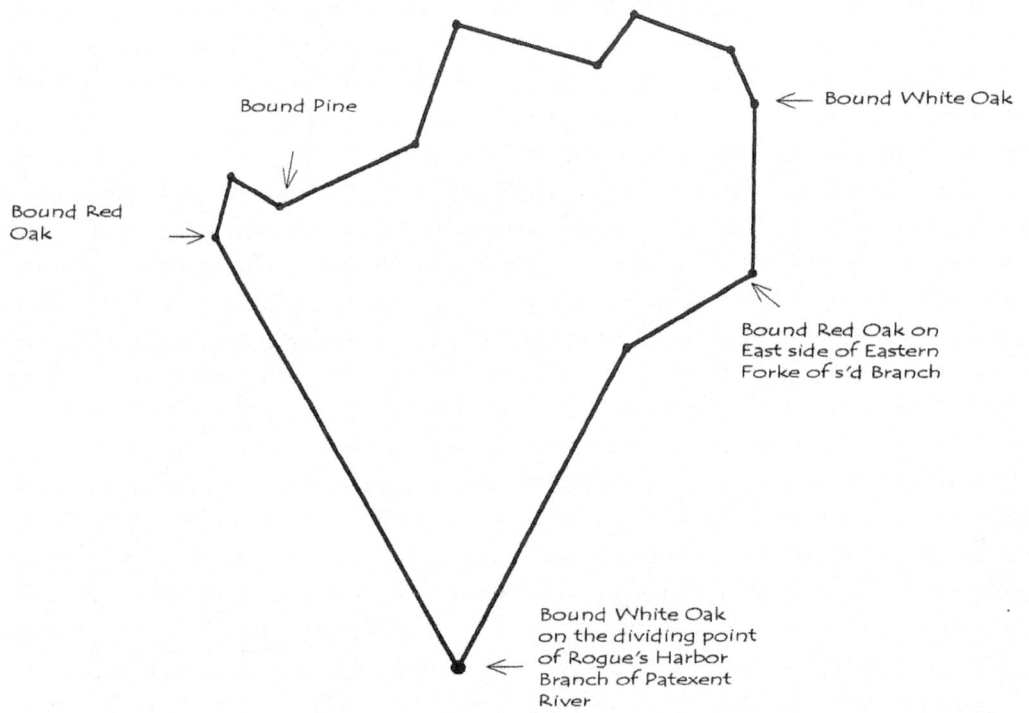

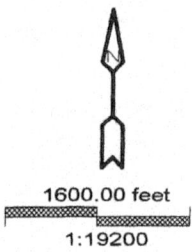

Bound Pine

← Bound White Oak

Bound Red
Oak →

Bound Red Oak on
East side of Eastern
Forke of s'd Branch

1600.00 feet
1:19200

Bound White Oak
on the dividing point
of Rogue's Harbor
Branch of Patexent
River

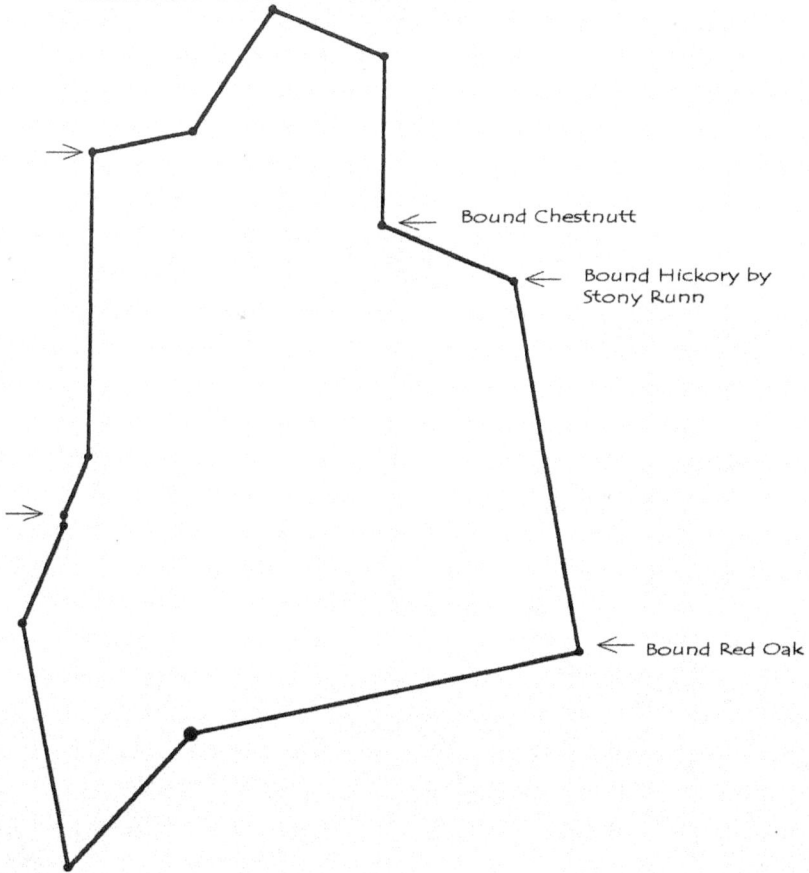

Ridgely's Forrest 264/259 Acres
Henry Ridgely 4/1/1696
(LC3i/340 SR7377)

Bound Hickory by a
Great Br. of Patux-
ent River

Bound Chestnutt

Bound Hickory by
Stony Runn

Bound White
Oak

Bound Red Oak

1200.00 feet
1:14400

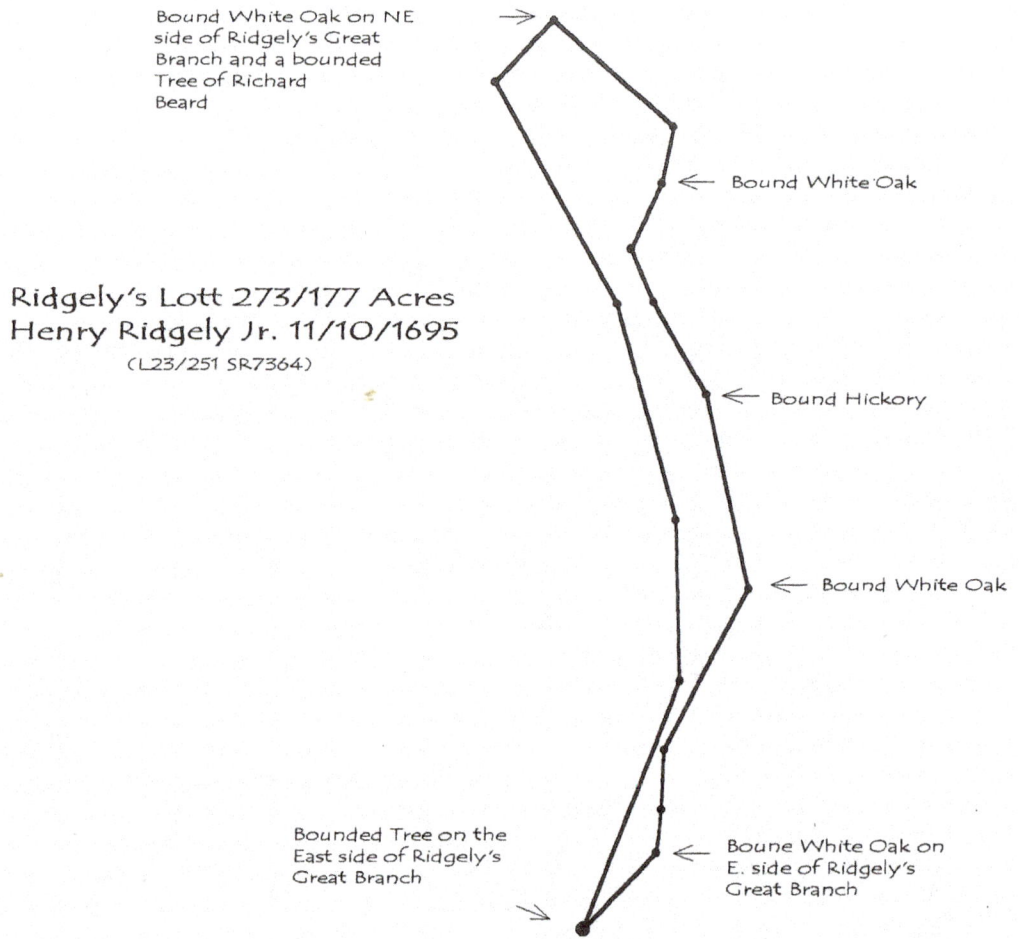

Bound White Oak on NE
side of Ridgely's Great
Branch and a bounded
Tree of Richard
Beard

← Bound White Oak

**Ridgely's Lott 273/177 Acres
Henry Ridgely Jr. 11/10/1695**
(L23/251 SR7364)

← Bound Hickory

← Bound White Oak

Bounded Tree on the
East side of Ridgely's
Great Branch

Boune White Oak on
E. side of Ridgely's
Great Branch

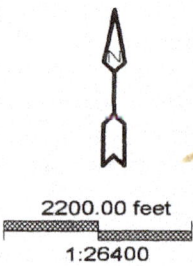

2200.00 feet

1:26400

Rosse 136/139 Acres
Guy Meeke 5/18/1679
(Liber 20/203 SR7361)

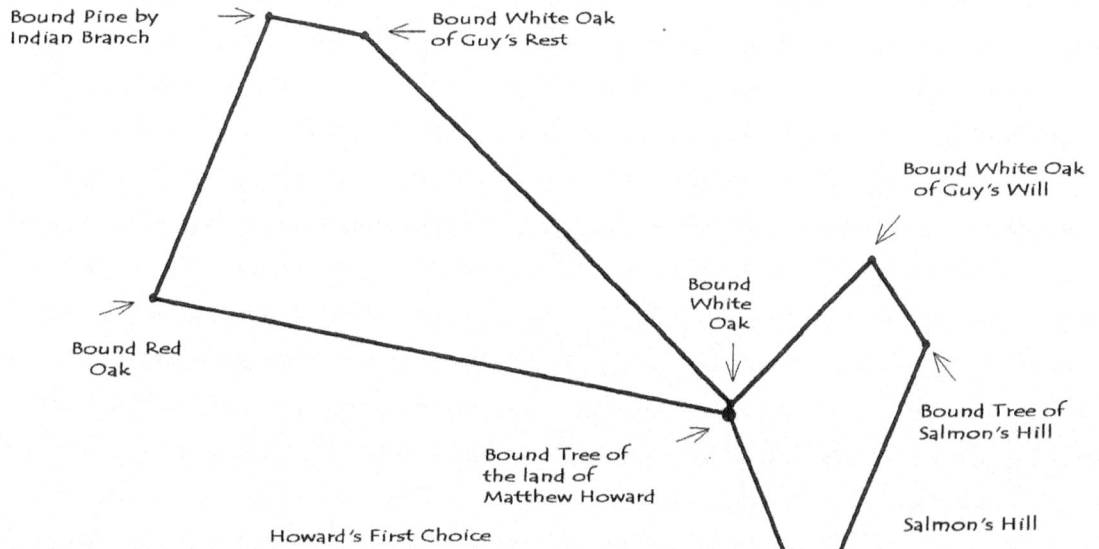

Bound Pine by
Indian Branch

Bound White Oak
of Guy's Rest

Bound White Oak
of Guy's Will

Bound
White
Oak

Bound Red
Oak

Bound Tree of
Salmon's Hill

Bound Tree of
the land of
Matthew Howard

Salmon's Hill

Howard's First Choice

1242.30 feet
1:14908

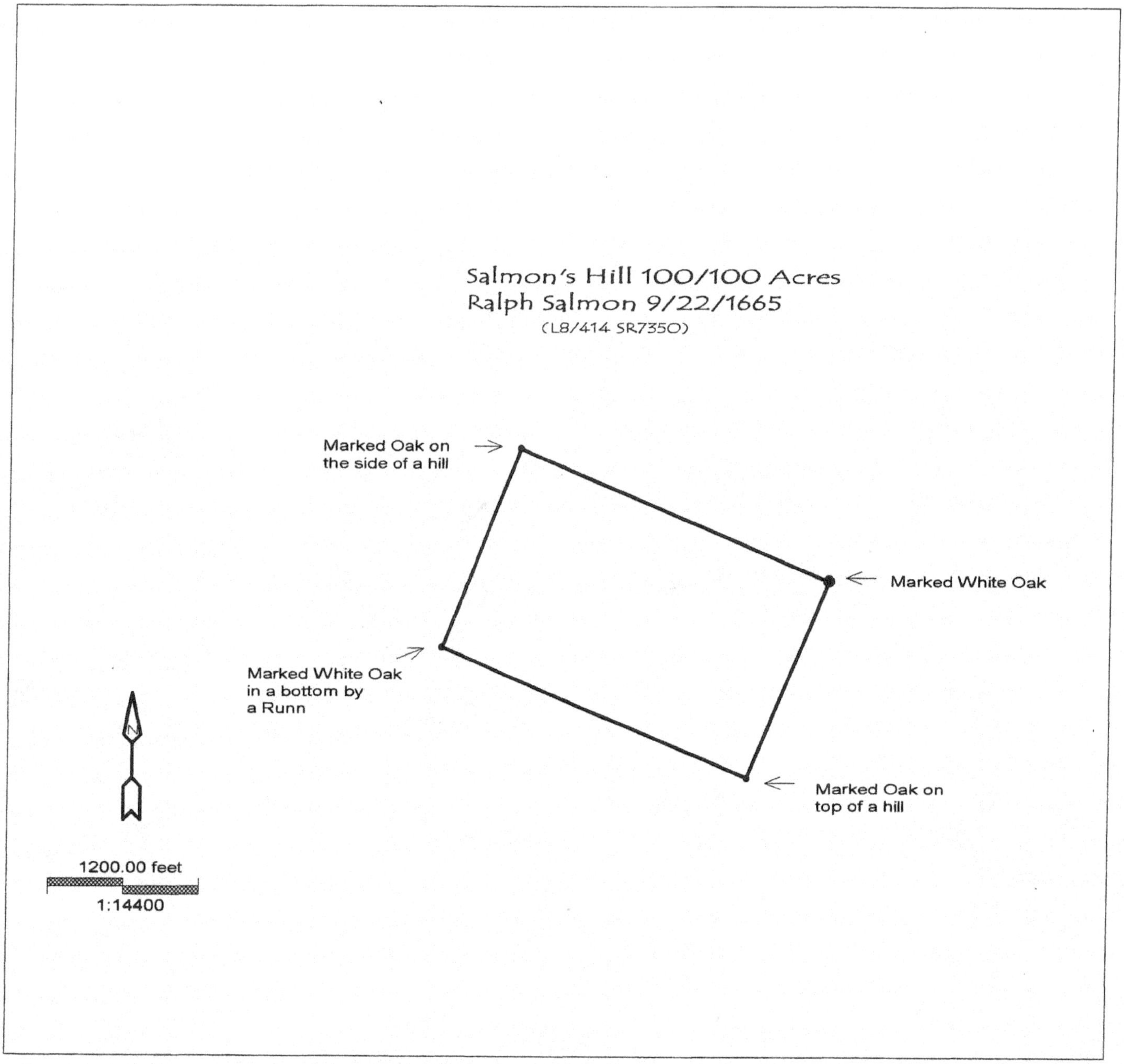

Salmon's Hill 100/100 Acres
Ralph Salmon 9/22/1665
(L8/414 SR7350)

Marked Oak on
the side of a hill

Marked White Oak

Marked White Oak
in a bottom by
a Runn

Marked Oak on
top of a hill

1200.00 feet

1:14400

Sewell's Encrease 500/509 Acres
Henry Sewell 5/25/1680
(L20/372 SR7361)

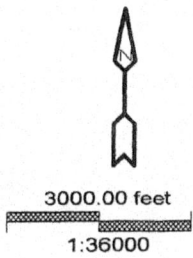

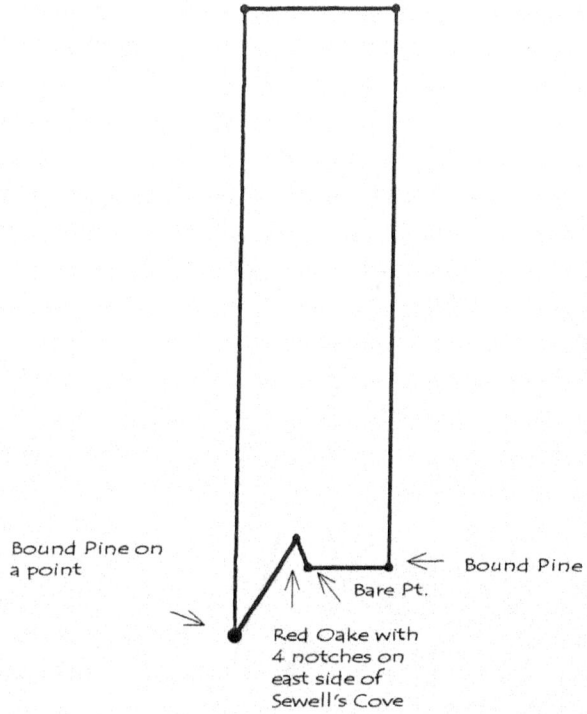

Bound Pine on
a point

Bound Pine

Bare Pt.

Red Oake with
4 notches on
east side of
Sewell's Cove

3000.00 feet
1:36000

Shepheard's Choice 240/240 Acres
Nicholas Shepheard 6/1/1687
(LNS2i/482 SR7371)

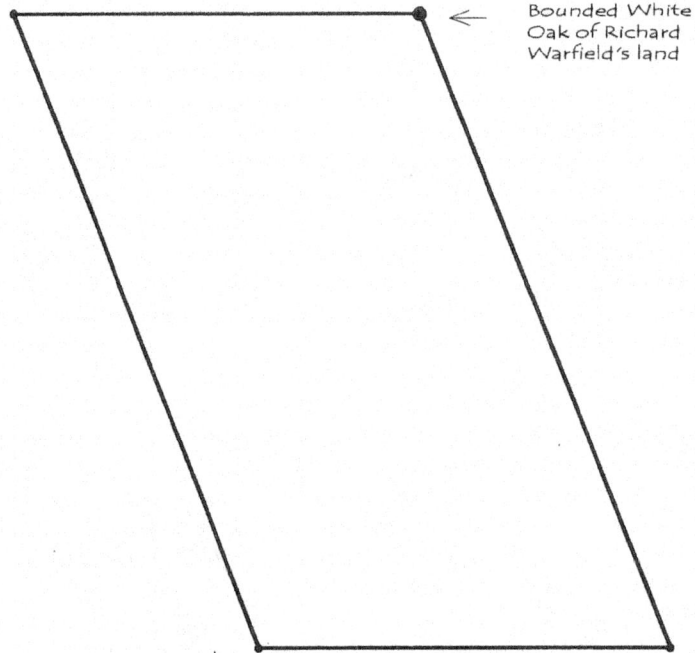

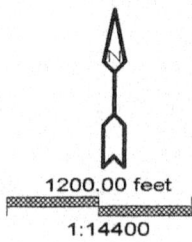

Bounded White
Oak of Richard
Warfield's land

1200.00 feet

1:14400

Shepheard's Grove 120/117 Acres
Nicholas Shepheard 8/10/1684
(LSDA/461 SR7369)

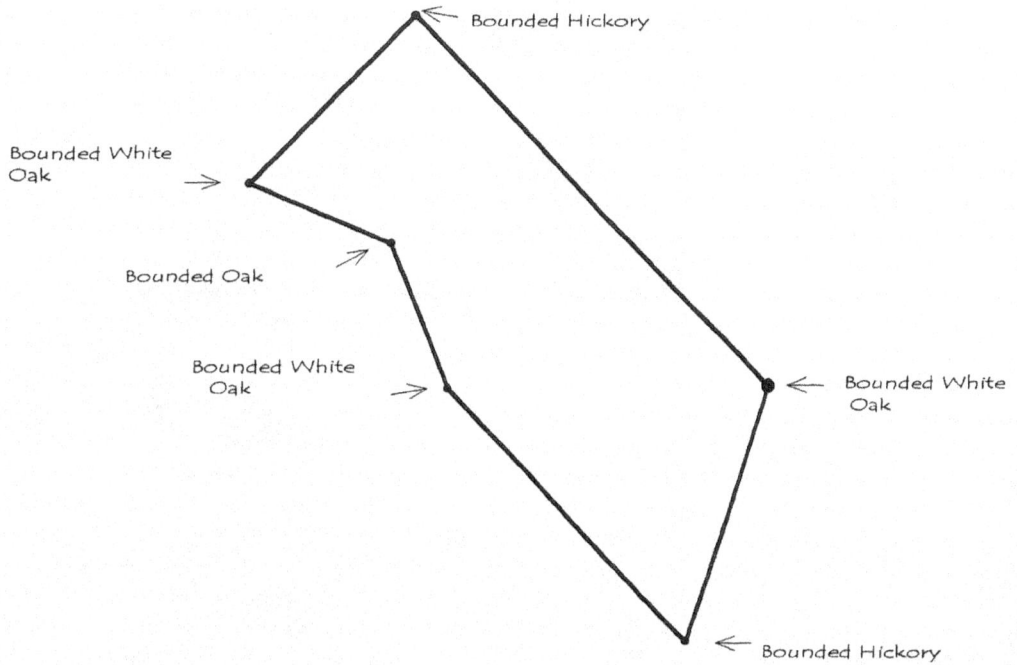

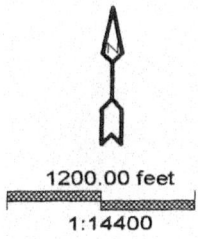

Bounded Hickory

Bounded White
Oak

Bounded Oak

Bounded White
Oak

Bounded White
Oak

Bounded Hickory

1200.00 feet

1:14400

Shepheard's Range 100/93 Acres
Nicholas Shepheard 10/1/1674
(L18/260 SR7359)

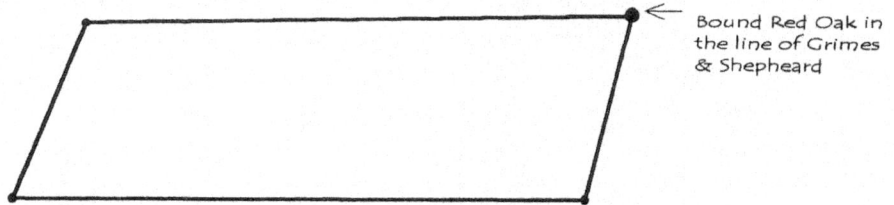

Bound Red Oak in
the line of Grimes
& Shepheard

N

1200.00 feet
1:14400

Shepley's Choice 200/205 Acres
Adam Shepley 1/20/1681
(LCB2i/463 SR7366)

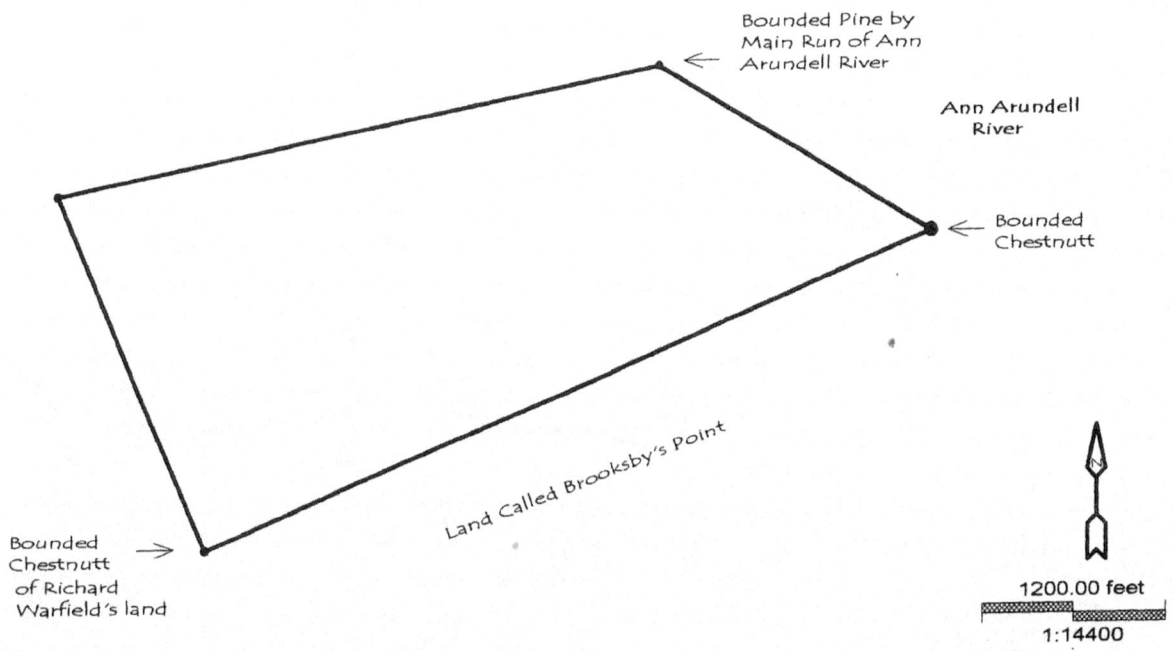

Bounded Pine by
Main Run of Ann
Arundell River

Ann Arundell
River

Bounded
Chestnutt

Land Called Brooksby's Point

Bounded
Chestnutt
of Richard
Warfield's land

1200.00 feet
1:14400

The Addition 50/51 Acres
William Jones 10/10/1704
(LDSF/517 SR7373-2)

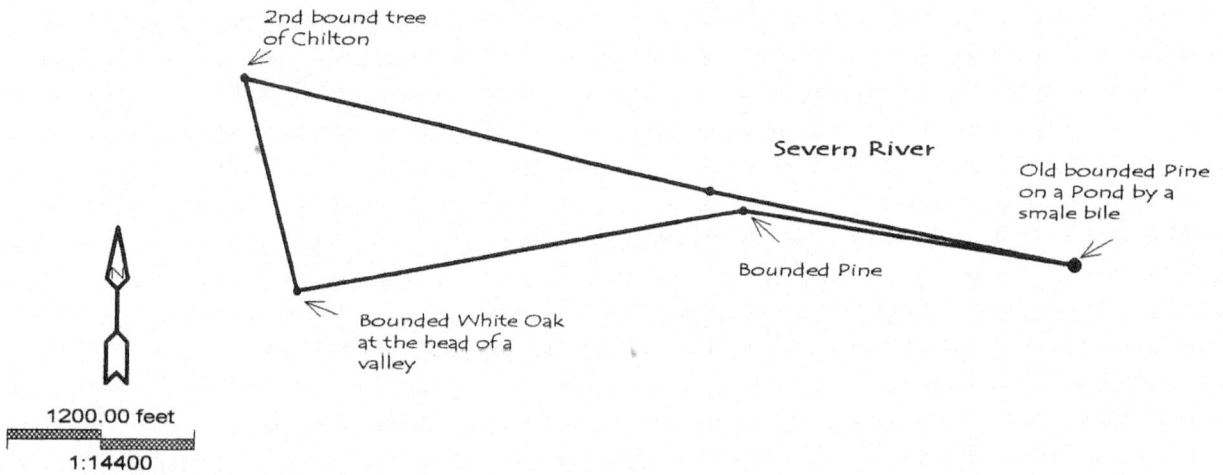

2nd bound tree
of Chilton

Severn River

Old bounded Pine
on a Pond by a
smale bile

Bounded Pine

Bounded White Oak
at the head of a
valley

1200.00 feet

1:14400

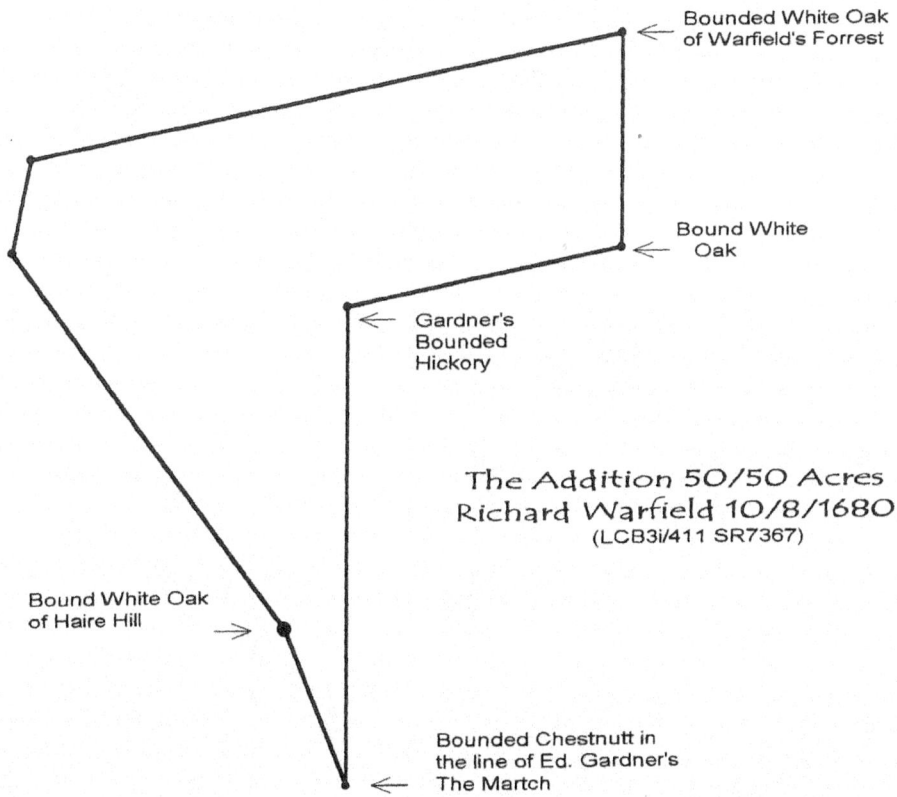

Bounded White Oak
of Warfield's Forrest

Bound White
Oak

Gardner's
Bounded
Hickory

The Addition 50/50 Acres
Richard Warfield 10/8/1680
(LCB3i/411 SR7367)

Bound White Oak
of Haire Hill

Bounded Chestnutt in
the line of Ed. Gardner's
The Martch

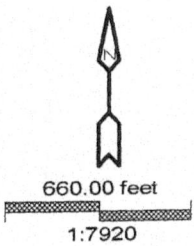

660.00 feet

1:7920

The Desert 148/138 Acres
Thomas Blackwell 6/12/1696
(LWD/124 SR7372-1)

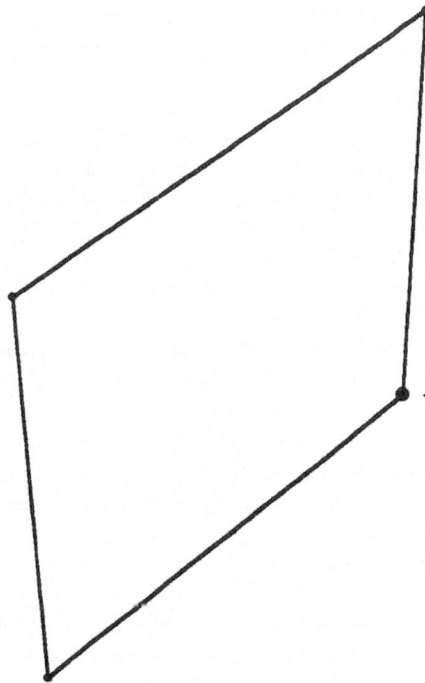

← Bounded Red Oak
of Thomas Browne

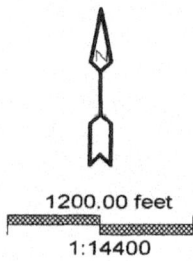

1200.00 feet

1:14400

The Diamond 200/207 Acres
Thomas Brown 8/10/1684
(LSDA/414 SR7369)

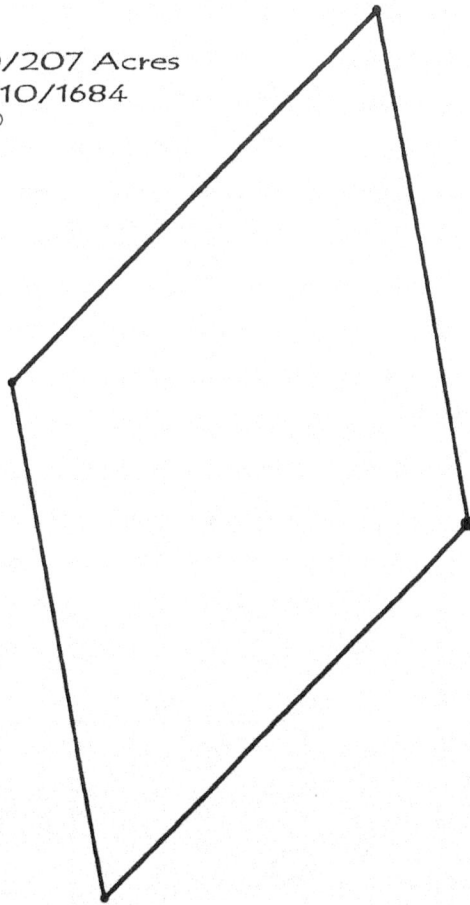

Bound Red Oak standing in a Marsh

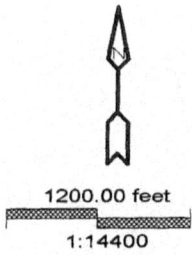

1200.00 feet
1:14400

d:\diamond.pla 03-13-2001

The Friend's Choice 100/92 Acres
William Grimes & Nicholas Shepherd 9/10/1672

(L17/298 SR7358)

Ann Arundell River

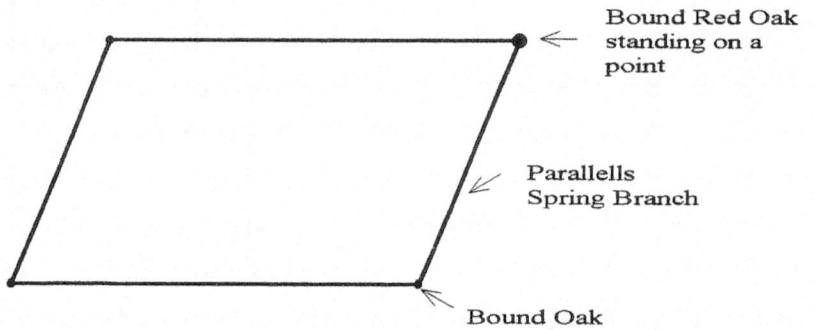

Bound Red Oak
standing on a
point

Parallells
Spring Branch

Bound Oak

1200.00 feet

1:14400

The Friendship 100/80 Acres
Thomas Browne and William Hopkins 5/26/1681
(LSDA/94 SR7369)

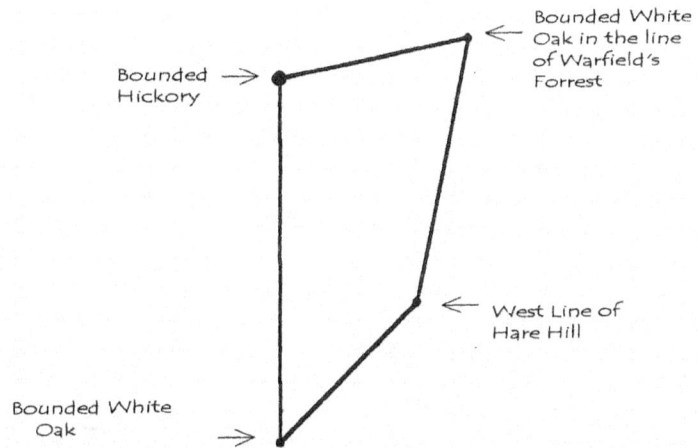

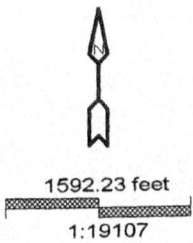

Bounded White
Oak in the line
← of Warfield's
Forrest

Bounded →
Hickory

← West Line of
Hare Hill

Bounded White
Oak

→

N

1592.23 feet

1:19107

Bound Tree of
Howard & Porters
Range

The Maiden 40/38 Acres
Mary Howard 11/5/1683
(LSDA/417 SR7369)

Howard &
Porter's Range

No. Runn of
South River

Line of Hammond's
Addition

660.00 feet
1:7920

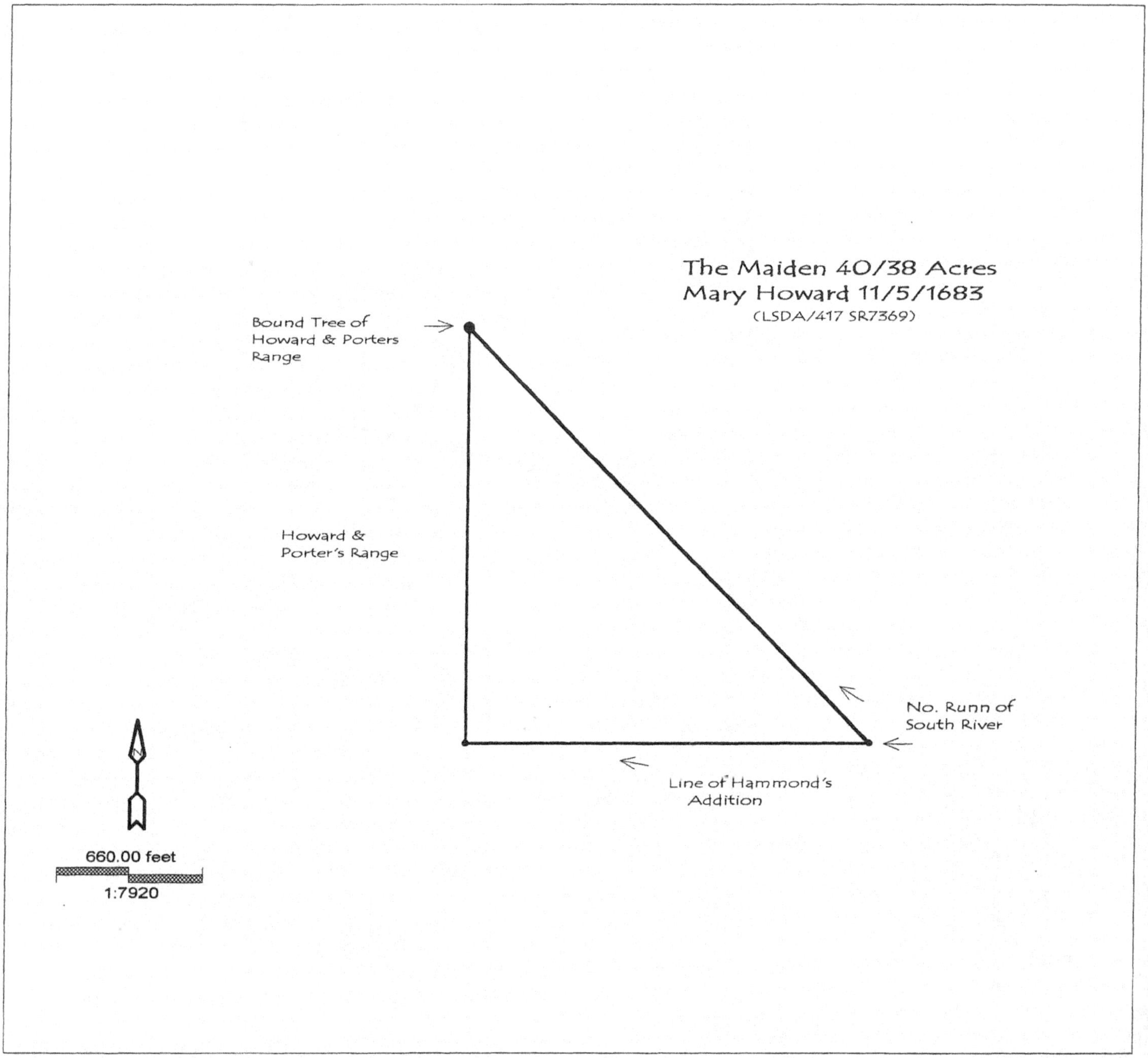

The March 110/113 Acres
Edward Gardner 6/1/1687
(LNS2i/280 SR7371)

Marked
Hickory

Line of
Warfield's
Plain

Bounded Oake of
Howard & Porter's
Range

Howard's
Hills

Bounded Red Oake
of Howard & Porter's
Fancy

1200.00 feet
1:14400

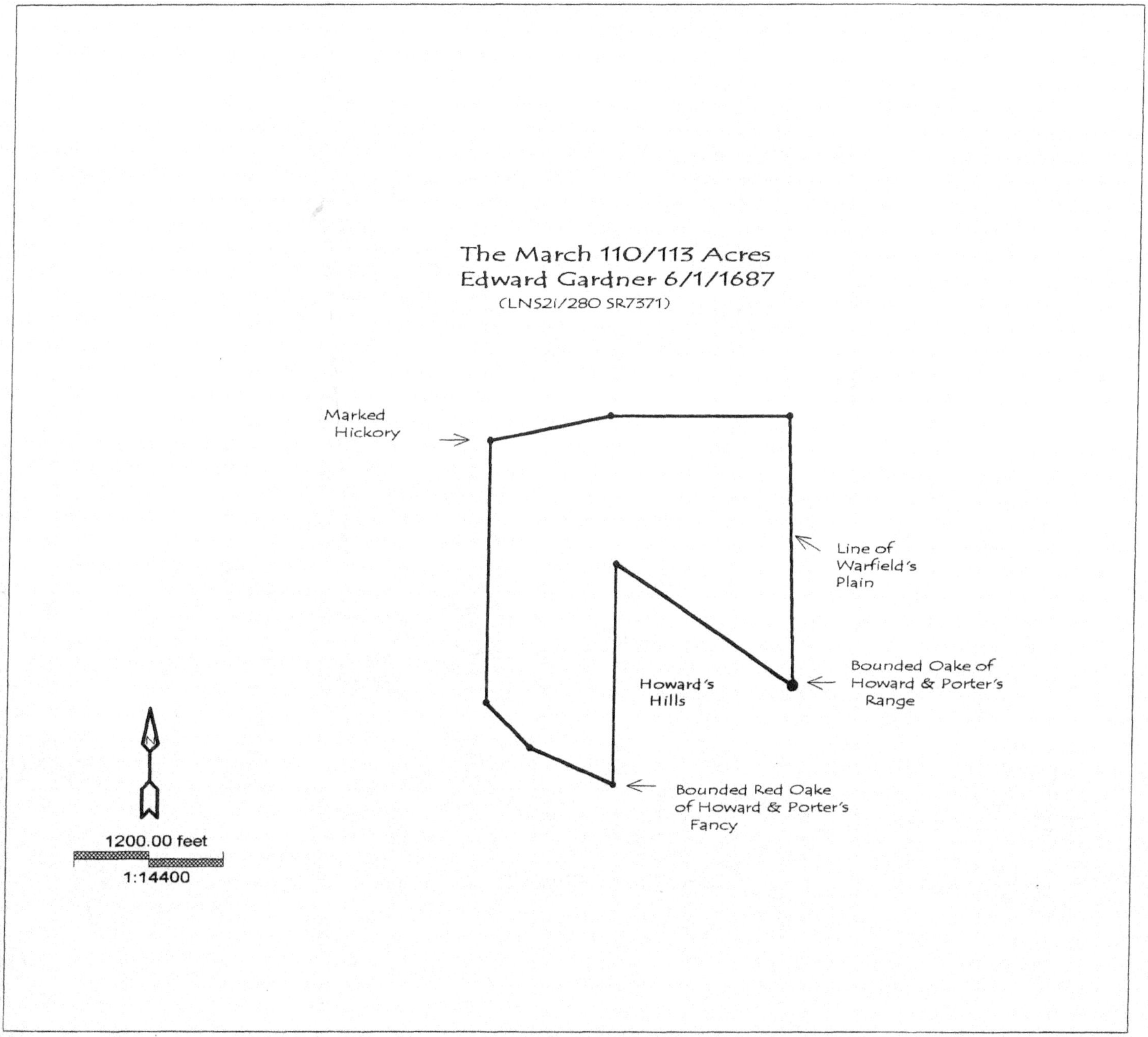

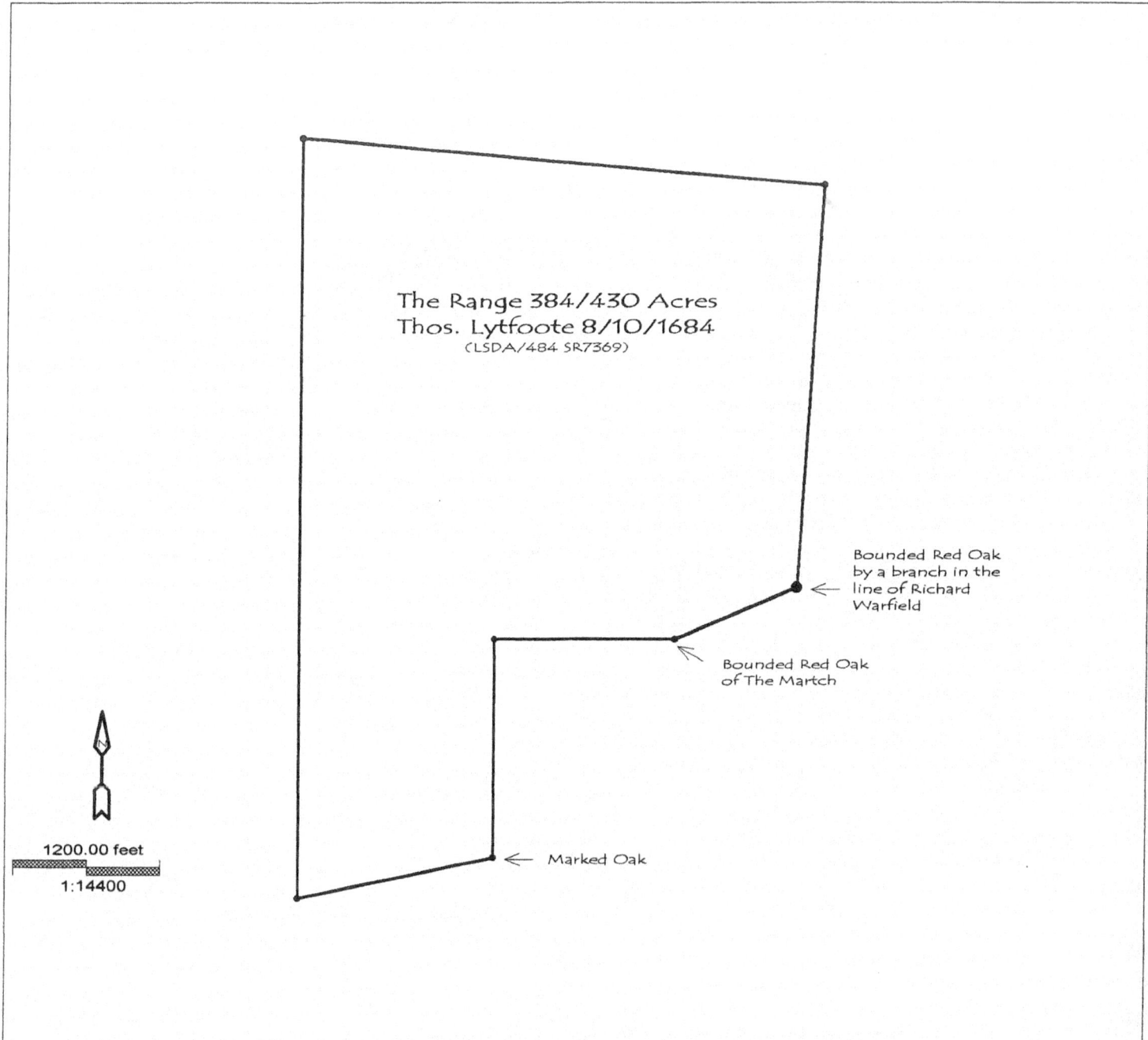

The Range 384/430 Acres
Thos. Lytfoote 8/10/1684
(LSDA/484 SR7369)

Bounded Red Oak
by a branch in the
line of Richard
Warfield

Bounded Red Oak
of The Martch

1200.00 feet

1:14400

Marked Oak

Timber Neck 303/298 Acres
Charles Stevens 11/10/1695
(LWD/143 SR7372-2)

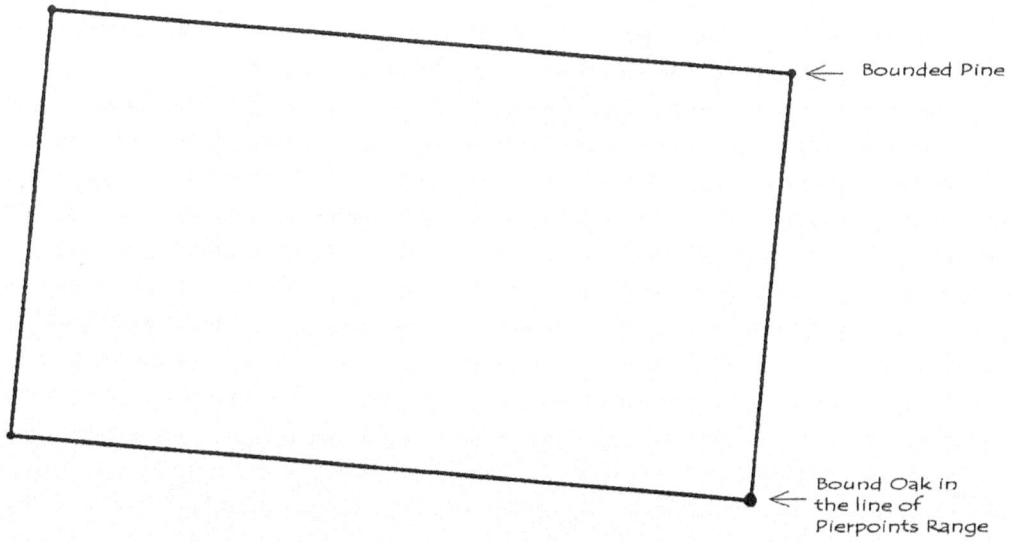

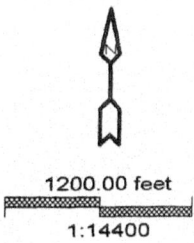

Bounded Pine

Bound Oak in
the line of
Pierpoints Range

1200.00 feet
1:14400

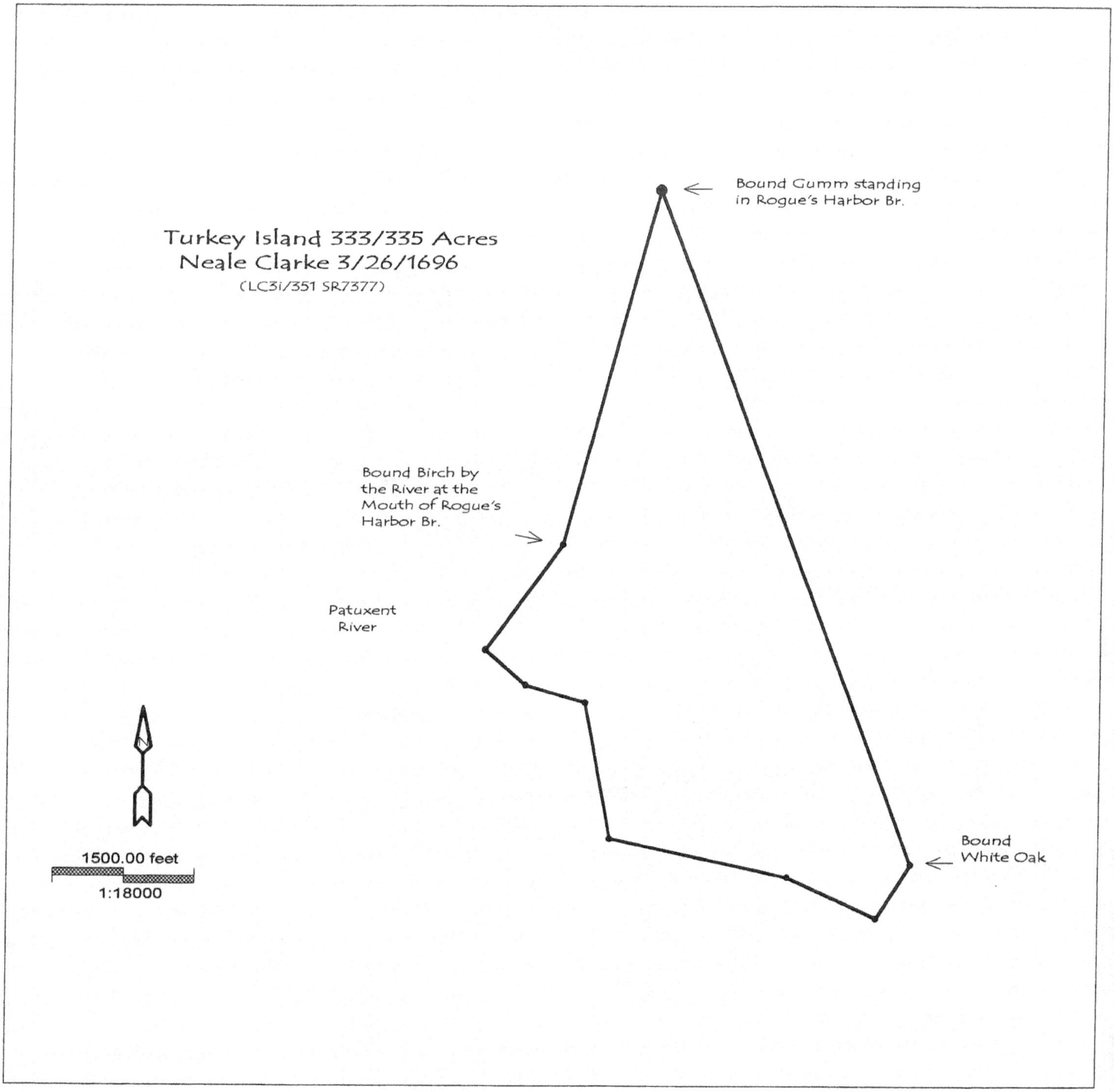

Turkey Island 333/335 Acres
Neale Clarke 3/26/1696
(LC3i/351 SR7377)

Bound Gumm standing
in Rogue's Harbor Br.

Bound Birch by
the River at the
Mouth of Rogue's
Harbor Br.

Patuxent
River

1500.00 feet
1:18000

Bound
White Oak

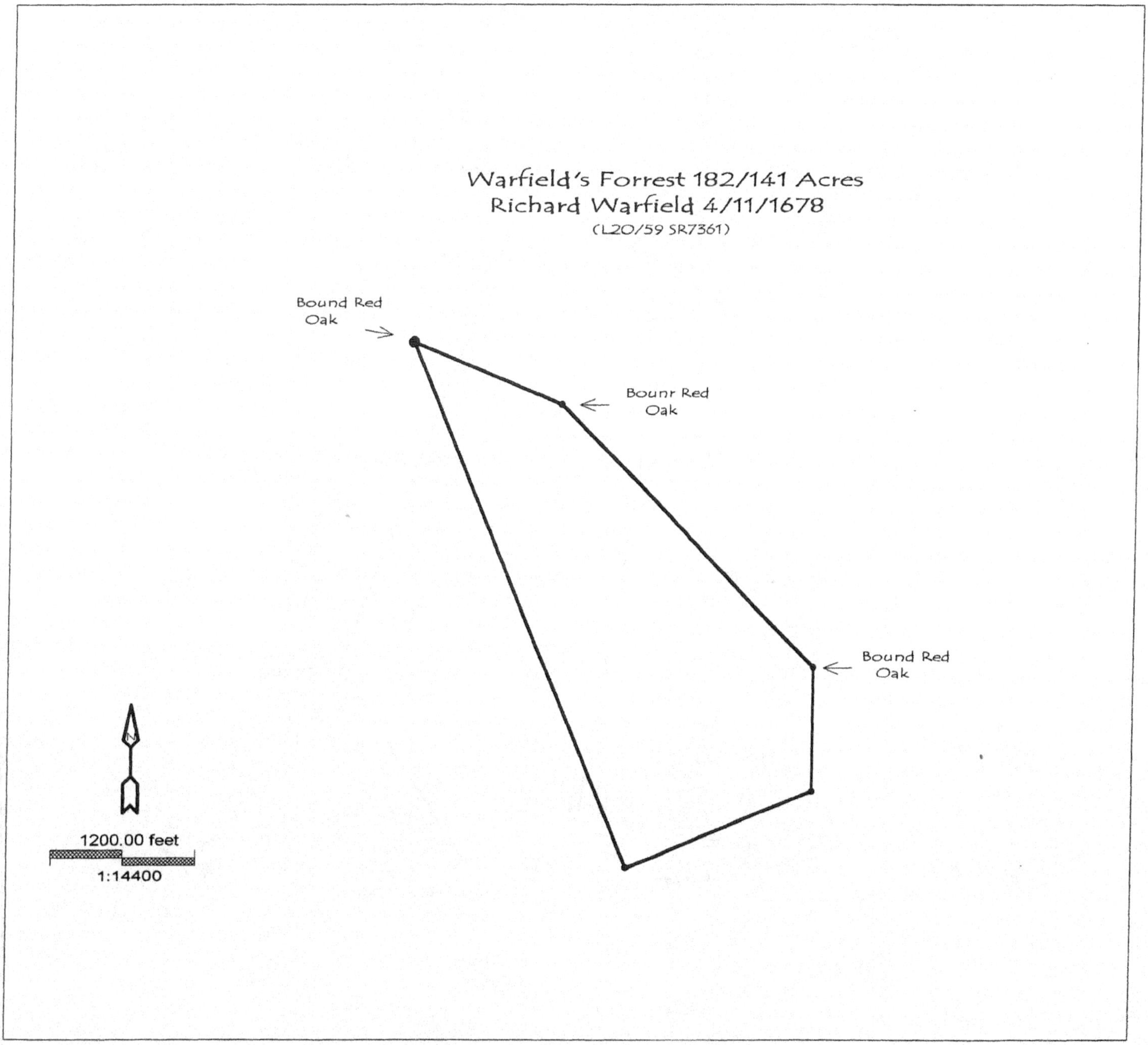

Warfield's Forrest 182/141 Acres
Richard Warfield 4/11/1678
(L20/59 SR7361)

Bound Red
Oak

Bounr Red
Oak

Bound Red
Oak

1200.00 feet
1:14400

Warfield's Plaines 300/315 Acres
Richard Warfield 1/6/1680
(LCB2i/412 SR7366)

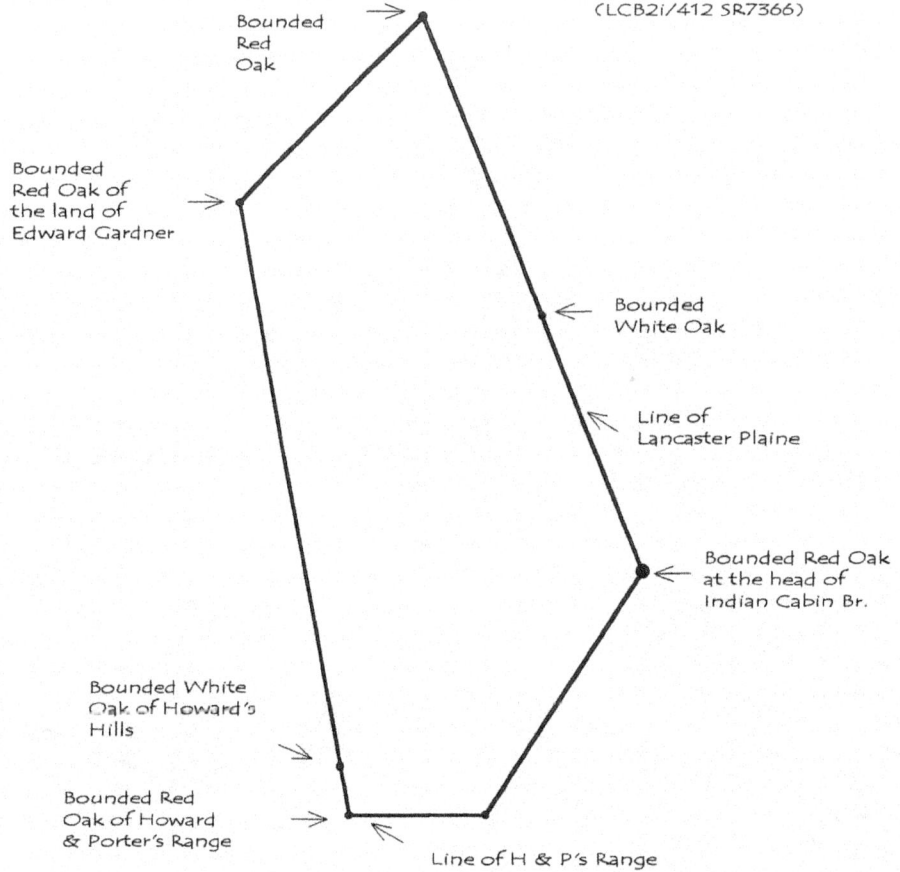

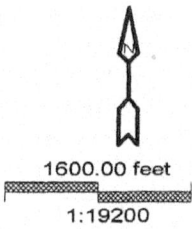

Bounded
Red
Oak

Bounded
Red Oak of
the land of
Edward Gardner

Bounded
White Oak

Line of
Lancaster Plaine

Bounded Red Oak
at the head of
Indian Cabin Br.

Bounded White
Oak of Howard's
Hills

Bounded Red
Oak of Howard
& Porter's Range

Line of H & P's Range

1600.00 feet

1:19200

Weston 130/129 Acres
Guy Meeke 8/14/1683
(LSDA/101 SR7369)

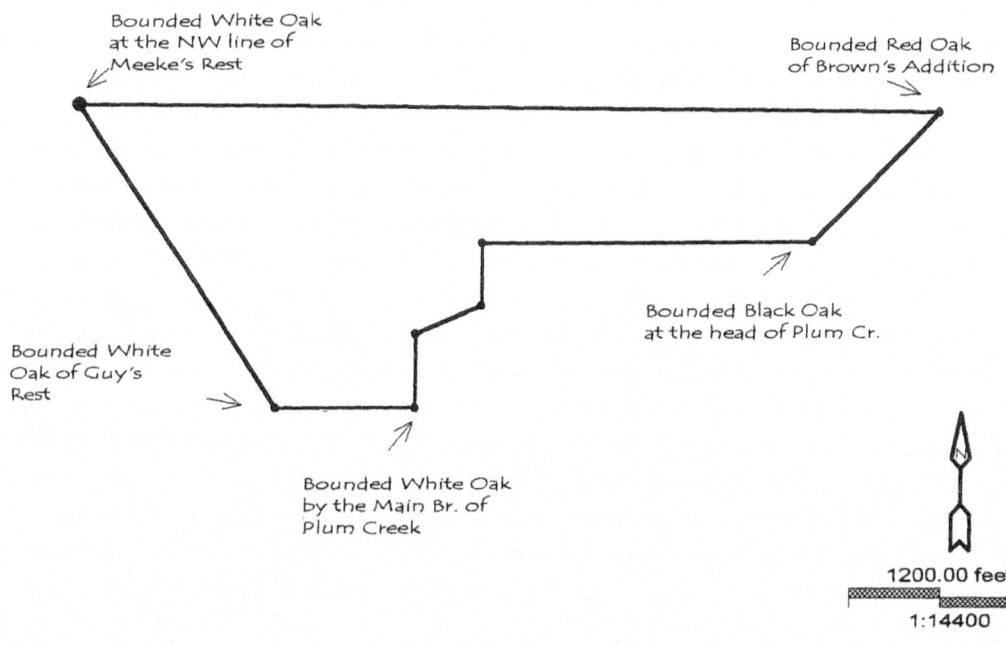

Bounded White Oak
at the NW line of
Meeke's Rest

Bounded Red Oak
of Brown's Addition

Bounded White
Oak of Guy's
Rest

Bounded Black Oak
at the head of Plum Cr.

Bounded White Oak
by the Main Br. of
Plum Creek

1200.00 feet
1:14400

What is Left 105/110 Acres
Amos Pierpoint 6/4/1702
(LSDF/403 SR7373-2)

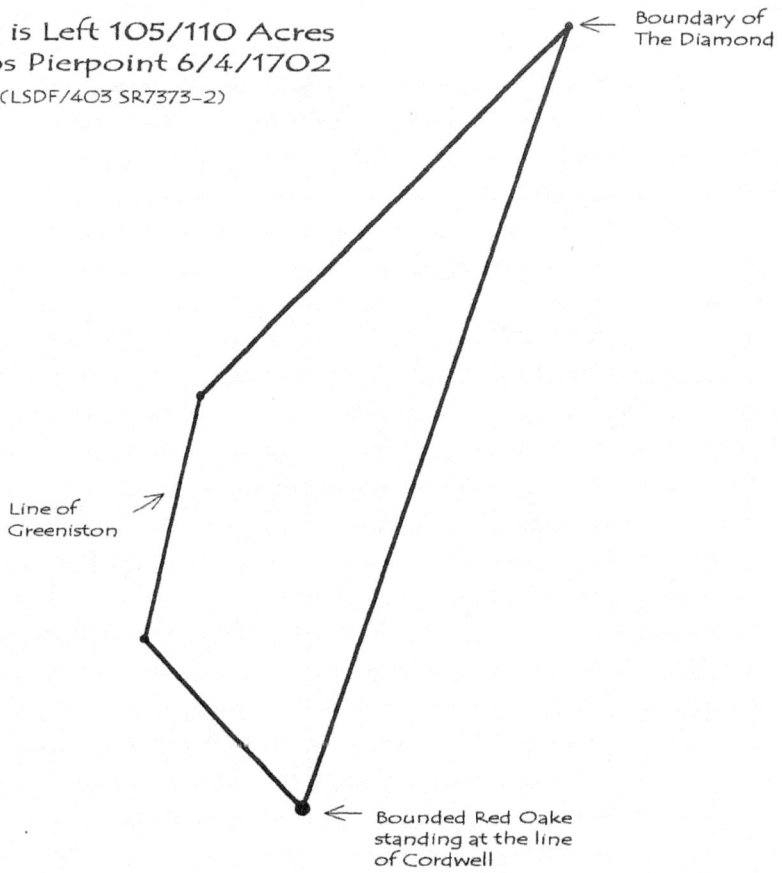

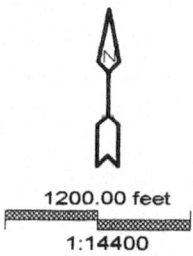

Boundary of
The Diamond

Line of
Greeniston

Bounded Red Oake
standing at the line
of Cordwell

1200.00 feet
1:14400

What You Please 72/48 Acres
Charles Stevens 11/10/1695
(LC3i/303 SR7377)

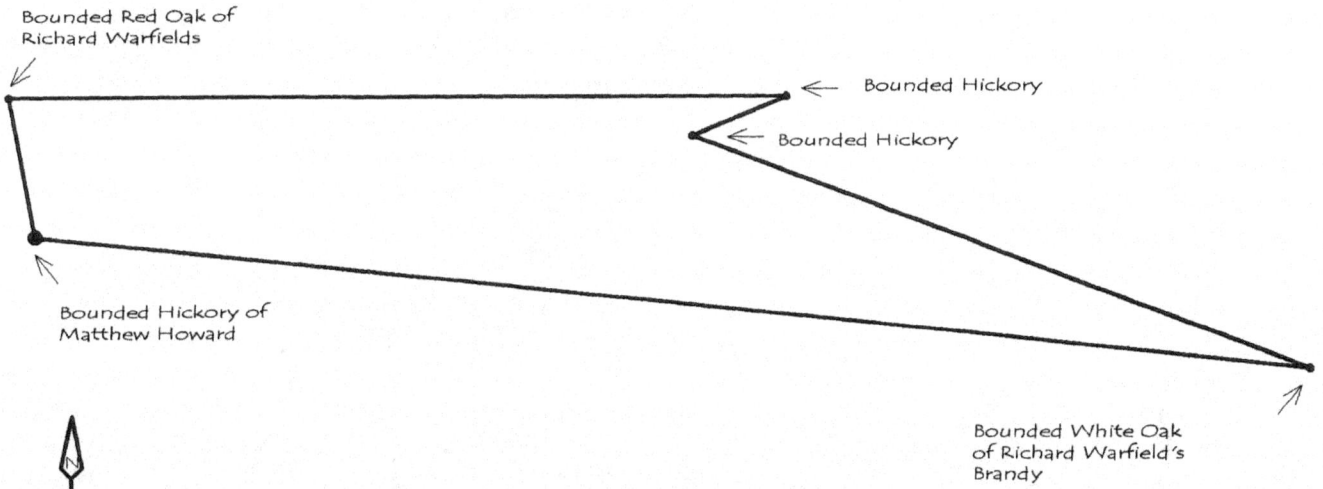

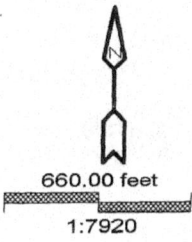

Bounded Red Oak of
Richard Warfields

← Bounded Hickory

← Bounded Hickory

Bounded Hickory of
Matthew Howard

Bounded White Oak
of Richard Warfield's
Brandy

N

660.00 feet

1:7920

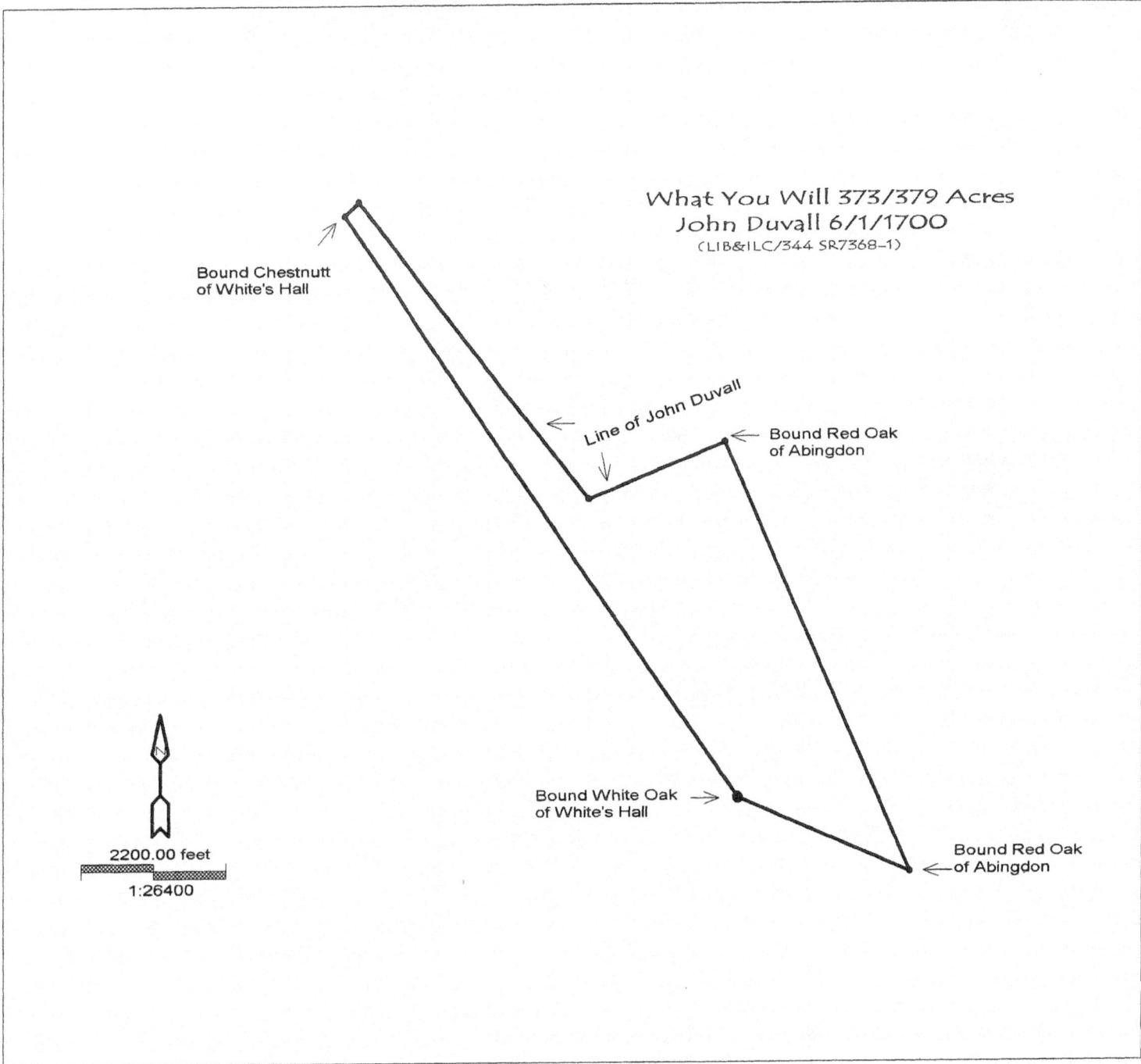

What You Will 373/379 Acres
John Duvall 6/1/1700
(LIB&ILC/344 SR7368-1)

Bound Chestnutt
of White's Hall

Line of John Duvall

Bound Red Oak
of Abingdon

Bound White Oak
of White's Hall

Bound Red Oak
of Abingdon

2200.00 feet
1:26400

146

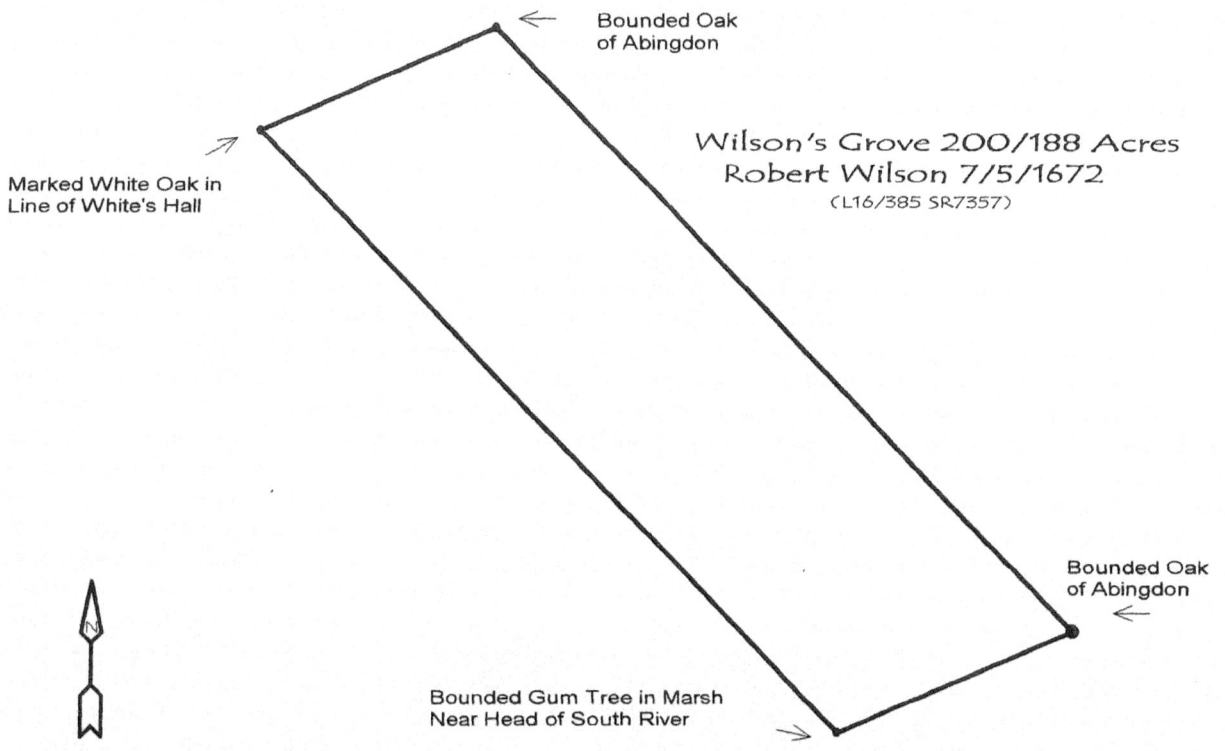

Bounded Oak
of Abingdon

Wilson's Grove 200/188 Acres
Robert Wilson 7/5/1672
(L16/385 SR7357)

Marked White Oak in
Line of White's Hall

Bounded Oak
of Abingdon

Bounded Gum Tree in Marsh
Near Head of South River

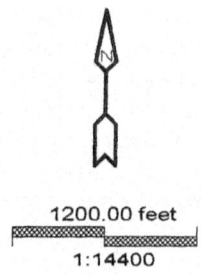

1200.00 feet
1:14400

Drawn and Placed Central Area Tracts

BC – Burnntwood Common
BH – Bruton's Hope
CL – Clarke's Enlargement
DA – Dorsey's Addition
FM – Free Manston
GW – Gardner's Warfield
HD – Howard's Discovery

HM – Howard's Mount
HML – Honest Man's Lott
HN – Hogg Neck
HS – Howard's Search
JI – Jane's Inheritance
LP – The Landing Place
MC – Medcalfe's Chance

MM – Medcalfe's Mount
ML – Mill Land
NN – Narrow Neck
PL – Pierpoint's Lott
PR – Pierpoint's Rocks
R – Rawling's Purchase
RB – Ridgely's Beginning

RH – Roundabout Hill
RP – Rocky Point
SH – Stony Hills
TA – The Adventure
TE – The Encresse (Minter)
TQ – Turkey Quarter
WF – Wayfield

6000.00 feet

1:72000

WH – Wyatt's Hills
WR – Warfield's Right

Bear Ridge 175/209 Acres
Nicholas Wyatt 8/11/1664
(L7/355 SR7349)

← Marked Oak

← Marked Oak

Line of Wyatt's Ridge
by a great Branch of
Broad Creek

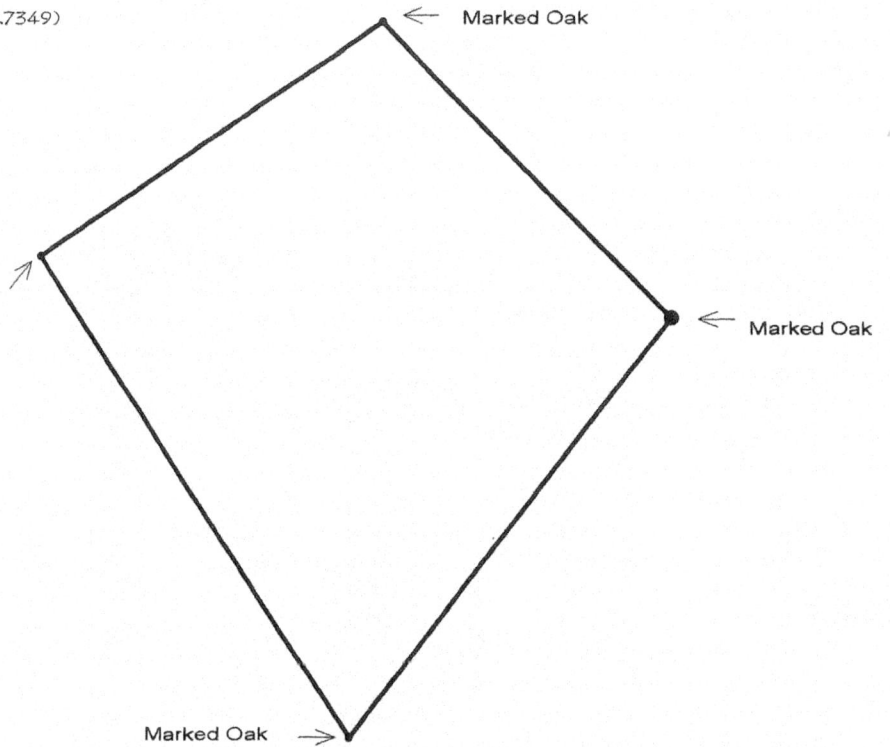

Marked Oak →

1200.00 feet

1:14400

150

Bell's Haven 100/122 Acres
Thomas Bell 8/25/1665
(L9/146 SR7351)

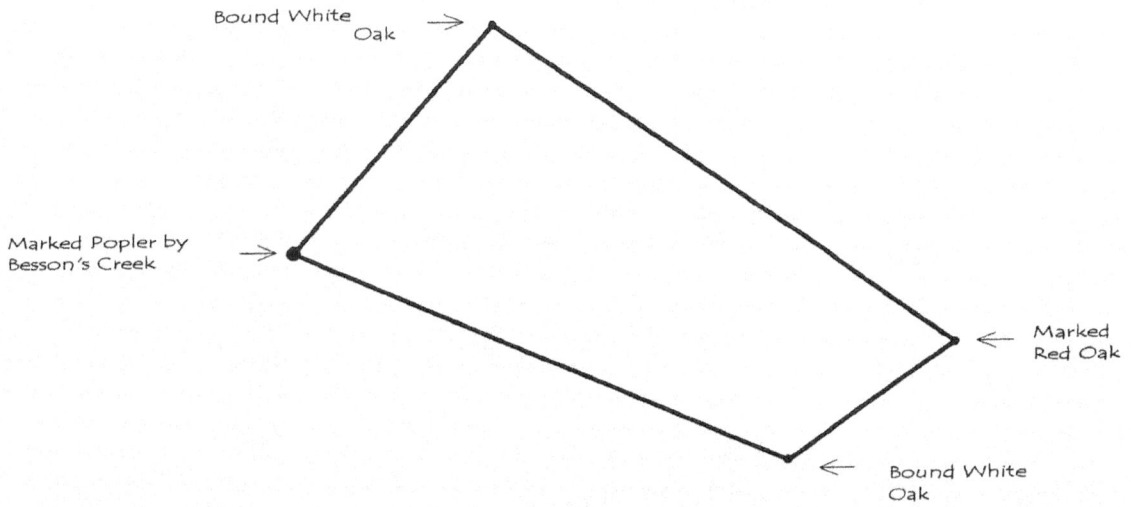

Bound White
Oak →

Marked Popler by
Besson's Creek →

Marked
Red Oak ←

Bound White
Oak ←

N

1200.00 feet
1:14400

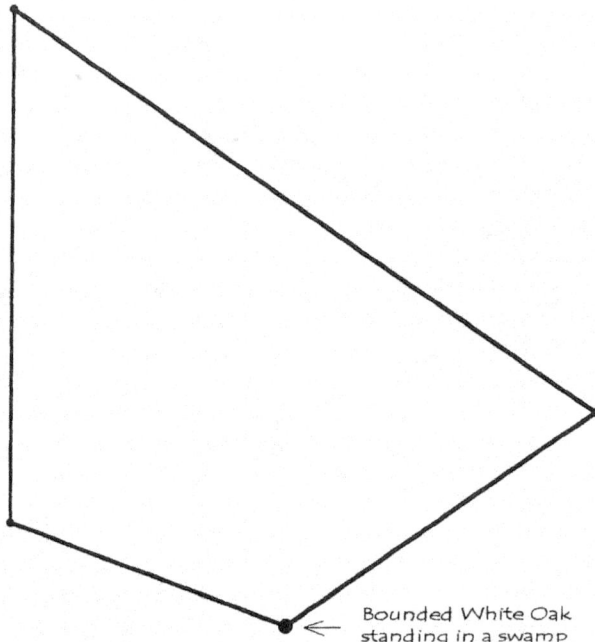

Bell's Haven Resurveyed 50/58 Acres
Richard & Elizabeth Bell 6/30/1684
(22/94 SR7363)

Bounded White Oak
standing in a swamp

660.00 feet
1:7920

Broome 200/202 Acres
Richard Beard 2/15/1659
(L4/441/SR7346)

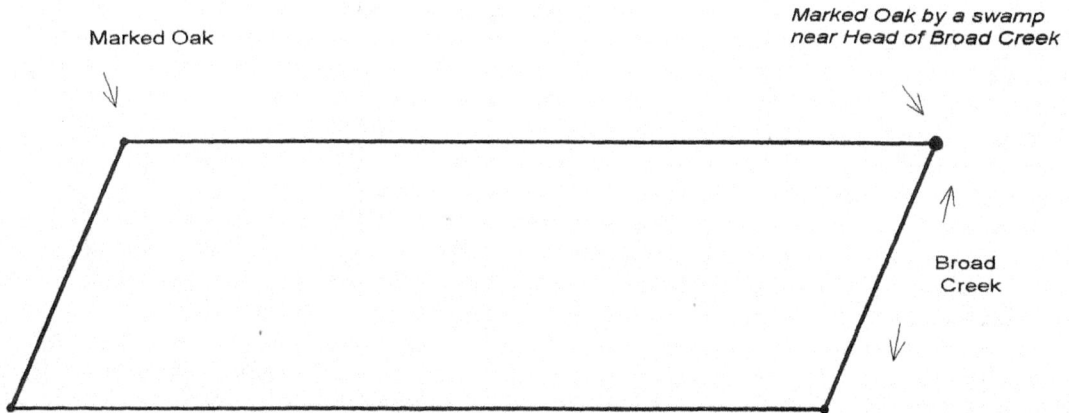

Marked Oak

Marked Oak by a swamp
near Head of Broad Creek

Broad
Creek

1200.00 feet

1:14400

153

Broome Resurveyed 220/153 Acres
Henry Ridgely 11/12/1670
(L16/23 SR7357)

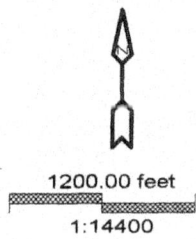

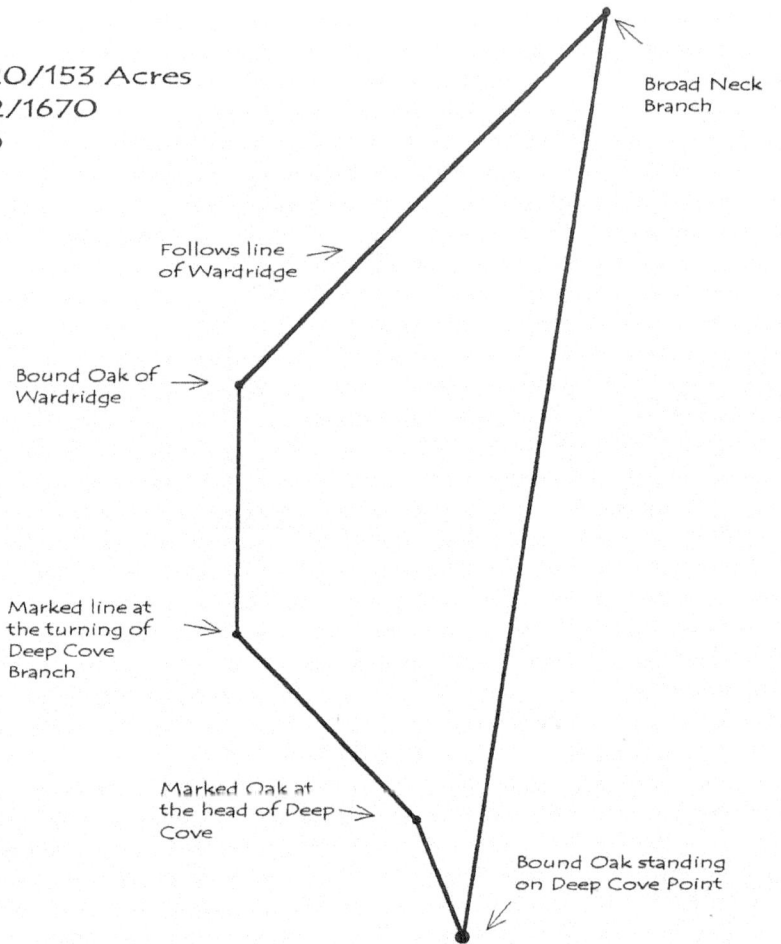

Broad Neck
Branch

Follows line
of Wardridge

Bound Oak of
Wardridge

Marked line at
the turning of
Deep Cove
Branch

Marked Oak at
the head of Deep
Cove

Bound Oak standing
on Deep Cove Point

1200.00 feet
1:14400

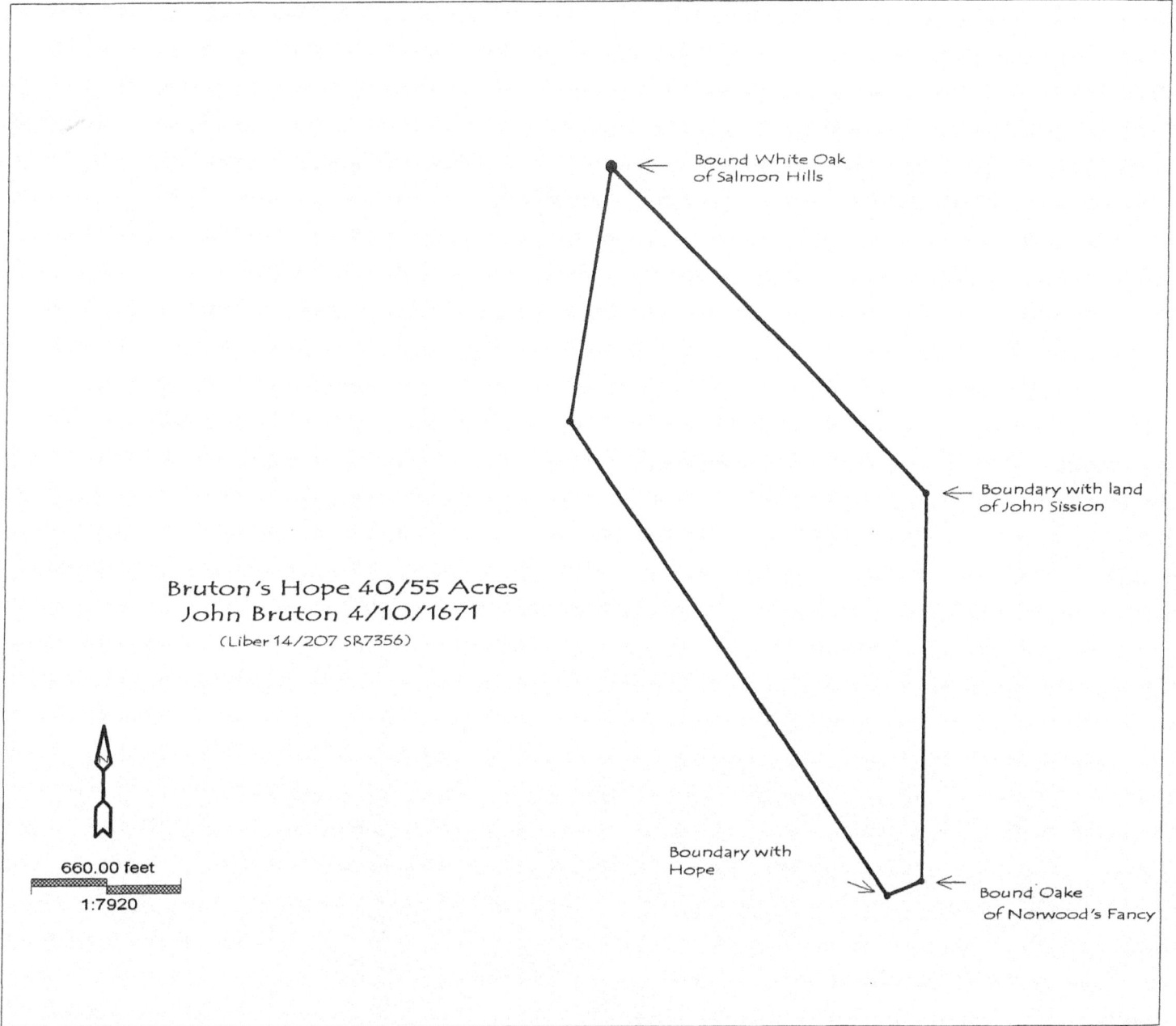

Bound White Oak
of Salmon Hills

Boundary with land
of John Sission

Bruton's Hope 40/55 Acres
John Bruton 4/10/1671
(Liber 14/207 SR7356)

660.00 feet

1:7920

Boundary with
Hope

Bound Oake
of Norwood's Fancy

155

Burntwood 100/176 Acres
Robert Gudgeon 5/1/1676
(Liber 19/350 SR7360)

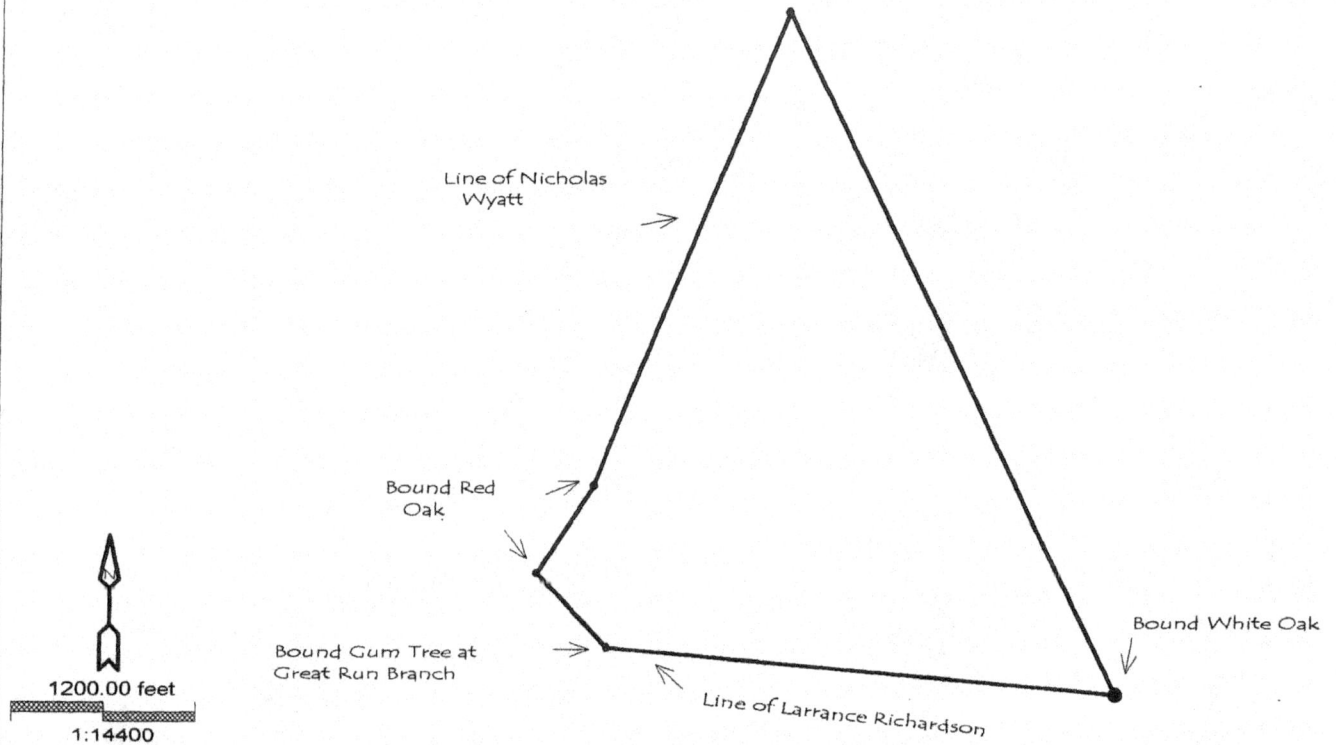

Line of Nicholas
Wyatt

Bound Red
Oak

Bound White Oak

Bound Gum Tree at
Great Run Branch

Line of Larrance Richardson

1200.00 feet

1:14400

Burntwood Common 50/55 Acres
Robert & Lawrence Gudgeon 6/1/1685)
(LIB&ILC/ 224 SR7368-2)

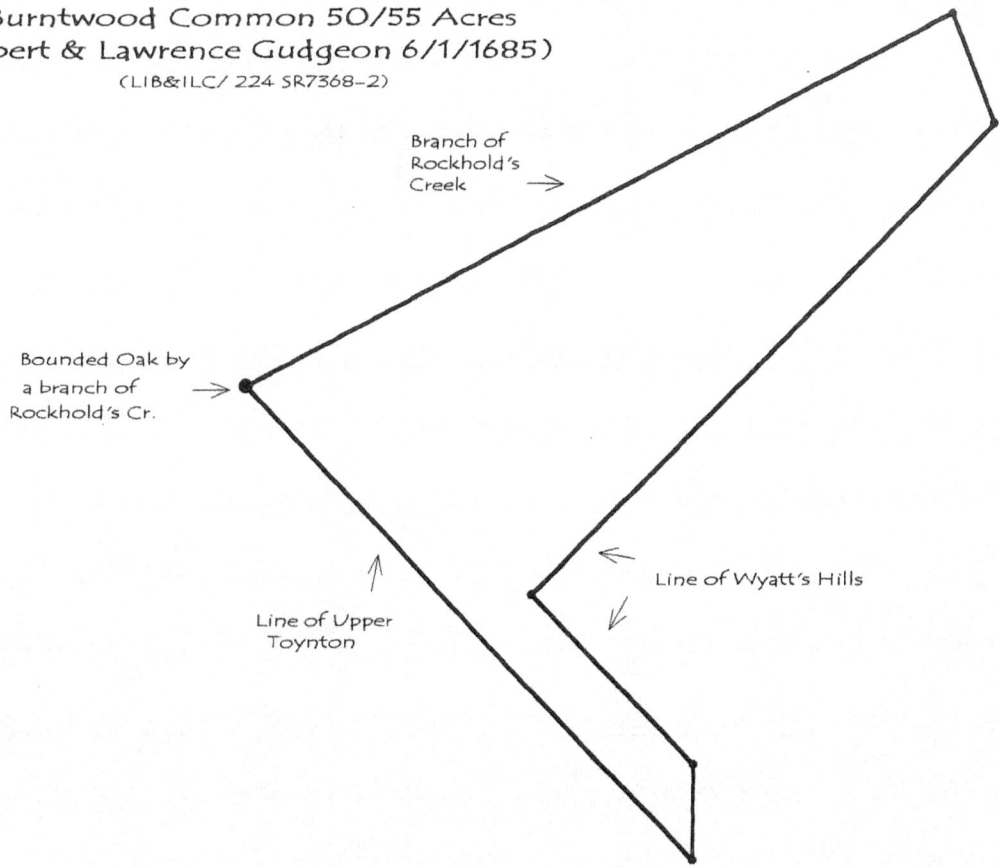

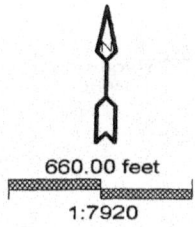

Branch of
Rockhold's
Creek

Bounded Oak by
a branch of
Rockhold's Cr.

Line of Wyatt's Hills

Line of Upper
Toynton

660.00 feet
1:7920

157

Charles's Hills 271/271 Acres
Charles Stevens 7/23/1679
(Liber 20/255 SR7361)

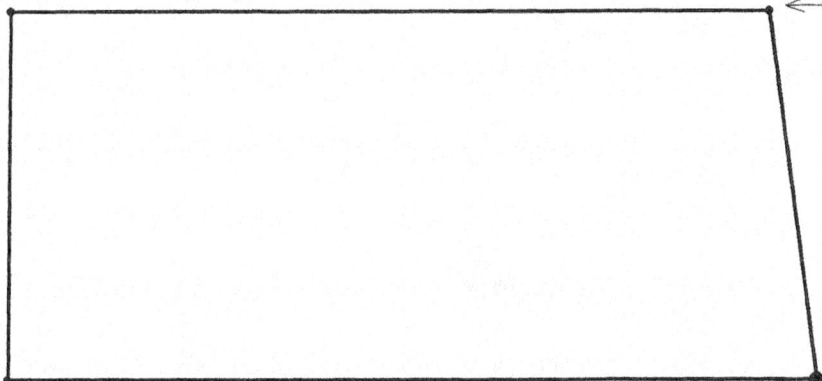

Bound Red
Oak →

Bound Chestnutt
← by the plantation
of Henry Sewell

← Bound White Oak
standing in a branch

Bound Oak
← standing on
a point

N

1200.00 feet
1:14400

Clarke's Enlargement 265/286 Acres
Neale Clarke 9/1/1687
(LNS2i/438 SR7371

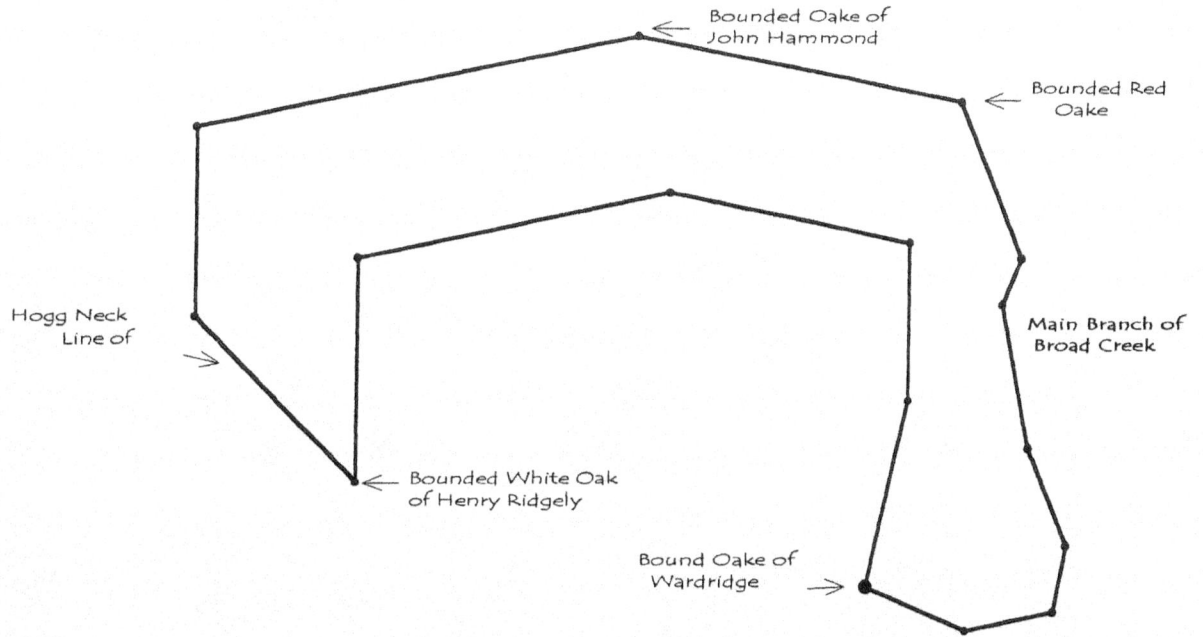

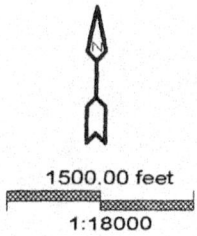

Bounded Oake of
John Hammond

Bounded Red
Oake

Hogg Neck
Line of

Main Branch of
Broad Creek

Bounded White Oak
of Henry Ridgely

Bound Oake of
Wardridge

1500.00 feet
1:18000

Clarke's Luck 60/60 Acres
Neale Clark 6/5/1685
(NSBi/415 SR7370)

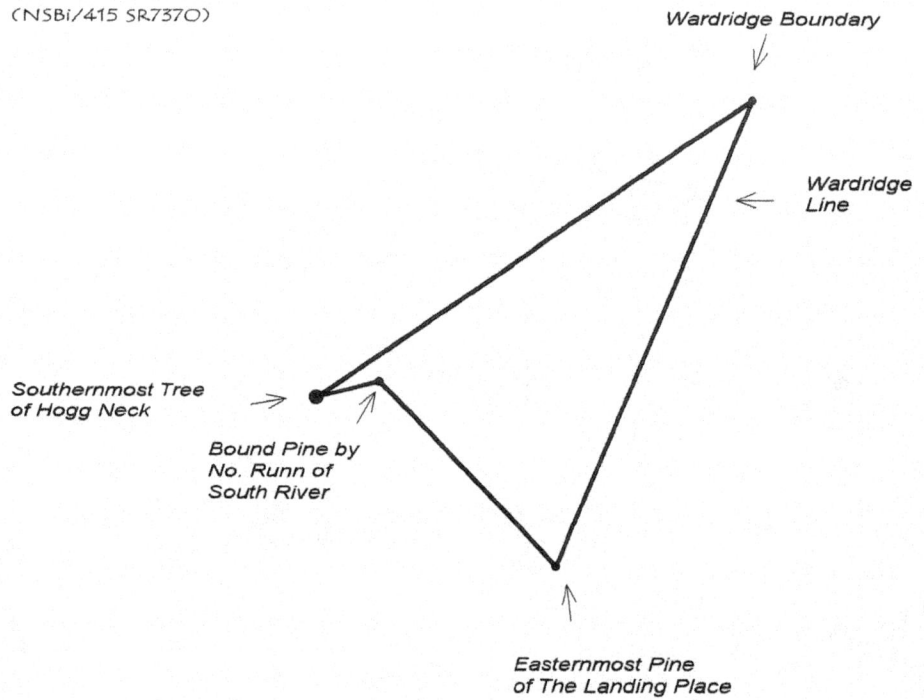

Wardridge Boundary

Wardridge
Line

Southernmost Tree
of Hogg Neck

Bound Pine by
No. Runn of
South River

Easternmost Pine
of The Landing Place

N

1200.00 feet

1:14400

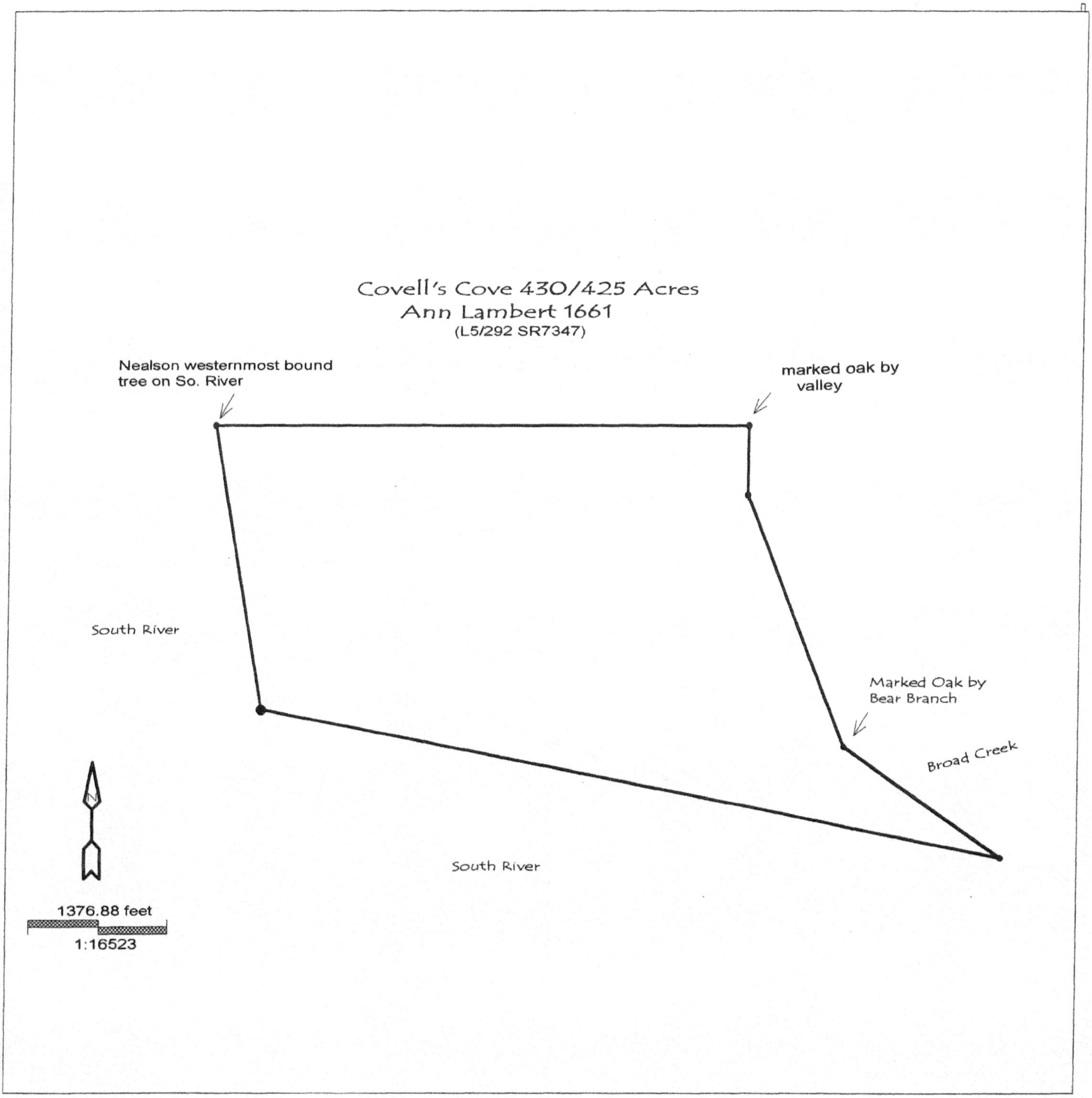

Covell's Cove 430/425 Acres
Ann Lambert 1661
(L5/292 SR7347)

Nealson westernmost bound
tree on So. River

marked oak by
valley

South River

Marked Oak by
Bear Branch

Broad Creek

South River

N

1376.88 feet

1:16523

Crouchfield 150/120 Acres
William Crouch 7/9/1659
(L4/87 SR7346)

Marked
pohicory →
tree

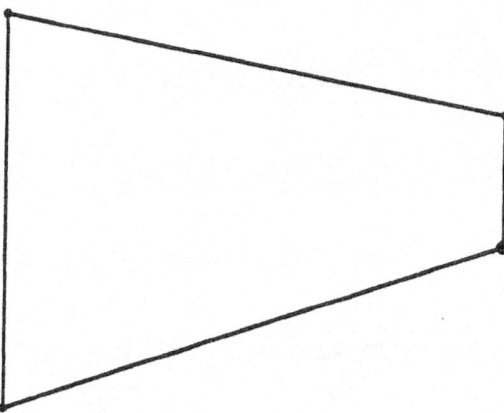

← Marked Wallnutt Tree

Marked Oak in
Crouche's Valley
near Marshe's ←
Swamp

Marked
Chestnutt in
Howard's →
Swamp

1200.00 feet

1:14400

Dorsey's Addition 50/50 Acres
Joshua Dorsey 5/10/1683
(LNSBi/433 SR7370)

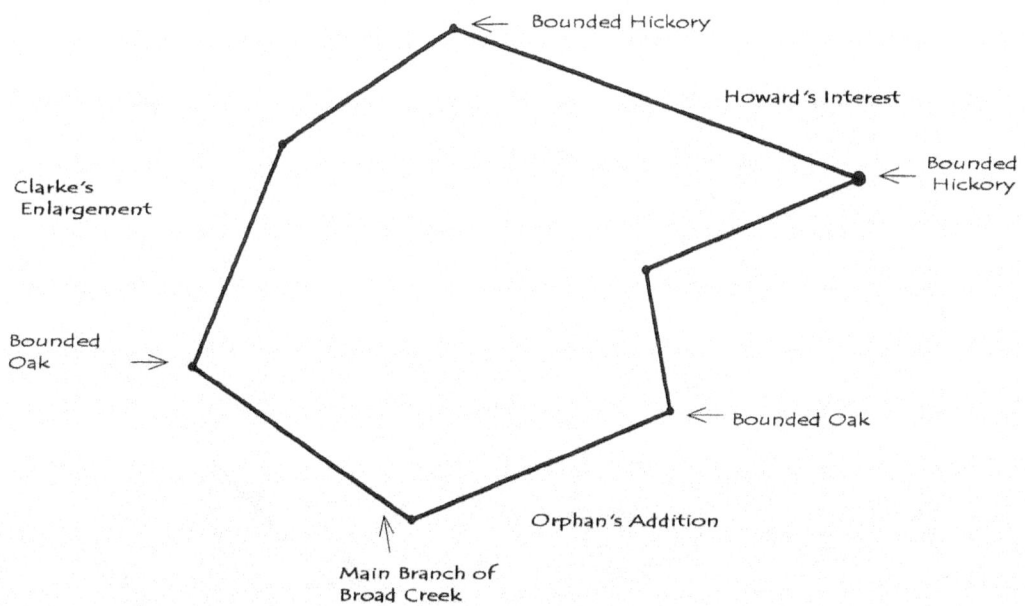

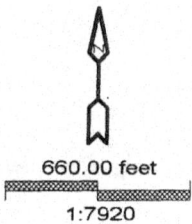

Bounded Hickory

Howard's Interest

Bounded
Hickory

Clarke's
Enlargement

Bounded
Oak

Bounded Oak

Orphan's Addition

Main Branch of
Broad Creek

660.00 feet

1:7920

163

Freeman's Fancy 300/250 Acres
John Freeman 5/27/1663
(L5/289 SR7347)

Bounds North
Swamp

line passes
thru swamp

Marked Oak by
South Swamp

Southernmost bounded Oak
of land foemerly conveyed to
him (John Freeman)

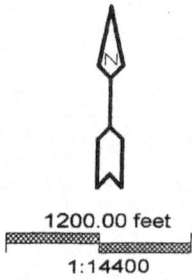

N

1200.00 feet
1:14400

Freemanston 150/131 Acres
John Freeman 2/15/1659
(L4/429 SR7346)

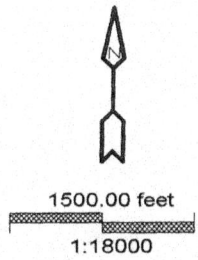

← Follows course of West
Banch of South River

Marked Pohikary on the
on the neck by the riverside
by the West Branch

1500.00 feet
1:18000

Marked on on the
East side of the
West Branch of So. River

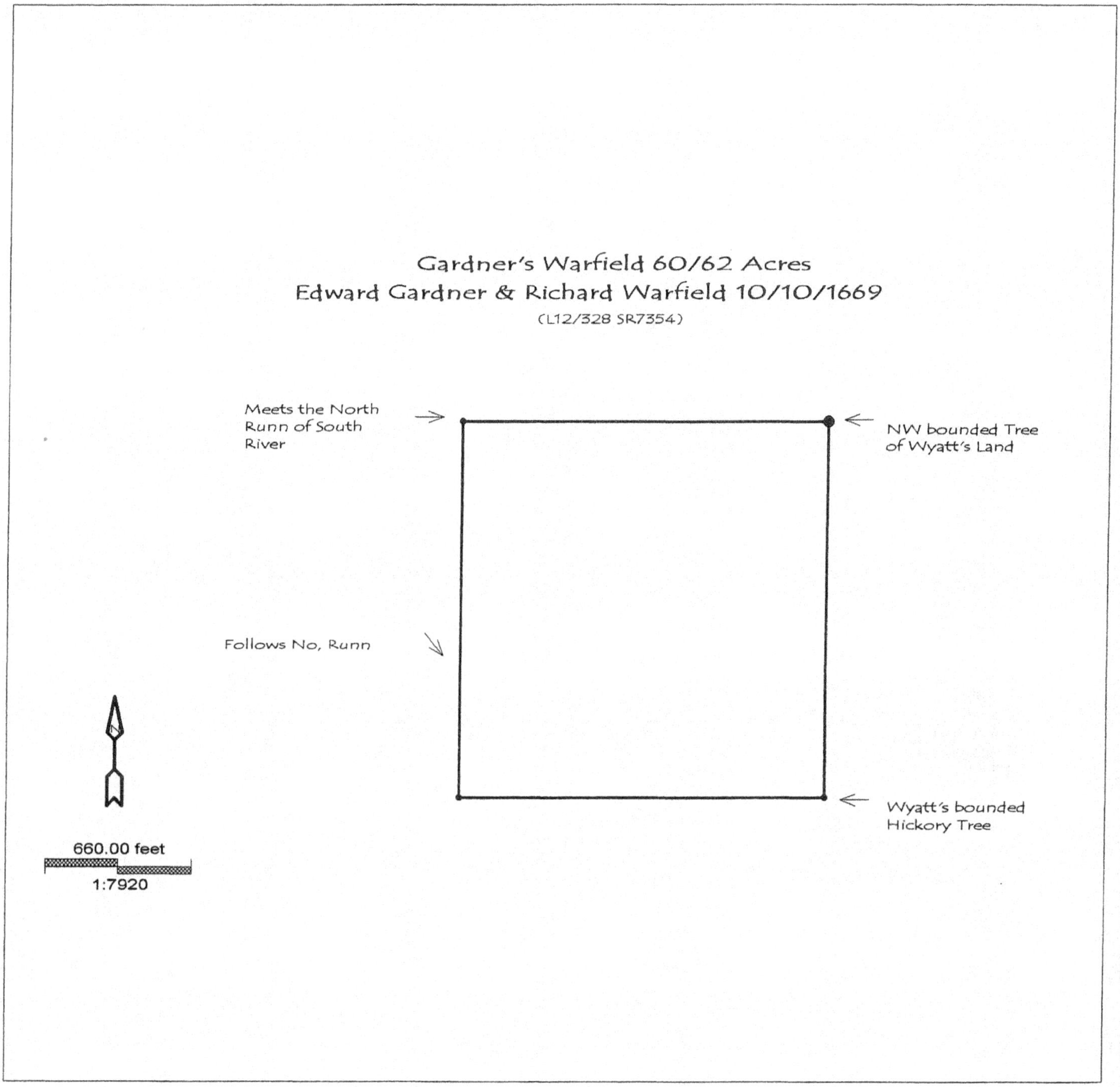

Gardner's Warfield 60/62 Acres
Edward Gardner & Richard Warfield 10/10/1669
(L12/328 SR7354)

Meets the North
Runn of South
River

NW bounded Tree
of Wyatt's Land

Follows No, Runn

Wyatt's bounded
Hickory Tree

660.00 feet

1:7920

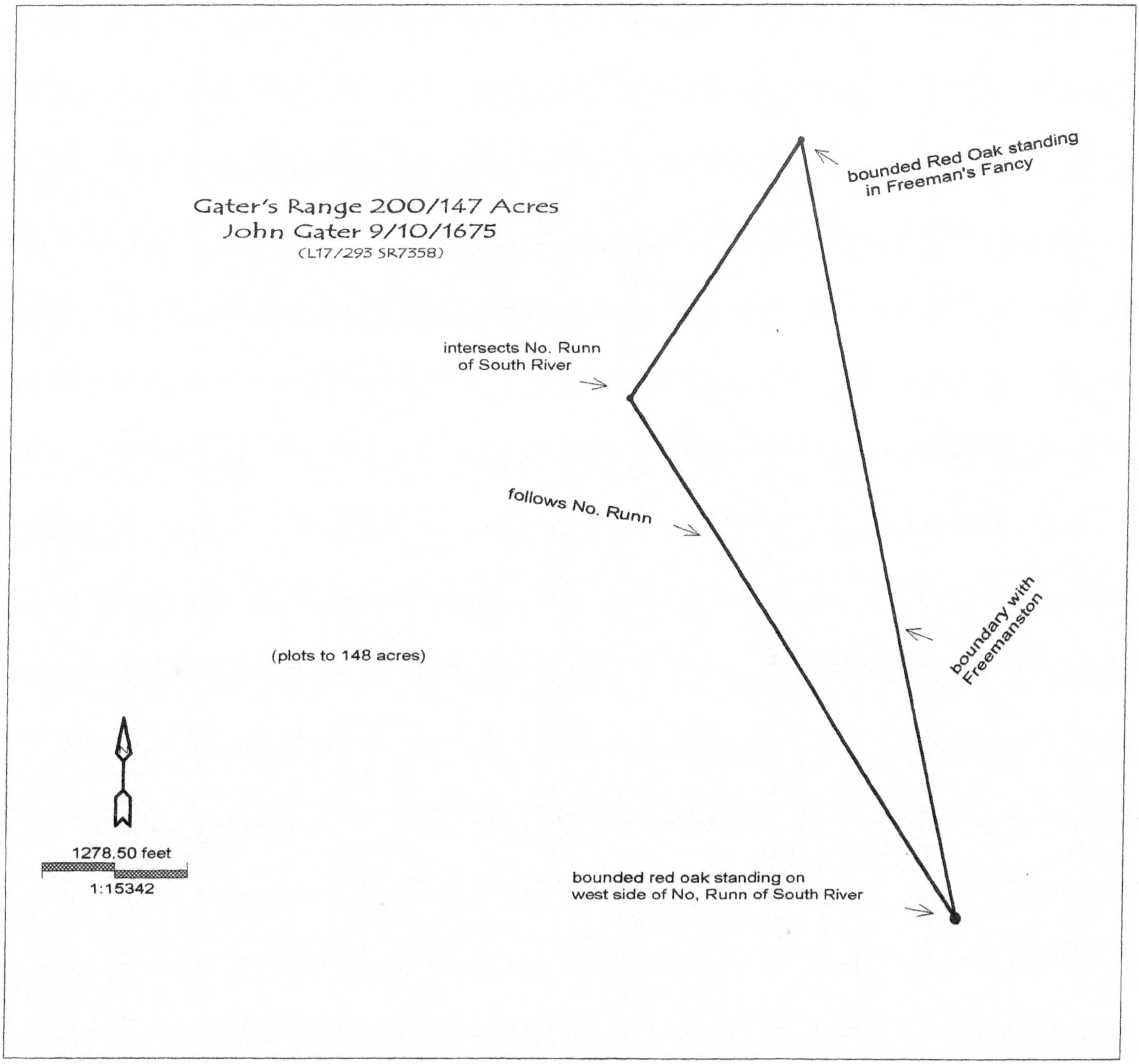

Gater's Range 200/147 Acres
John Gater 9/10/1675
(L17/293 SR7358)

bounded Red Oak standing
in Freeman's Fancy

intersects No. Runn
of South River

follows No. Runn

boundary with
Freemanston

(plots to 148 acres)

1278.50 feet

1:15342

bounded red oak standing on
west side of No, Runn of South River

Hog Neck 250/233 Acres
Edward Hope 6/24/1663
(L5/353 SR7347)

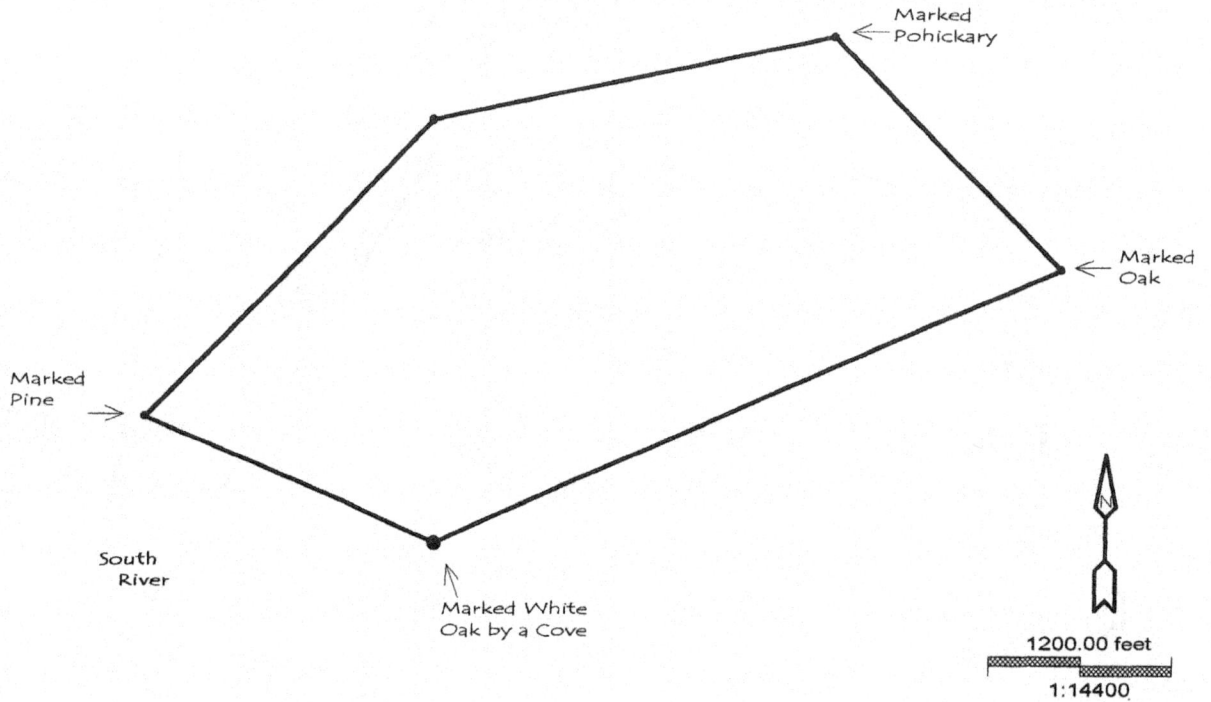

Marked
Pohickary

Marked
Oak

Marked
Pine

South
River

Marked White
Oak by a Cove

N

1200.00 feet
1:14400

Bound Poplar by
a road leading from
Richard Warfield's
House to house of
Mrs. Ruth Howard

Honest Man's Lot 110/119 Acres
John Duvall 7/23/1704
(LCDi/220 SR7376)

Beechnut Tree by
East side of a
branch

Bound Tree of
The Good Mother's
Endeavor

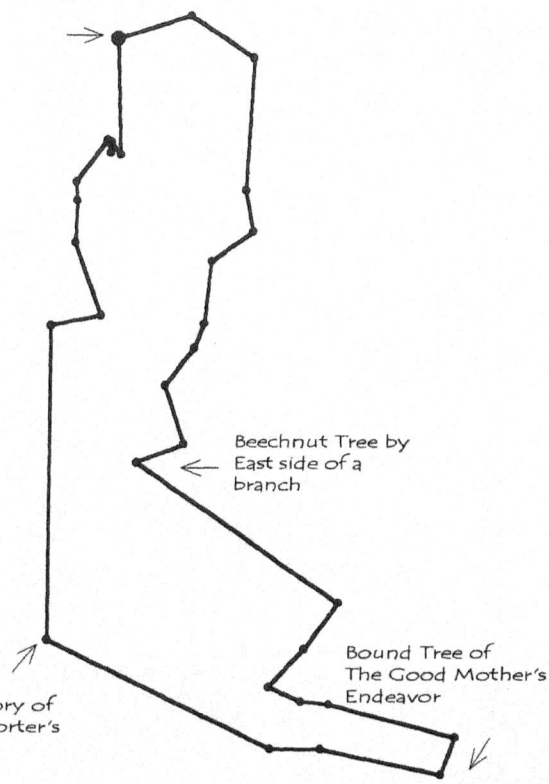

N

Bound Hickory of
Howard & Porter's
Range

1200.00 feet
1:14400

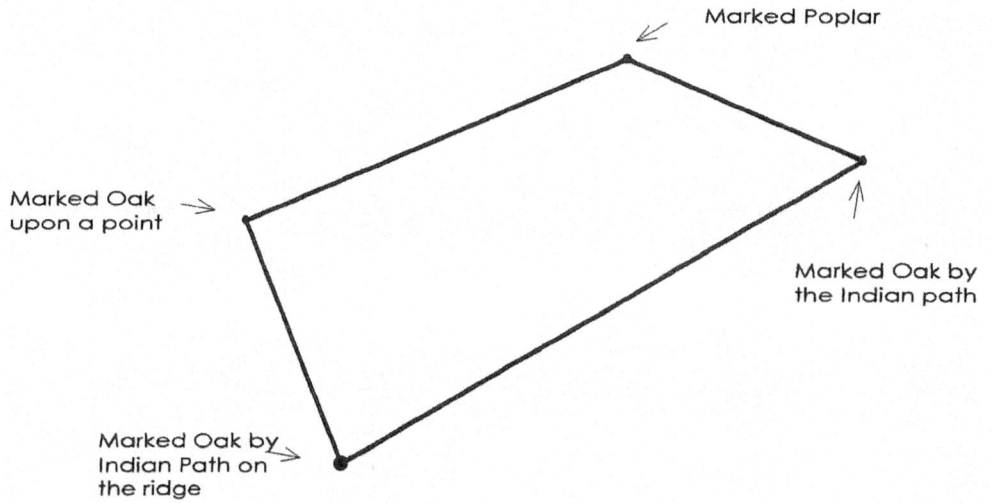

Hope 100/107 Acres
Henry Sewell 8/8/1664
(L7/343 SR7349)

Marked Poplar

Marked Oak
upon a point

Marked Oak by
the Indian path

Marked Oak by
Indian Path on
the ridge

1200.00 feet

1:14400

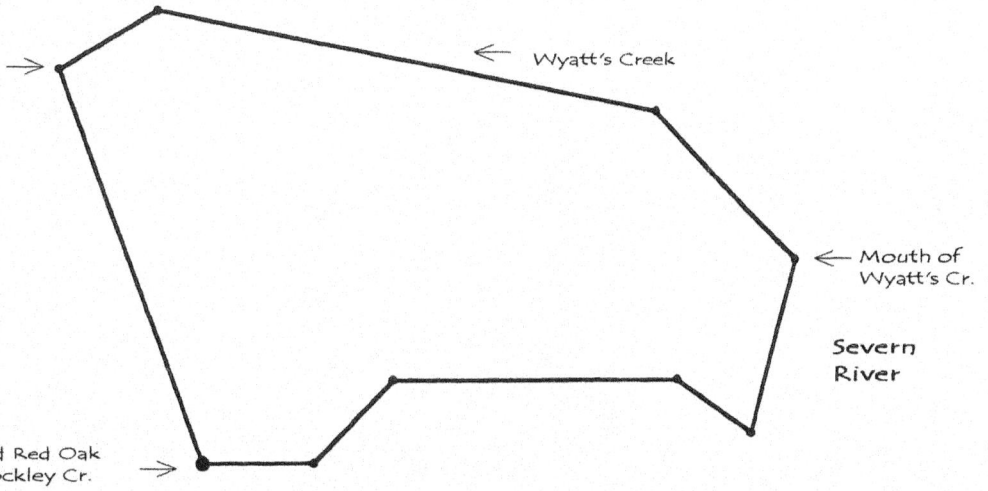

Howard's Discovery 50/50 Acres
John Howard 5/1/1697
(LCD/18 SR7376)

Bound Red Oake
by Creekside

Wyatt's Creek

Mouth of
Wyatt's Cr.

Severn
River

Bound Red Oak
by Hockley Cr.

600.00 feet

1:7200

Howard's Interest 150/209 Acres
John Howard 8/4/1664
(L7/252 SR7349)

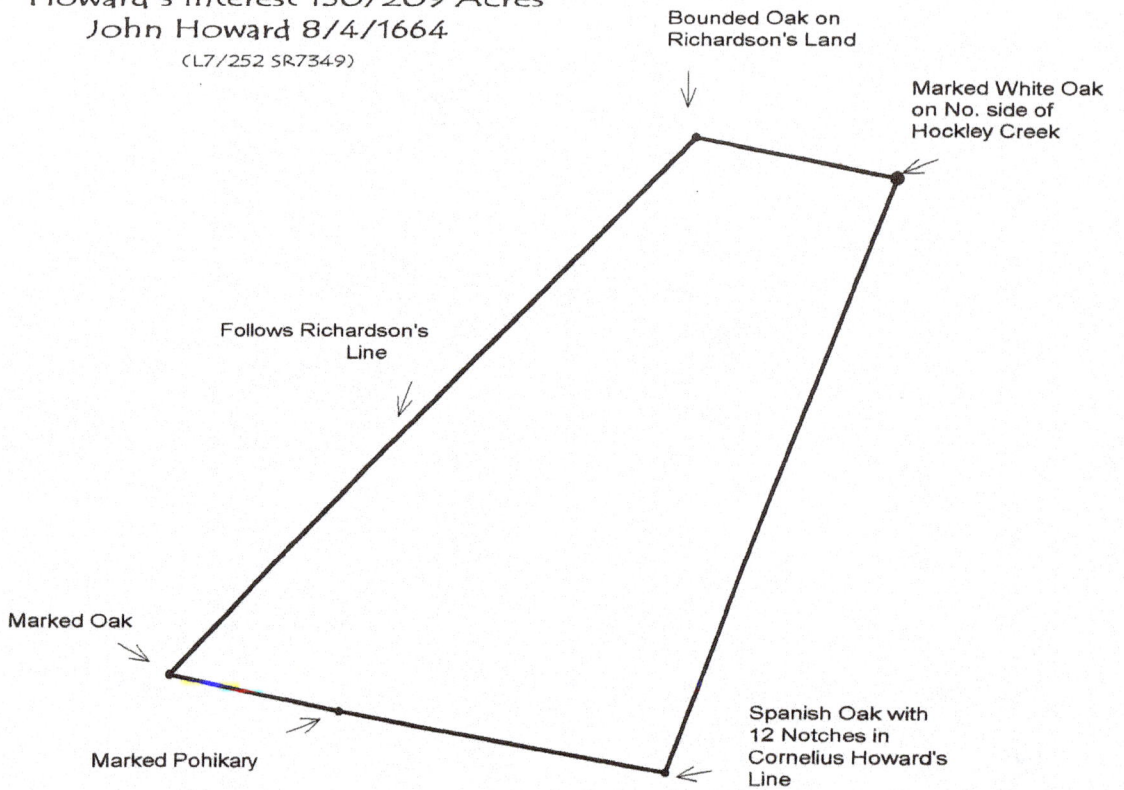

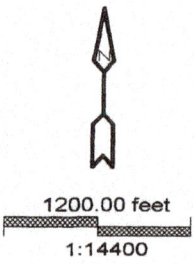

Bounded Oak on
Richardson's Land

Marked White Oak
on No. side of
Hockley Creek

Follows Richardson's
Line

Marked Oak

Marked Pohikary

Spanish Oak with
12 Notches in
Cornelius Howard's
Line

1200.00 feet
1:14400

Howard's Mount 80/76 Acres
John Howard 4/12/1678
(Liber 20/69 SR7361)

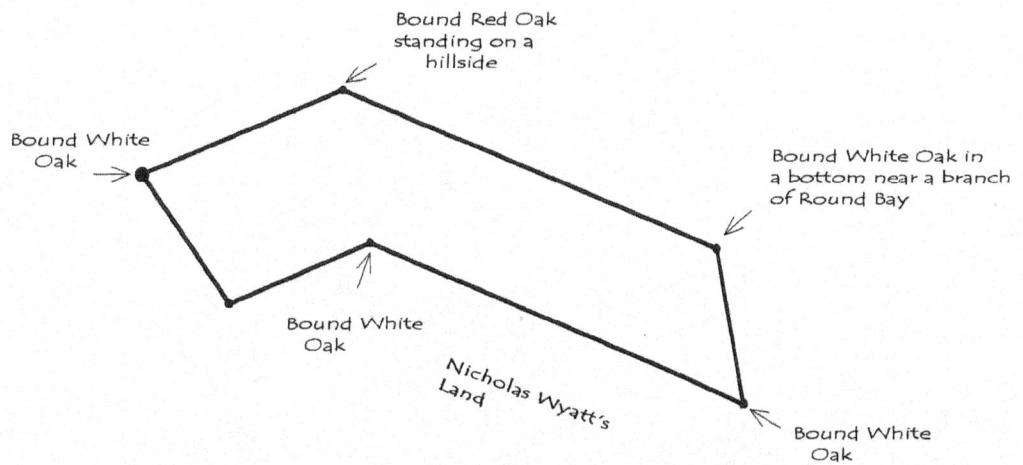

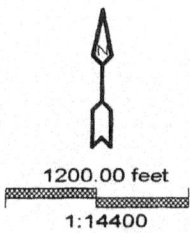

Bound Red Oak
standing on a
hillside

Bound White
Oak

Bound White Oak in
a bottom near a branch
of Round Bay

Bound White
Oak

Nicholas Wyatt's
Land

Bound White
Oak

1200.00 feet

1:14400

Howard's Search 121/119 Acres
John Howard 12/10/1690
(LCC4/13 SR7375)

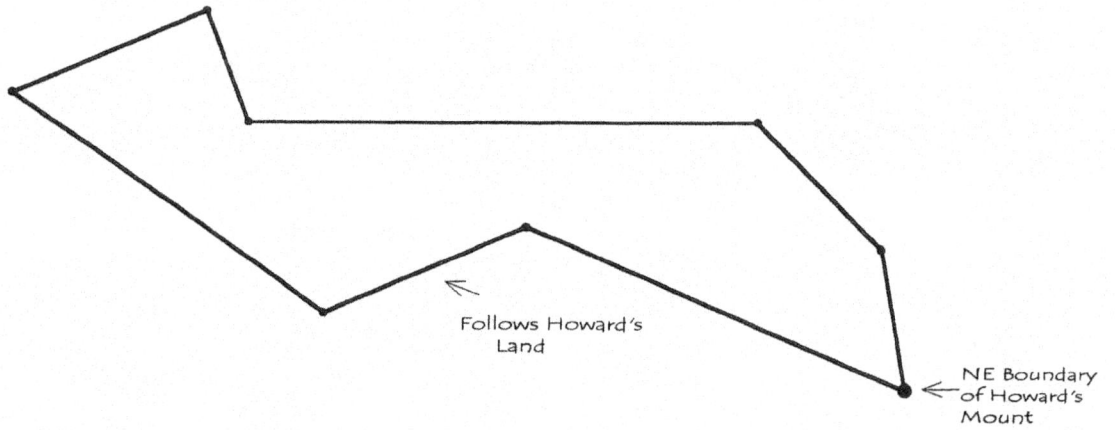

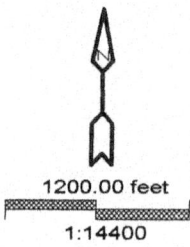

Follows Howard's
Land

NE Boundary
of Howard's
Mount

1200.00 feet

1:14400

Jane's Inheritance 50/51 Acres
Jane Sisson 6/20/1668
(L12/28 SR7354)

Bounded Red Oak
on Sunken Ground
Creek

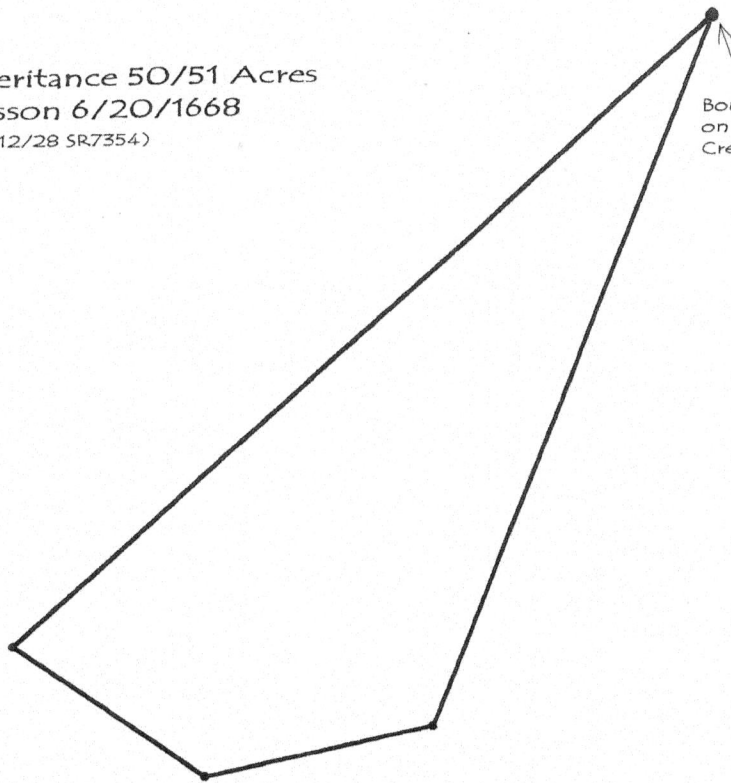

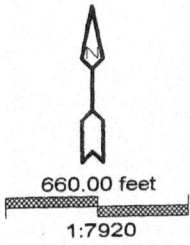

660.00 feet
1:7920

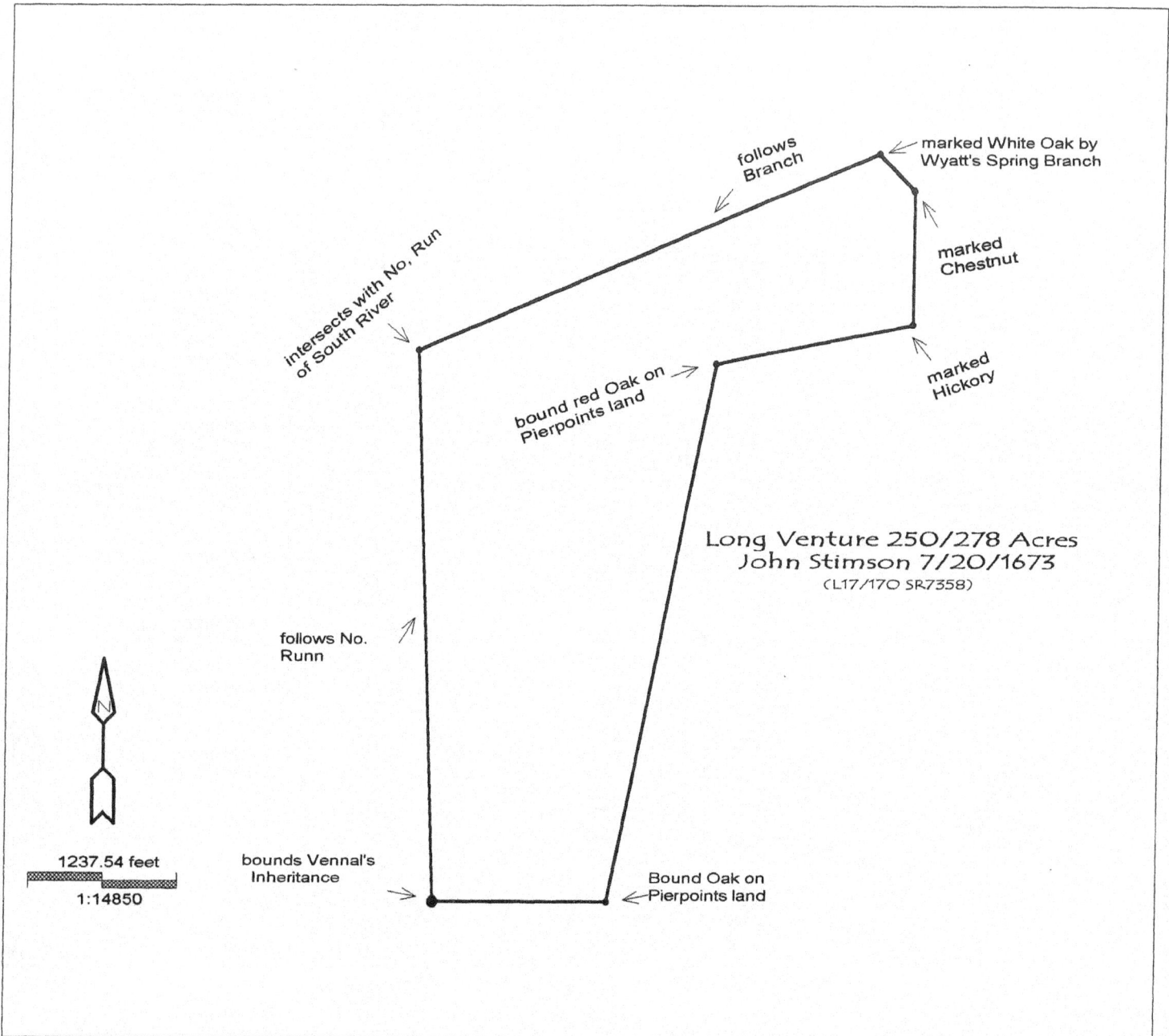

follows
Branch

marked White Oak by
Wyatt's Spring Branch

marked
Chestnut

intersects with No. Run
of South River

bound red Oak on
Pierpoints land

marked
Hickory

Long Venture 250/278 Acres
John Stimson 7/20/1673
(L17/170 SR7358)

follows No.
Runn

N

1237.54 feet

1:14850

bounds Vennal's
Inheritance

Bound Oak on
Pierpoints land

Medcalfe's Chance 80/71 Acres
John Medcalfe 8/10/1683
(LSDA/104 SR7369)

Bound Hickory of
Howard & Porter's
Range

Bound White Oake
at the turning point
of a branch

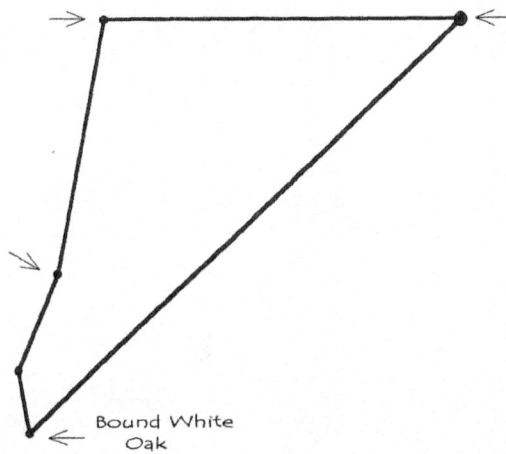

Bound White
Oak

1200.00 feet

1:14400

Medcalfe's Mount 70/70 Acres
John Medcalfe 5/10/1685
(LNSBi/174 SR7370)

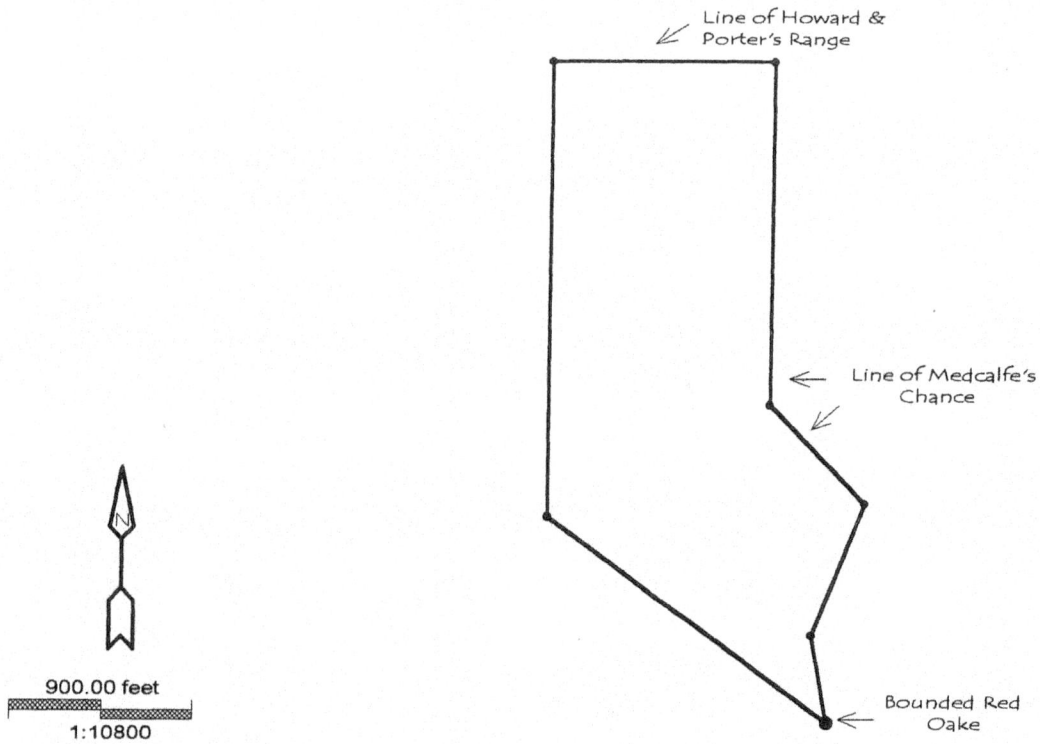

Line of Howard &
Porter's Range

Line of Medcalfe's
Chance

Bounded Red
Oake

900.00 feet

1:10800

Mill Land 100/101 Acres
Robert Proctor 5/10/1683
(LNS2i/111 SR7371)

Line of Hockley
In The Hole

Main Branch of
Broad Creek

1200.00 feet

1:14400

Bounded Oak by
Main Br. of Broad
Creek

Bounded Oak of
Hockley In The
Hole

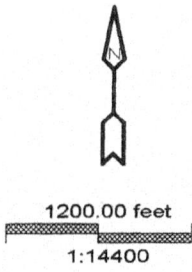

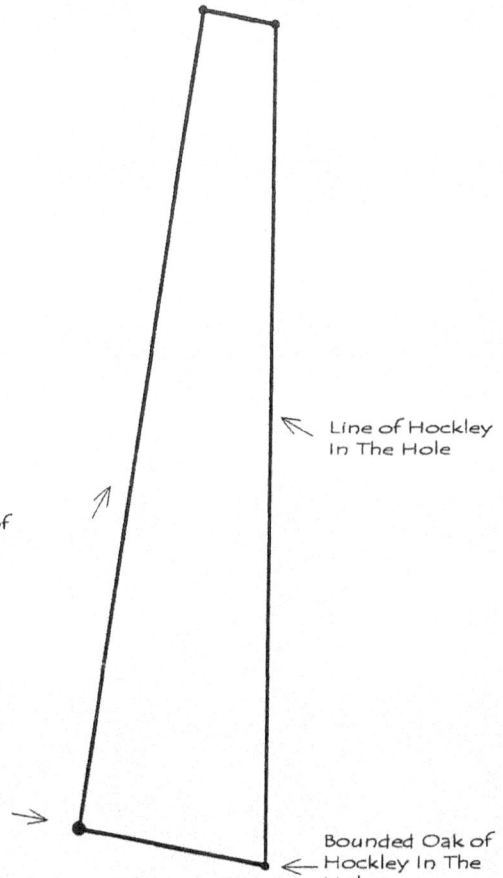

Narrow Neck 41/39 Acres
Wm. Yieldhall 10/5/1683
(LSDA/420 SR7369)

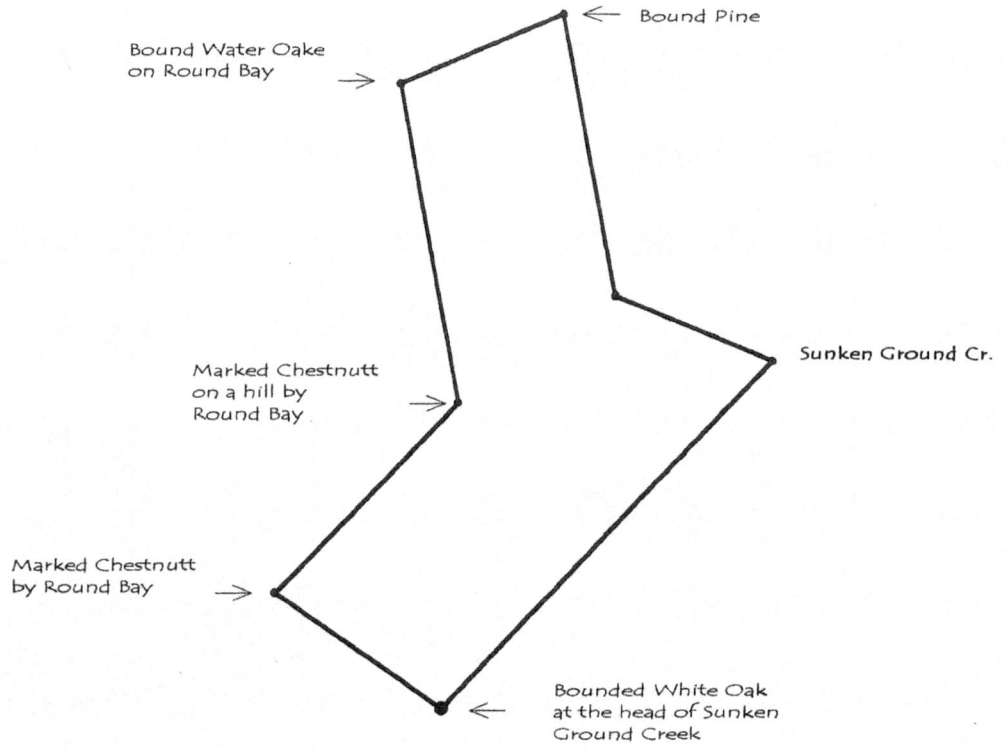

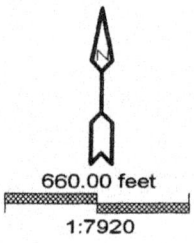

Bound Pine

Bound Water Oake
on Round Bay

Marked Chestnutt
on a hill by
Round Bay

Sunken Ground Cr.

Marked Chestnutt
by Round Bay

Bounded White Oak
at the head of Sunken
Ground Creek

660.00 feet

1:7920

Nealson 100/100 Acres
Neale Clarke 2/15/1659
(L4/383 SR7346)

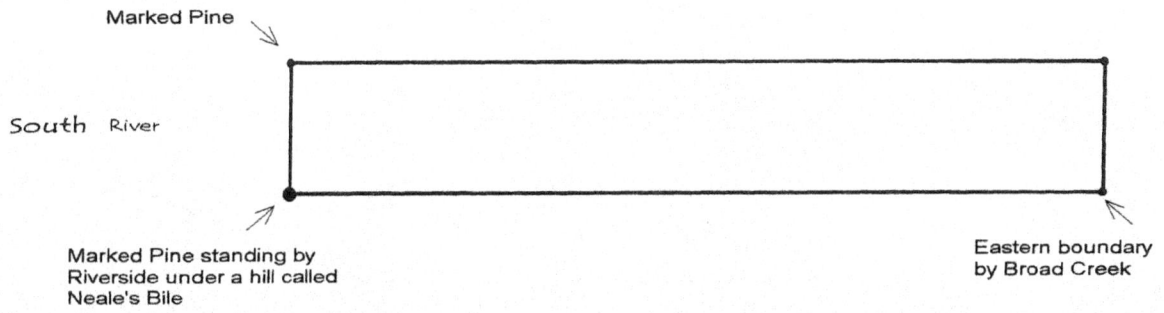

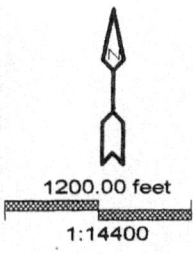

Marked Pine

South River

Marked Pine standing by
Riverside under a hill called
Neale's Bile

Eastern boundary
by Broad Creek

1200.00 feet

1:14400

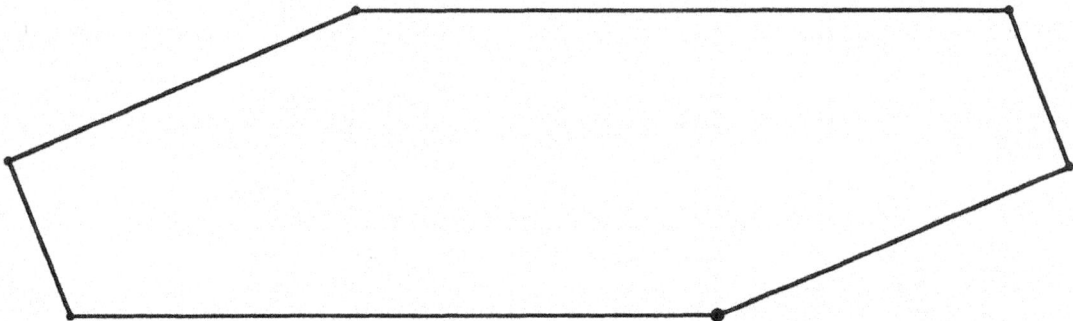

Norwood's Fancy 420/381 Acres
John Norwood 2/16/1659
(L4/426 SR7346)

Marked Oak
by a Creek

Marked Ash standing
by a fresh branch

Round
Bay

1500.00 feet
1:18000

Pierpoint's Lott 150/207 Acres
Henry Pierpoint 9/15/1666
(L10/106 SR7352)

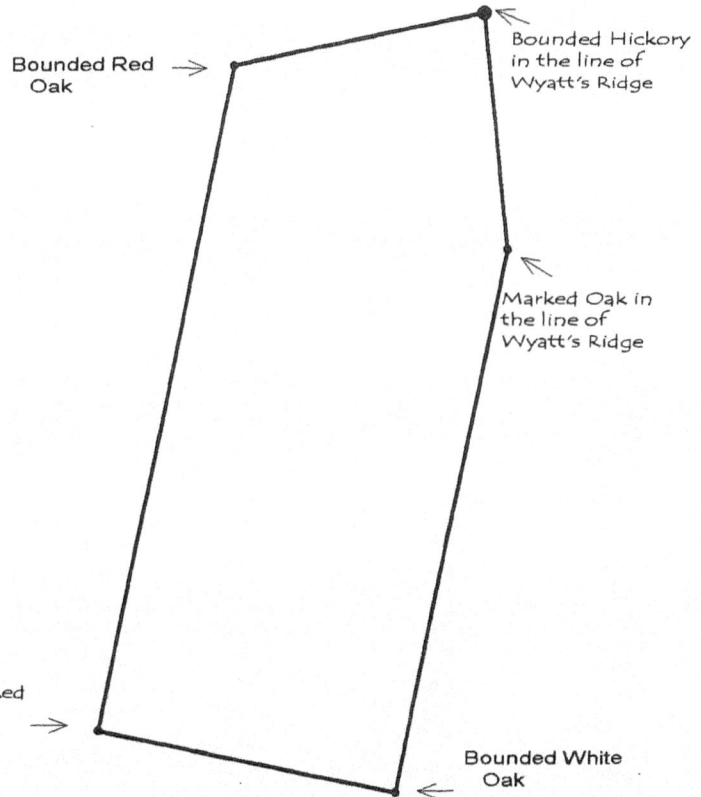

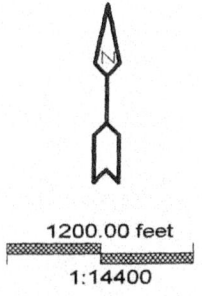

Bounded Red Oak

Bounded Hickory in the line of Wyatt's Ridge

Marked Oak in the line of Wyatt's Ridge

1200.00 feet
1:14400

Bounded Red Oak

Bounded White Oak

Pierpoint's Rocks 80/57 Acres
Henry Pierpoint 4/1/1672
(L14/489 SR7456)

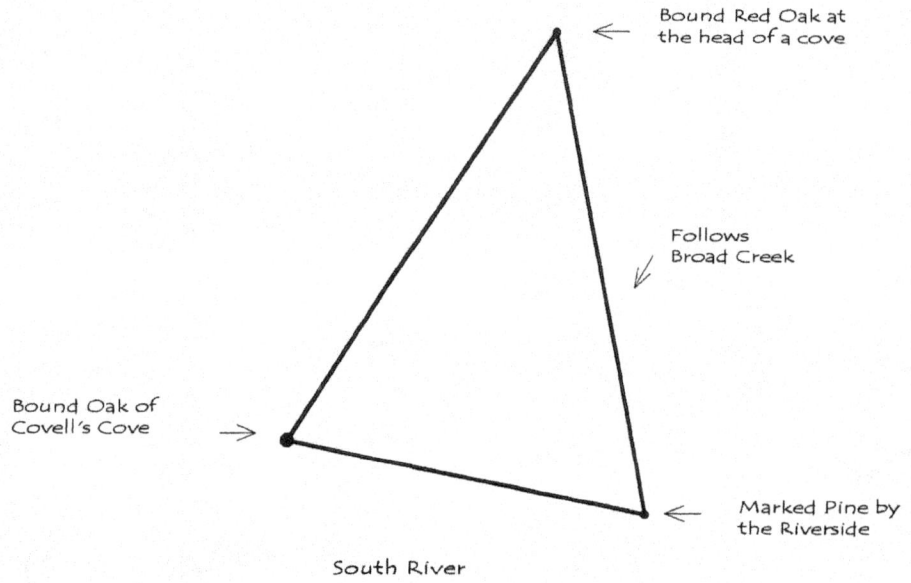

Bound Red Oak at
the head of a cove

Follows
Broad Creek

Bound Oak of
Covell's Cove

Marked Pine by
the Riverside

South River

1028.39 feet

1:12341

Providence 200/200 Acres
Amos Garrett 8/20/1710
(LDD5i/633 SR7378)

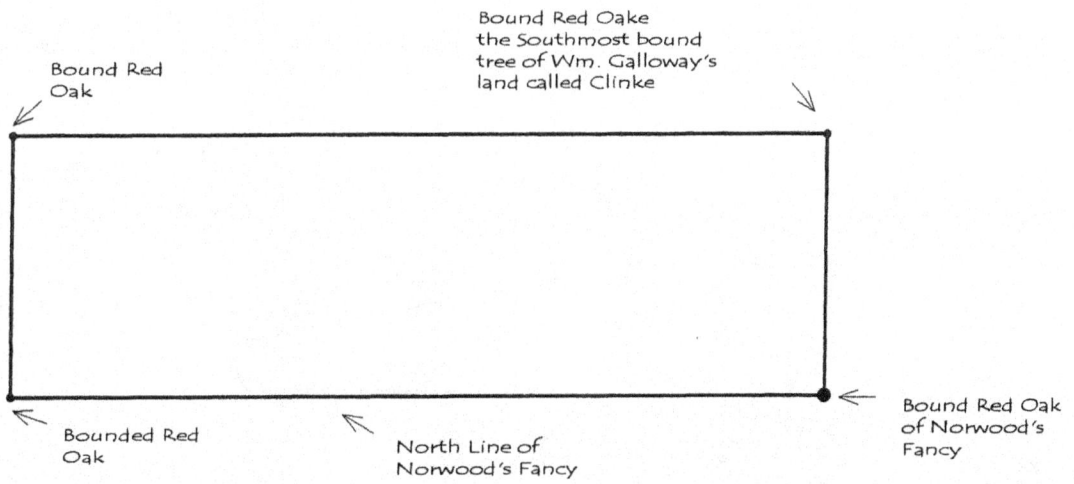

Bound Red Oake
the Southmost bound
tree of Wm. Galloway's
land called Clinke

Bound Red
Oak

Bound Red Oak
of Norwood's
Fancy

Bounded Red
Oak

North Line of
Norwood's Fancy

N

1200.00 feet

1:14400

Rawling's Purchase 50/48 Acres
Richard Rawlings 8/30/1682
(LCB3i/146 SR7367)

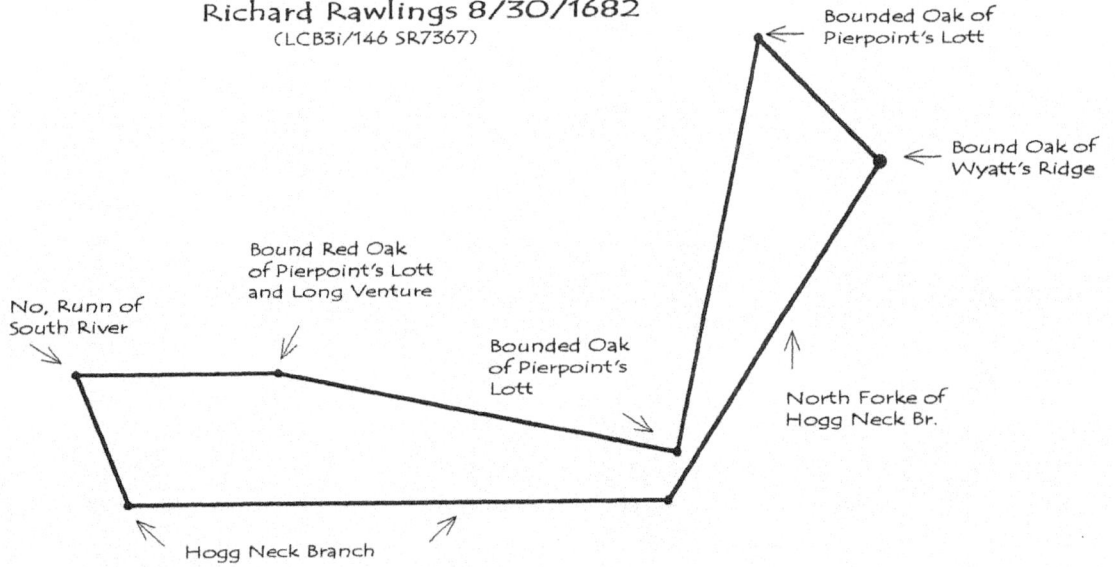

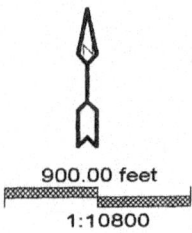

Bounded Oak of
Pierpoint's Lott

Bound Oak of
Wyatt's Ridge

Bound Red Oak
of Pierpoint's Lott
and Long Venture

No, Runn of
South River

Bounded Oak
of Pierpoint's
Lott

North Forke of
Hogg Neck Br.

Hogg Neck Branch

900.00 feet

1:10800

Richardson's Joy 200/195 Acres
Lawrence Richardson 6/23/1663
(Liber 5/344 SR7347)

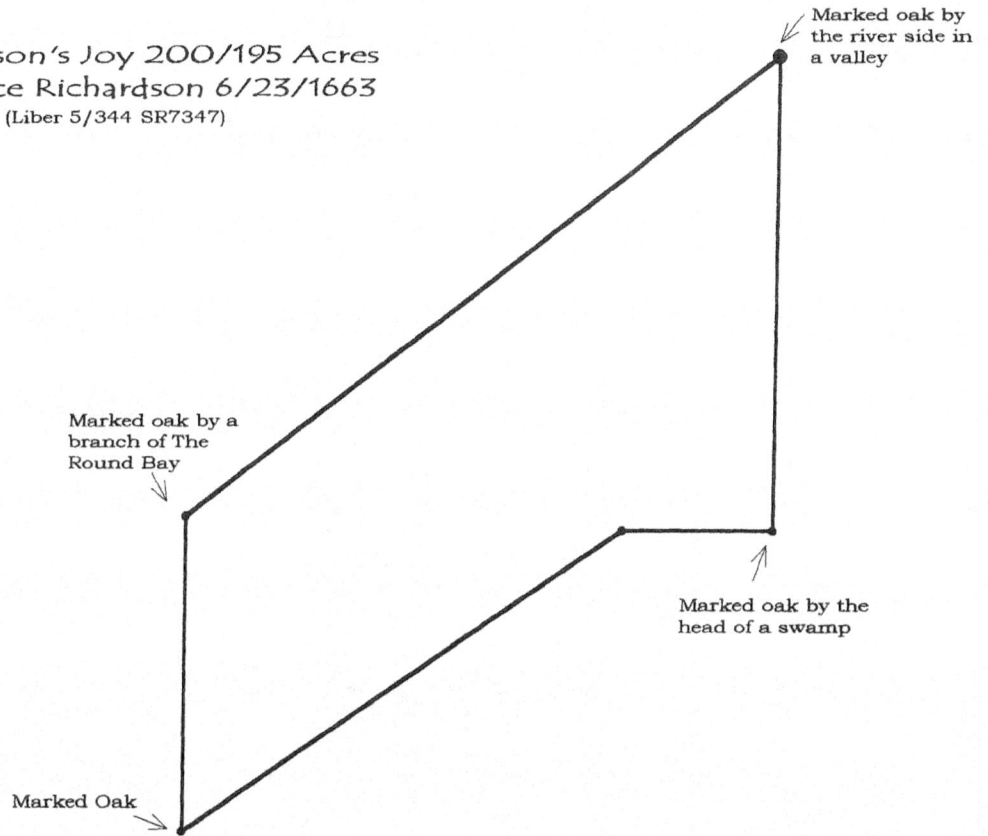

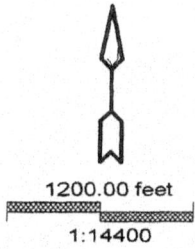

Marked oak by
the river side in
a valley

Marked oak by a
branch of The
Round Bay

Marked oak by the
head of a swamp

Marked Oak

1200.00 feet

1:14400

Ridgely's Beginning 40/60 Acres
William Ridgely 5/18/1679
(L20/205 SR7361)

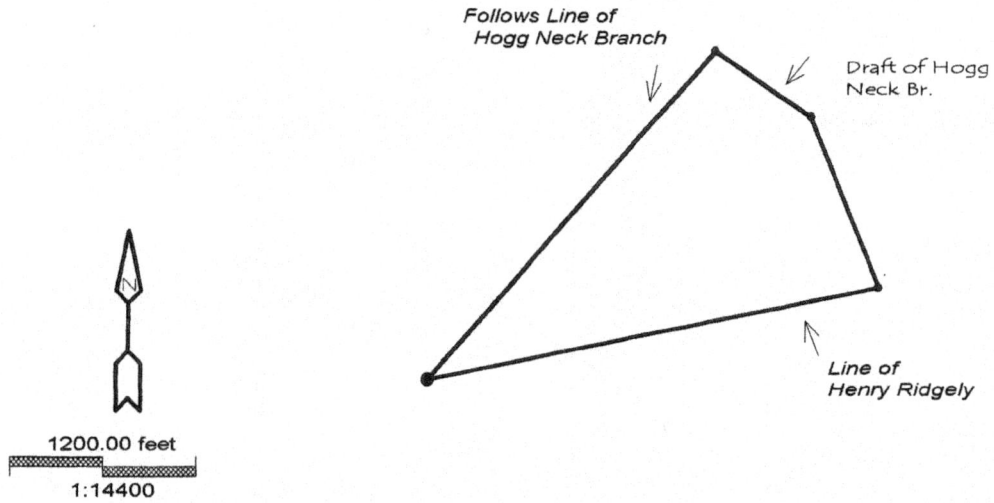

Follows Line of
Hogg Neck Branch

Draft of Hogg
Neck Br.

Line of
Henry Ridgely

N

1200.00 feet
1:14400

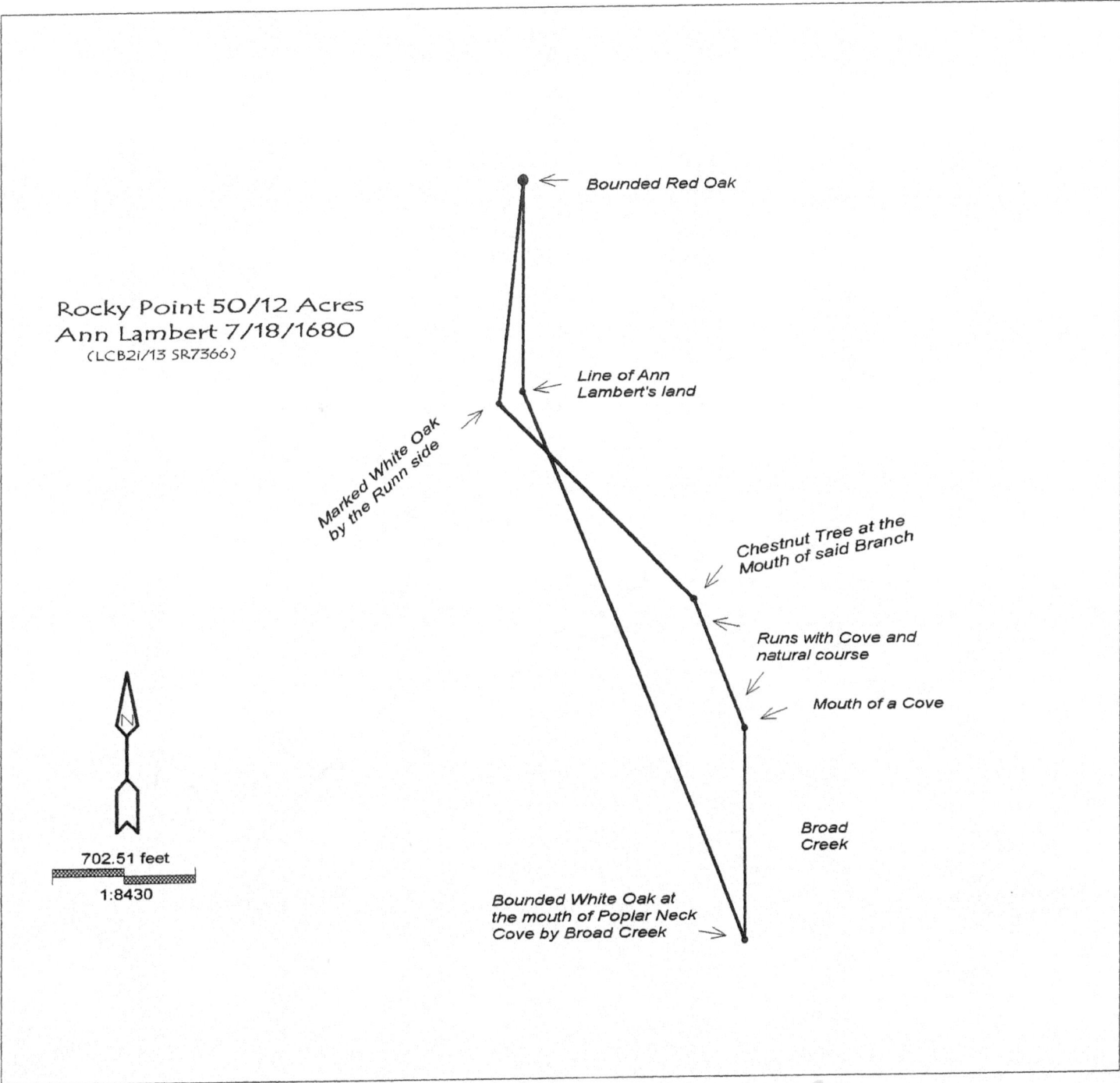

Rocky Point 50/12 Acres
Ann Lambert 7/18/1680
(LCB2i/13 SR7366)

Bounded Red Oak

Line of Ann
Lambert's land

Marked White Oak
by the Runn side

Chestnut Tree at the
Mouth of said Branch

Runs with Cove and
natural course

Mouth of a Cove

Broad
Creek

702.51 feet
1:8430

Bounded White Oak at
the mouth of Poplar Neck
Cove by Broad Creek

189

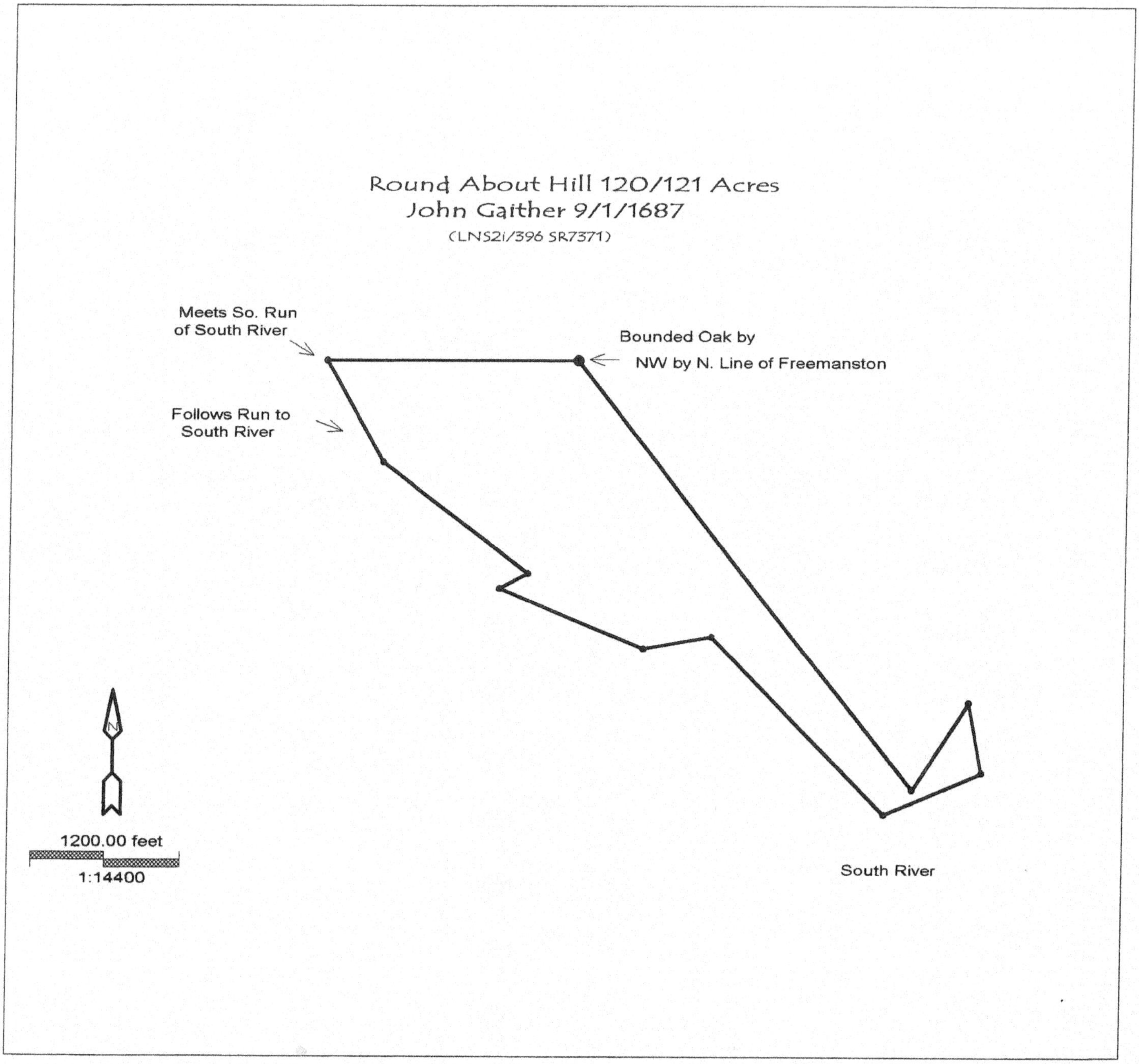

Round About Hill 120/121 Acres
John Gaither 9/1/1687
(LNS2i/396 SR7371)

Meets So. Run
of South River

Bounded Oak by
NW by N. Line of Freemanston

Follows Run to
South River

N

1200.00 feet

1:14400

South River

Stony Hills 36/26 Acres
Richard Everet 1/10/1695
(LWD/126 SR7372-2)

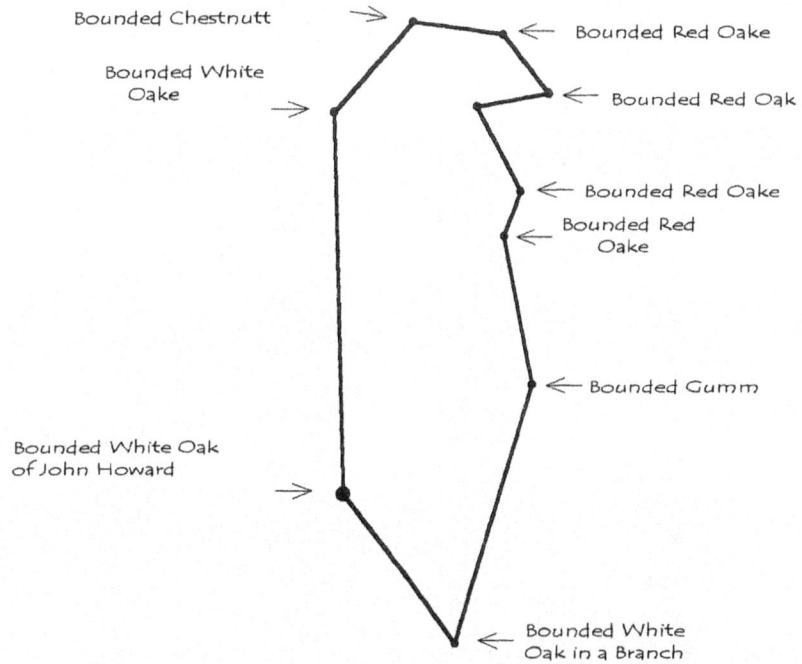

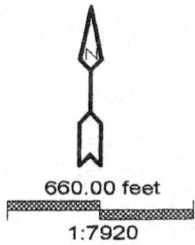

Bounded Chestnutt

Bounded Red Oake

Bounded White Oake

Bounded Red Oak

Bounded Red Oake

Bounded Red Oake

Bounded Gumm

Bounded White Oak of John Howard

Bounded White Oak in a Branch

N

660.00 feet

1:7920

The Adventure 50/43 Acres
William Frizzell 9/13/1663
(L5/574 SR7347)

Follows West line of
Wyatt's Ridge

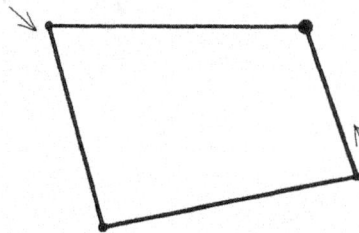

follows Branch of
Broad Creek

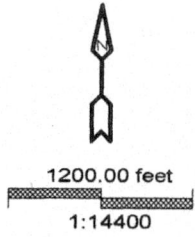

1200.00 feet

1:14400

The Coombe 150/149 Acres
Tobias Butler 1/22/1659
L6/432 SR7346)

1200.00 feet

1:14400

*Oak standing in marsh
by fresh run of River*

Marked Oak by
South River →

← *Runs Along
South River*

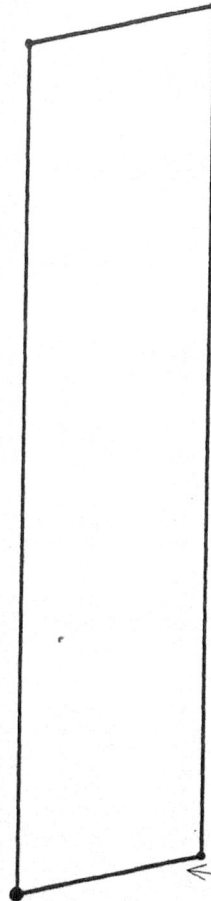

The Encrease 50/33 Acres
John Minter 5/15/1668
(L11/407 SR7353)

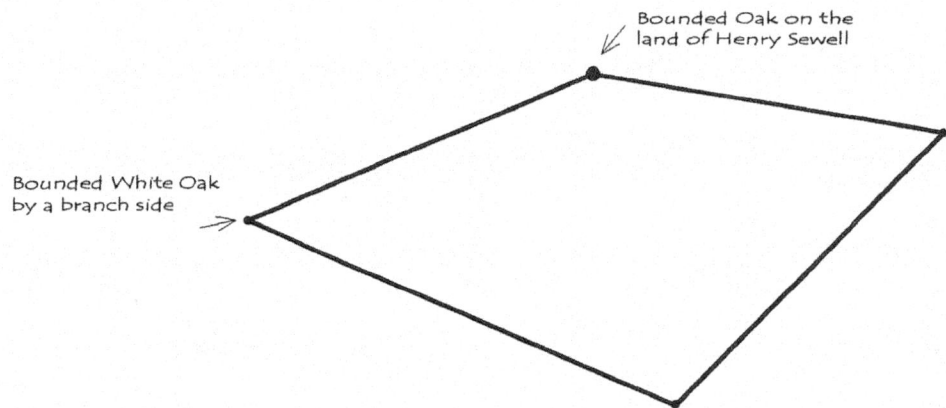

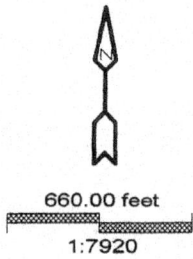

Bounded Oak on the
land of Henry Sewell

Bounded White Oak
by a branch side

N

660.00 feet

1:7920

The Good Mother's Endeavor 285/285 Acres
Elinor Howard 6/1/1698
(LBBB3i/537 SR7374)

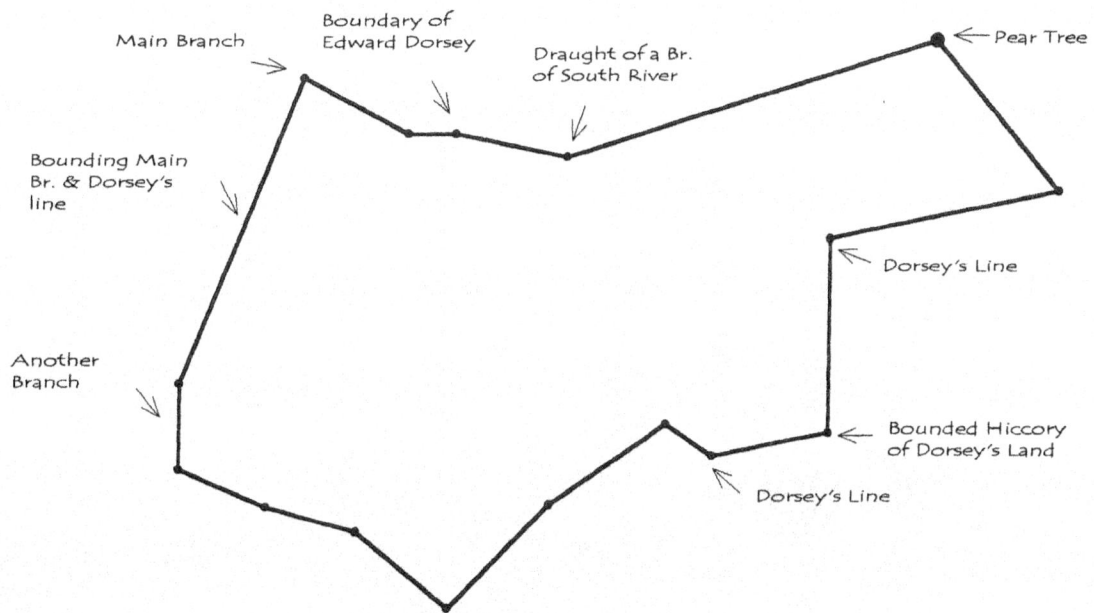

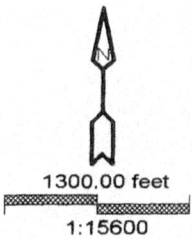

Main Branch

Boundary of
Edward Dorsey

Draught of a Br.
of South River

Pear Tree

Bounding Main
Br. & Dorsey's
line

Dorsey's Line

Another
Branch

Bounded Hiccory
of Dorsey's Land

Dorsey's Line

1300.00 feet

1:15600

195

The Landing Place 50/31 Acres
Neale Clarke 9/25/1663
(L5/597 SR7347)

South River

N

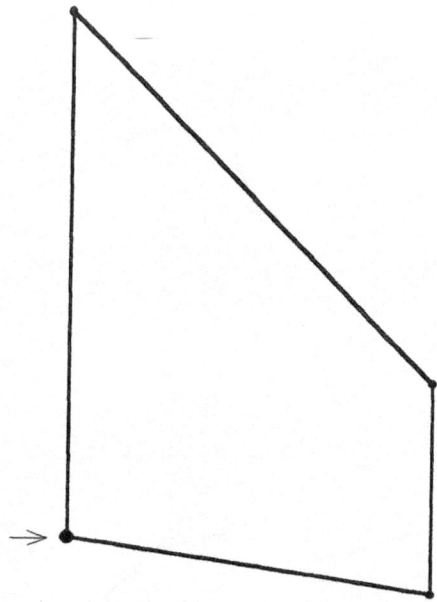

Northernmost Bound Tree
of Clarke's "home Plantation"

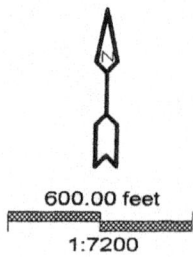

600.00 feet

1:7200

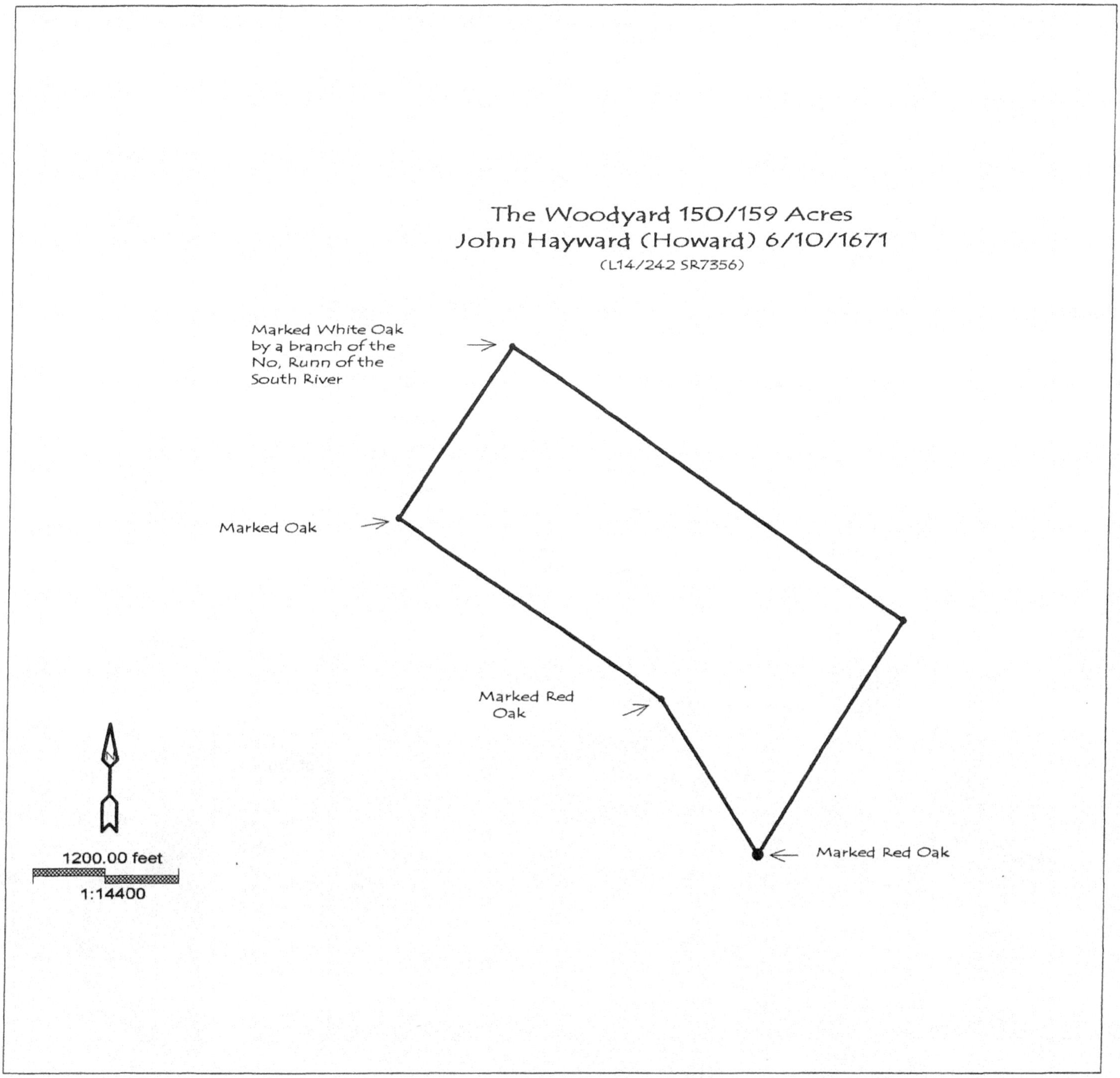

The Woodyard 150/159 Acres
John Hayward (Howard) 6/10/1671
(L14/242 SR7356)

Marked White Oak
by a branch of the
No, Runn of the
South River

Marked Oak

Marked Red
Oak

Marked Red Oak

1200.00 feet
1:14400

Turkey Quarter 150/176 Acres
Neale Clarke 9/25/1663
(L5/598 SR7347)

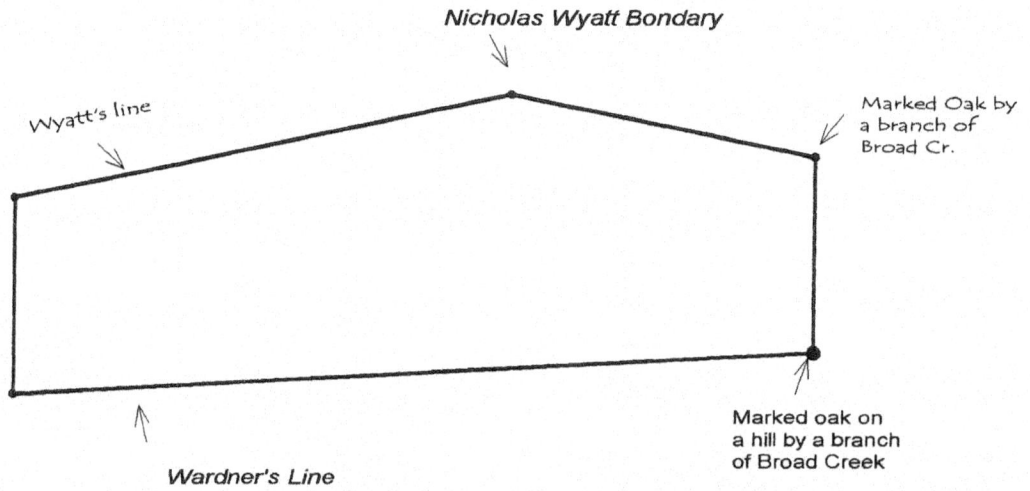

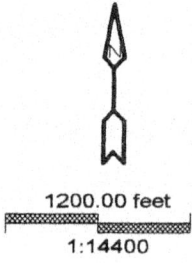

Nicholas Wyatt Bondary

Wyatt's line

Marked Oak by
a branch of
Broad Cr.

Wardner's Line

Marked oak on
a hill by a branch
of Broad Creek

1200.00 feet
1:14400

Upper Toynton 280/280 Acres
Larrance Richardson 8/15/1666
(L10/20 SR7352)

Marked Red Oak
on land he now
liveth upon

Marked Red
Oak

Marked White Oak
with 12 notches
standing in a branch

1200.00 feet
1:14400

Marked White Oak on
the side of a hill by a
Spring on the East side
of a branch

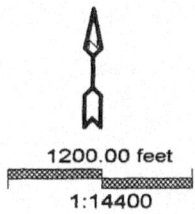

Wardridge 600/524 Acres
Jas Wardner & Henry Ridgely 6/26/1663
(L5/355 SR7347)

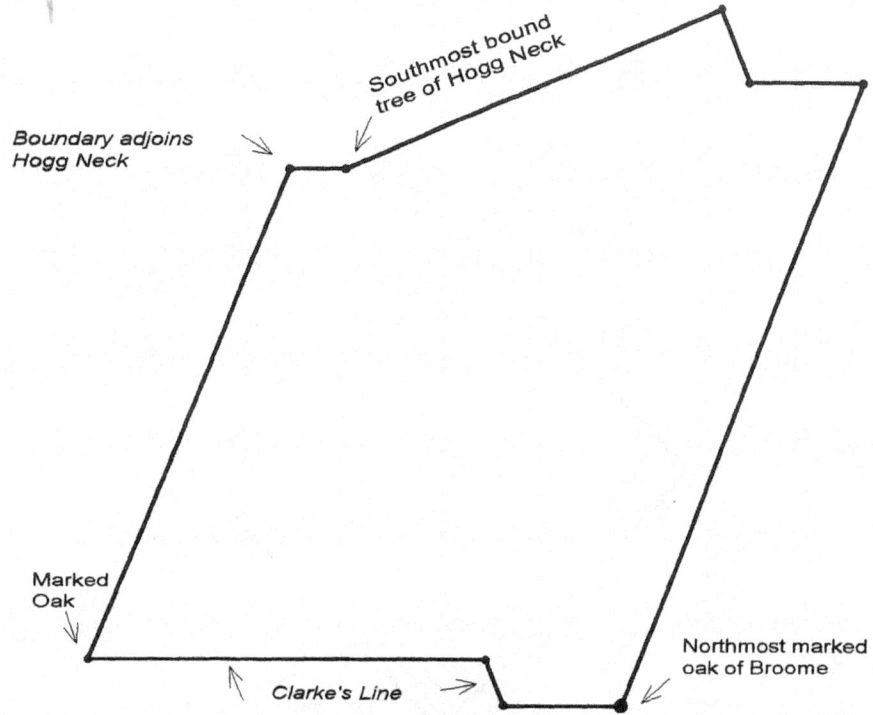

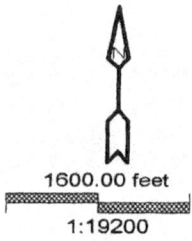

Southmost bound
tree of Hogg Neck

Boundary adjoins
Hogg Neck

Marked
Oak

Northmost marked
oak of Broome

Clarke's Line

1600.00 feet
1:19200

Warfield's Right 50/37 Acres
Richard Warfield 7/14/1675
(L19/45 SR7360)

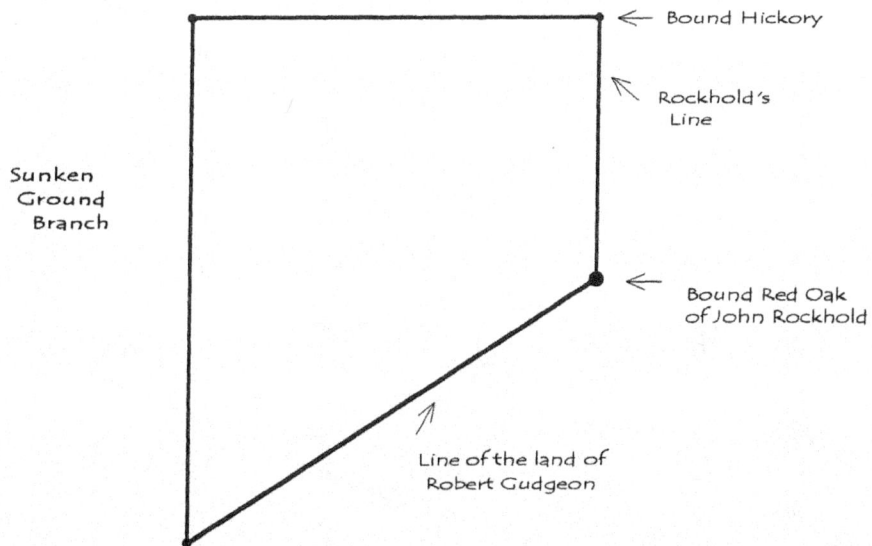

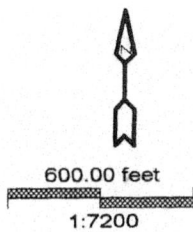

← Bound Hickory

↖ Rockhold's
Line

Sunken
Ground
Branch

← Bound Red Oak
of John Rockhold

↗
Line of the land of
Robert Gudgeon

600.00 feet
1:7200

Wayfield 100/80 Acres
Nicholas Wyatt 8/11/1664
(L7/353 SR7349)

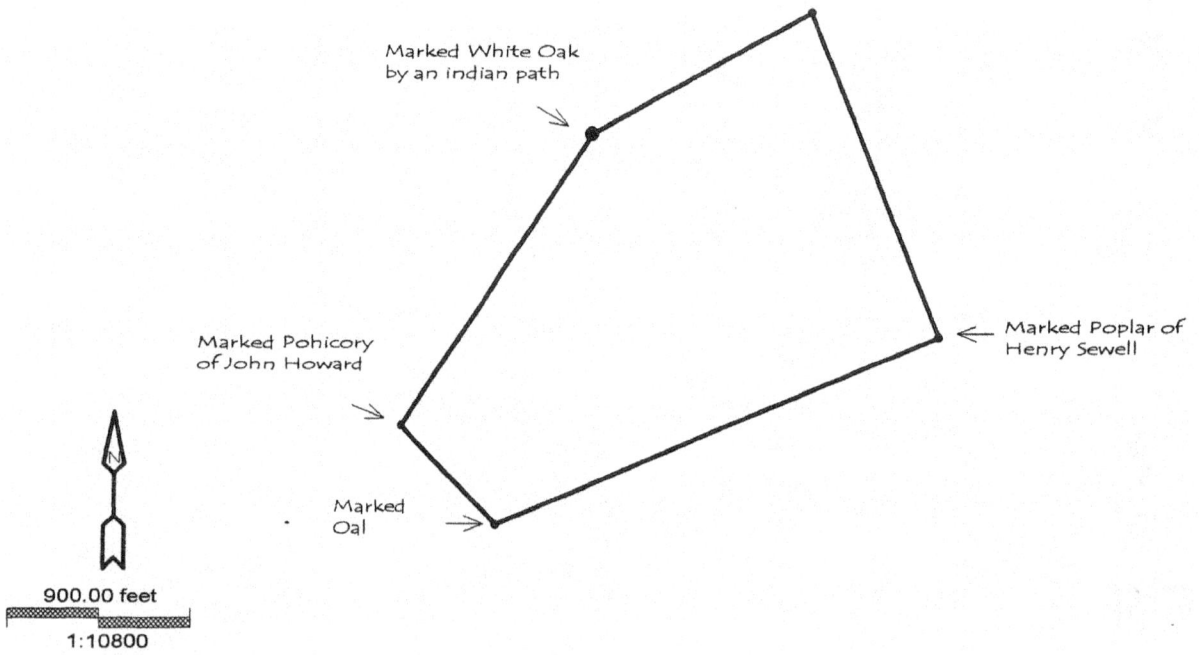

Marked White Oak
by an indian path

Marked Poplar of
Henry Sewell

Marked Pohicory
of John Howard

Marked
Oal

N

900.00 feet
1:10800

Wyatt's Hills 60/54 Acres
Nicholas Wyatt 8/8/1681
(L7/345 SSR7349)

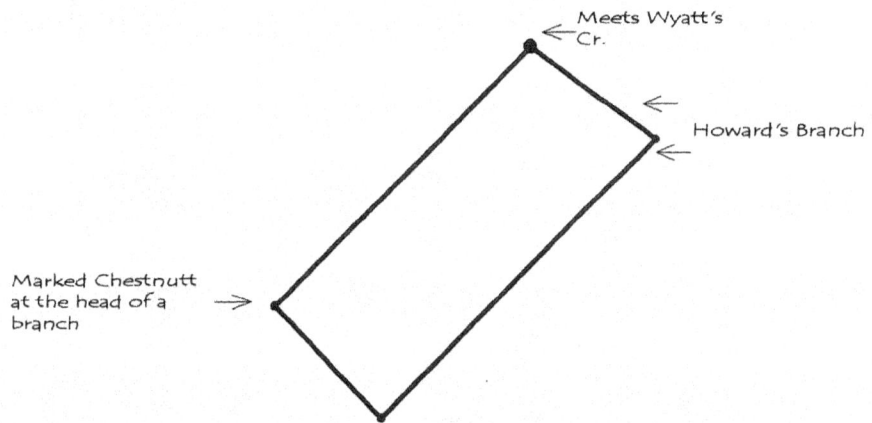

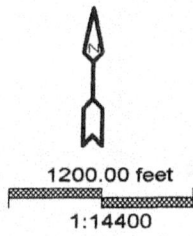

Meets Wyatt's
← Cr.

Howard's Branch

Marked Chestnutt
at the head of a
branch →

1200.00 feet

1:14400

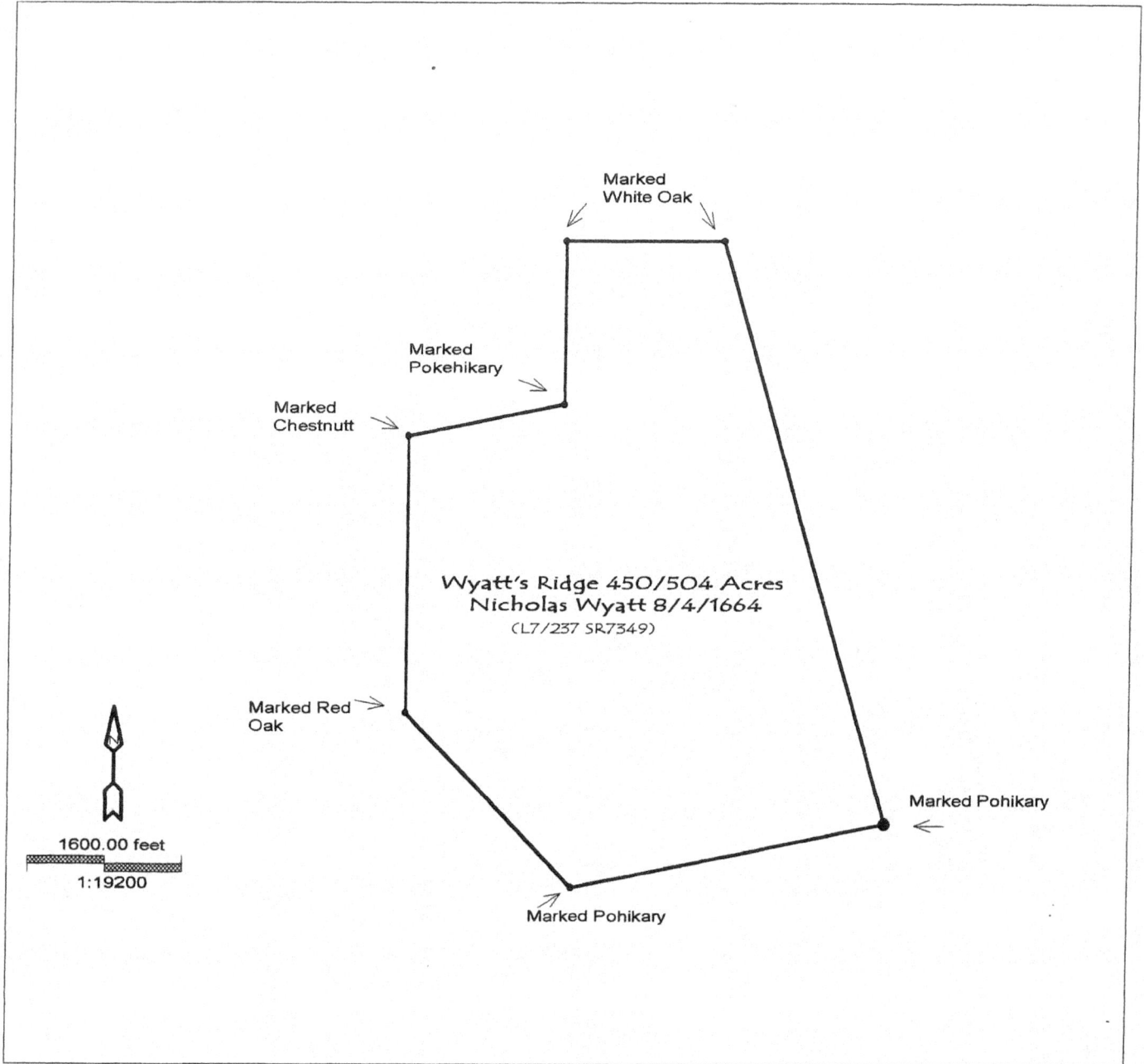

Marked
White Oak

Marked
Pokehikary

Marked
Chestnutt

Wyatt's Ridge 450/504 Acres
Nicholas Wyatt 8/4/1664
(L7/237 SR7349)

Marked Red
Oak

Marked Pohikary

Marked Pohikary

1600.00 feet

1:19200

d:\zsouth.pls 03-14-2001

Drawn and Placed Southern Area Tracts

A - Acton
B- Brampton
BA Baldwin's Addn.
BC - Baldwin's Chance
BN - Brushy Neck (Baldwin)
C - Chelsy
CBC - Come By Chance

CF - Chance (Frizzell)
CL - Clarkson
DL - Dunkin's Luck
EA - Edge's Addn.
EN - Edward His Neck
FE - Freeborne's Enlgt.
FP - Fuller's Point

G - Georgeston
GT - Gatenby
GTT - Garret's Town
HH - Howard's Hope
HHC - Howard's Hills (C)
HP - Hammond's Pasture
I - Intacke

JE - Jeffe's Enlgt.
JH - Jame's Hill
LR - Lydia's Rest
MC - Maiden Croft
MN1 - Mount. Neck 1
MN2 - Mount. Neck 2
NA - Norwood's Angles

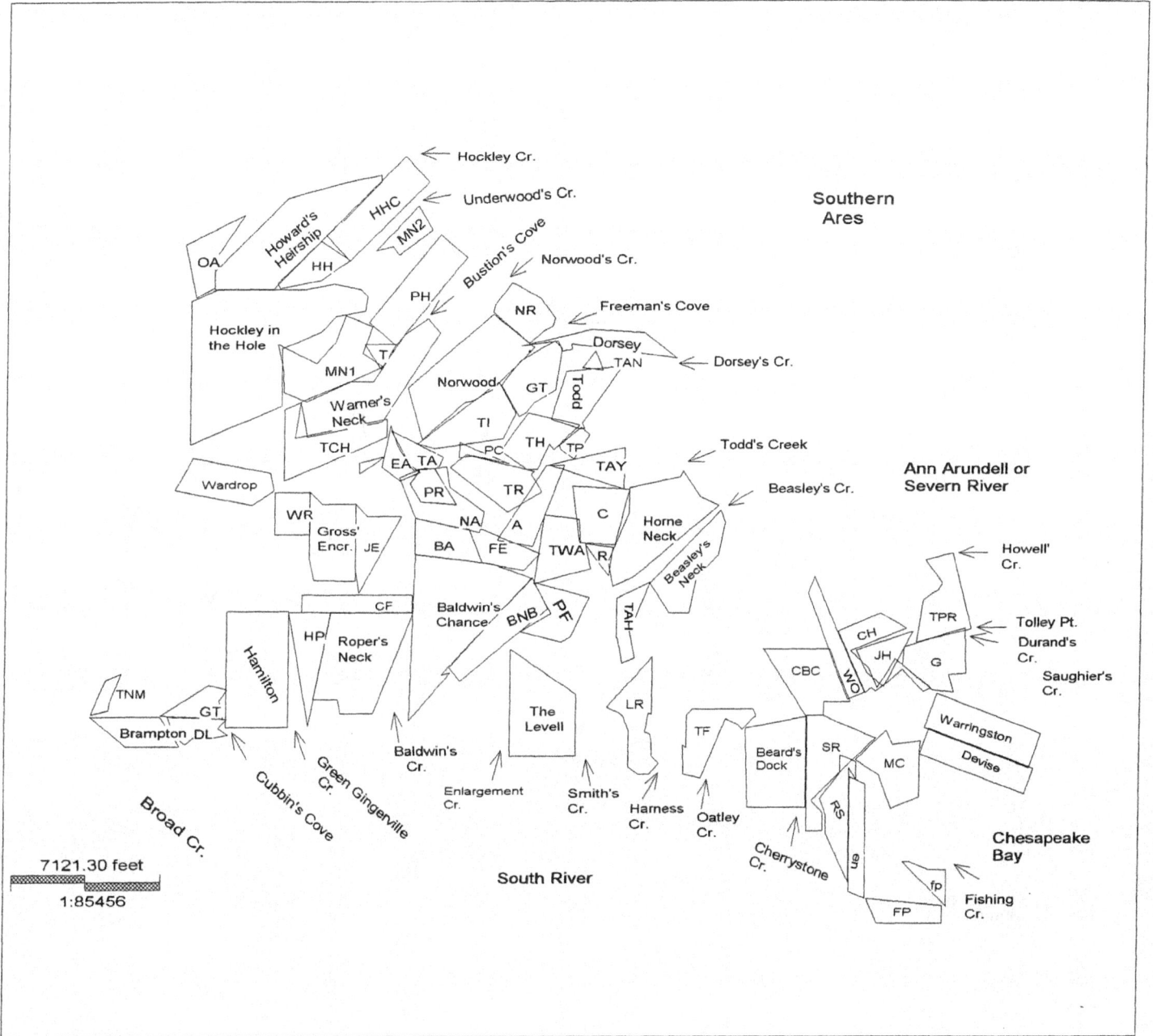

Southern Ares

Hockley Cr.
Underwood's Cr.
Bustion's Cove
Norwood's Cr.
Freeman's Cove
Dorsey's Cr.
Todd's Creek
Beasley's Cr.
Howell' Cr.
Tolley Pt.
Durand's Cr.
Saughier's Cr.

Ann Arundell or Severn River

HHC
Howard's Heirship
MN2
OA
HH
PH
Hockley in the Hole
NR
Dorsey
TAN
T
MN1
Norwood
GT
Todd
Warner's Neck
TI
TH
TP
TCH
PC
TAY
Wardrop
EA TA
PR
C
Horne Neck
WR
TR
Gross' Encr.
JE
NA
A
BA
FE
TWA
R
Beasley's Neck
TPR
CF
Baldwin's Chance
BNB
PF
CH
JH
G
HP
Roper's Neck
TAH
CBC
WO
TNM
Hamilton
Warringston
Devise
GT
Brampton DL
The Levell
LR
SR
MC
Baldwin's Cr.
TF
Beard's Dock
RS
Green Gingerville Cr.
Cubbin's Cove
Enlargement Cr.
Smith's Cr.
Harness Cr.
Oatley Cr.
Cherrystone Cr.
fp
FP
Fishing Cr.
Broad Cr.
South River
Chesapeake Bay

7121.30 feet
1:85456

NR - Norwood's Recovery
OA - Orphan's Addition
PC - Proctor's Chance
PF - Proctor's Forrest
PH - Porter's Hills
PR - Petticoate's Rest
RL - Reade's Lott

RS - Ruly's Search
SR - Smith's Rest
T - The Addn. (Hammond)
TA - The Advance (Edge)
TAH - The Addn. (Hill)
TAN - The Angle (Hill)
TAY - The Addn. (Young)

TCF - The Chance (Frizzell)
TCH - The Chance (Howard)
TF - The Favor
TH - Todd's Harbor
TN - The Neglect
TPR - Tolly Pt. Res
TR - Todd's Range

TWA - Widow's Addn.
W - Warringston
WO - Wither's Outlet
WR - Wardrop Ridge

Acton 100/107 Acres
Richard Acton 8/11/1658
(LQ/117 SR7345)

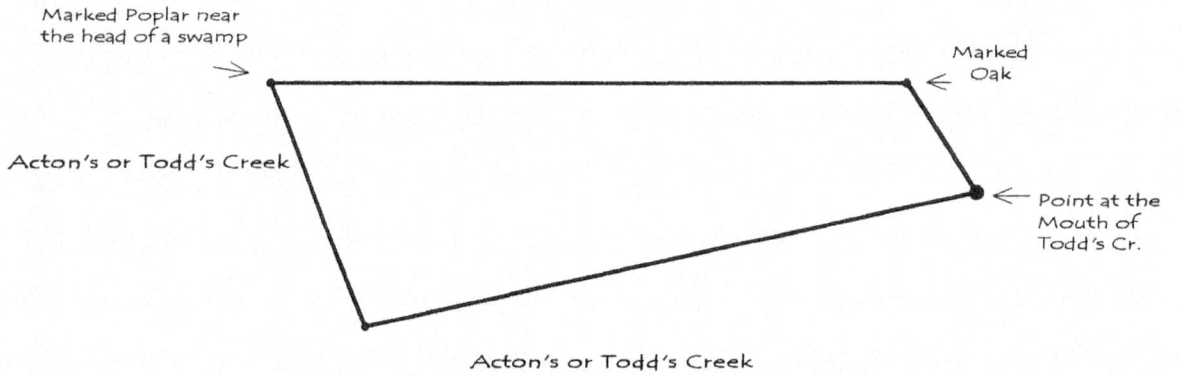

Marked Poplar near
the head of a swamp

Marked
Oak

Acton's or Todd's Creek

← Point at the
Mouth of
Todd's Cr.

Acton's or Todd's Creek

N

1200.00 feet

1:14400

Baldwin's Addition 120/102 Acres
John Baldwin 8/11/1664
(L7/356 SR7349)

Marked White Oak
at the head of a
swamp

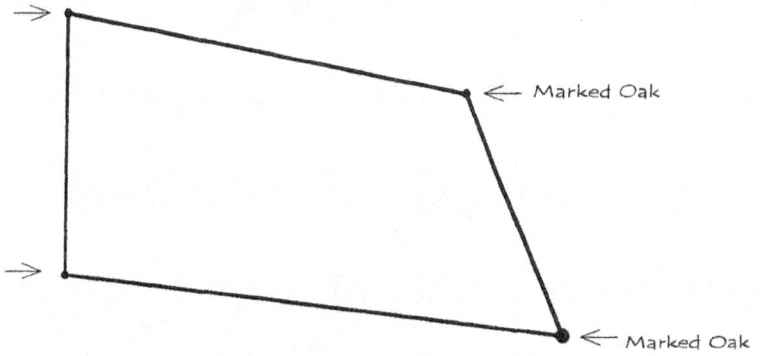

← Marked Oak

Adjoins Baldwin's Neck
at Baldwin's Creek

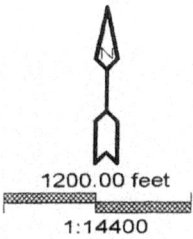

← Marked Oak

1200.00 feet

1:14400

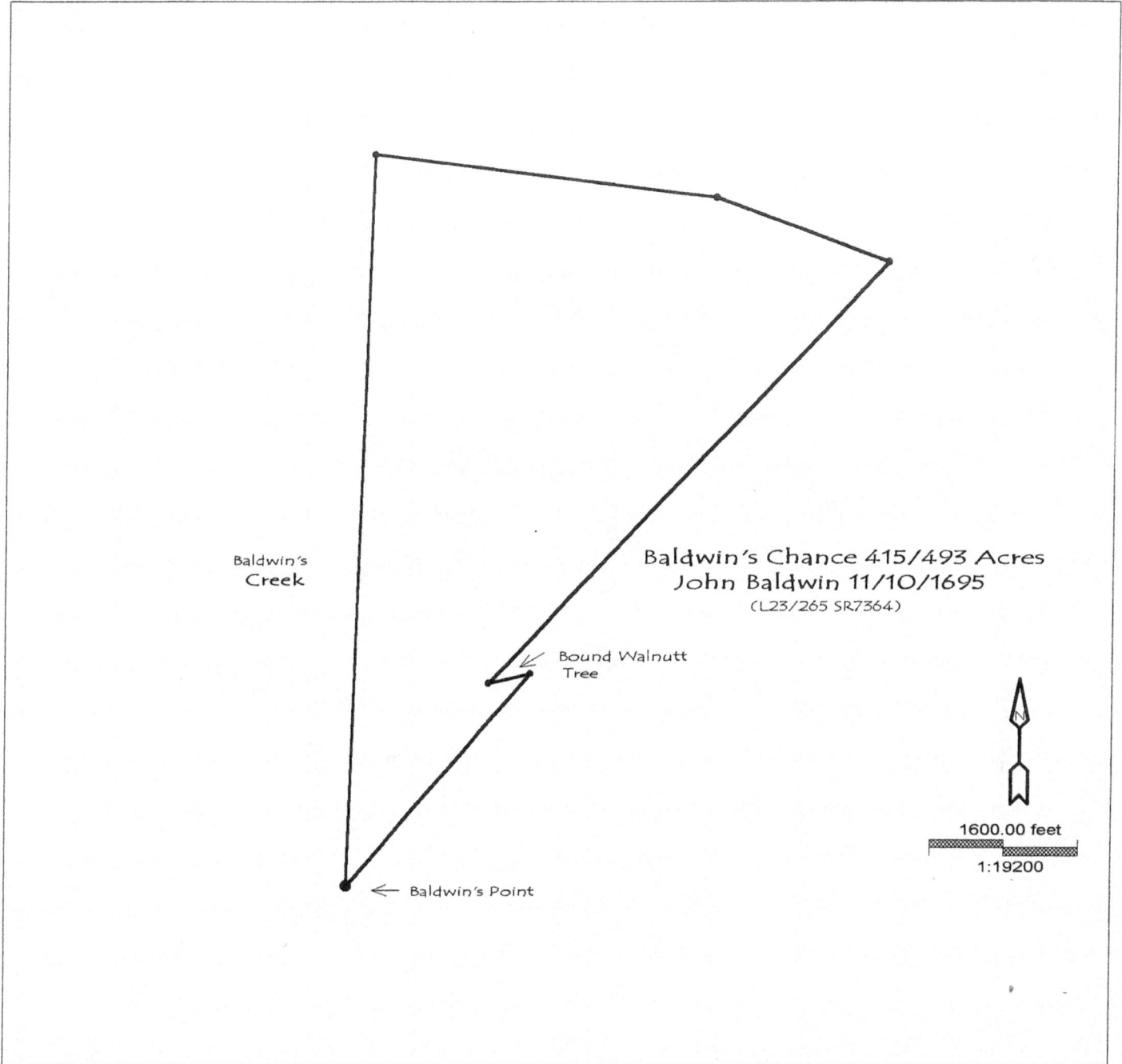

Baldwin's
Creek

Baldwin's Chance 415/493 Acres
John Baldwin 11/10/1695
(L23/265 SR7364)

Bound Walnutt
Tree

N

1600.00 feet
1:19200

← Baldwin's Point

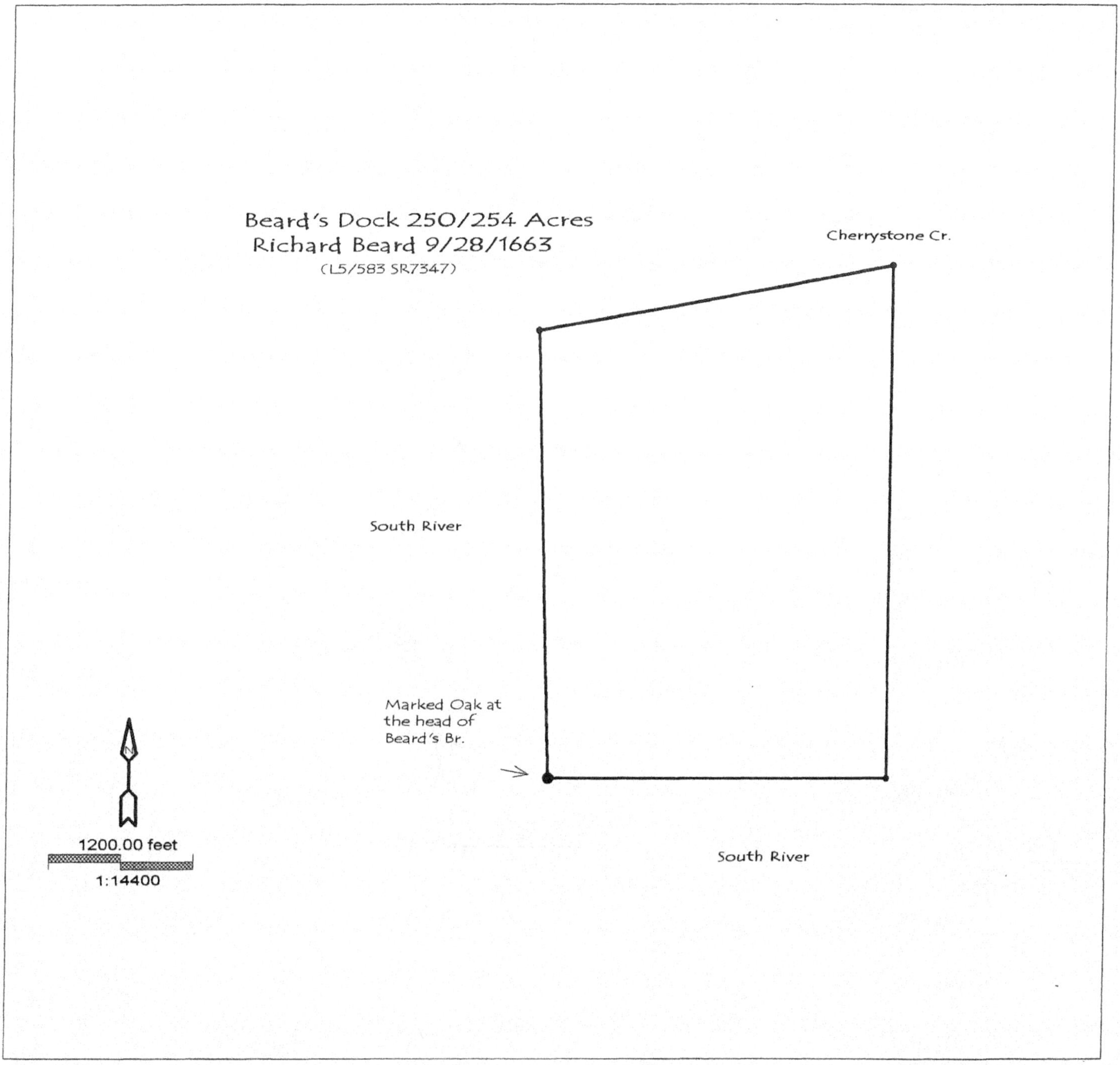

Beard's Dock 250/254 Acres
Richard Beard 9/28/1663
(L5/583 SR7347)

Cherrystone Cr.

South River

Marked Oak at
the head of
Beard's Br.

1200.00 feet

1:14400

South River

Beasley's Neck Resurveyed 150/162 Acres
Richard Hill 2/3/1673
(L15/347 SR4327)

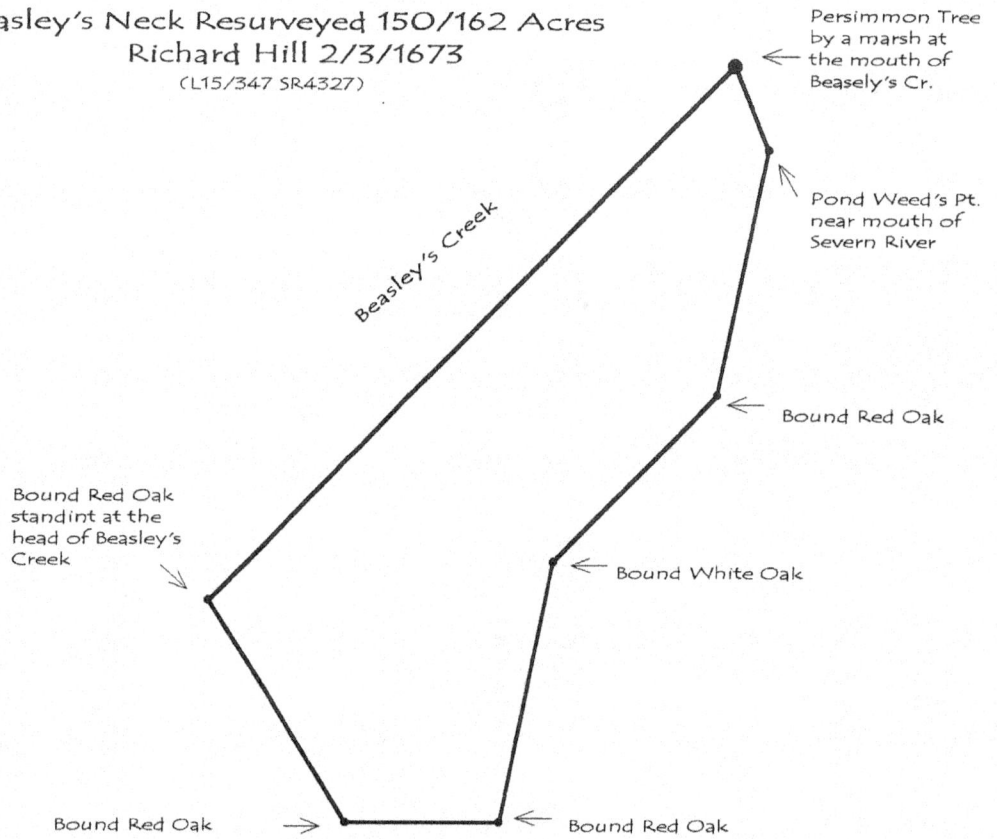

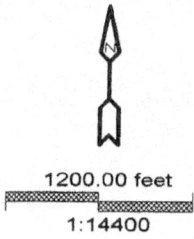

Persimmon Tree
by a marsh at
the mouth of
Beasely's Cr.

Pond Weed's Pt.
near mouth of
Severn River

Bound Red Oak

Beasley's Creek

Bound Red Oak
standint at the
head of Beasley's
Creek

Bound White Oak

1200.00 feet

1:14400

Bound Red Oak

Bound Red Oak

210

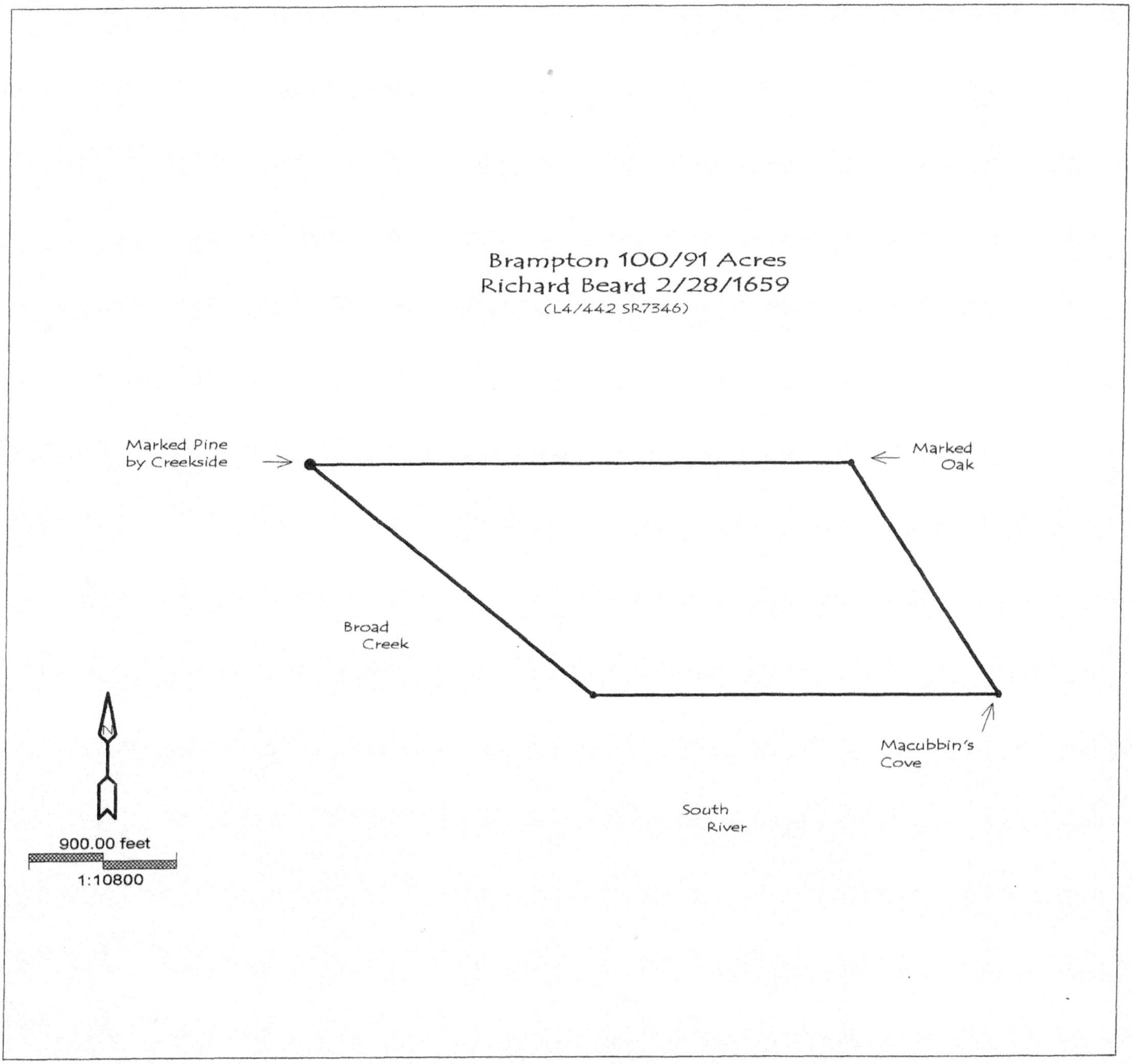

Brampton 100/91 Acres
Richard Beard 2/28/1659
(L4/442 SR7346)

Marked Pine
by Creekside

Marked
Oak

Broad
Creek

Macubbin's
Cove

South
River

N

900.00 feet
1:10800

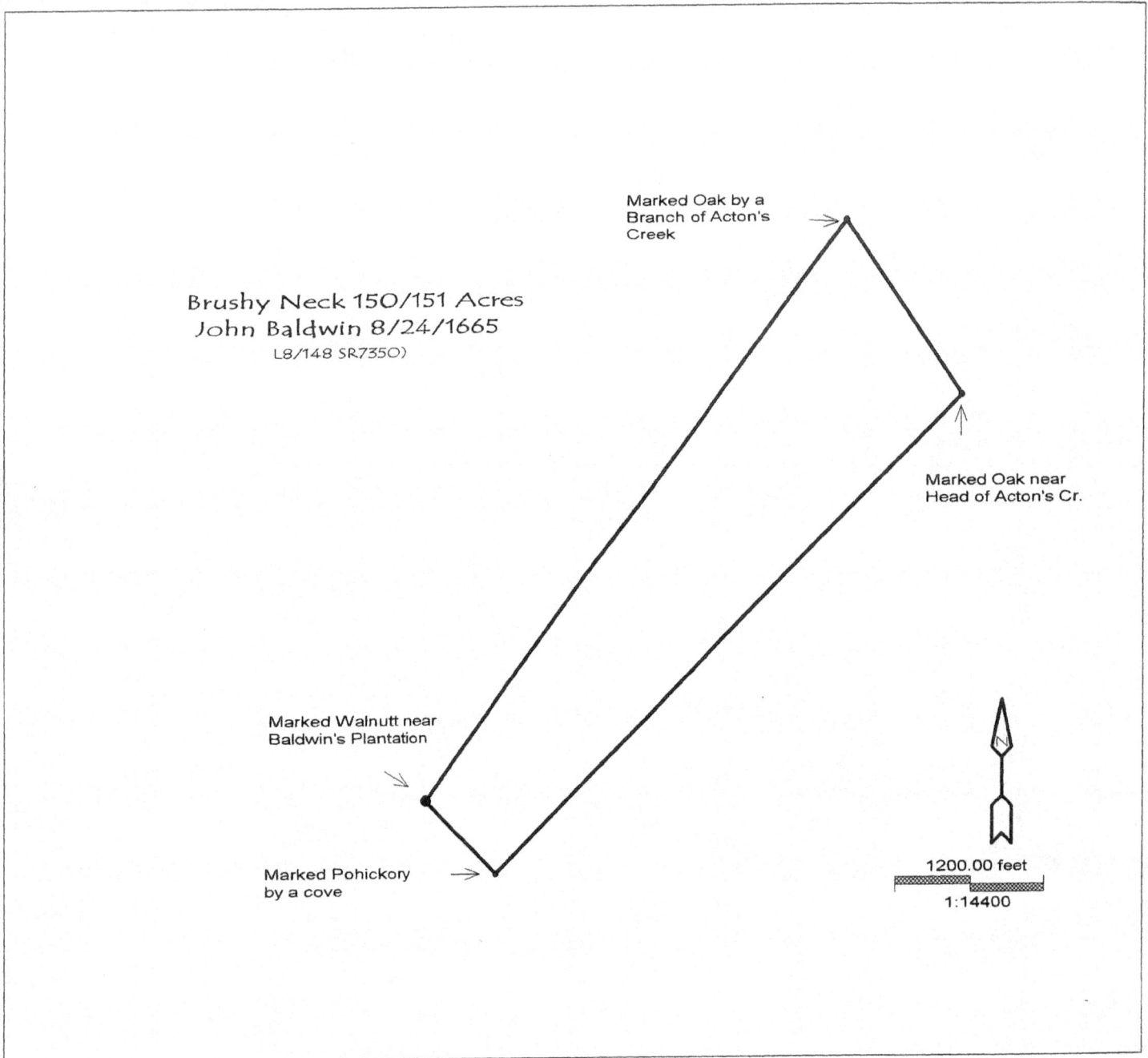

Brushy Neck 150/151 Acres
John Baldwin 8/24/1665
L8/148 SR7350)

Marked Oak by a
Branch of Acton's
Creek

Marked Oak near
Head of Acton's Cr.

Marked Walnutt near
Baldwin's Plantation

Marked Pohickory
by a cove

N

1200.00 feet
1:14400

212

Brushy Neck Resurveyed 390/390 Acres
Thomas Francis 10/7/1683
(L22/106 SR7363)

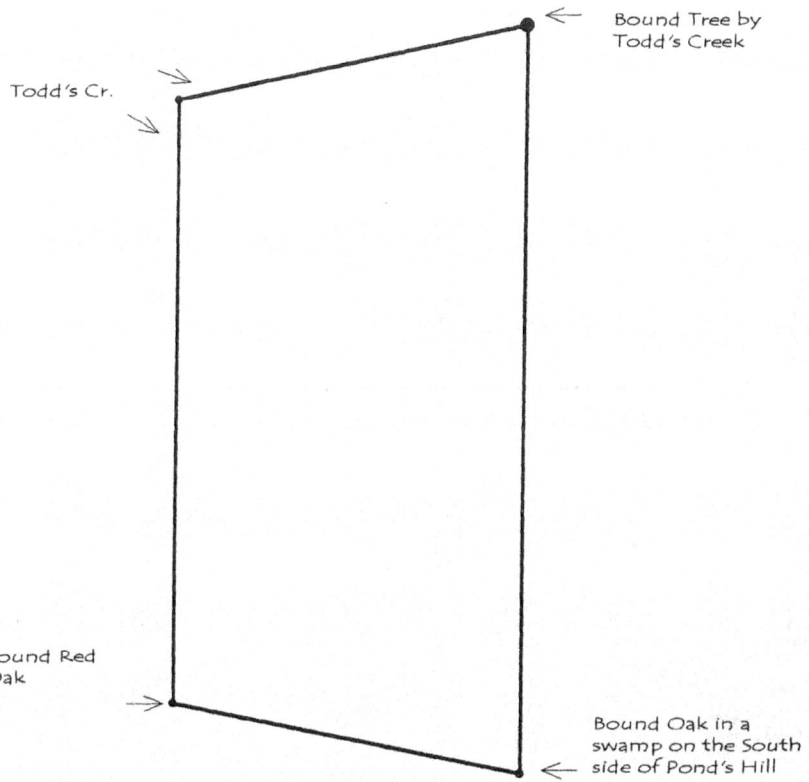

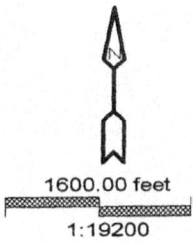

Bound Tree by
Todd's Creek

Todd's Cr.

Bound Red
Oak

Bound Oak in a
swamp on the South
side of Pond's Hill

1600.00 feet

1:19200

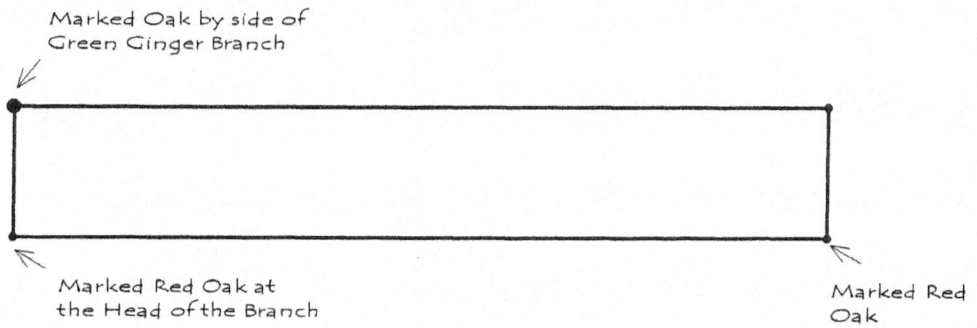

Chance 100/100 Acres
William Frizzell 8/6/1664
(L7/342 SR7349)

Marked Oak by side of
Green Ginger Branch

Marked Red Oak at
the Head of the Branch

Marked Red
Oak

1200.00 feet
1:14400

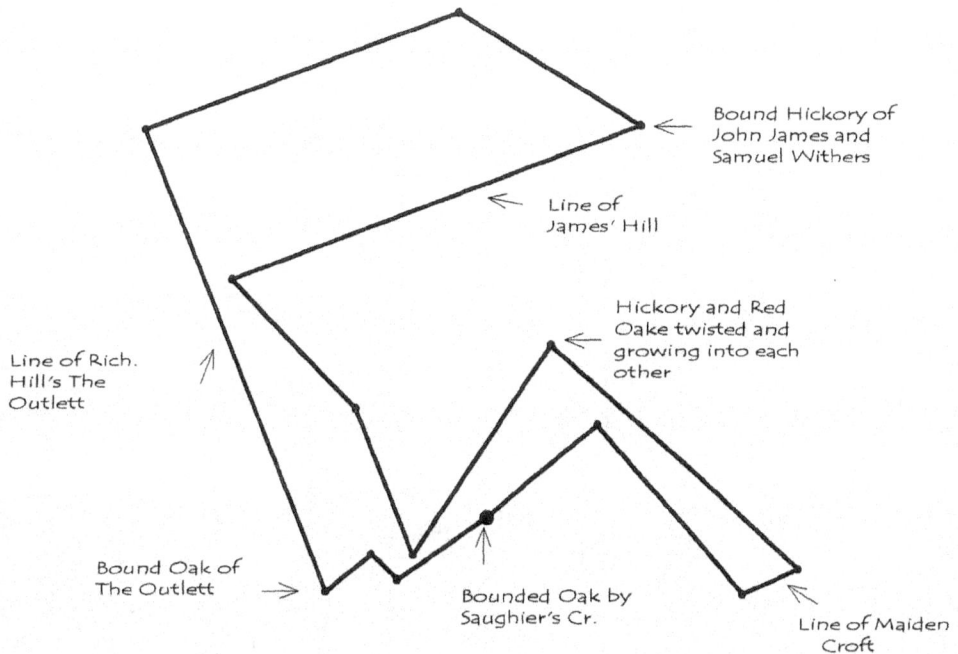

Chelsy 117/108 Acres
Lawrence Draper 3/26/1695
(LWD/132 SR7372-2)

Bound Hickory of
John James and
Samuel Withers

Line of
James' Hill

Hickory and Red
Oake twisted and
growing into each
other

Line of Rich.
Hill's The
Outlett

Bound Oak of
The Outlett

Bounded Oak by
Saughier's Cr.

Line of Maiden
Croft

1200.00 feet

1:14400

Clarkston 100/130 Acres
Matthew Clarke 2/28/1659
(L4/490 SR7346)

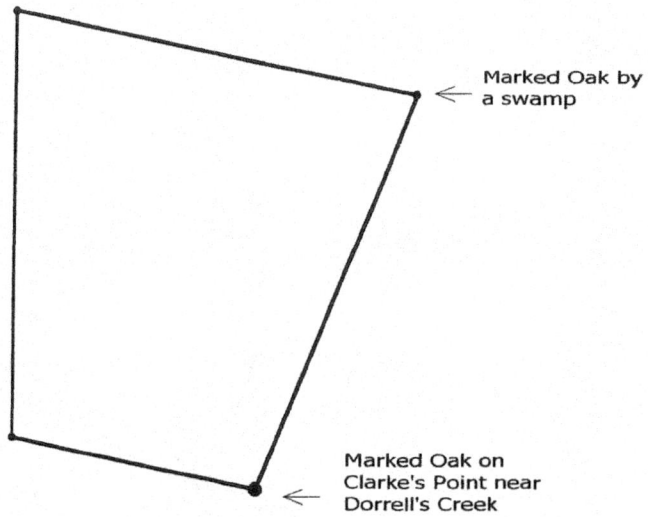

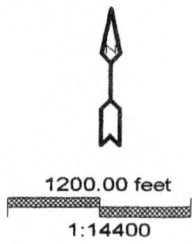

Marked Oak by
a swamp

Marked Oak on
Clarke's Point near
Dorrell's Creek

1200.00 feet

1:14400

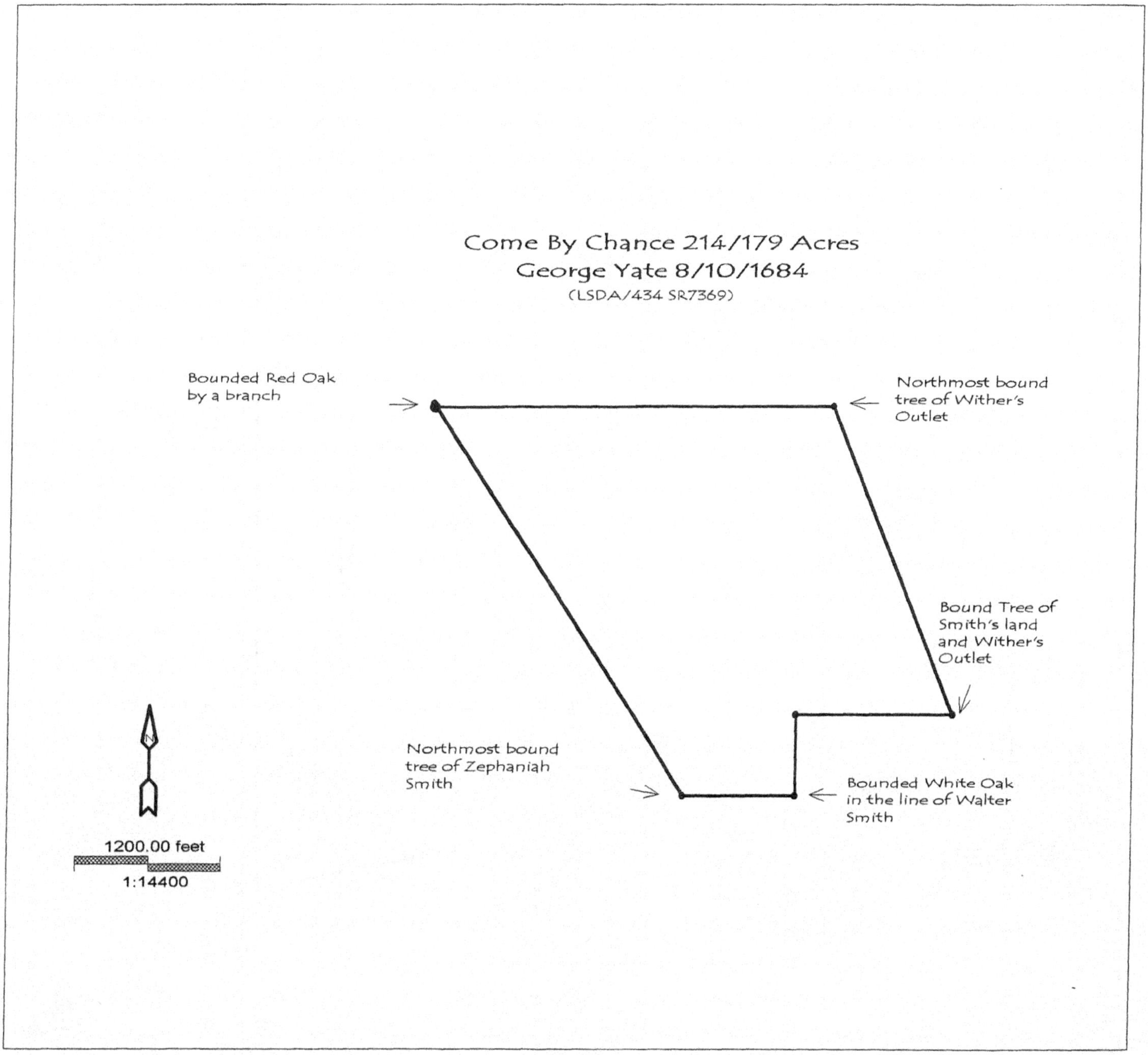

Come By Chance 214/179 Acres
George Yate 8/10/1684
(LSDA/434 SR7369)

Bounded Red Oak
by a branch

Northmost bound
tree of Wither's
Outlet

Bound Tree of
Smith's land
and Wither's
Outlet

Northmost bound
tree of Zephaniah
Smith

Bounded White Oak
in the line of Walter
Smith

N

1200.00 feet

1:14400

217

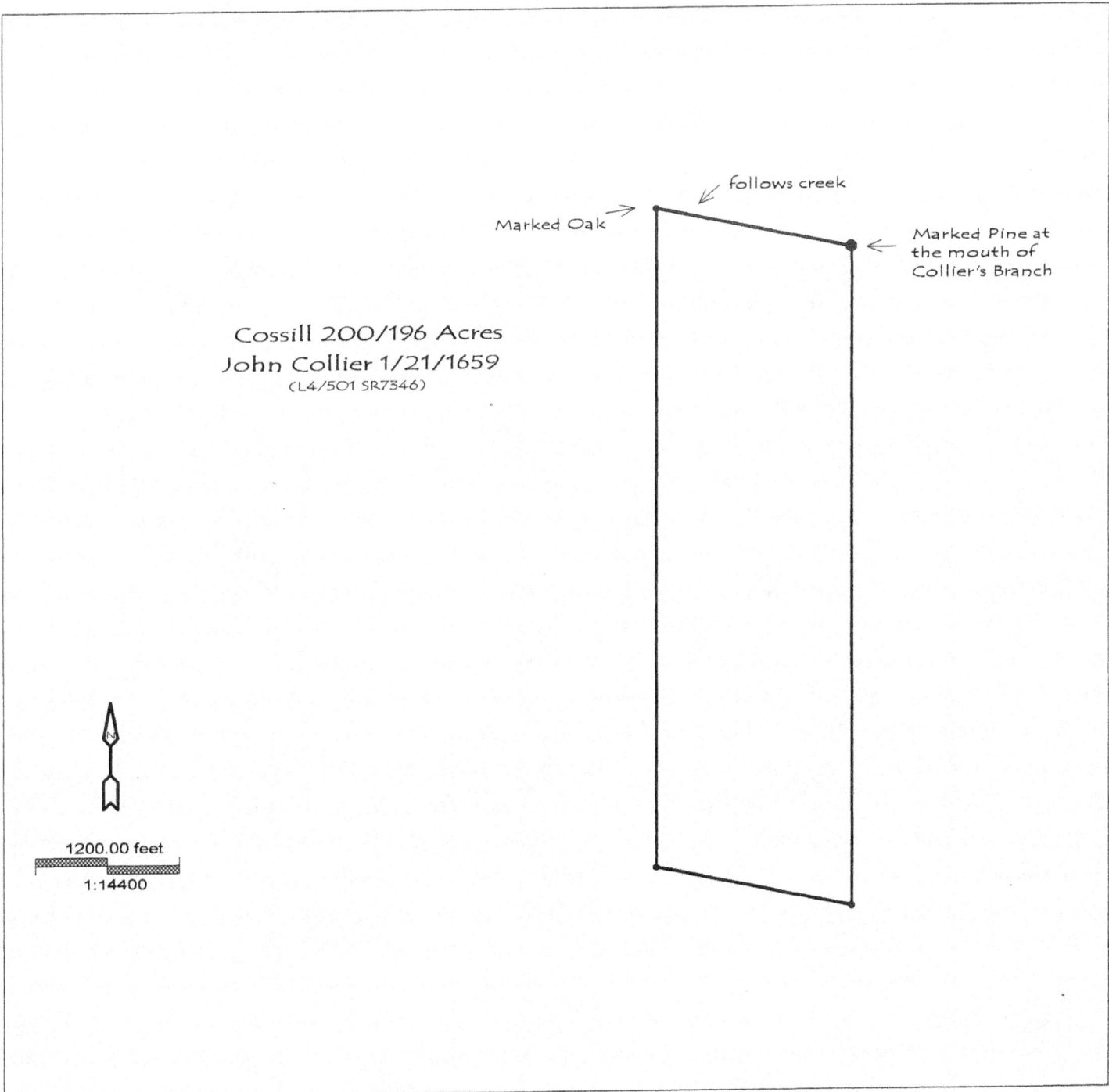

follows creek

Marked Oak

Marked Pine at
the mouth of
Collier's Branch

Cossill 200/196 Acres
John Collier 1/21/1659
(L4/501 SR7346)

1200.00 feet
1:14400

Devise 150/150 Acres
Thomas Davies 2/22/1659
(L4/527 SR7346)

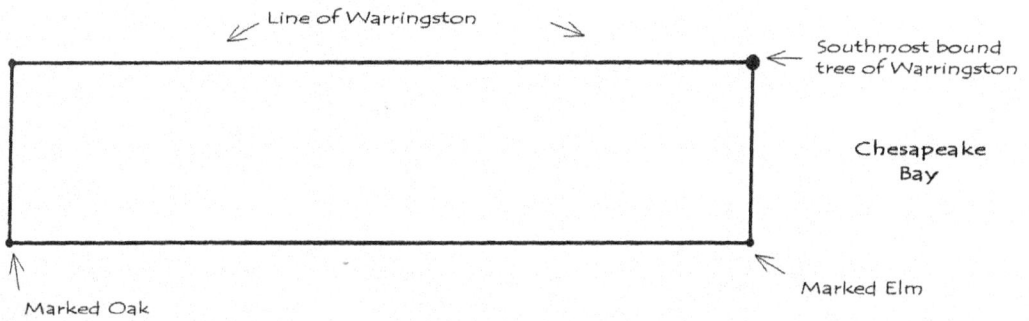

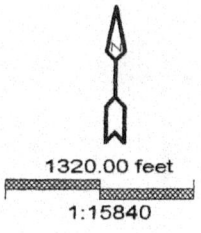

Line of Warringston

Southmost bound
tree of Warringston

Chesapeake
Bay

Marked Oak

Marked Elm

1320.00 feet
1:15840

Dorsey 60/93 Acres
Edward Dorsey 9/16/1668
(L12/136 SR7354)

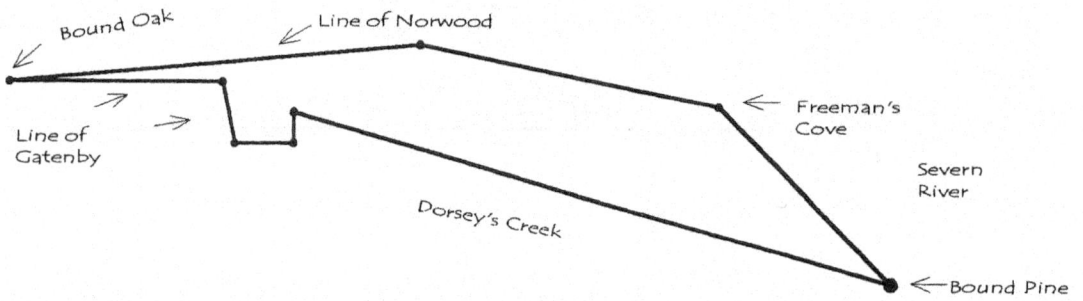

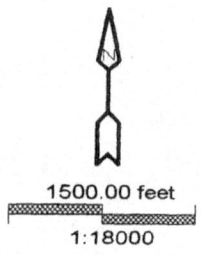

Bound Oak

Line of Norwood

Line of
Gatenby

Freeman's
Cove

Severn
River

Dorsey's Creek

Bound Pine

N

1500.00 feet

1:18000

Dunken's Luck 52/52 Acres
Patrick Dunken 9/1/1687
(LNS2i/399 SR7371)

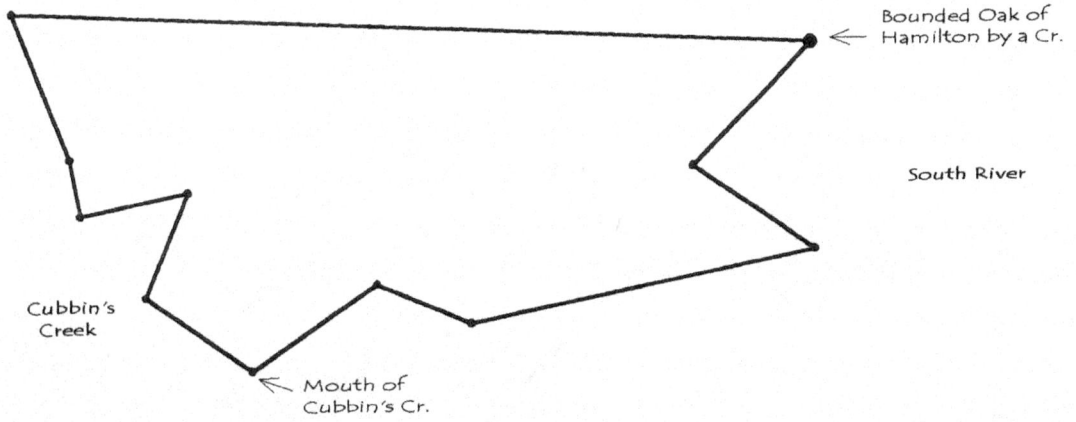

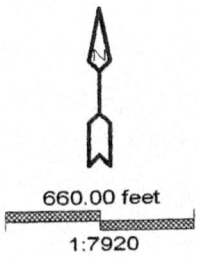

Bounded Oak of
Hamilton by a Cr.

South River

Cubbin's
Creek

Mouth of
Cubbin's Cr.

660.00 feet
1:7920

Edge's Addition 50/42 Acres
Daniel Edge 9/10/1684
(LSDA/456 SR7369)

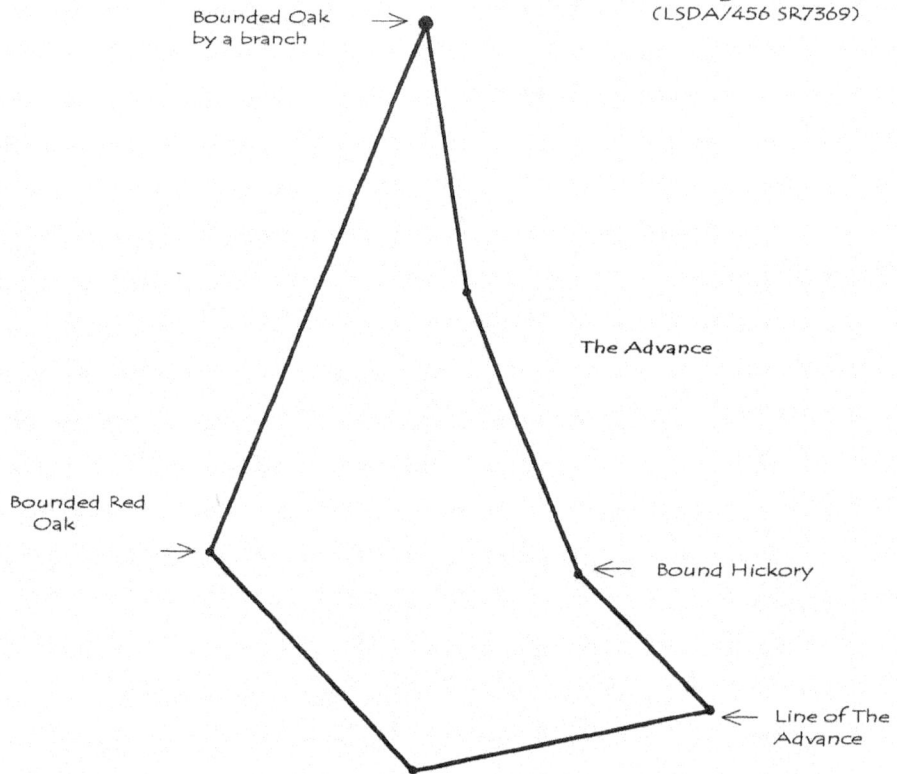

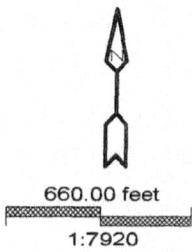

Bounded Oak
by a branch →

The Advance

Bounded Red
Oak →

← Bound Hickory

← Line of The
Advance

660.00 feet
1:7920

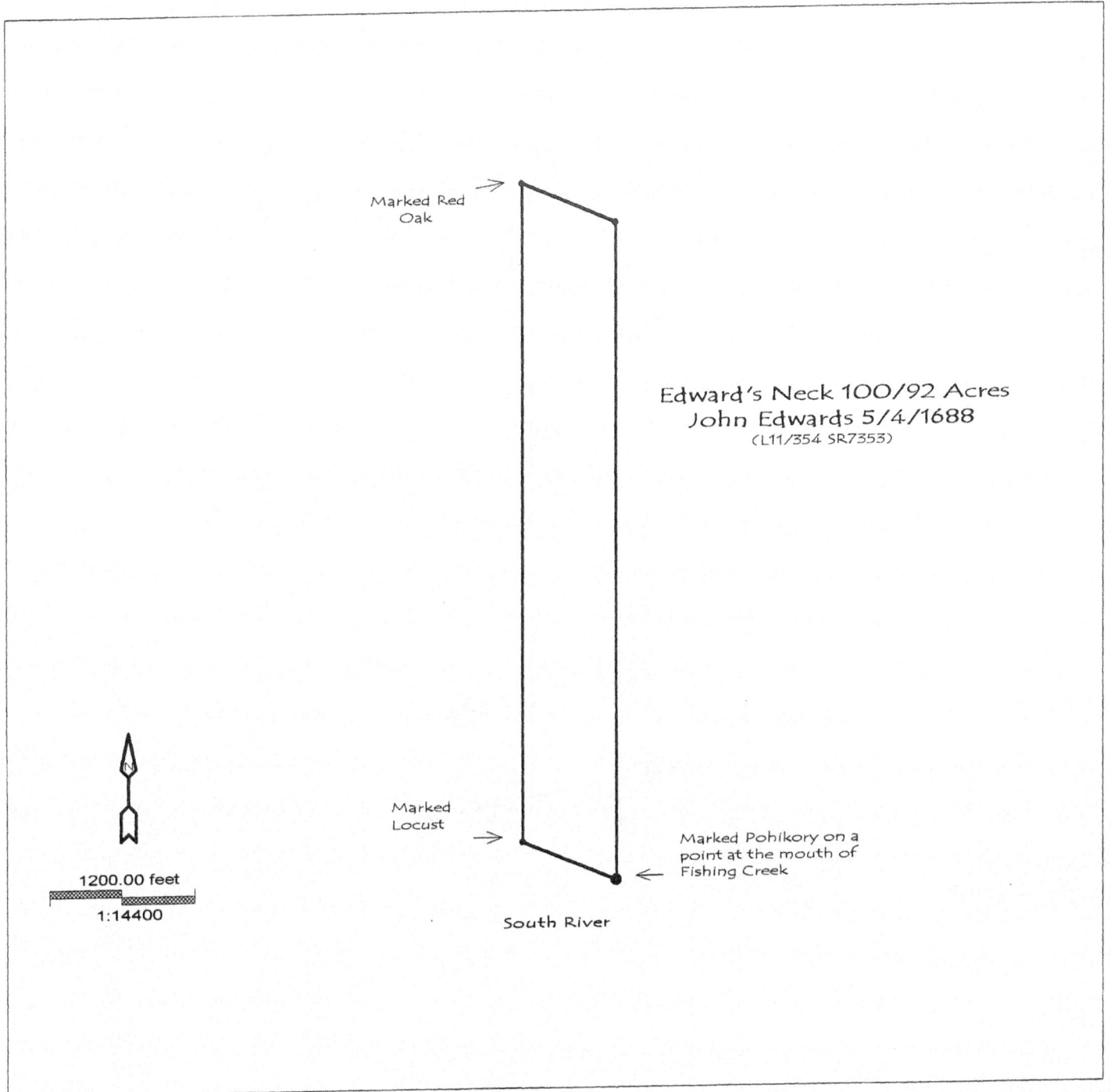

Marked Red
Oak

Edward's Neck 100/92 Acres
John Edwards 5/4/1688
(L11/354 SR7353)

Marked
Locust

Marked Pohikory on a
point at the mouth of
Fishing Creek

1200.00 feet

1:14400

South River

Freeborne's Enlargement 80/81 Acres
Thomas Freeborne 10/7/1694
(123/260 SR7364)

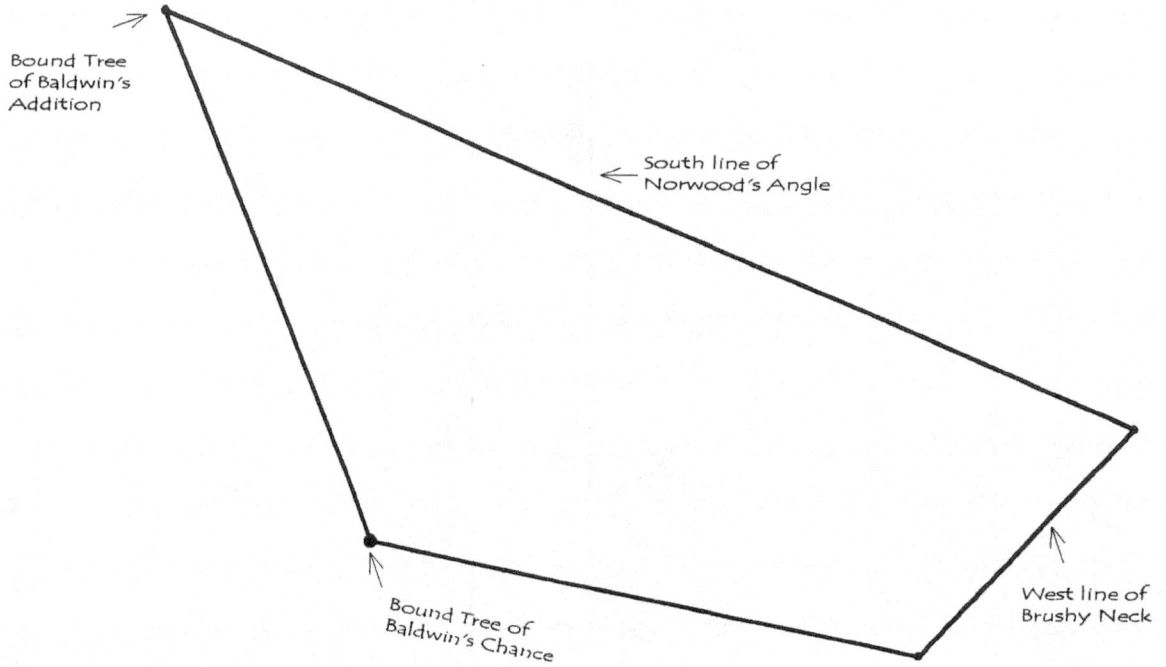

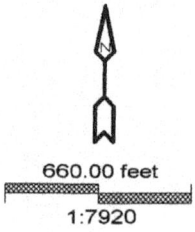

Bound Tree
of Baldwin's
Addition

South line of
Norwood's Angle

Bound Tree of
Baldwin's Chance

West line of
Brushy Neck

660.00 feet

1:7920

Fuller's Point 120/113 Acres
Phillip Thomas 4/12/1664
(Liber 9/292 SR7351)

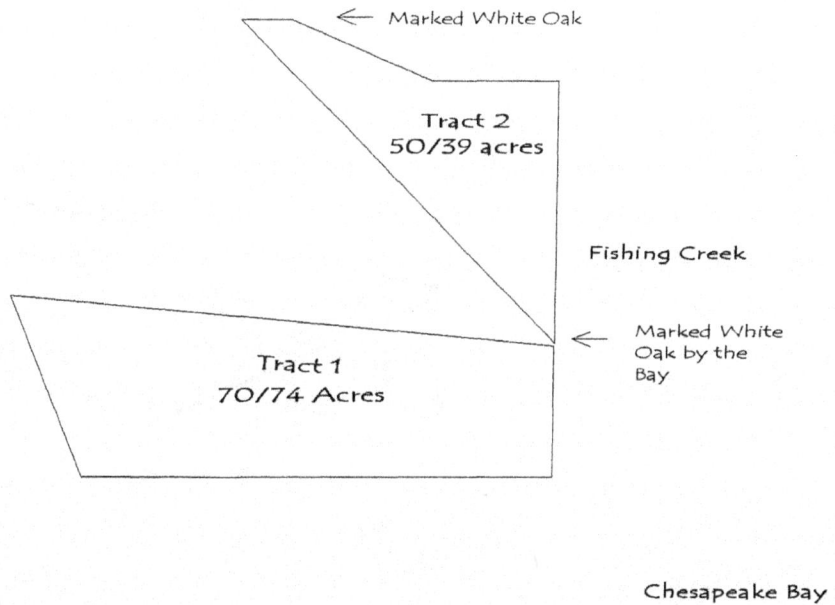

← Marked White Oak

Tract 2
50/39 acres

Fishing Creek

← Marked White
Oak by the
Bay

Tract 1
70/74 Acres

South
River

Chesapeake Bay

1200.00 feet
1:14400

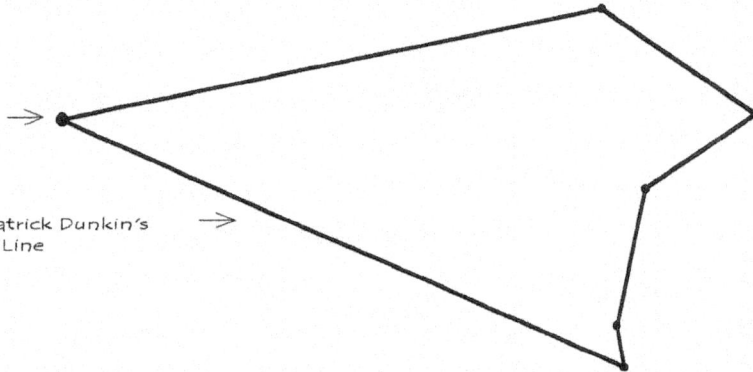

Garrets Town 59/59 Acres
Michael Cussack 8/12/1685
(LSNBi/414 SR7370)

Bounded Red
Oake at the
head of a Cove

Patrick Dunkin's
Line

900.00 feet
1:10800

Gatenby 100/121 Acres
Ensign Thomas Gates 2/7/1650
(LQ/392 SR7345)

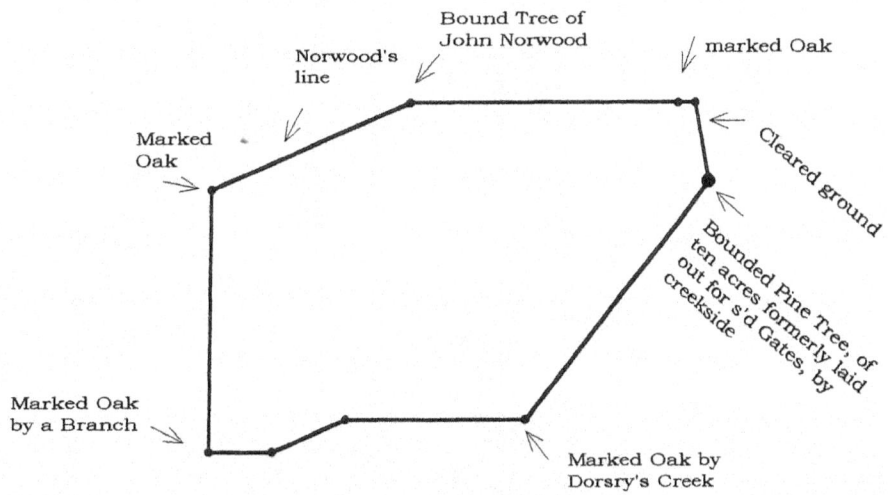

Bound Tree of
John Norwood

marked Oak

Norwood's
line

Marked
Oak

Cleared ground

Bounded Pine Tree, of
ten acres formerly laid
out for s'd Gates, by
creekside

Marked Oak
by a Branch

Marked Oak by
Dorsry's Creek

1200.00 feet
1:14400

227

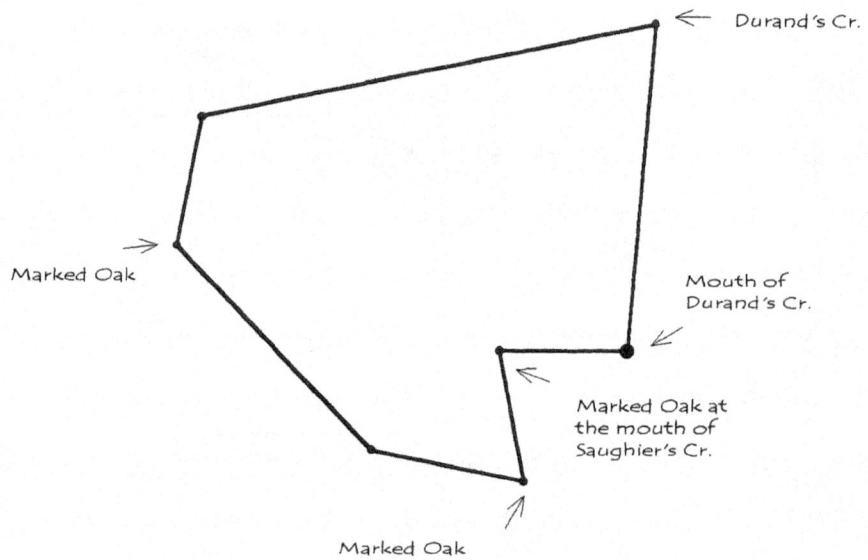

Georgeston 190/132 Acres
George Saughier 2/16/1659
(L4/503 SR7346)

Durand's Cr.

Marked Oak

Mouth of
Durand's Cr.

Marked Oak at
the mouth of
Saughier's Cr.

Marked Oak

1200.00 feet
1:14400

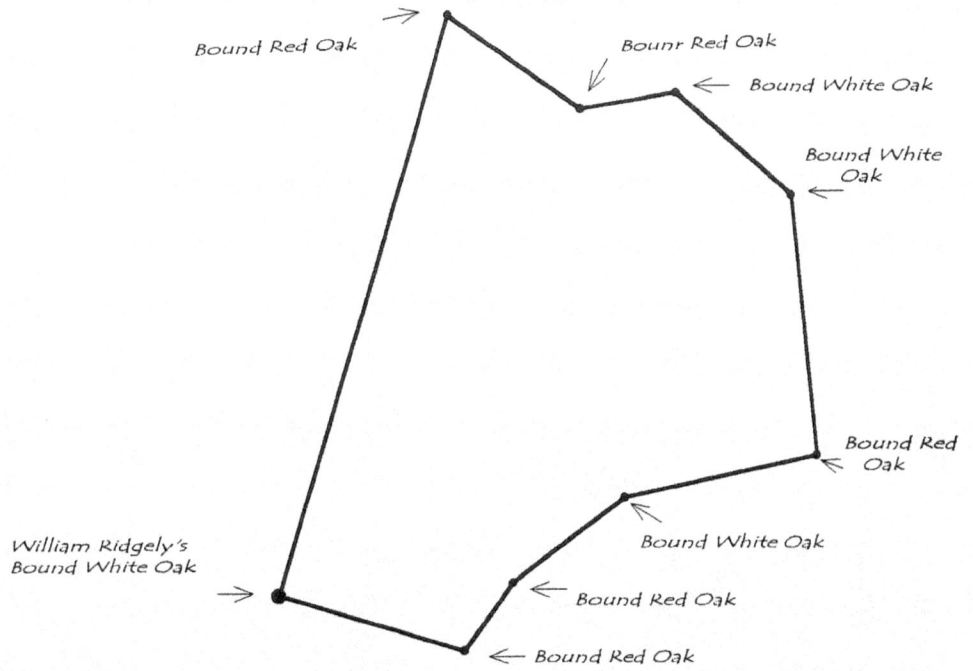

Griffith's Lott 197/190 Acres
William Griffith 11/10/1695
(L23/256 SR7364)

Bound Red Oak

Bounr Red Oak

Bound White Oak

Bound White Oak

Bound Red Oak

Bound White Oak

Bound Red Oak

Bound Red Oak

William Ridgely's
Bound White Oak

1200.00 feet
1:14400

Gross's Increase 180/182 Acres
Thomas Gross 6/1/1685
(LNS2i/116 SR7371)

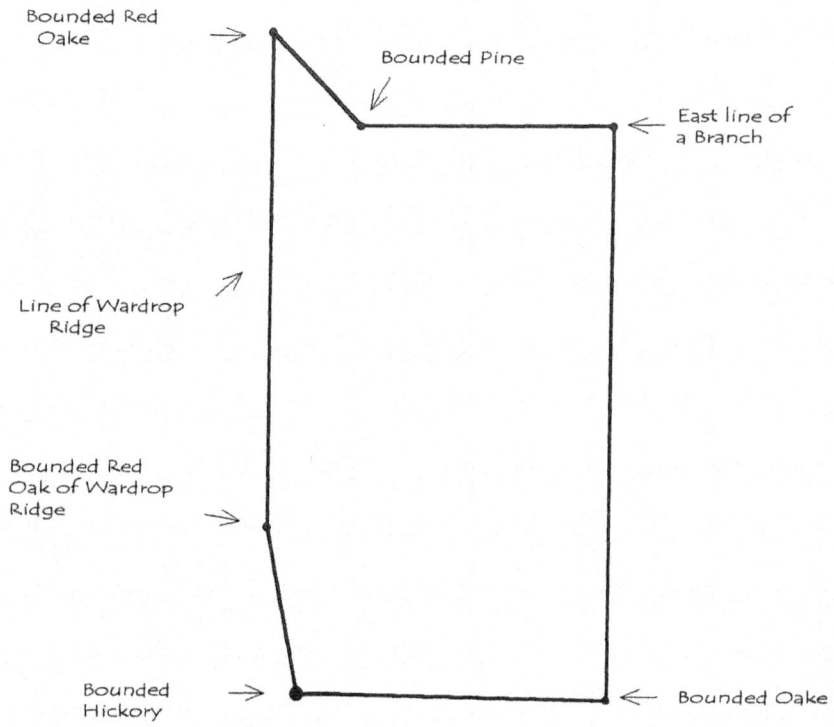

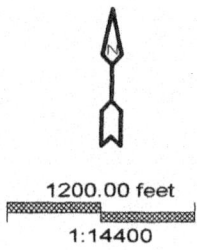

Bounded Red
Oake

Bounded Pine

East line of
a Branch

Line of Wardrop
Ridge

Bounded Red
Oak of Wardrop
Ridge

1200.00 feet

1:14400

Bounded
Hickory

Bounded Oake

Intersects McCubbin's West Line

White Oak

Hamilton 350/350 Acres
Edward Skidmore 8/4/1665
(L7/238 SR7349)

Follows Creek

N

1300.00 feet

1:15600

Marked Pine at mouth of McCubbin's Cove

Marked Pine at Mouth of Hamilton's Creek

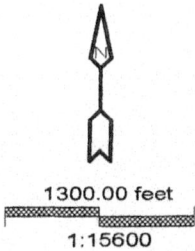

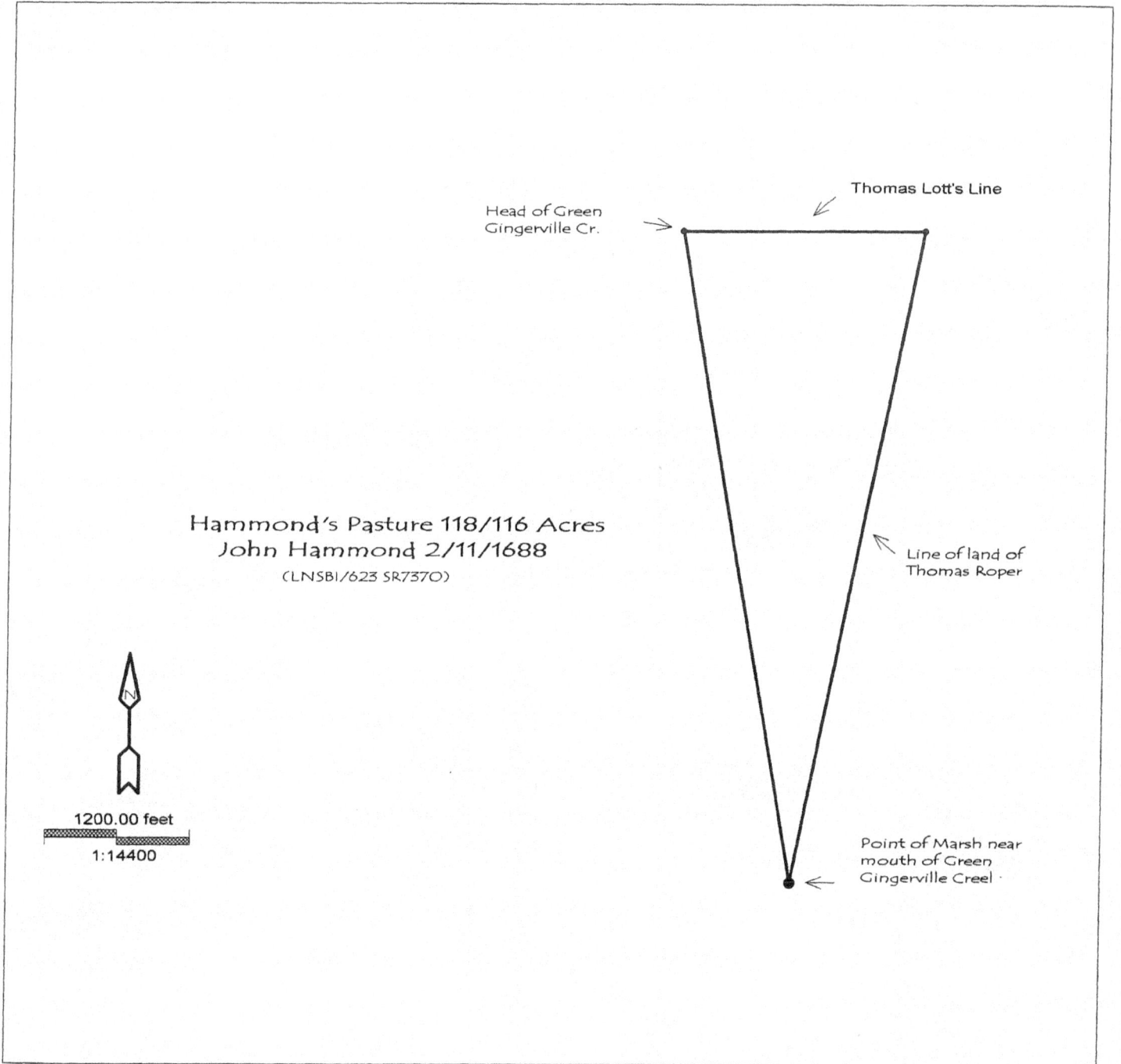

Head of Green
Gingerville Cr.

Thomas Lott's Line

Hammond's Pasture 118/116 Acres
John Hammond 2/11/1688
(LNSBI/623 SR7370)

Line of land of
Thomas Roper

N

1200.00 feet
1:14400

Point of Marsh near
mouth of Green
Gingerville Creel

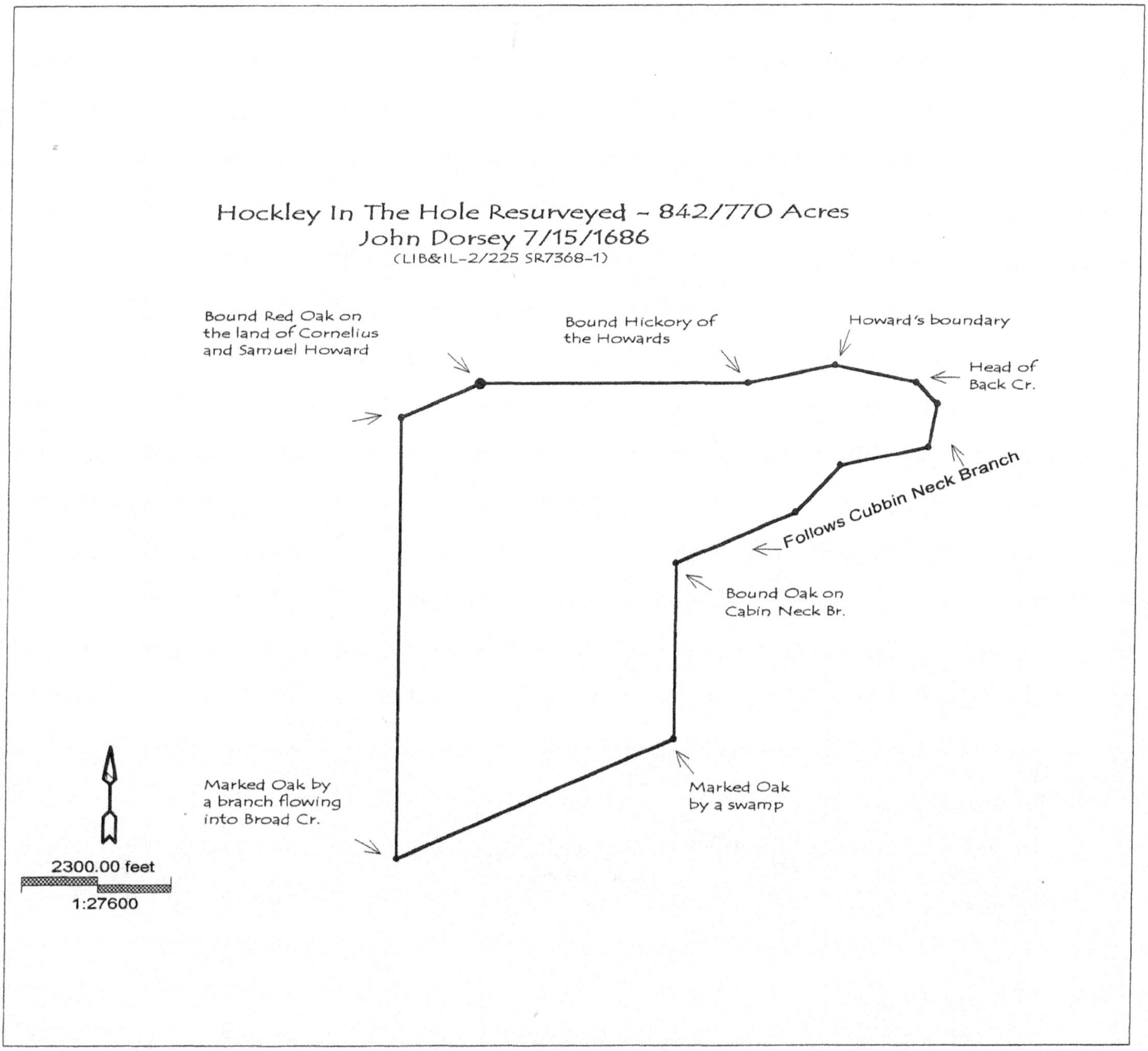

Hockley In The Hole Resurveyed ~ 842/770 Acres
John Dorsey 7/15/1686
(LIB&IL-2/225 SR7368-1)

Bound Red Oak on
the land of Cornelius
and Samuel Howard

Bound Hickory of
the Howards

Howard's boundary

Head of
Back Cr.

Follows Cubbin Neck Branch

Bound Oak on
Cabin Neck Br.

Marked Oak by
a branch flowing
into Broad Cr.

Marked Oak
by a swamp

2300.00 feet

1:27600

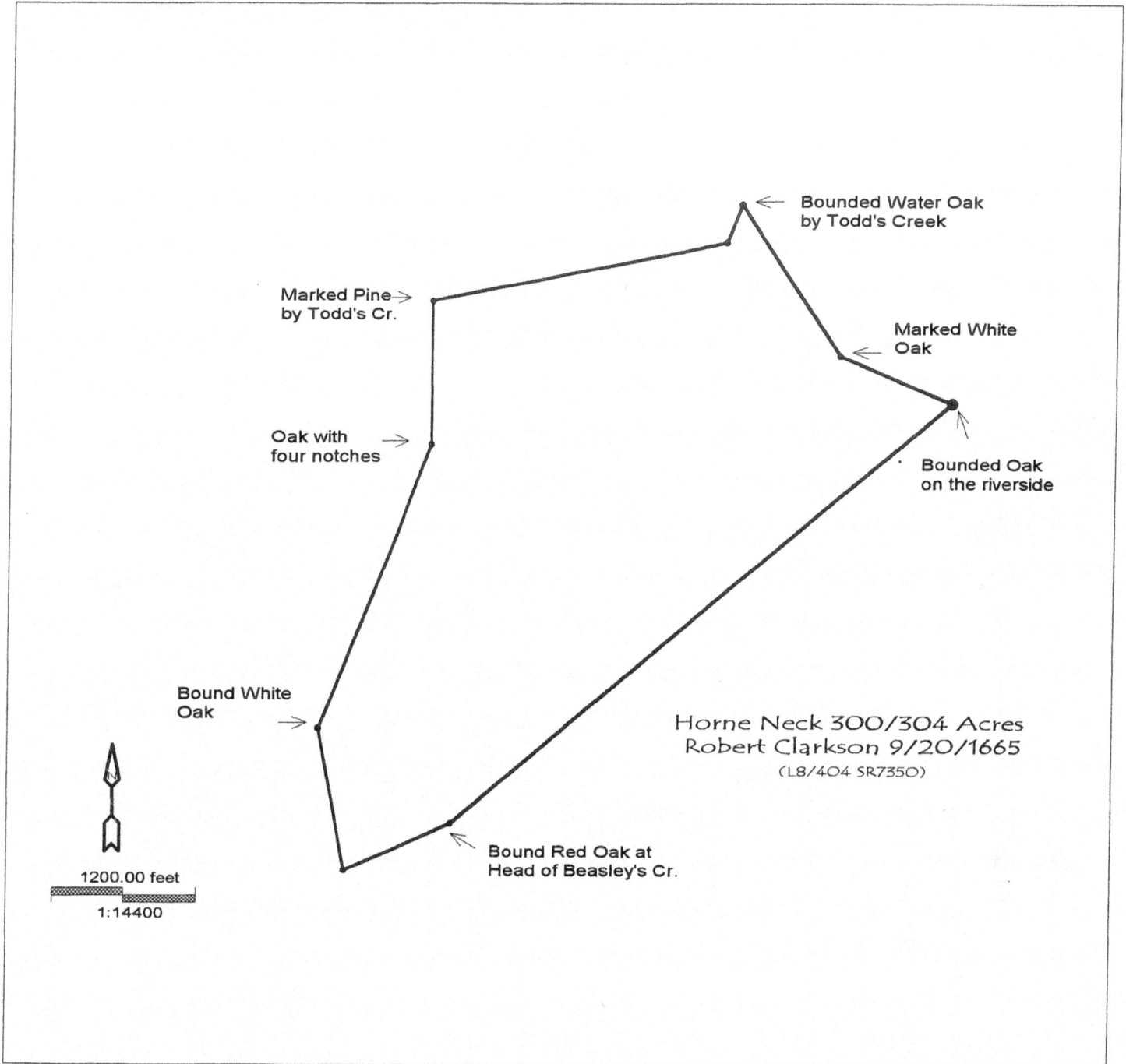

Bounded Water Oak
by Todd's Creek

Marked Pine →
by Todd's Cr.

Marked White
Oak

Oak with   →
four notches

Bounded Oak
on the riverside

Bound White
Oak
→

Horne Neck 300/304 Acres
Robert Clarkson 9/20/1665
(L8/404 SR7350)

1200.00 feet

1:14400

Bound Red Oak at
Head of Beasley's Cr.

234

Howard's Heirship 420/390 Acres
Cornelius Howard 8/4/1664
(L7/249 SR7349)

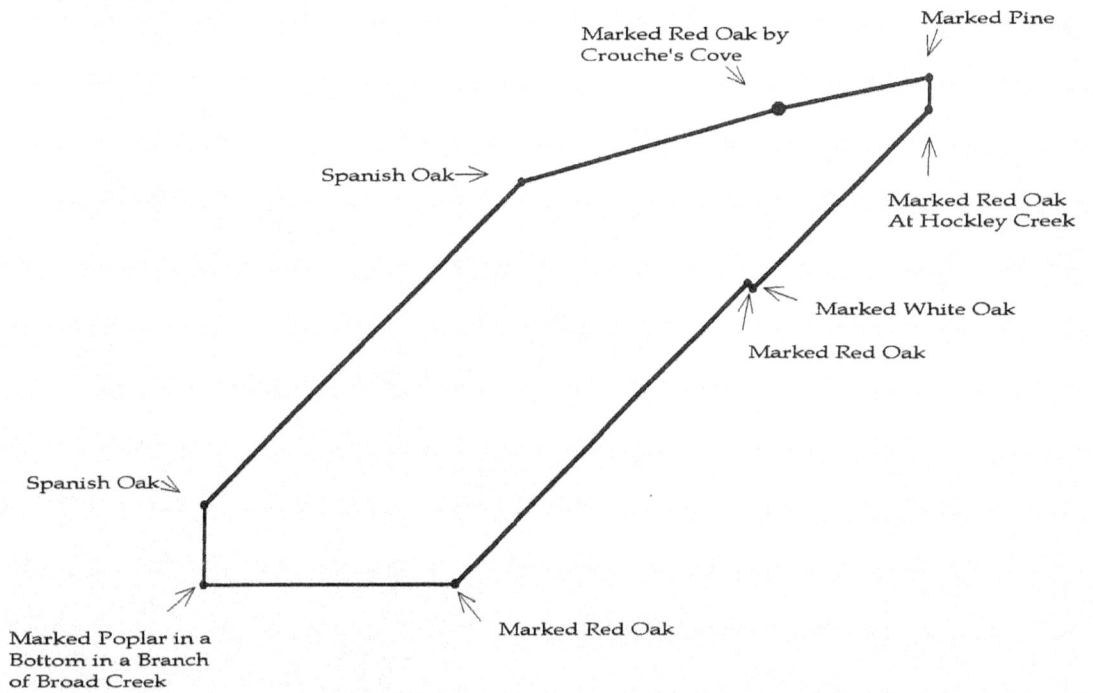

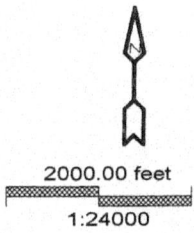

Marked Red Oak by
Crouche's Cove

Marked Pine

Spanish Oak→

Marked Red Oak
At Hockley Creek

Marked White Oak

Marked Red Oak

Spanish Oak

Marked Poplar in a
Bottom in a Branch
of Broad Creek

Marked Red Oak

2000.00 feet

1:24000

235

Howard's Hill 200/200 Acres
Cornelius Howard 9/10/1672

(L17/297 SR7358)

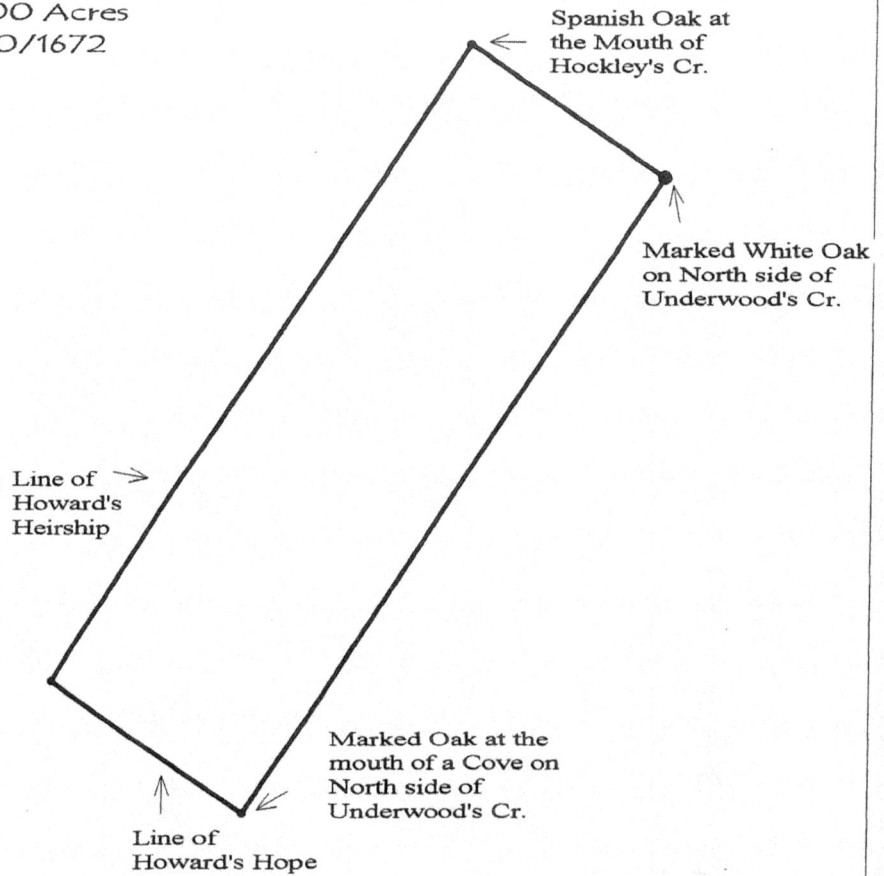

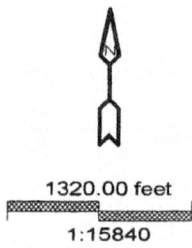

Spanish Oak at
the Mouth of
Hockley's Cr.

Marked White Oak
on North side of
Underwood's Cr.

Line of
Howard's
Heirship

Marked Oak at the
mouth of a Cove on
North side of
Underwood's Cr.

Line of
Howard's Hope

1320.00 feet

1:15840

Howard's Hope 100/77 Acres
Samuell Howard 8/4/1664
(L7/251 SR7349)

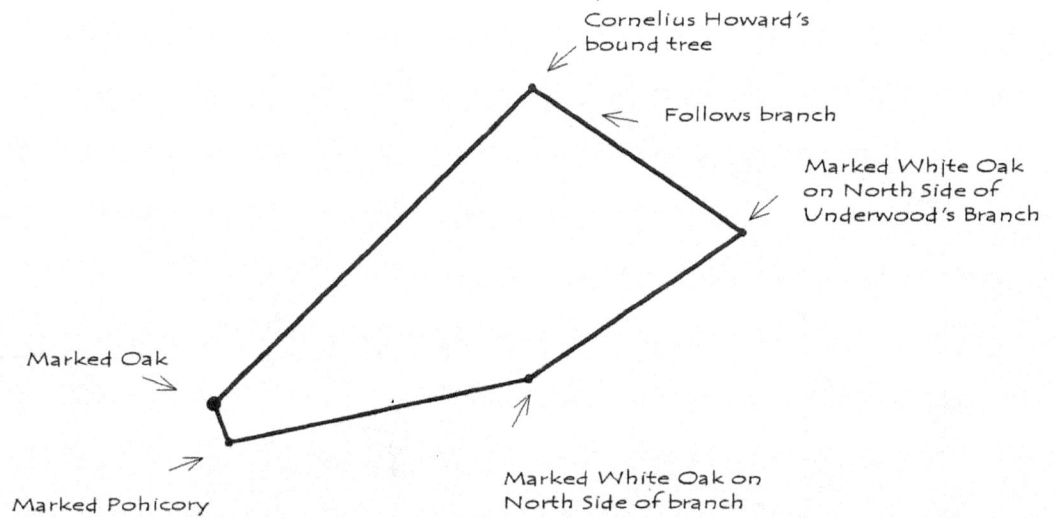

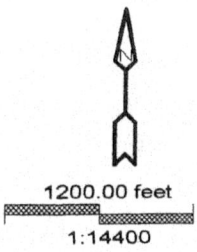

Cornelius Howard's
bound tree

Follows branch

Marked White Oak
on North Side of
Underwood's Branch

Marked Oak

Marked Pohicory

Marked White Oak on
North Side of branch

N

1200.00 feet

1:14400

Howard's Inheritance 449/446 Acres
Samuel Howard 5/1/1700
(LCD/45 SR7376)

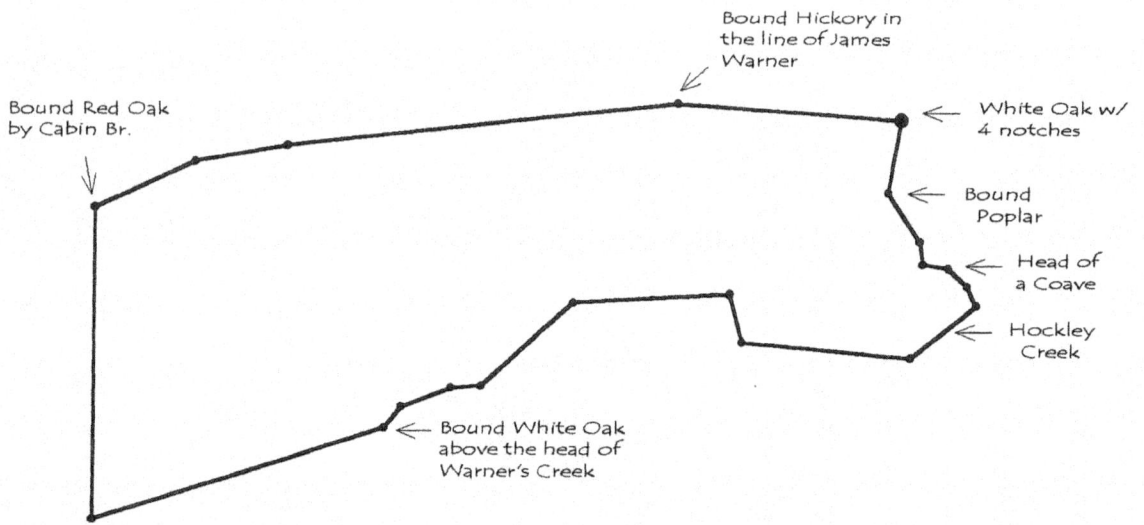

Bound Hickory in
the line of James
Warner

Bound Red Oak
by Cabin Br.

White Oak w/
4 notches

Bound
Poplar

Head of
a Coave

Hockley
Creek

Bound White Oak
above the head of
Warner's Creek

1800.00 feet
1:21600

James' Hill 100/69 Acres
John James 8/4/1664
(L7/225 SR7349)

Sam Wiither's
bound Sassafras
Tree

Marked Poplar
at Head of
Jame's Creek

Follows Sam Wither's line

Marked Oak .
by a path

Marked Oak by
a marsh

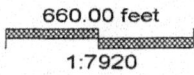

660.00 feet

1:7920

Jeffe's Encrease 180/100 Acres
Thomas Jeffe 10/5/1683
(LSDA/176 SR7369)

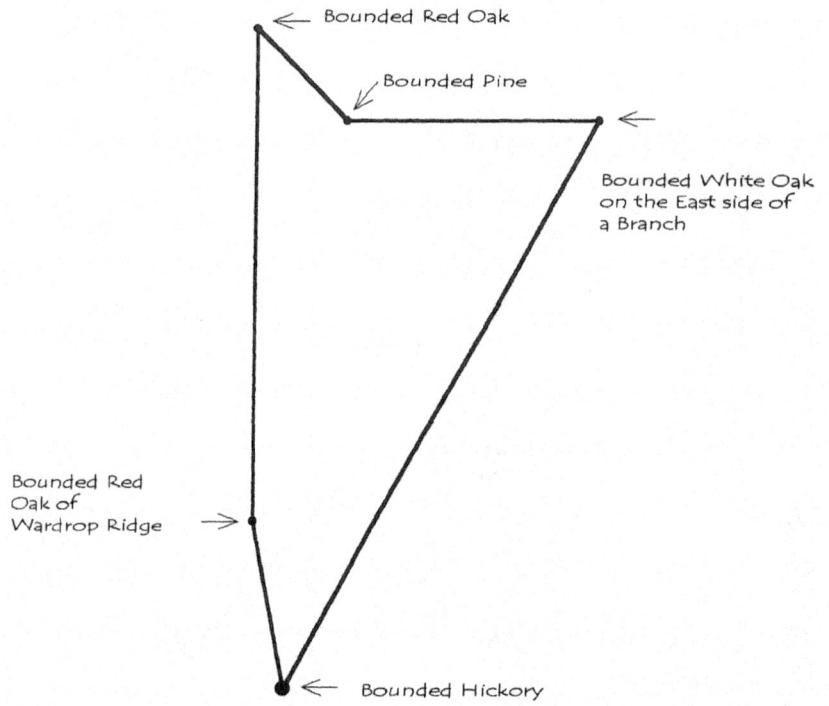

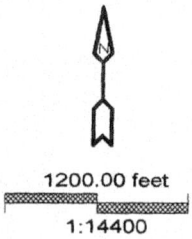

← Bounded Red Oak

Bounded Pine

Bounded White Oak
on the East side of
a Branch

Bounded Red
Oak of
Wardrop Ridge →

← Bounded Hickory

N

1200.00 feet

1:14400

Jeff's Search 39/39 Acres
William Jeff 2/18/1688
(LNSBi/676 SR7370)

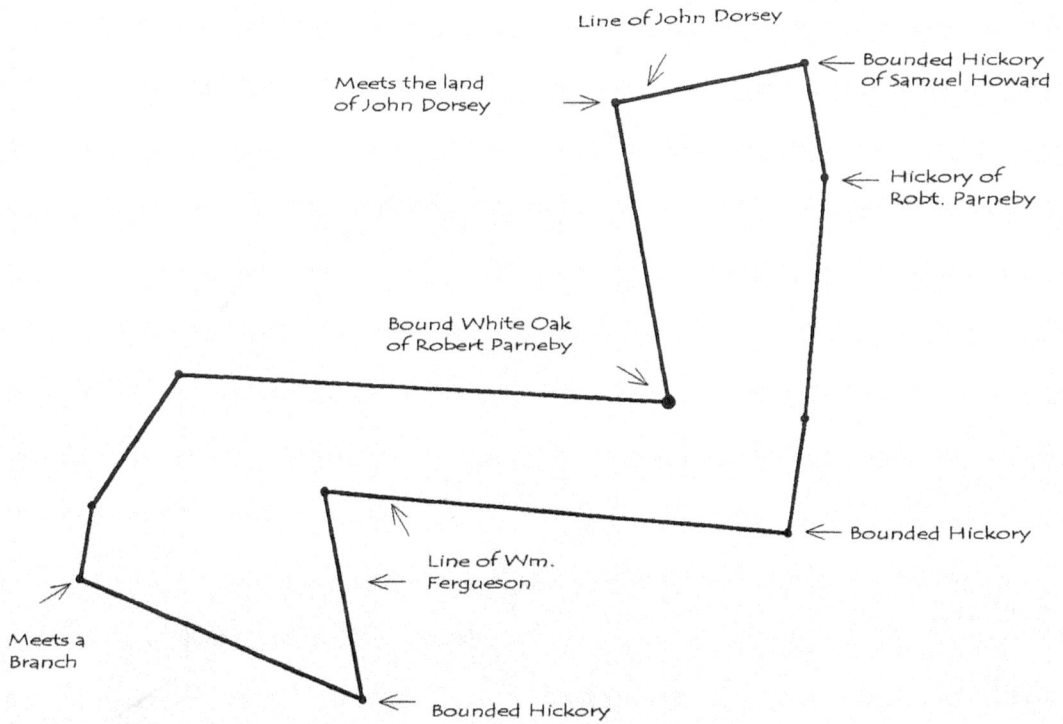

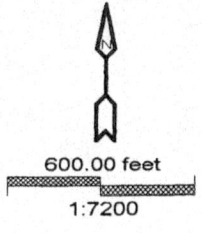

Line of John Dorsey

Meets the land
of John Dorsey

Bounded Hickory
of Samuel Howard

Hickory of
Robt. Parneby

Bound White Oak
of Robert Parneby

Bounded Hickory

Line of Wm.
Fergueson

Meets a
Branch

Bounded Hickory

N

600.00 feet
1:7200

Lydia's Rest Resurveyed 210/134 Acres
John Baldwin 7/8/1681
(LCB2i/148 SR7366)

Bound Water
Oak on a Br.
of Oatley's Cr.

Oatley Poynt the Eastern
most point on the N. side
of Oatley Creek

Beetenson's
Pt.

Small
Water
Oake

South River

Bound
Hickory

Bound Water Oake
at Hollowing Pt.

Mouth of
Harness's
Cr.

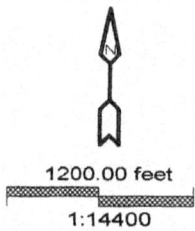

Bound Chestnutt

N

1200.00 feet

1:14400

242

Major's Fancy 186/187 Acres
Maj. Edward Dorsey 11/10/1695
(L23/257 SR7364)

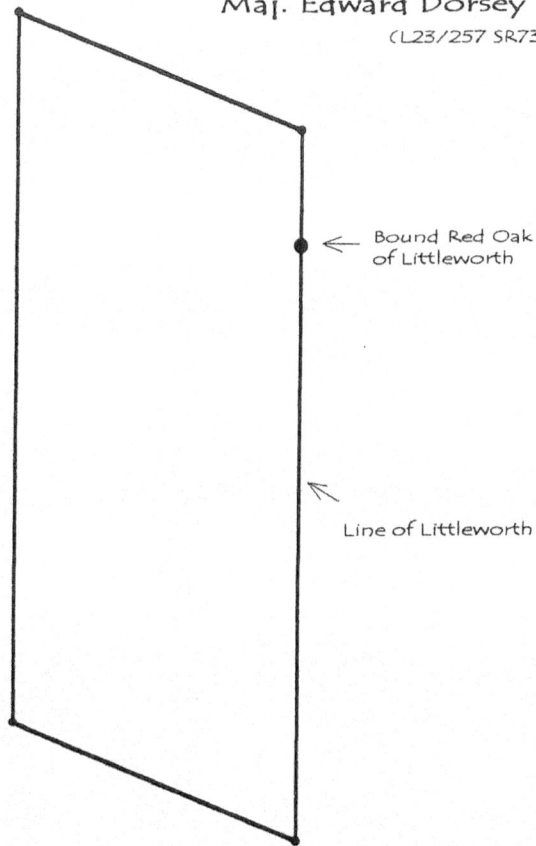

← Bound Red Oak
of Littleworth

Line of Littleworth

1200.00 feet
1:14400

Mayden Croft 128/139 Acres
Lawrence Draper 2/11/1688
(LNSBi/618 SR7370)

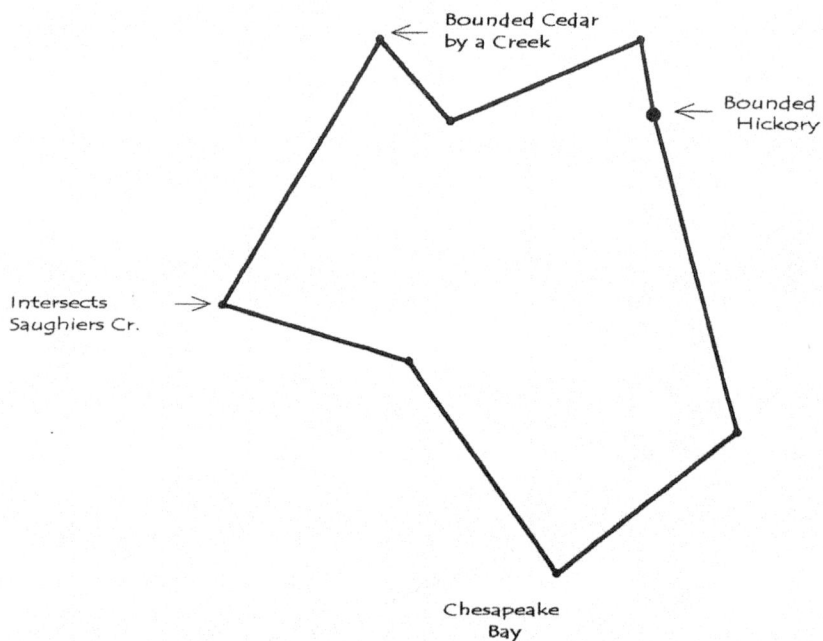

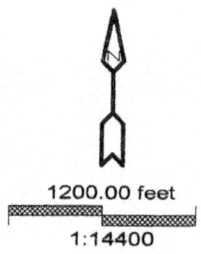

Bounded Cedar
by a Creek

Bounded
Hickory

Intersects
Saughiers Cr.

Chesapeake
Bay

N

1200.00 feet

1:14400

Mountain Neck 190/266 Acres
Thomas Hammond 8/24/1665
(L8/115 SR7350)

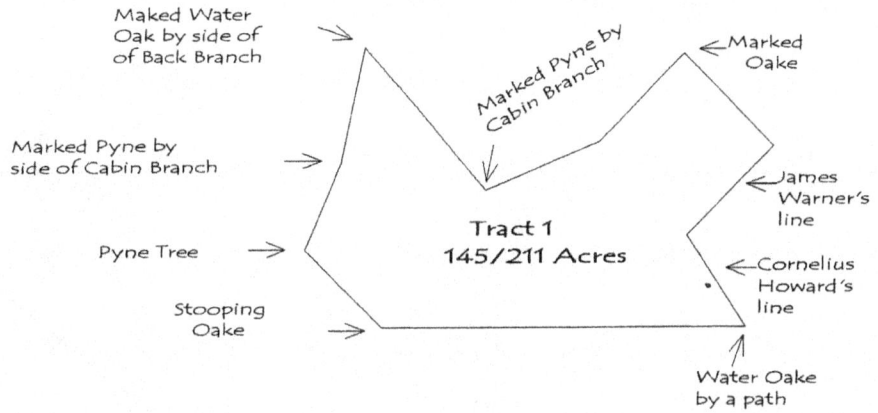

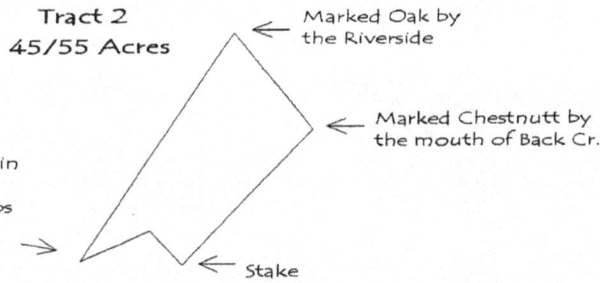

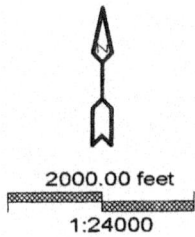

Maked Water
Oak by side of
of Back Branch

Marked Pyne by
Cabin Branch

Marked
Oake

Marked Pyne by
side of Cabin Branch

James
Warner's
line

Pyne Tree

Tract 1
145/211 Acres

Cornelius
Howard's
line

Stooping
Oake

Water Oake
by a path

Tract 2
45/55 Acres

Marked Oak by
the Riverside

Marked Chestnutt by
the mouth of Back Cr.

Marked Pyne in
the line of
Matthew Gibbs

2000.00 feet

Stake

1:24000

245

Norwood 250/333 Acres
John Norwood 2/8/1650
(LQ/396 SR7345)

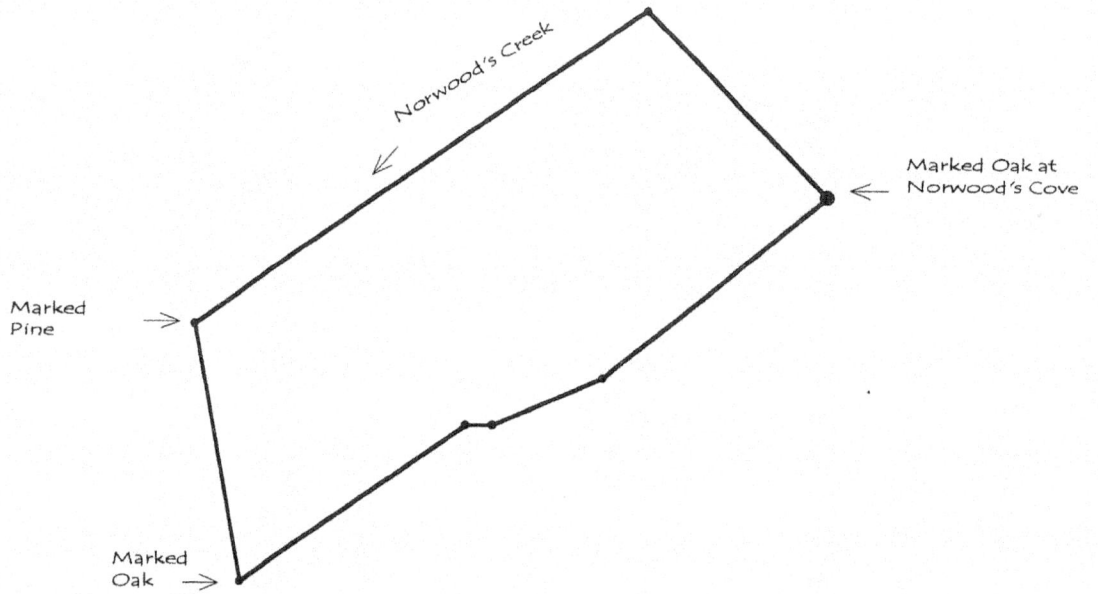

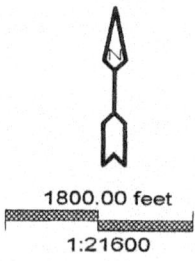

Norwood's Creek

Marked Oak at
Norwood's Cove

Marked
Pine

Marked
Oak

1800.00 feet
1:21600

Norwood's Angles 103/109 Acres
Andrew Norwood 8/10/1684
(LSDA/446 SR7369)

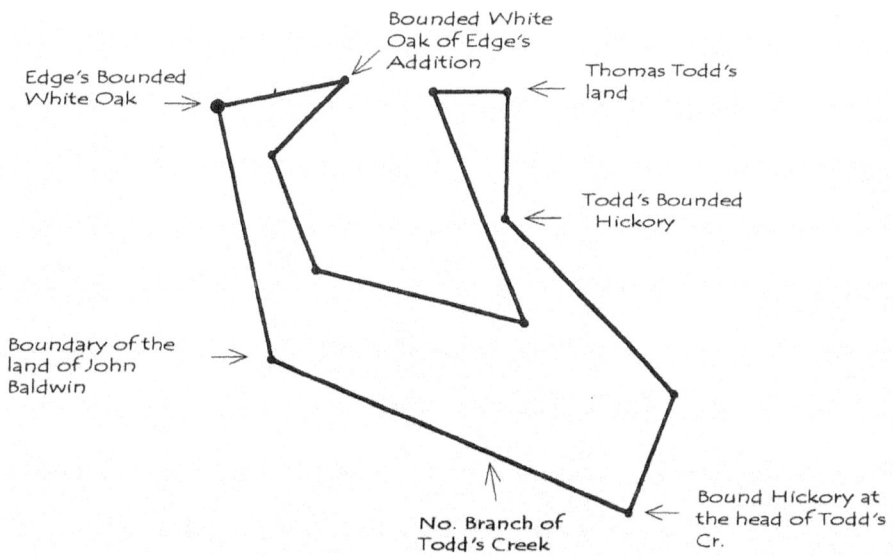

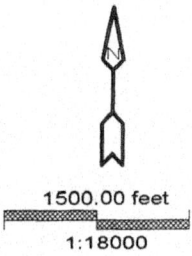

Bounded White
Oak of Edge's
Addition

Thomas Todd's
land

Edge's Bounded
White Oak

Todd's Bounded
Hickory

Boundary of the
land of John
Baldwin

No. Branch of
Todd's Creek

Bound Hickory at
the head of Todd's
Cr.

N

1500.00 feet

1:18000

Norwood's Recovery 104/103 Acres
Andrew Norwood 6/10/1686

(LIB&ILCi/229 SR7368-2)

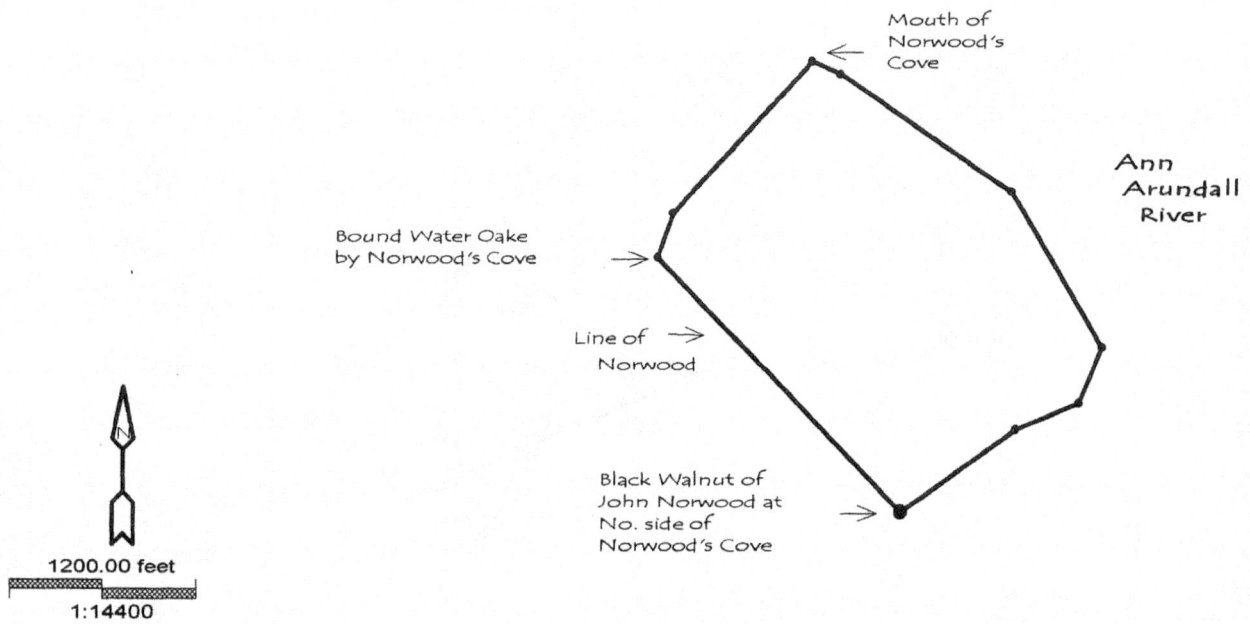

Mouth of
Norwood's
Cove

Ann
Arundall
River

Bound Water Oake
by Norwood's Cove

Line of
Norwood

Black Walnut of
John Norwood at
No. side of
Norwood's Cove

1200.00 feet

1:14400

Orphans Addition 85/90 Acres
Robert & Lawrence Guggon 5/10/1685
(LNSBi/150 SR7370)

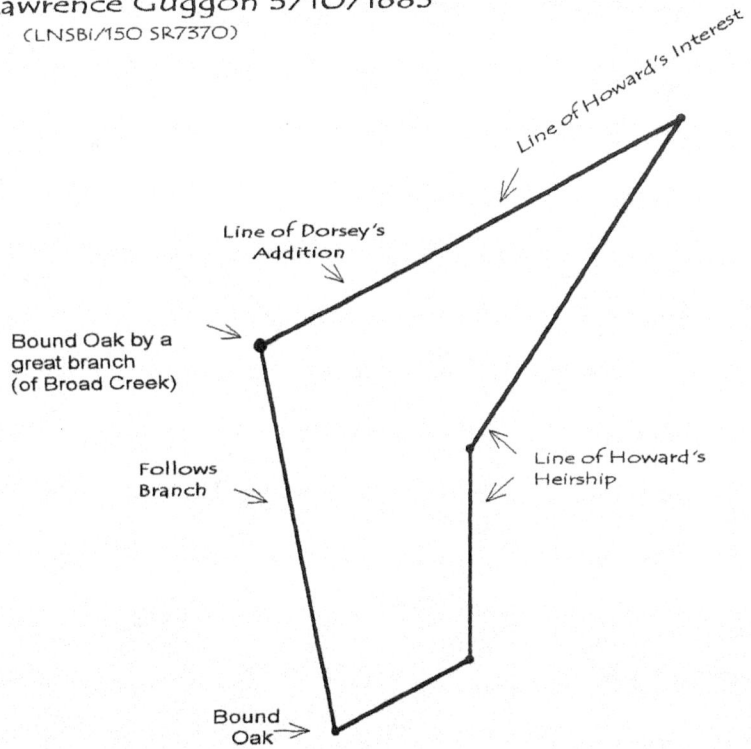

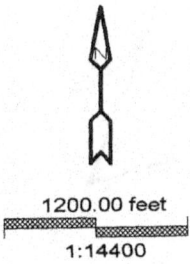

Line of Howard's Interest

Line of Dorsey's
Addition

Bound Oak by a
great branch
(of Broad Creek)

Line of Howard's
Heirship

Follows
Branch

Bound
Oak

1200.00 feet

1:14400

Petticoate's Rest 100/52 Acres
William Petticoate 9/9/1679
(L21/99 SR7362)

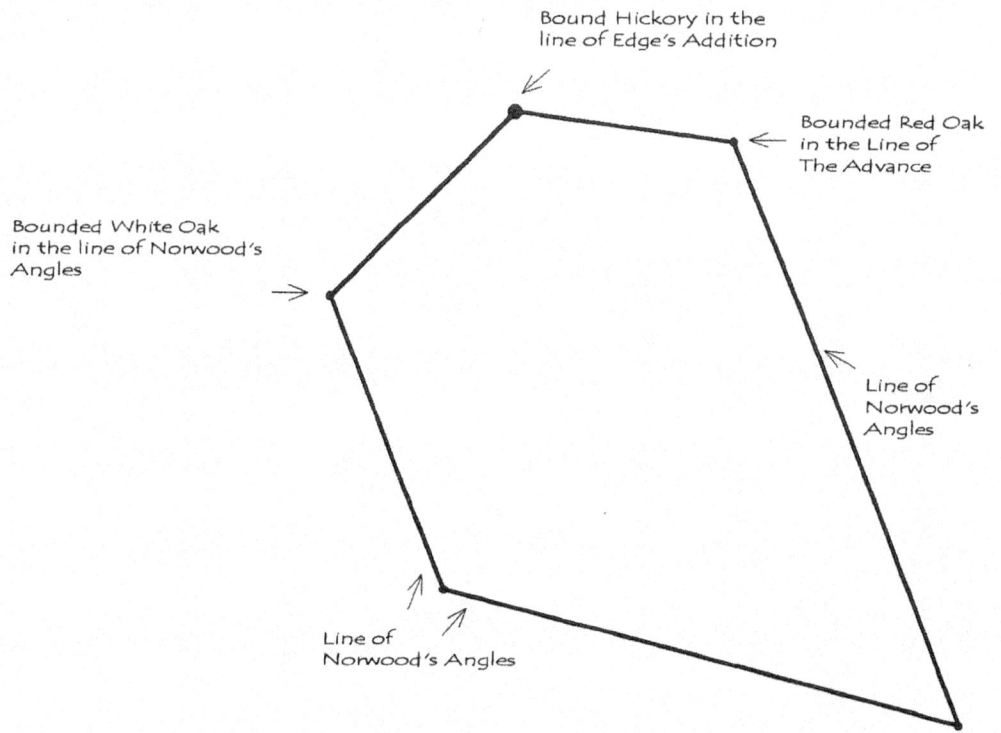

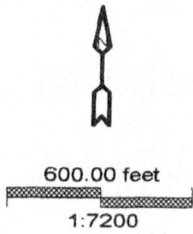

Bound Hickory in the
line of Edge's Addition

Bounded Red Oak
in the Line of
The Advance

Bounded White Oak
in the line of Norwood's
Angles

Line of
Norwood's
Angles

Line of
Norwood's Angles

600.00 feet

1:7200

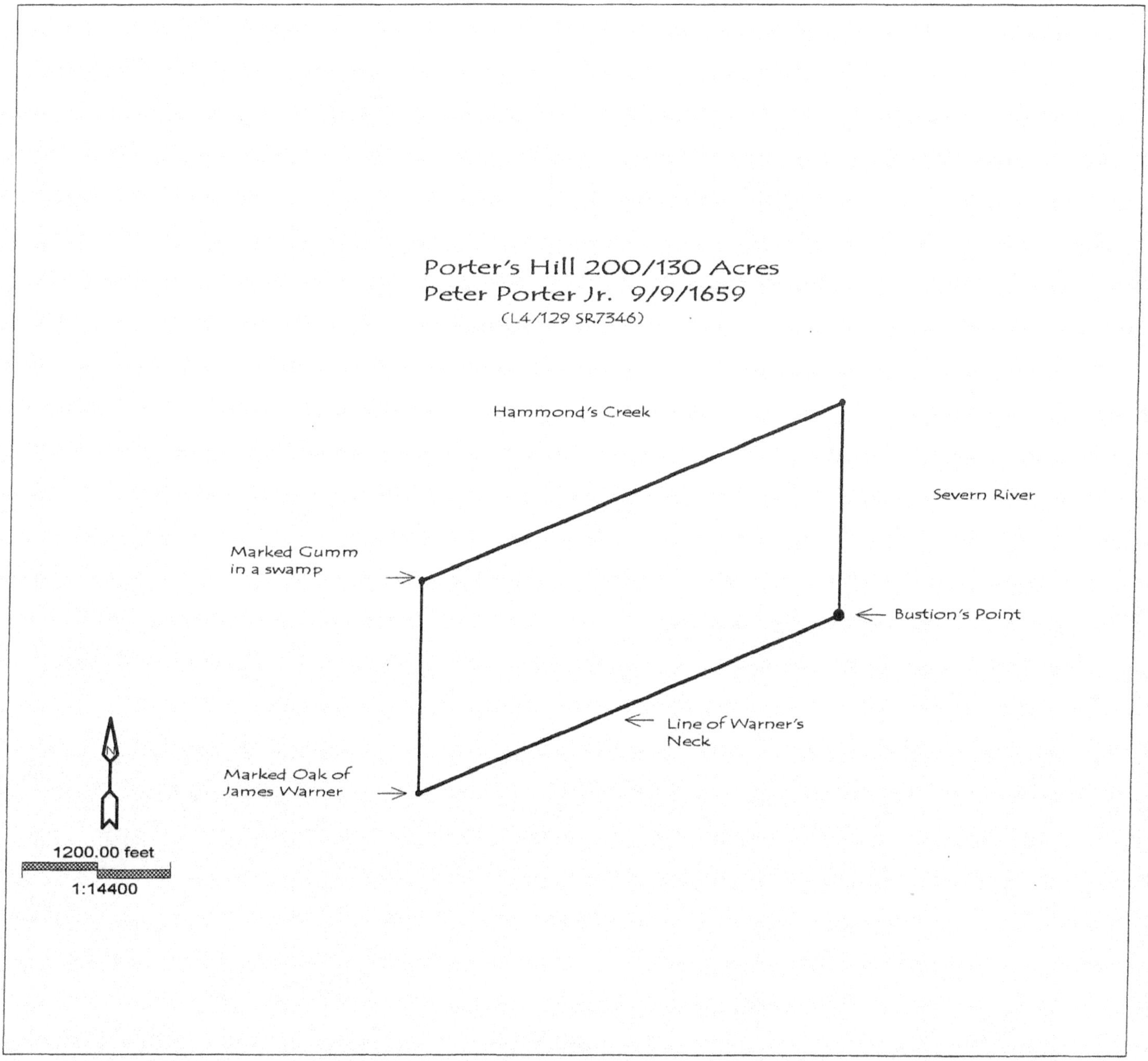

Porter's Hill 200/130 Acres
Peter Porter Jr. 9/9/1659
(L4/129 SR7346)

Hammond's Creek

Severn River

Marked Gumm
in a swamp

Bustion's Point

Marked Oak of
James Warner

Line of Warner's
Neck

N

1200.00 feet

1:14400

Proctor's Chance 30/14 Acres
Robert Proctor 6/28/1680
(LCB2i/13 SR7366)

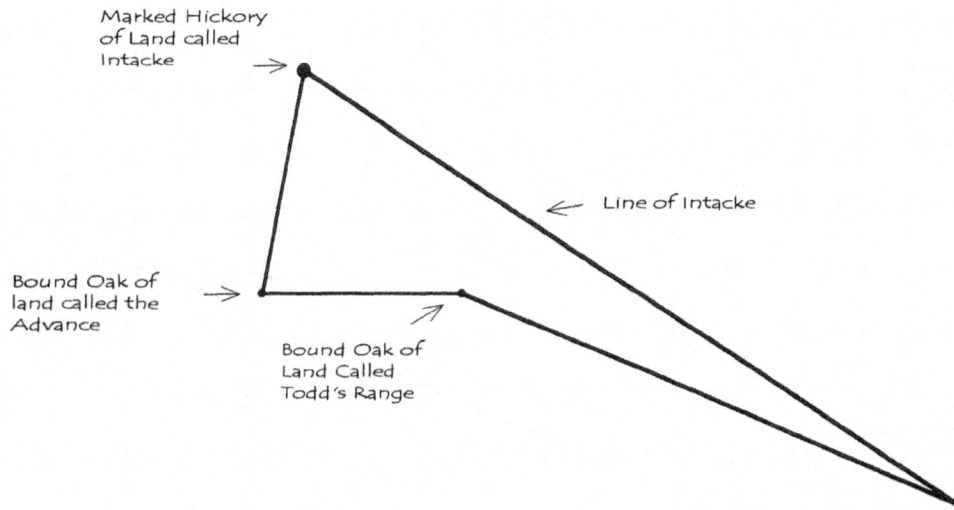

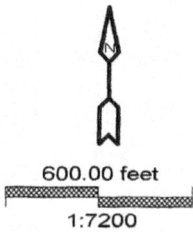

Marked Hickory
of Land called
Intacke

Line of Intacke

Bound Oak of
land called the
Advance

Bound Oak of
Land Called
Todd's Range

N

600.00 feet
1:7200

Proctor's Forrest 100/100 Acres
Robert Proctor 7/20/1673
(L15/87 SR4327)

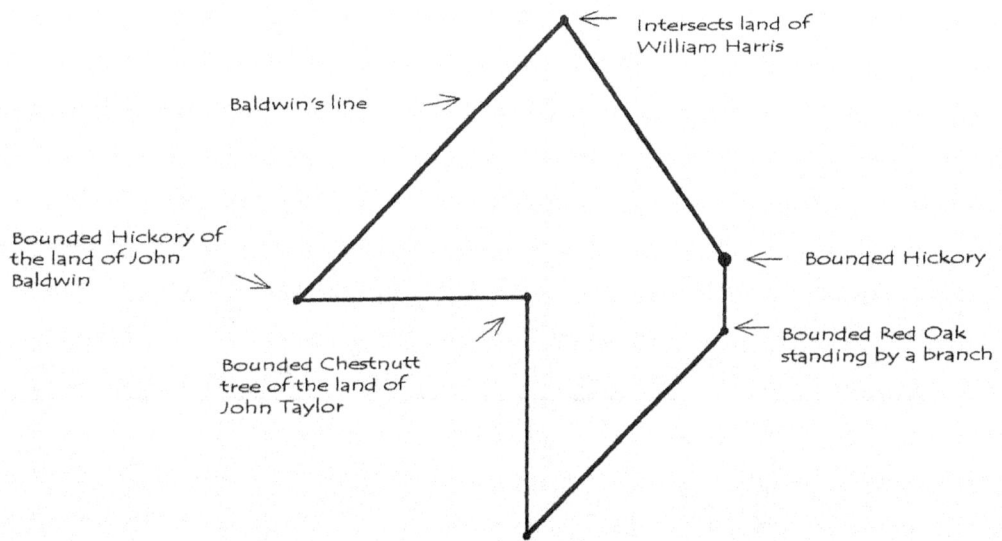

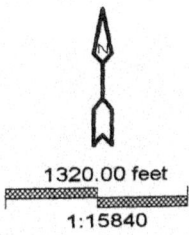

Intersects land of
William Harris

Baldwin's line

Bounded Hickory of
the land of John
Baldwin

Bounded Hickory

Bounded Red Oak
standing by a branch

Bounded Chestnutt
tree of the land of
John Taylor

1320.00 feet
1:15840

Range 75/45 Acres
John Medcalfe 4/2/1706
(LWD/512 SR7372–2)

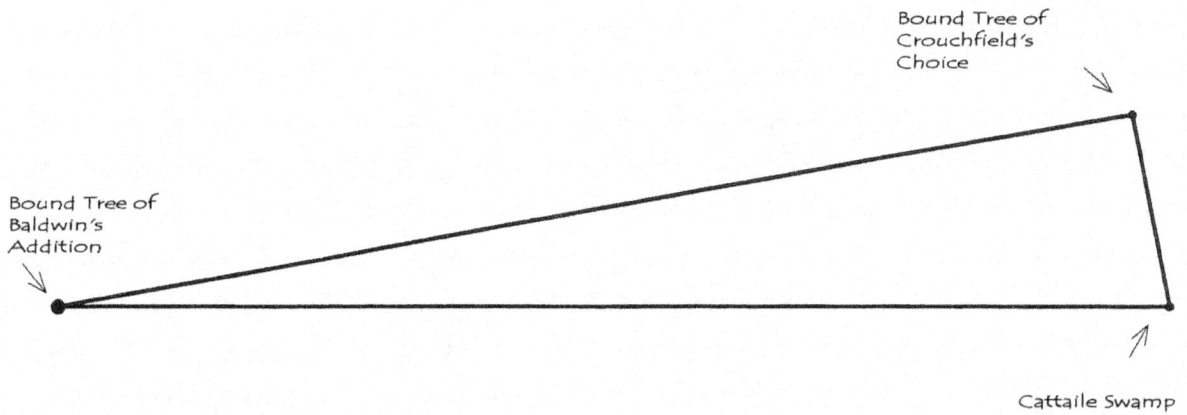

Bound Tree of
Crouchfield's
Choice

Bound Tree of
Baldwin's
Addition

Cattaile Swamp

N

800.00 feet
1:9600

Read's Lott 40/20 Acres
William Read 9/15/1665
(L8/290 SR7350)

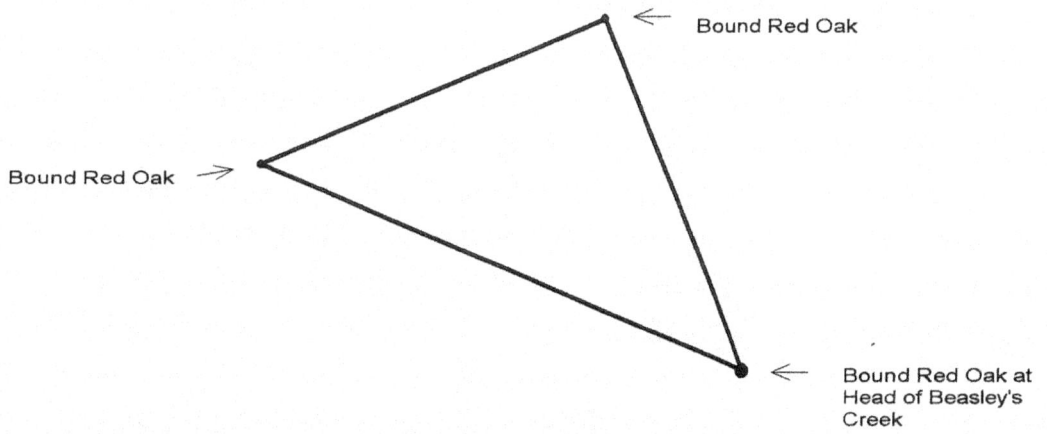

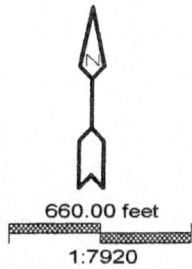

← Bound Red Oak

Bound Red Oak →

← Bound Red Oak at
Head of Beasley's
Creek

660.00 feet

1:7920

Roper's Neck Resurveyed 300/348 Acres
Thomas Roper 3/1/1673
(L15/153 SR4327)

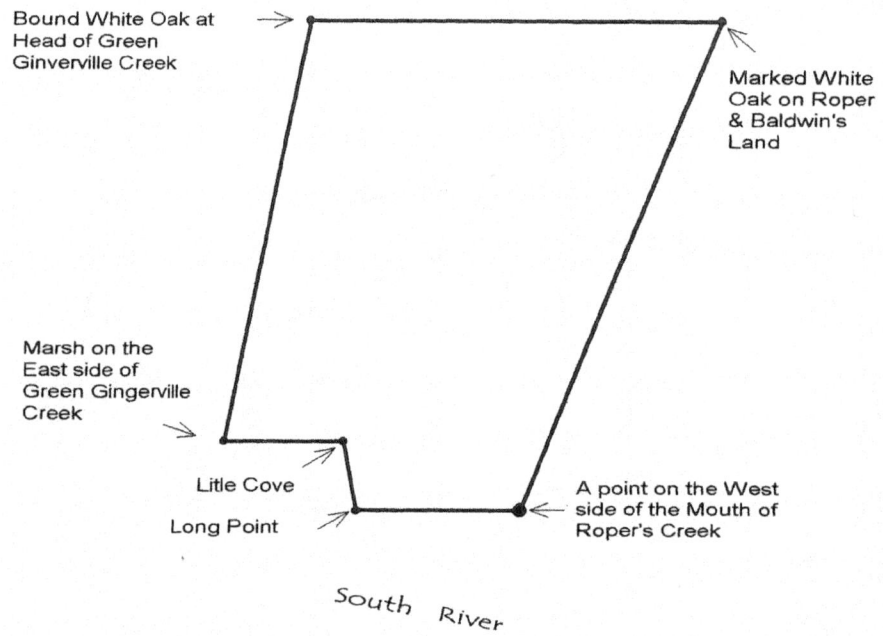

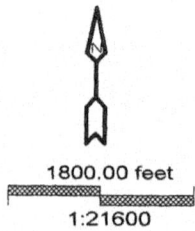

Bound White Oak at
Head of Green
Ginverville Creek

Marked White
Oak on Roper
& Baldwin's
Land

Marsh on the
East side of
Green Gingerville
Creek

Litle Cove

Long Point

A point on the West
side of the Mouth of
Roper's Creek

South River

1800.00 feet

1:21600

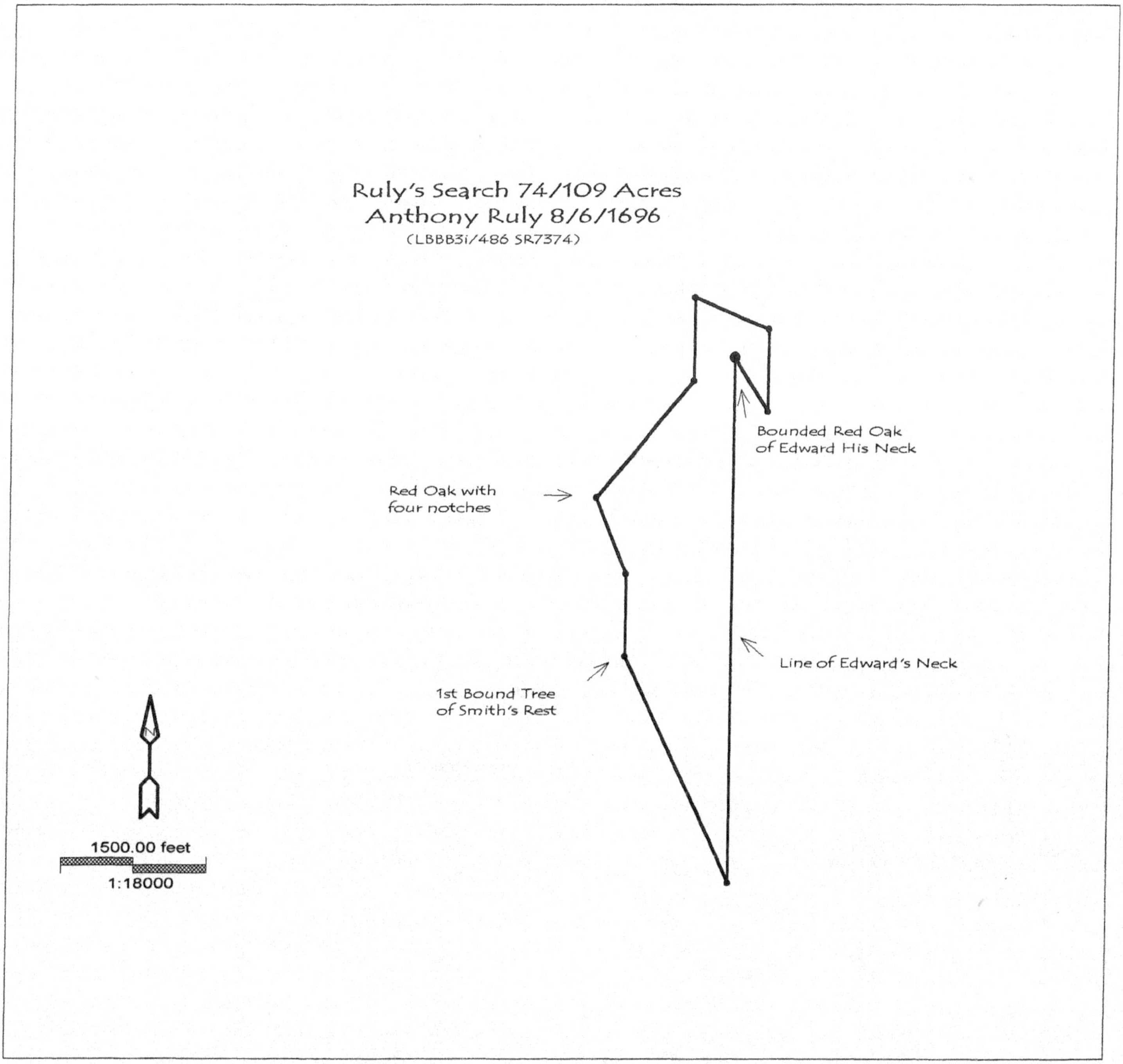

Ruly's Search 74/109 Acres
Anthony Ruly 8/6/1696
(LBBB3i/486 SR7374)

Bounded Red Oak
of Edward His Neck

Red Oak with
four notches

Line of Edward's Neck

1st Bound Tree
of Smith's Rest

1500.00 feet

1:18000

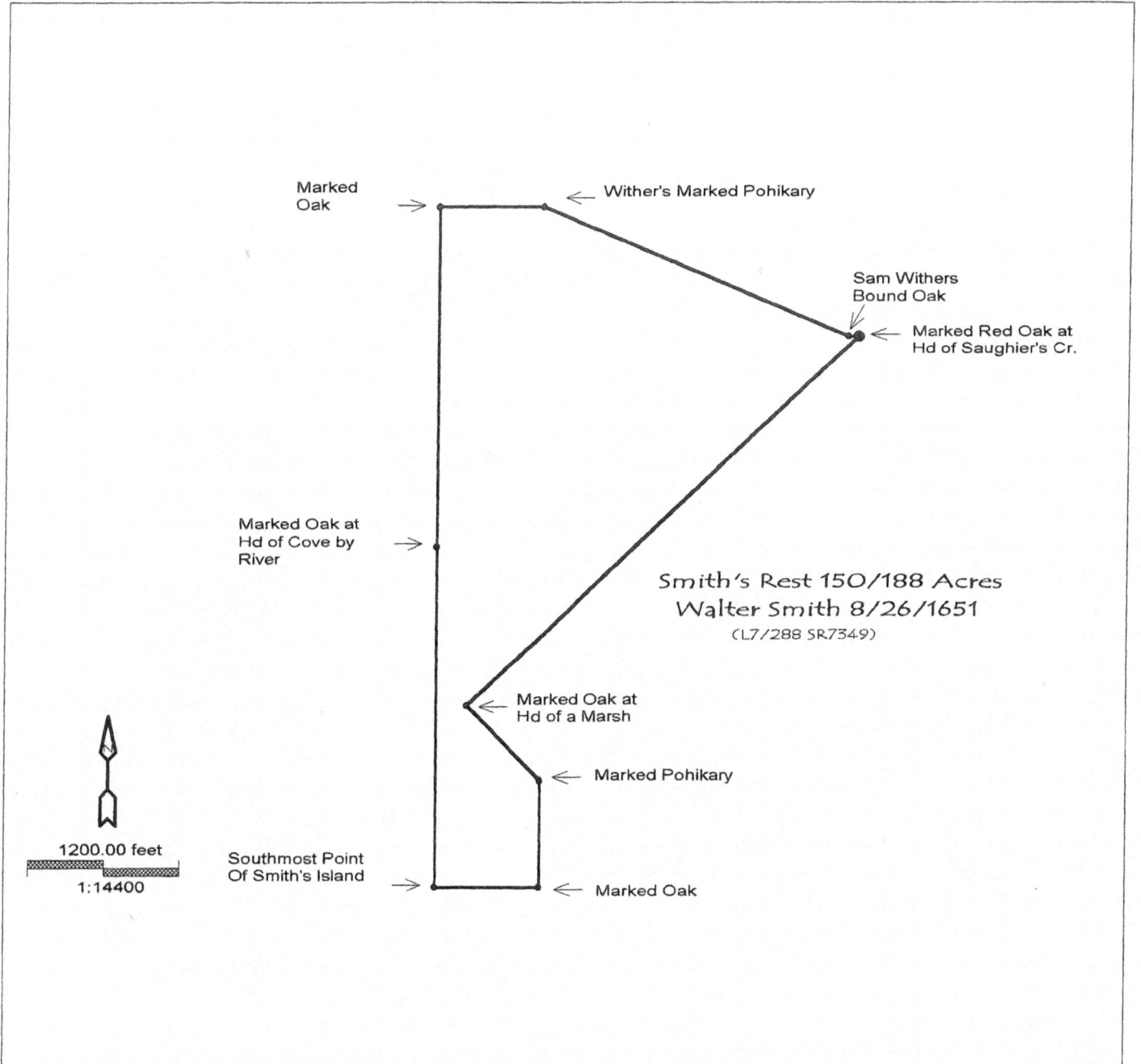

Marked
Oak

Wither's Marked Pohikary

Sam Withers
Bound Oak

Marked Red Oak at
Hd of Saughier's Cr.

Marked Oak at
Hd of Cove by
River

Smith's Rest 150/188 Acres
Walter Smith 8/26/1651
(L7/288 SR7349)

Marked Oak at
Hd of a Marsh

Marked Pohikary

1200.00 feet

1:14400

Southmost Point
Of Smith's Island

Marked Oak

The Addition 22/20 Acres
John Hammond 1/5/1687
(LIB&ILC/315 SR7368-1)

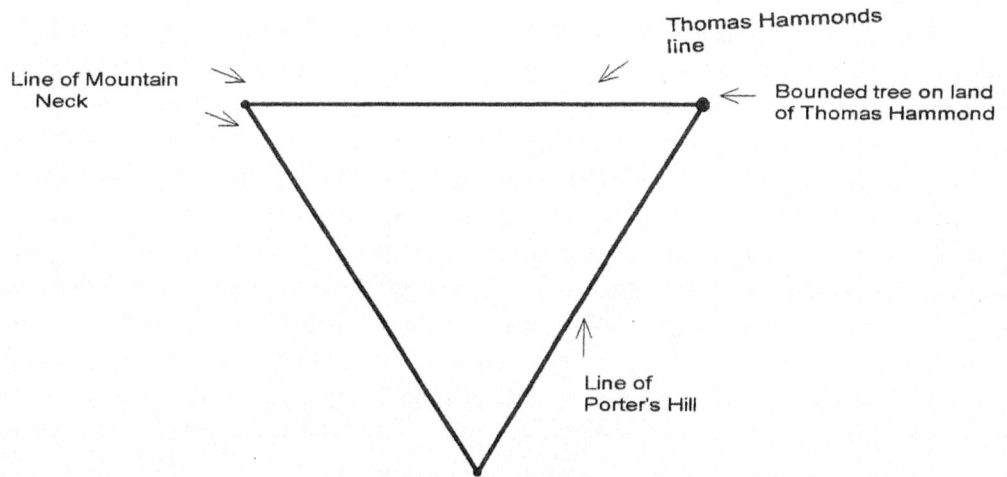

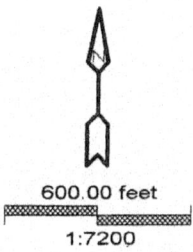

Thomas Hammonds
line

Line of Mountain
Neck

Bounded tree on land
of Thomas Hammond

Line of
Porter's Hill

600.00 feet

1:7200

The Addition 60/60 Acres
Capt. Richard Hill 6/1/1687
(LNS2i/321 SR7371)

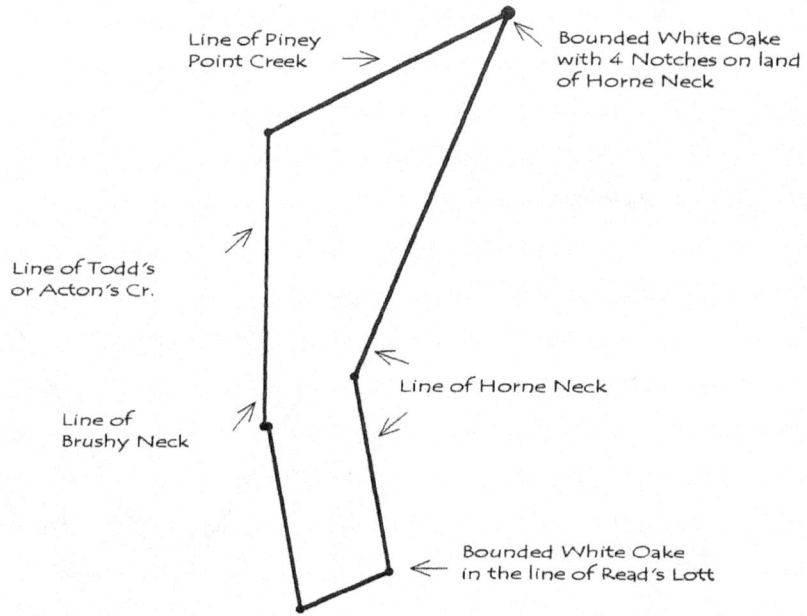

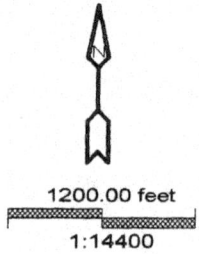

Line of Piney
Point Creek →

Bounded White Oake
with 4 Notches on land
of Horne Neck

Line of Todd's
or Acton's Cr.

Line of Horne Neck

Line of
Brushy Neck

Bounded White Oake
in the line of Read's Lott ←

1200.00 feet

1:14400

260

The Addition 80/80 Acres
Samuel Young 10/20/1704
(LDSF/540 SR7373-2)

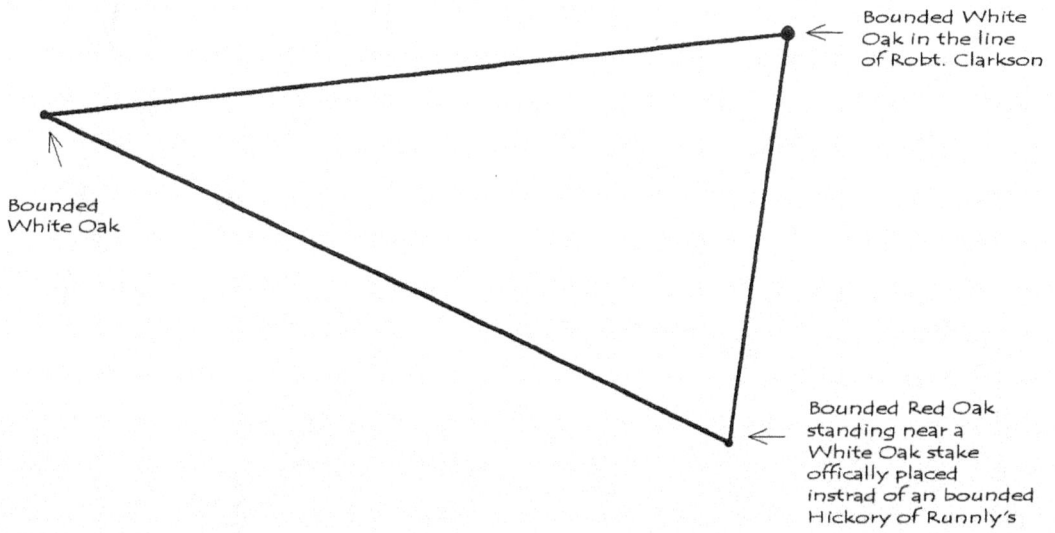

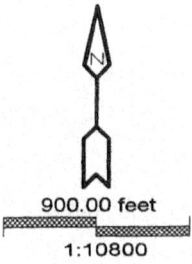

Bounded White
Oak in the line
of Robt. Clarkson

Bounded
White Oak

Bounded Red Oak
standing near a
White Oak stake
offically placed
instrad of an bounded
Hickory of Runnly's

N

900.00 feet

1:10800

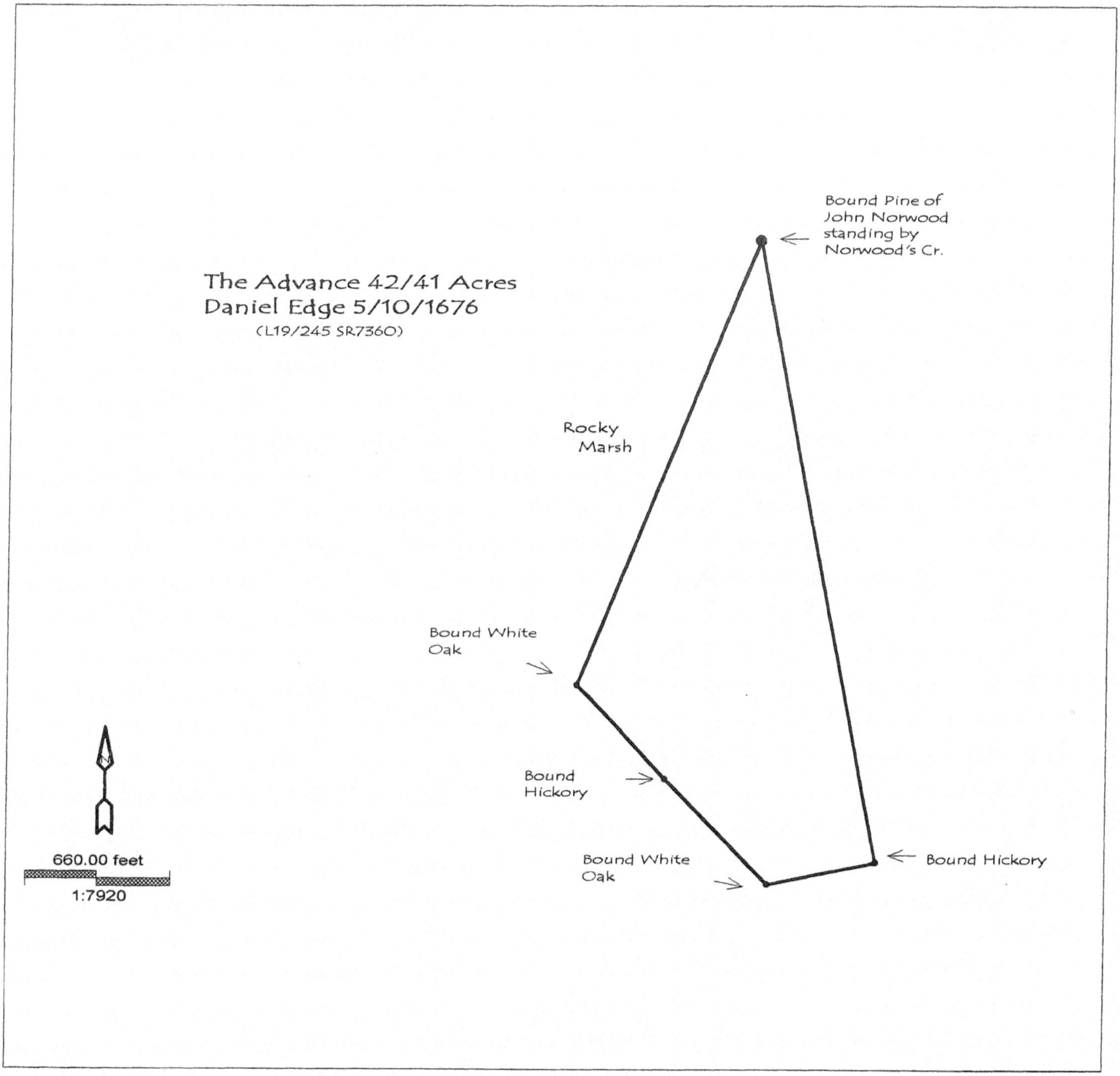

The Advance 42/41 Acres
Daniel Edge 5/10/1676
(L19/245 SR7360)

Bound Pine of
John Norwood
standing by
Norwood's Cr.

Rocky
Marsh

Bound White
Oak

Bound
Hickory

Bound White
Oak

Bound Hickory

N

660.00 feet
1:7920

The Advantage 40/23 Acres
Richard Moss 8/24/1665
(L8/110 SR7350)

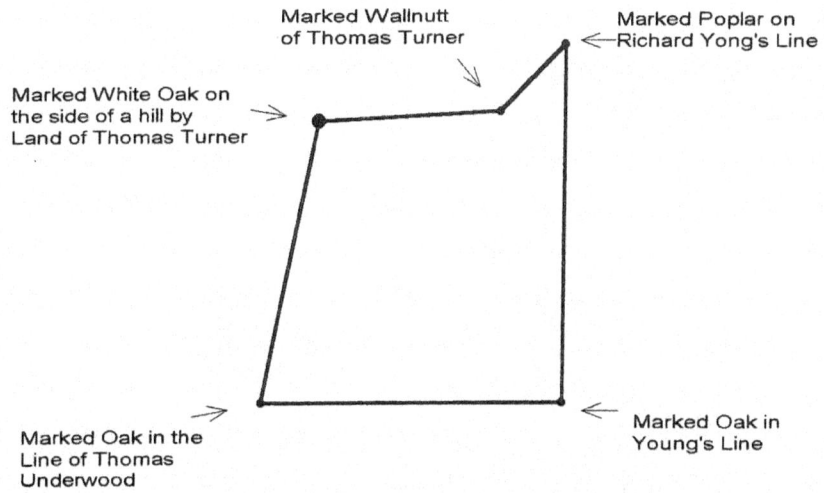

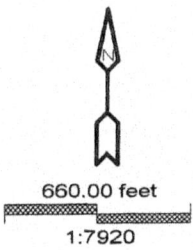

Marked Wallnutt
of Thomas Turner

Marked Poplar on
←Richard Yong's Line

Marked White Oak on
the side of a hill by
Land of Thomas Turner →

Marked Oak in the
Line of Thomas
Underwood →

Marked Oak in
Young's Line ←

N

660.00 feet

1:7920

The Angle 7/7 Acres
Capt. Richard Hill 6/1/1687
(LNS2i/321 SR7371)

Bounded Pine
by Dorsey's Cr.

Dorsey's Creek

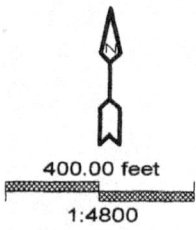

Marked Elm

400.00 feet

1:4800

The Chance 200/173 Acres
Cornelius Howard 8/25/1664
(L7/379 SR7349)

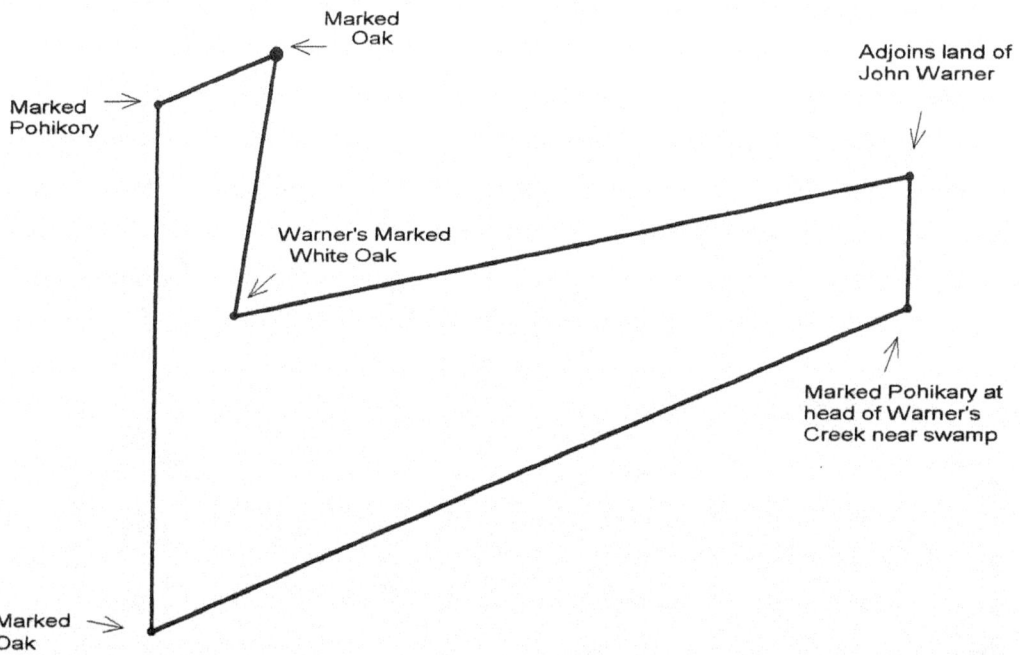

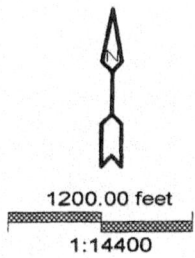

Marked
Oak

Adjoins land of
John Warner

Marked
Pohikory

Warner's Marked
White Oak

Marked Pohikary at
head of Warner's
Creek near swamp

1200.00 feet
1:14400

Marked
Oak

265

The Chance 15/10 Acres
Thomas Roper 9/10/1665
(L8/408 SR7350)

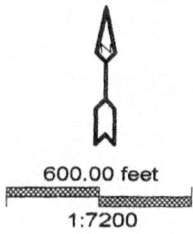

Bound White Oak on
the Land of Wm,
Frizzell and John
Baldwin

Bound Pine Tree
on creek side

Bound Red Oak on
land already laid out
for Thomas Roper

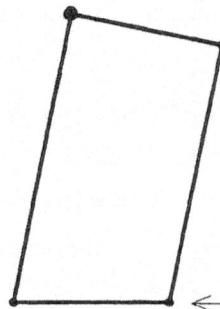

600.00 feet

1:7200

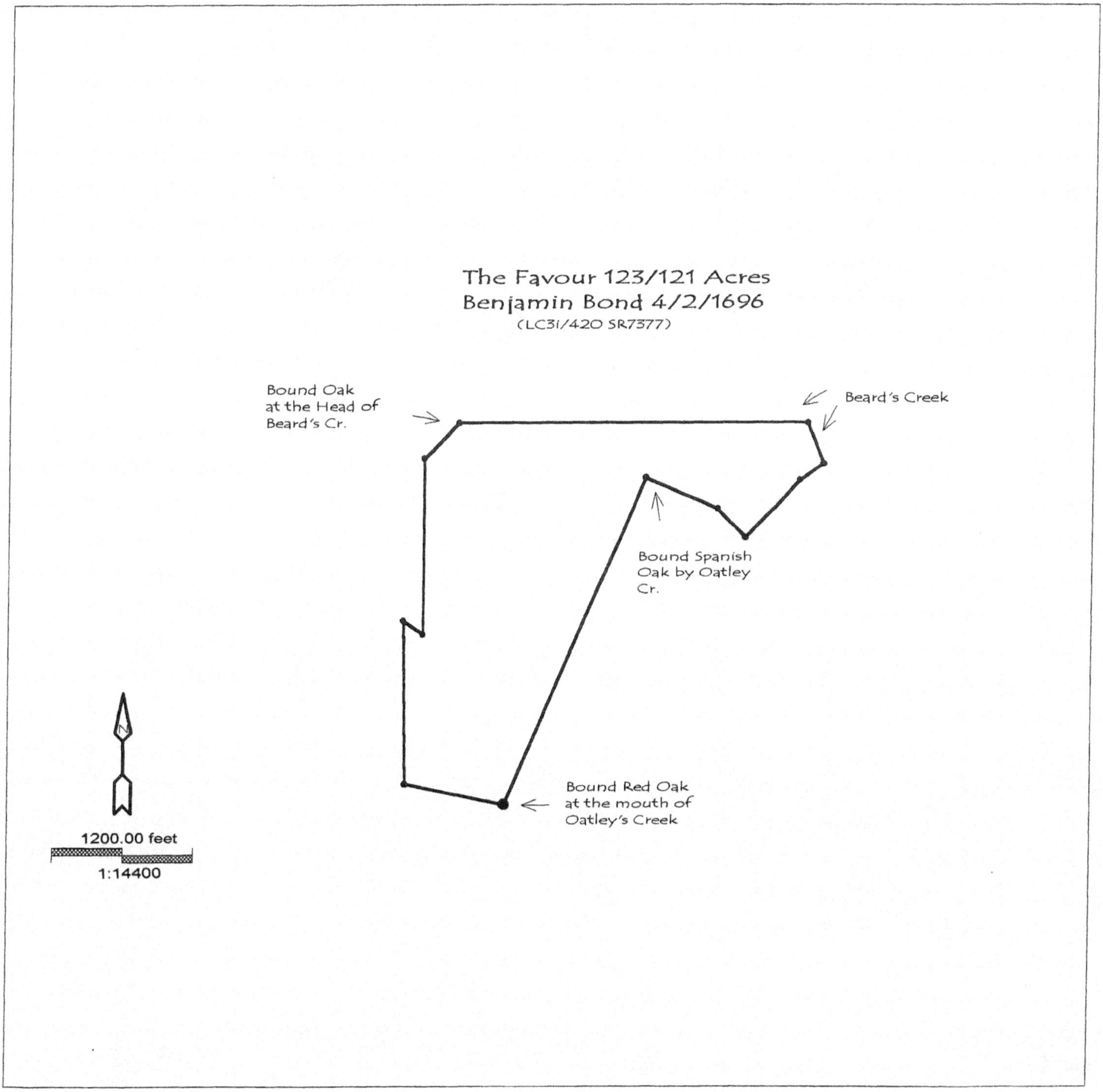

The Favour 123/121 Acres
Benjamin Bond 4/2/1696
(LC3i/420 SR7377)

Bound Oak
at the Head of
Beard's Cr.

Beard's Creek

Bound Spanish
Oak by Oatley
Cr.

Bound Red Oak
at the mouth of
Oatley's Creek

1200.00 feet
1:14400

The Intacke 100/155 Acres
John Norwood 1/18/1659
(L4/425 SR7346)

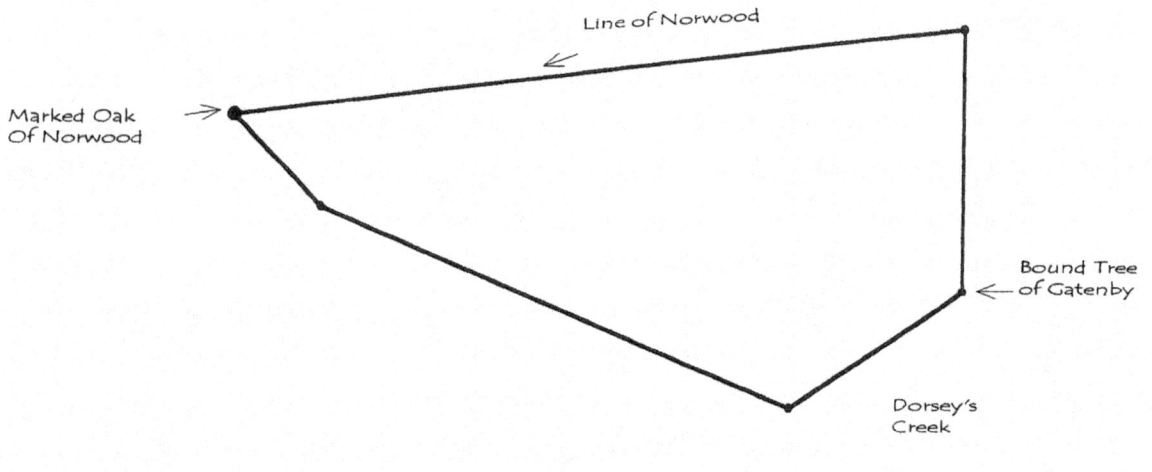

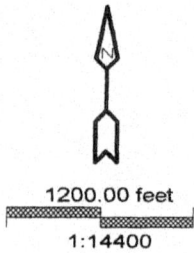

Line of Norwood

Marked Oak
Of Norwood

Bound Tree
of Gatenby

Dorsey's
Creek

N

1200.00 feet

1:14400

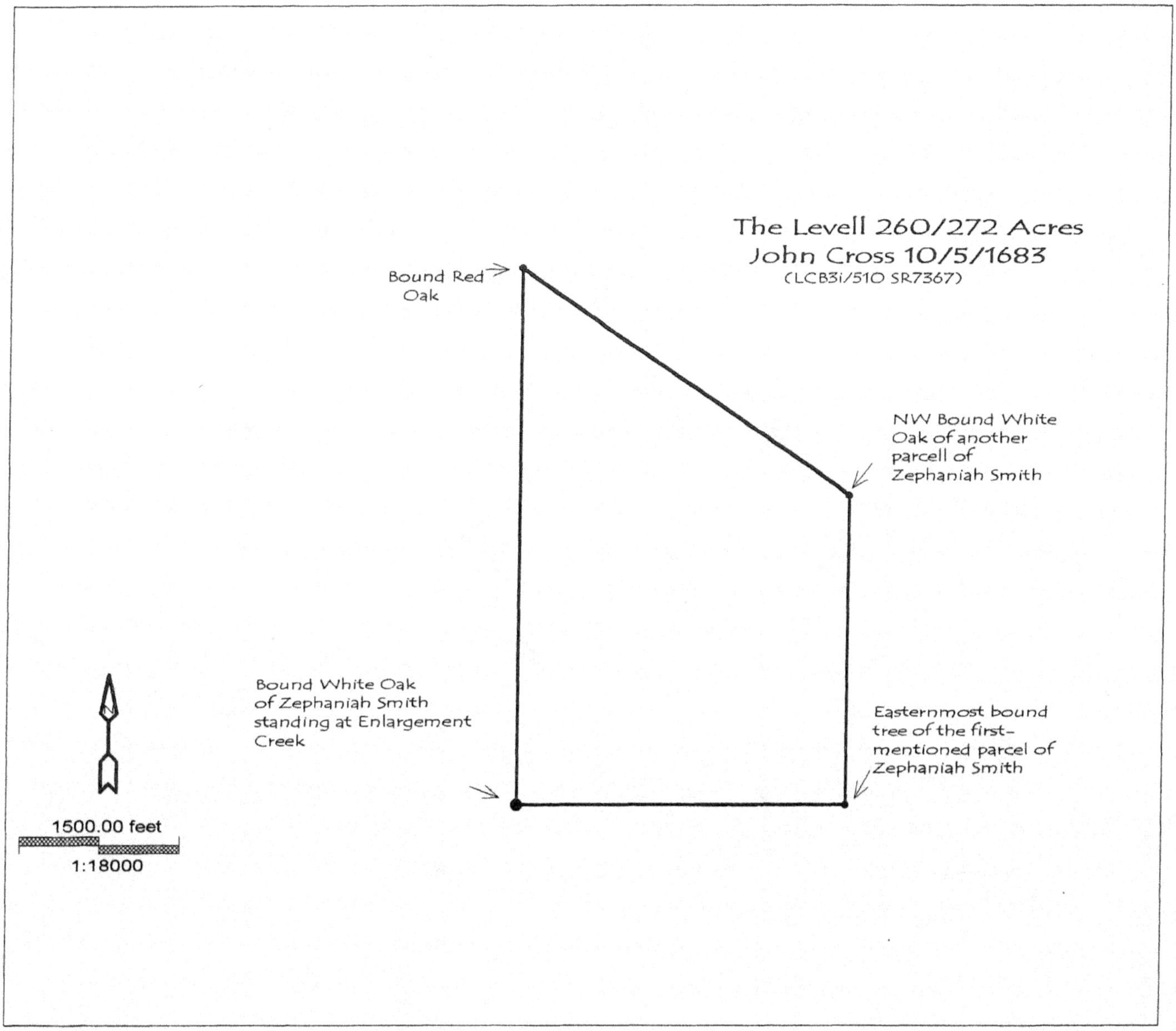

The Levell 260/272 Acres
John Cross 10/5/1683
(LCB3i/510 SR7367)

Bound Red
Oak

NW Bound White
Oak of another
parcell of
Zephaniah Smith

Bound White Oak
of Zephaniah Smith
standing at Enlargement
Creek

Easternmost bound
tree of the first-
mentioned parcel of
Zephaniah Smith

1500.00 feet

1:18000

The Neglect 30/9 Acres
Patrick Dunkin 5/4/1683
(LCB3i/280 SR7367)

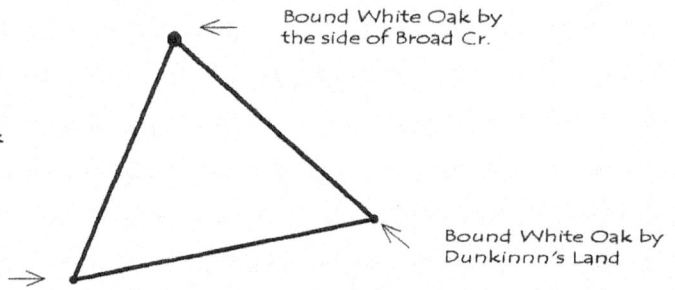

Bound White Oak by
the side of Broad Cr.

Broad Creek

Bound White Oak by
Dunkinnn's Land

Bounded White Oak
by the side of a cove

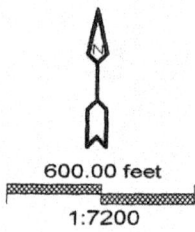

600.00 feet

1:7200

Timber Neck 40/24 Acres
John Maccubin 9/15/1665
(L8/294 SR7350)

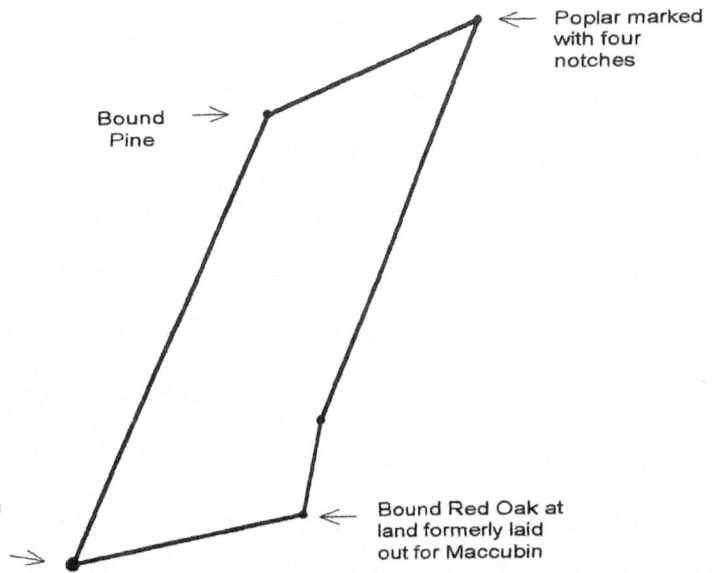

← Poplar marked with four notches

Bound Pine →

→ Bound Red Oak at land formerly laid out for Maccubin

Bound Pine of John Maccubin near mouth oof Broad Creek →

660.00 feet
1:7920

Todd 100/117 Acres
Thomas Todd 6/8/1651
(LAB&H/288 SR7344)

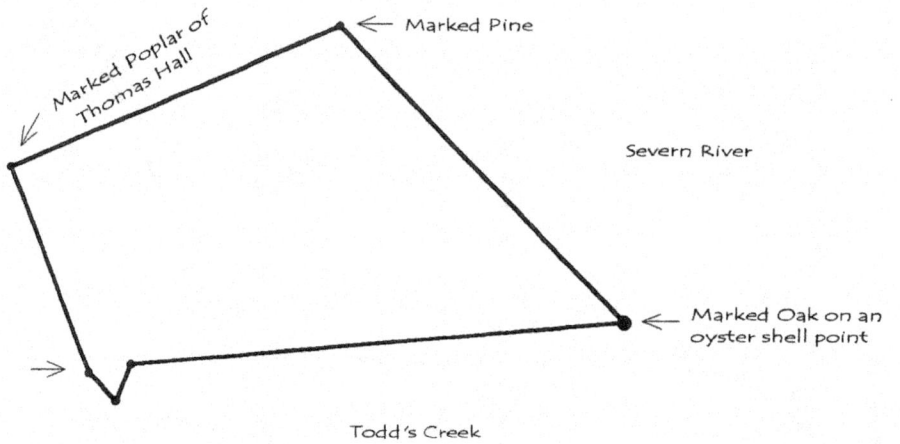

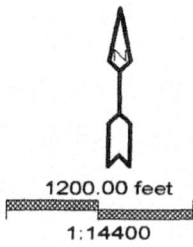

Marked Poplar of
Thomas Hall

← Marked Pine

Severn River

← Marked Oak on an
oyster shell point

Acton's Marked
Oak

Todd's Creek

N

1200.00 feet

1:14400

Todd's Harbour 120/113 Acres
Thomas Todd 4/10/1671
(L14/191 SR7356)

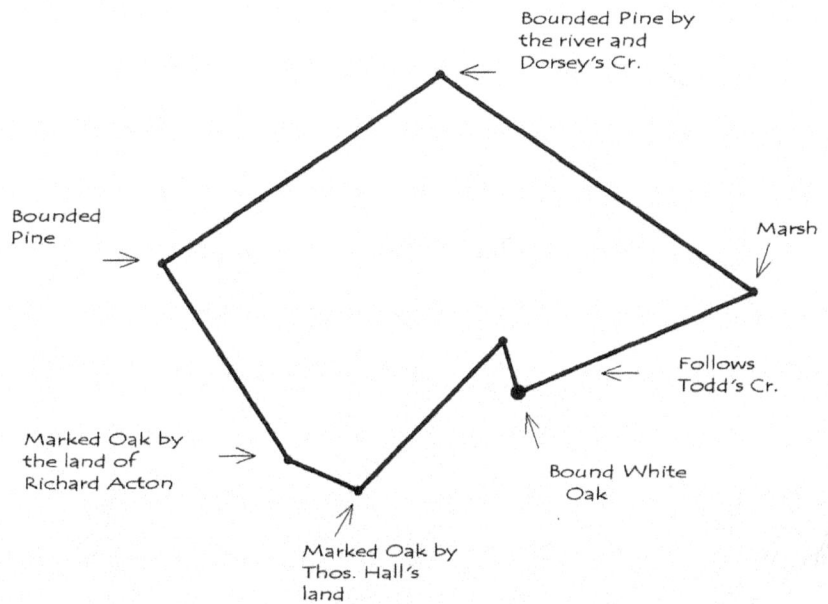

Bounded Pine by
the river and
Dorsey's Cr.

Bounded
Pine

Marsh

Follows
Todd's Cr.

Marked Oak by
the land of
Richard Acton

Bound White
Oak

Marked Oak by
Thos. Hall's
land

N

1200.00 feet
1:14400

273

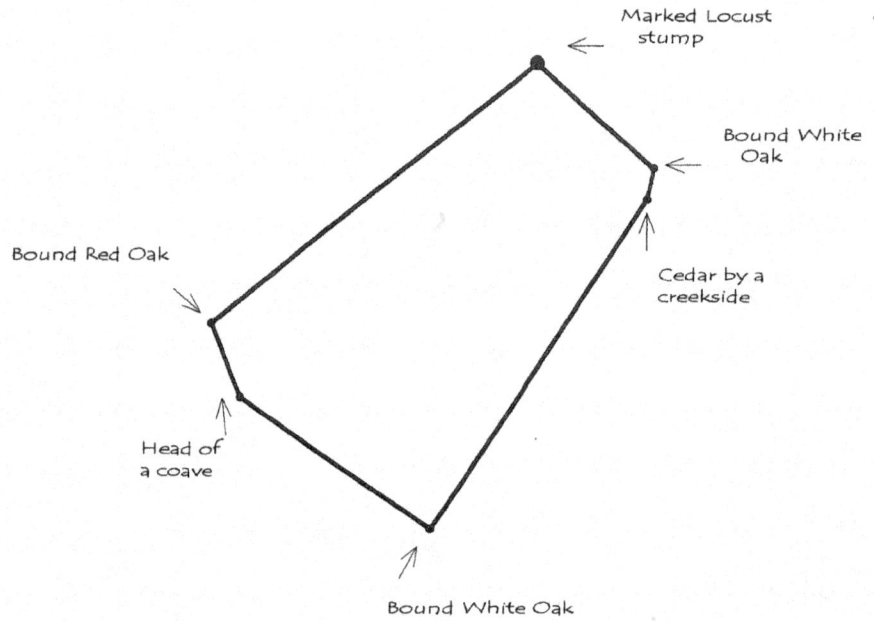

Todd's Pasture 29/24 Acres
Thomas Todd 6/29/1675
(L19/122 SR7360)

Marked Locust stump

Bound White Oak

Cedar by a creekside

Bound Red Oak

Head of a coave

Bound White Oak

600.00 feet
1:7200

Todd's Range 120/136 Acres
Thomas Todd 5/4/1664
(L7/244 SR7349)

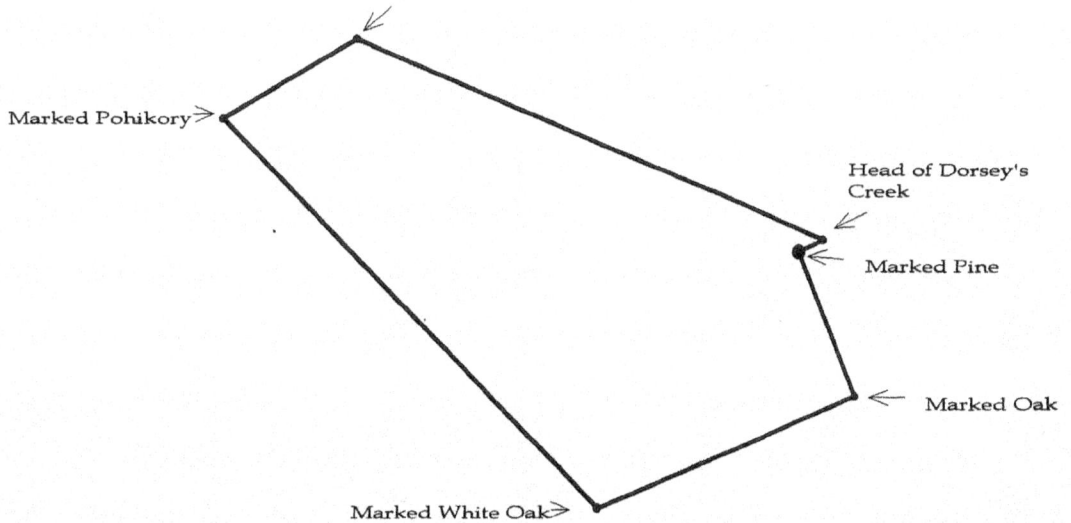

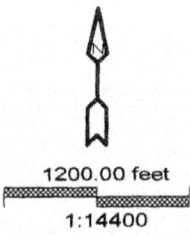

Marked Pohikory

Head of Dorsey's Creek

Marked Pine

Marked Oak

Marked White Oak

1200.00 feet

1:14400

Tolley's Point Resurveyed 140/141 Acres
Capt. Richard Hill 4/6/1684
(LSDA/319 SR7369)

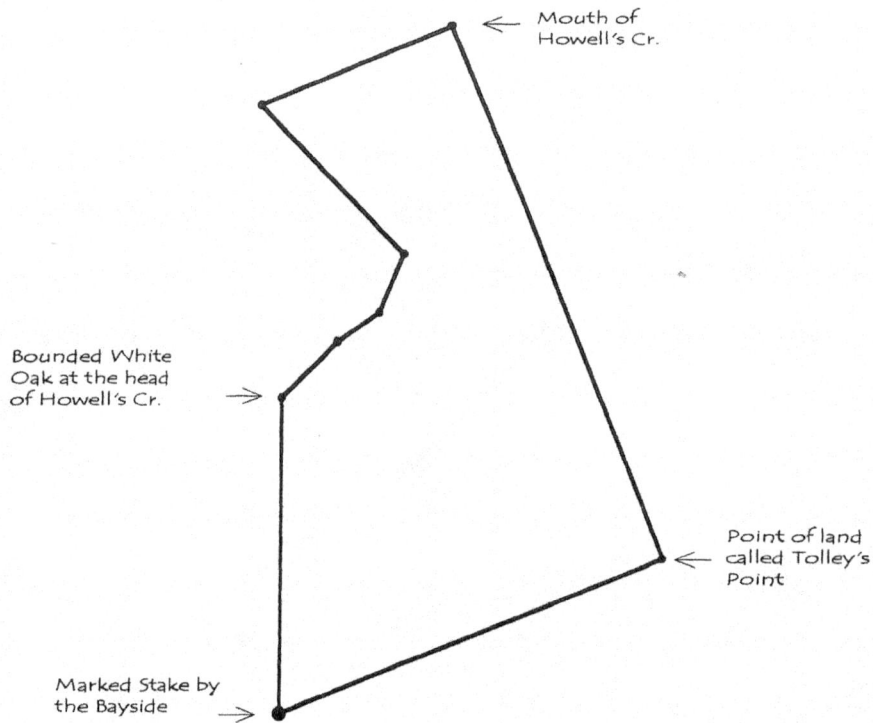

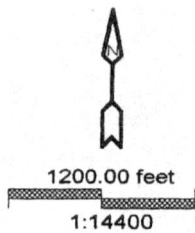

Mouth of Howell's Cr.

Bounded White Oak at the head of Howell's Cr.

Point of land called Tolley's Point

Marked Stake by the Bayside

1200.00 feet
1:14400

Wardner's Neck Resurveyed 320/293 Acres
James Wardner 6/20/1668
(Liber 12/24 SR7354)

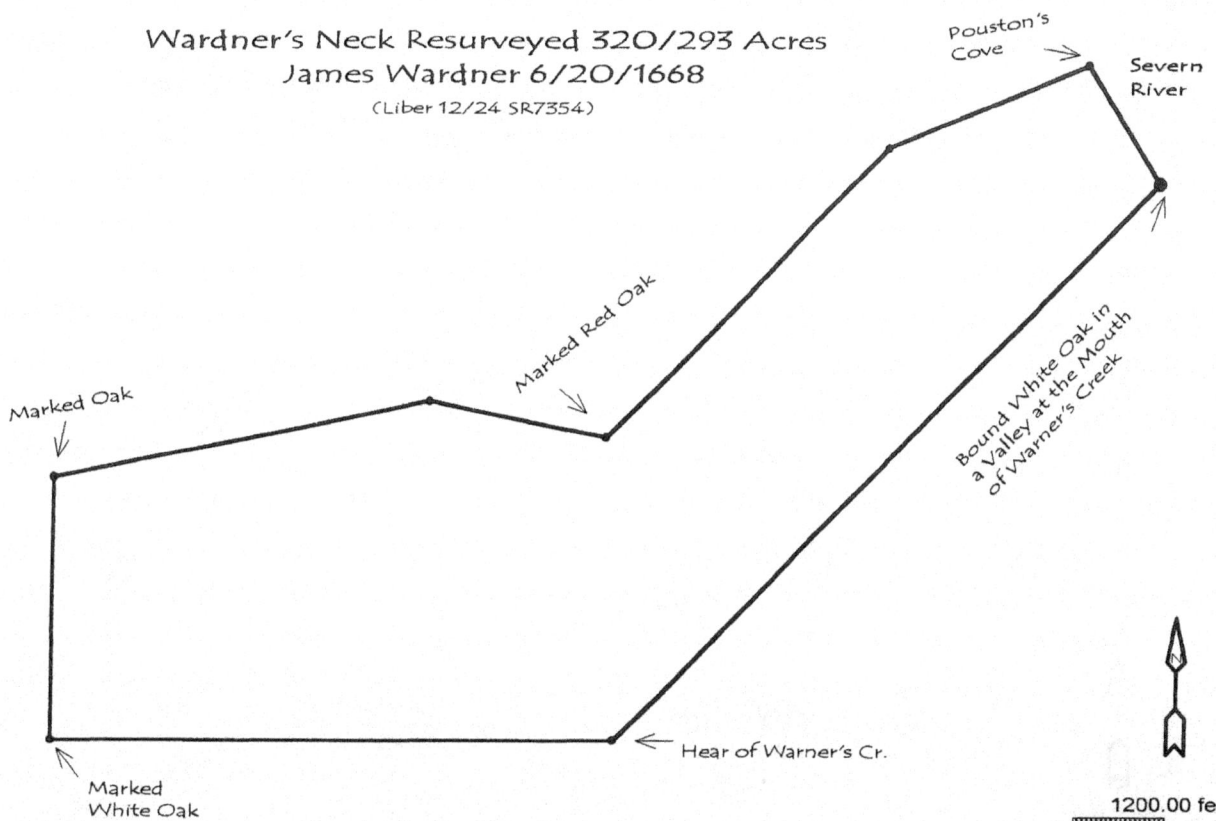

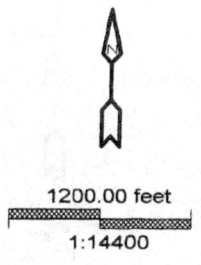

Pouston's Cove

Severn River

Marked Red Oak

Marked Oak

Bound White Oak in a Valley at the Mouth of Warner's Creek

Hear of Warner's Cr.

Marked White Oak

1200.00 feet
1:14400

Wardrop 200/150 Acres
James Wardner 6/26/1663
(Liber 5/354 SR7347)

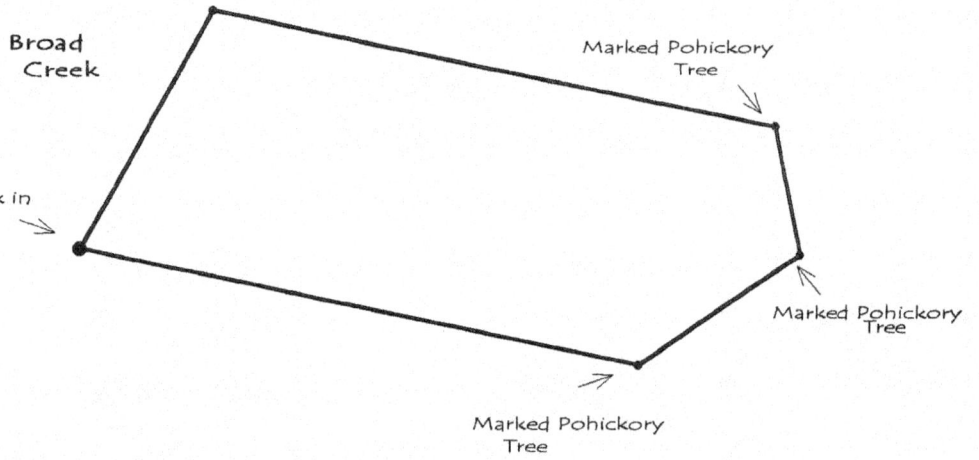

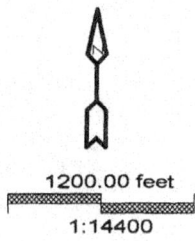

Broad
Creek

Marked Pohickory
Tree

Marked Oak in
a bile by a
swamp

Marked Pohickory
Tree

Marked Pohickory
Tree

1200.00 feet
1:14400

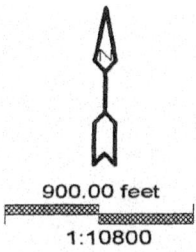

Wardrop Ridge 100/75 Acres
Patrick Dunkin 5/12/1663
(LCB3i/283 SR7367)

Marked White Oak

Marked Oak on the West side of a Branch

Marked Oak

900.00 feet
1:10800

Warringston 200/200 Acres
Sampson Warring 9/2/1663
(Liber 7/75 SR7349)

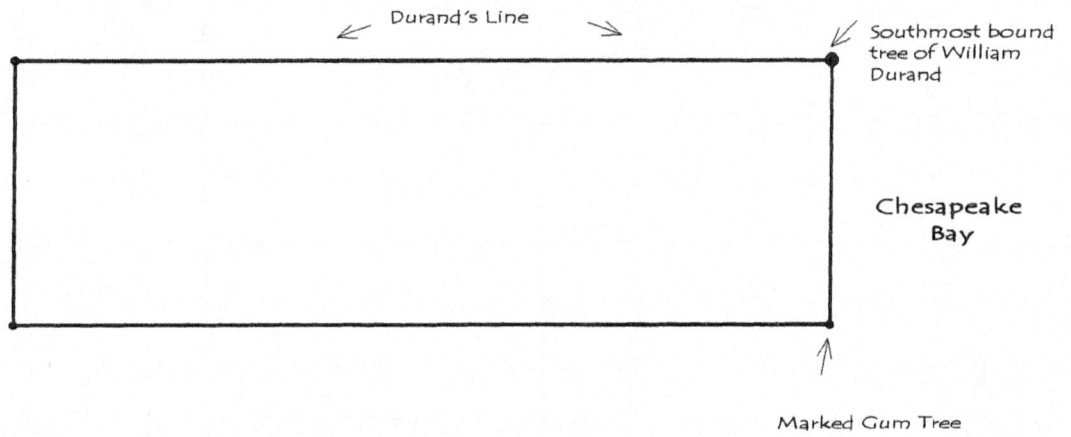

Durand's Line

Southmost bound
tree of William
Durand

Chesapeake
Bay

Marked Gum Tree

1200.00 feet
1:14400

West Quarter 100/100 Acres
Jacob Brimingham 6/20/1663
(L5/352 SR7347)

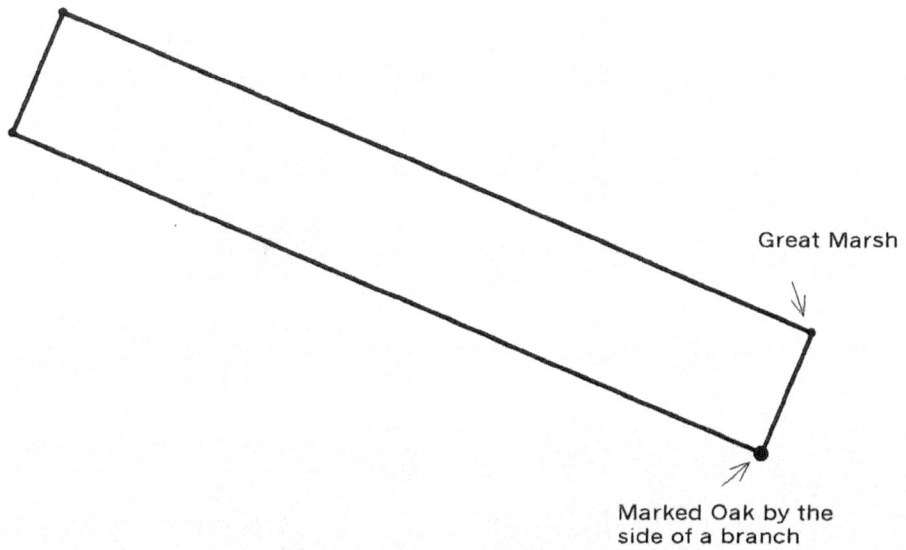

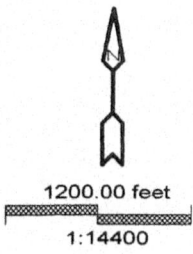

Great Marsh

Marked Oak by the
side of a branch

1200.00 feet

1:14400

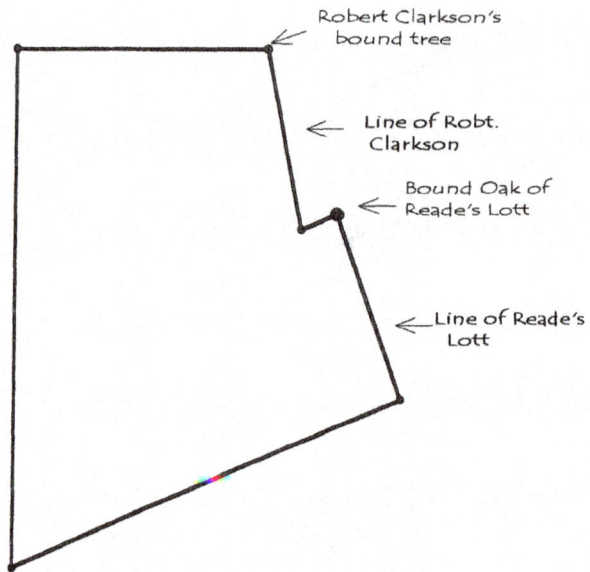

Widow's Addition 130/134 Acres
Elizabeth Reade 5/18/1679
(Liber 20/199 SR7361)

Robert Clarkson's
bound tree

Line of Robt.
Clarkson

Bound Oak of
Reade's Lott

Line of Reade's
Lott

1200.00 feet

1:14400

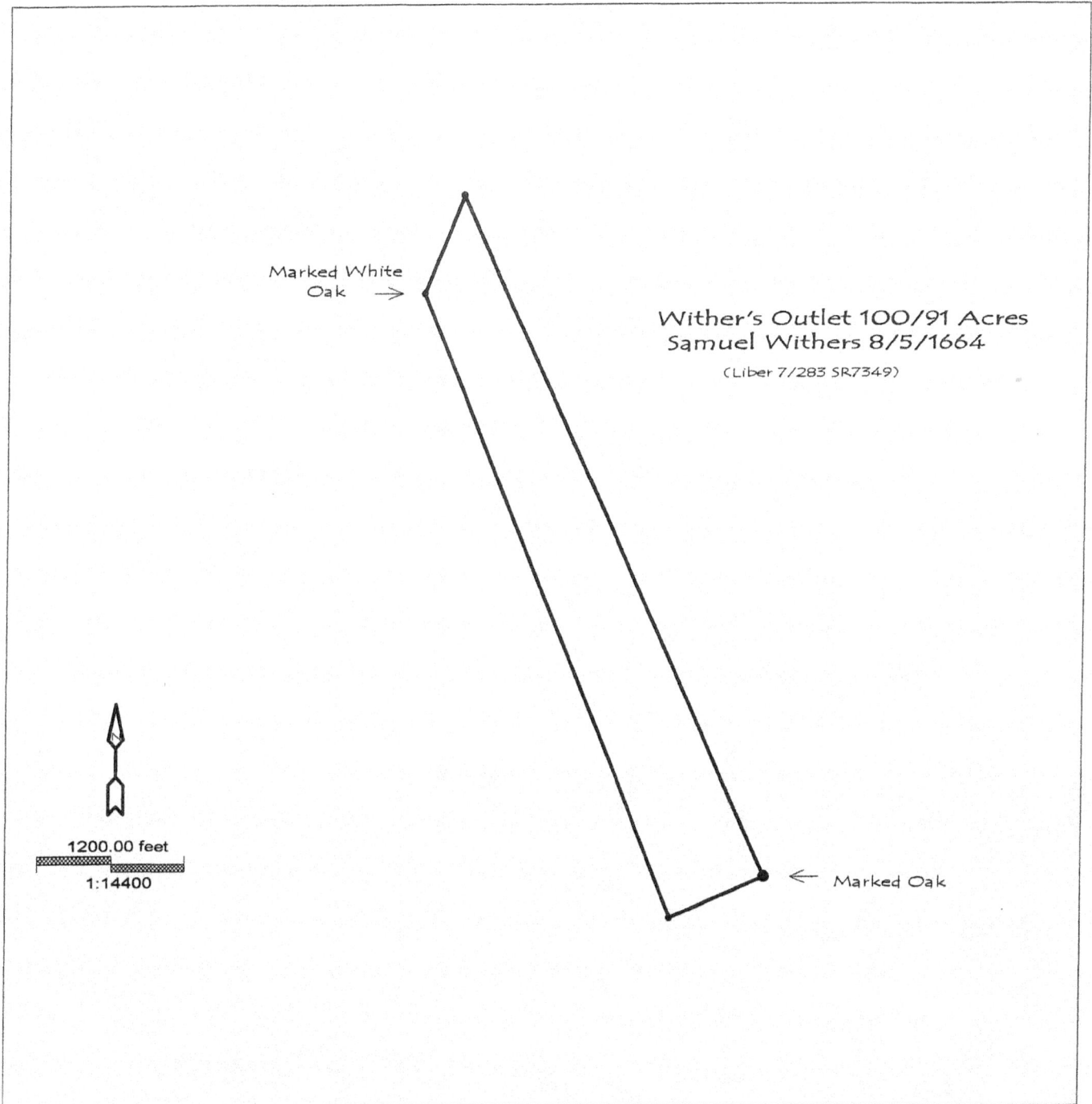

Marked White Oak →

Wither's Outlet 100/91 Acres
Samuel Withers 8/5/1664

(Liber 7/283 SR7349)

← Marked Oak

1200.00 feet

1:14400

Bibliography

Anne Arundel County Church Records of the 17th & 18th Centuries, F. Edward Wright, Family Line Publications, Westminster, MD 1994

Abstracts of Anne Arundel County Land Records, Vols. 1-4, Rosemary Dodd and Patricia Bausell, Anne Arundel Genealogical Society, Pasadena MD.

First Families of Anne Arundel County, MD 1649-1658, Vol. 1, Donna Valley Russell. Catoctin Press, 1999

Foundations of Representative Government in Maryland 1632-1715, David W. Jordan. Cambridge Press, 1987

Map- Original Landgrants on the South Side of the Severn River, Caleb Dorsey, 1958 (held at Maryland State Archives)

Maryland, A History 1632-1974, Walsh and Fox, Maryland Historical Society, Baltimore, 1974

Maryland Rent Roll's Baltimore and Anne Arundel County 1700-1707, 1705-1724, reprinted by Clearfield, 1996

Providence Ye Lost Town at Severn in Maryland, James E. Moss, distributed by the Maryland Historical Society, Baltimore, MD 1976

The Evolution of a Tidewater Settlement System – All Hallows Parish, MD, 1650-1783, Carville V. Earle, University of Chicago Press, 1975

The Founders of Anne Arundel and Howard Counties, J.D. Warfield, Kohn & Pollock, Baltimore, 1905, reprinted by Heritage Books Inc., Bowie, MD 1995

The Making of England 55BC-1399, 2nd Edition. C. Warren Holliston. D.C. Heath & Co., Lexington, Mass 1971

The Placenames of Maryland, Their Origin and Meaning, Hamill Kenny, Ph. D. Museum and Library of Maryland History, Maryland Historical Society, Baltimore, MD 1984

Index of Tract Owners
Ann Arundel County
1650-1704

Acton, Richard
Baldwin, John
Beard, Richard
Bell, Thomas
Beetenson, John
Birmingham, Michael
Blackwell, Thomas
Bond, Benjamin
Boyde, John
Birmingham, Jacob
Brooksby, John
Brown, Richard
Brown (e), Thomas
Bruton (Burton), John
Butler, Tobias

Carroll, Charles
Child, Abraham
Clark, Matthew
Clark, Richard
Clarke, Neale
Clarkson, Robert
Collier, John
Covell, Ann (aka Covill, Lambert, Mott)
Cross, John
Crouch, William
Cussack, Michael

Davies, Thomas
Davis, Thomas
Davis, William
Dorsey, Edward
Dorsey, John
Dorsey, Joshua
Draper, Lawrence
Dryer, Samuel
Dunken, Patrick
Duvall, John
Duvall, Marin

Edge, Daniel
Edwards, John
Everett, Richard
Francis, Thomas

Freeborn, Thomas
Freeman, John
Frizzell, William
Gaither (Gater, Gather), John
Galloway, William
Gardner, Edward
Garrett, Amos
Gates, Thomas
Greeniston, James
Griffith, William
Grimes, William
Gross, Thomas
Gudgeon, Lawrence
Gudgeon, Robert

Hammond, John
Hammond, Thomas
Harness, Jacob
Harris, John
Harris, William
Hill, Richard
Hope, Edward
Hopkins, William
Horner, James
Howard, Cornelius
Howard, Elenor
Howard, John
Howard, Mary
Howard, Matthew
Howard, Phillip
Howard, Samuel
Hudson, John

James, John
James, William
Jeffe, Thomas
Lambert, Ann (aka Covell, Covill, Mott)
Lytfoot, Thomas
McCubbin, John
Medcalfe (Metcalfe), John
Meeke (Meeks), Guy
Meriott, John
Minter, John
Moss, Richard
Mott, Ann (aka Covell, Covill, Lambert)
Norwood, Andrew
Norwood, John

Oatley, Christopher
Owen, Ann
Owen, Richard

Peasley, Francis
Petticoate, William
Phelps, Thomas
Pierpoint, Amos (Arnis)
Pierpoint, Henry
Pierpoint, Jabes
Porter, Peter
Porter, Richard
Proctor, Robert

Rawlings, Richard
Read, Elizabeth
Read, Thomas
Read, William
Richardson, Lawrence
Ridgely, Henry
Ridgely, Henry Jr.
Ridgely, William
Roper, Thomas
Ruly, Anthony
Salmon, Ralph
Saughier, George
Sewell, Henry
Shepheard, Nicholas
Shipley (Shepley), Adam
Sisson, Jane
Skidmore, Edward,
Smith, Walter
Stephens (Stevens), Charles

Thomas, Phillip
Todd, Thomas
Tolley, Thomas
Underwood, Thomas
Vennel, James
Walker, George
Wardner (Warner), James
Warfield, Benjamin
Warfield, Richard
Waring, Sampson
Wilson, Robert
Withers, Samuel
Wyatt, Nicholas
Yate, George
Young, Samuel

Index of People

Brooke, Baker Esq. 10, 42
Brooksby, John 3,
Brown. T. 4,
Brown(e), Thomas 3, 4(4), 5, 6(2), 7, 10, 18, 34
Browne(e), Elizabeth 34
Bruton, John 5(2),
Burges, Edward 19
Burges(s), William (Coll) 2, 7, 13. 18, 20, 21(2), 28(2), 31, 56
Burin, Matthew 65
Burton, John 25
Butler, Thobey 26, 29, 38
Butler, Tobias 36
Calvert, Charles (Esq), 19, 45, 59
Calvert, Phillip Esq. 63
Camell, Quentin 64
Caplyn, Elizabeth 53
Caplyn, Henry 54
Carroll, Charles 5, 43, 67
Cattline, Henry 4, 56
Cattline, Josie Elizabeth 56
Chilcott, James 62
Child (s), Abraham 5, 16
Child, Lucy 6
Clark, Matthew 44
Clarke, Elizabeth 28
Clark(e), Neal(e) 21, 26, 27, 32, 37(2)
Clarke, Rachel Beard 37, 38
Clarkson, Robert 33, 45, 51, 57, 58(2), 61(2)
Collier, John 45
Combs, Mary 67
Conaway, James Capt. 45
Cook, William 12
Copes, James 59
Covell (Covill), John 26, 33, 67
Cross, John 63
Crouch, Elizabeth 27
Crouch, Josias 27
Crouch, Mary 27
Crouch, Rachell 27
Crouch, William 27, 34
Cussack, Michael 41, 47
Darcy, Sarah 12,
Darnall, Henry Coll 2, 37, 52
Davies, Thomas 6, 45
Davis, Evan
Davis, Mary 9,
Davis, Thomas
Deaver, Richard 36
Desapp, Adam 62
Dodderidge, John 7,
Dolphin, Nathaniel 37, 38

Gearfe, Thomas 42
Gedgeon, Lawrence
Gibbs, Mary 67
Gleve, Thomas 12
Godfrey, Elias 49
Gossum, Ester 62
Gray, John 16
Green, Nicholas 61
Gremmell, Ann 36
Greeniston, James 7,
Griffin, Catherine Baldwin 42
Griffin, Charles 42
Griffith, Thomas 40
Griffith, William 26, 32, 48
Grimes, Ann 8
Grimes, William 7, 8(2), 17, 18
Gross, Thomas 49
Gudgeon (Guggeon), Robert 25 (2), 56
Gudgeon (Guggeon), Lawrence 25, 56
Hage, John 32
Hall, Edward 25, 26
Hall, Thomas 32, 64(2)
Hammond, John (Coll) (Maj) 5, 9, 11(2),14, 26, 36, 37, 49, 60
Hammond, Thomas 55, 60
Hanslap, Henry 2, 6, 7, 13(2), 17, 18(2), 19, 21, 31, 32, 53, 63
Harness, Ellinor 50
Harness, Isaac 50
Harness, Jacob 50(2)
Harness, Susan 50
Harness, William 50
Harness, William Jr. 50
Harrington, John 55
Harris, Elizabeth 50
Harris, John 9
Harris, William 50
Hedge, Thomas 12, 25
Hermon, John 31
Hill, Joseph 50
Hill, Richard 41, 42, 48, 57, 58. 68
Hill, Richard Capt. 13, 20, 54, 60, 61, 65
Hills, Elizabeth 21
Holland, George 4(2), 10, 35, 57
Holloway, John 48
Honorable Charles 41, 47
Hope, Edward 26, 29
Hopkins, Charles 35
Hopkins, William 3, 4(2),
Horner, James 12
Howard, Cornelius 10, 11(2), 18, 30, 37, 44, 51(3), 52(3), 62
Howard, Cornelius Jr. 20
Howard, Eleanor (Elinor) 36

Index of Tracts

Heritage Books by Robert W. Hall

Early Landowners of Maryland

Volume 1: Anne Arundel County, 1650–1704

Volume 2: Prince George's County, 1650–1710

Volume 3: Calvert County, 1640–1710
Robert W. Hall and Sandy Hall

Volume 4: Charles County, 1640–1710

Volume 5: St. Mary's County, 1633–1710
Robert W. Hall and Sandy Hall

Volume 6: Kent County, 1640–1710
Robert W. Hall and Sandy Hall

Volume 7: Baltimore County, 1658–1710
Robert W. Hall and Sandy Hall

Volume 8: Talbot County, 1650–1710

Volume 9: Queen Anne's County, 1640–1710

Volume 10: Cecil County, 1640–1710

Volume 11: Dorchester County, 1655–1710

Volume 12: Old Somerset County 1655–1710

*Land Grants in Anne Arundel County,
Maryland, 1650–1704: South River Hundred*

*Land Grants of the Middle Neck Hundred of
Anne Arundel County, Maryland, 1650–1704*

www.ingramcontent.com/pod-product-compliance
Lightning Source LLC
Chambersburg PA
CBHW080413270326
41929CB00018B/3007